CW00925212

# China and Globalization

**Series Editors**

Huiyao Wang, Center for China and Globalization, Beijing, China

Lu Miao, Center for China and Globalization, Bejing, China

This series are designed to address the evolution of China's global orientation, challenges of globalization and global governance facing China and the rest of the world, actions and proposals for the future of sustainable development, prospects of China's further capital and market liberalization, and China's globalizing trajectories as experienced by the world.

This book series seek to create a balanced global perspective by gathering the views of highly influential policy scholars, practitioners, and opinion leaders from China and around the world.

More information about this series at http://www.springer.com/series/16735

Huiyao Wang · Alistair Michie
Editors

# Consensus or Conflict?

China and Globalization in the 21st Century

 Springer

*Editors*
Huiyao Wang
Center for China and Globalization (CCG)
Beijing, China

Alistair Michie
Center for China and Globalization (CCG)
Beijing, China

ISSN 2730-9983 ISSN 2730-9991 (electronic)
China and Globalization
ISBN 978-981-16-5390-2 ISBN 978-981-16-5391-9 (eBook)
https://doi.org/10.1007/978-981-16-5391-9

© The Editor(s) (if applicable) and The Author(s) 2021. This book is an open access publication.

**Open Access** This book is licensed under the terms of the Creative Commons Attribution-NonCommercial-NoDerivatives 4.0 International License (http://creativecommons.org/licenses/by-nc-nd/4.0/), which permits any noncommercial use, sharing, distribution and reproduction in any medium or format, as long as you give appropriate credit to the original author(s) and the source, provide a link to the Creative Commons license and indicate if you modified the licensed material. You do not have permission under this license to share adapted material derived from this book or parts of it.

The images or other third party material in this book are included in the book's Creative Commons license, unless indicated otherwise in a credit line to the material. If material is not included in the book's Creative Commons license and your intended use is not permitted by statutory regulation or exceeds the permitted use, you will need to obtain permission directly from the copyright holder.

This work is subject to copyright. All commercial rights are reserved by the author(s), whether the whole or part of the material is concerned, specifically the rights of translation, reprinting, reuse of illustrations, recitation, broadcasting, reproduction on microfilms or in any other physical way, and transmission or information storage and retrieval, electronic adaptation, computer software, or by similar or dissimilar methodology now known or hereafter developed. Regarding these commercial rights a non-exclusive license has been granted to the publisher.

The use of general descriptive names, registered names, trademarks, service marks, etc. in this publication does not imply, even in the absence of a specific statement, that such names are exempt from the relevant protective laws and regulations and therefore free for general use.

The publisher, the authors and the editors are safe to assume that the advice and information in this book are believed to be true and accurate at the date of publication. Neither the publisher nor the authors or the editors give a warranty, expressed or implied, with respect to the material contained herein or for any errors or omissions that may have been made. The publisher remains neutral with regard to jurisdictional claims in published maps and institutional affiliations.

This Springer imprint is published by the registered company Springer Nature Singapore Pte Ltd.
The registered company address is: 152 Beach Road, #21-01/04 Gateway East, Singapore 189721, Singapore

# Recommendations for readers about this book

*"Multilateral co-operation is critically important to address the many challenges we face, from tackling the pandemic, dealing with climate change and fostering sustainable development. This collection of essays is a very useful contribution for those seeking to understand our rapidly changing and globally connected economies and societies."* **Sir Danny Alexander, Vice President, Asian Infrastructure Investment Bank (AIIB) and former Chief Secretary, H M Treasury**

*"If anybody is in doubt that we all live in a global, interconnected world then consider the impact of global warming, covid, social media etc. To live in this world, we must embrace free and open dialogue between peoples and nations. This collection explains some Why's and How's. A must read to get a balanced view of the world today."* **Sir Peter Bonfield, CBE, FREng, Chairman, NXP Semiconductors**

*"If we are to negotiate the next decade in peace, we cannot just trade with China and compete geo-strategically. We need to understand her far better. This collection of essays from across the political spectrum is a major contribution to that understanding."* **Sir Andrew Cahn, former CEO of UK Trade and Investment**

*"The rise of China is leading to shifts in the global landscape not seen since the Industrial Revolution that started in Europe. Anyone who wants to understand, and thus benefit from these changes, needs to delve deep into China's millennial long experience of governing a complex state. This exceptional and powerful collection of essays holds the key to that new understanding."* **Tim Clissold, author of the global best-seller, 'Mr China'**

*"We wish the book every success and hope very much that it contributes to a more balanced view of China in the world."* **Sir Angus Deaton, winner of the 2015 Nobel Memorial Prize in Economics and Anne Case, Professor of Economics and Public Affairs Emeritus at Princeton University**

*"The world is changing, of that there is no doubt. Within the frighteningly fluid global ecosystem of governance, capital markets and business, the place of a pure, rules based, approach could be seen as out of step with the changes already upon us and those about to descend. China's place in this emerging new world order is little understood. Any contribution which assists in addressing this misunderstanding is to be welcomed."* **Jon Geldart, Director General, Institute of Directors**

*"Managing our relationships with an emerging Chinese superpower with very different values, history and political systems to our own, yet huge shared economic interests, is likely to be one of the great challenges for the medium-sized Western democracies, like the UK, over the next three decades. This collection of essays will be an important contribution to that debate".* **Lord Philip Hammond, former British Chancellor of the Exchequer**

*"The Atlantic community is being driven herd-like towards some simplistic assumptions about China, the apparent threat it poses and the choices we are being asked to make. Such analysis does not get us very far which is why this book is an important antidote and an invaluable guide to a more rational and realistic future— of course we need to mitigate the risk that China poses the west, but we also need to understand where our interests are aligned with Beijing."* **Lord Peter Mandelson, Chairman, Global Counsel; former European Trade Commissioner and British First Secretary of State**

*"This is an original, wide-ranging and stimulating set of essays. The relationship between China and the west is one of the most important in contemporary geopolitics, and these authors give us a range of productive and thoughtful ways to address its future."* **Rana Mitter, Professor, History and Politics of Modern China, University of Oxford and author of 'Forgotten Ally: China's World War II, 1937– 1945'**

*"The world is not flat ... for nations and economies to succeed and stay safe in this increasingly interconnected world, we must be willing to embrace change and be more tolerant of cultures and ideologies which appear different. Global climate change is undoubtedly a crisis which needs all nations to work together if we are to protect the lives and livelihoods of future generations ... therefore reaching a global consensus on issues of this magnitude is essential. This book provides a compelling insight into China, the world's second biggest economy, and the role it is likely to play in the future ... as such this is a must-read publication."* **Sir John Peace, Chairman of the Midlands Engine and former Chairman of Standard Chartered, Experian and Burberry**

*"The world, and the west in particular, needs to recognise that we are moving to a different global dynamic, economically, politically and militarily, and that we have to engage with China in a balanced and pragmatic manner leaving ideology at the door. This is essential if we are to work together to deal with the enormous economic, climatic and health challenges the world faces in the short and long term. This book should help build understanding in this essential dialogue."* **Sir Mike Rake, Former President of the Confederation of British Industry (CBI)**

*"For anyone wanting to understand what role China will play in the emerging world, as Western global domination weakens, this book is essential reading. It provides a soundly based framework for understanding the political, economic and military forces at work in the transition."* **John Russell, Chairman, Henderson Far East Income Limited**

# Preface

## The Genesis of a Unique Book

Our first task as co-editors is to express our profound thanks to all those who accepted our invitation to contribute essays for this book. We are deeply grateful that so many distinguished leaders and scholars gave so freely of their time.

The generosity of our writers has resulted in what we believe is a truly unique book. Never before has such an authoritative group of essayists come together to develop deep new thinking about global governance that is relevant to current shared global challenges. Our writers hail from across the globe and share views with great authority thanks to their wealth of professional experience. In their essays, they express deep concerns about the historically unprecedented upheavals in the world. They describe the unparalleled turbulence that mankind is facing in the form of multiple crises, any one of which has the potential to bring civilization to its knees. The most obvious of these is the threat posed by climate change.

In this book, leaders and scholars spell out why these perils pose a stark choice for the human race. They stress how any path that leads to conflict increases the risk of catastrophe. In this context, the common thread is that a consensus must be reached about the future of our world. Our writers have put forward many ideas and potential new policies, reflecting their vision of what this consensus should be and how it is the only way forward for the human race. We believe that, given the sentiments expressed by our essayists, and the turmoil visible in the world in 2021, the publication of this book is extremely timely.

## The Spirit of Globalization

Our motivation for creating this book draws on the spirit and core culture of CCG. The first element of this book springs from the concept of "globalization," which is not just part of our name but a deeply held belief that all of us at CCG share, We believe that a globalized world is a core component for the creation of a peaceful and sustainable world order that contributes to the mutual benefit of all mankind. The COVID-19 pandemic has unleashed forces that pose great challenges to the realization of a peaceful and sustainable world order, but it was also a major catalyst that motivated us to collaborate and co-edit this book.

As co-editors, we take pride in the fact that CCG is not only China's leading non-governmental think tank but has also been granted official special consultative status by the Economic and Social Council of the United Nations (ECOSOC).[1] Unsurprisingly China takes a central role in many of the essays you can read in this book, but we believe that as China now represents almost 18.5% of the world's population, this balance in the book is proportionate. In addition, China has been changing, and continues to advance at a very rapid rate, as reflected in data published in 2020 by the Brookings Institute in the United States:

> In the 1950s, over 90% of the global middle class resided in Europe and North America. Today, over 20% live in China. China is experiencing the fastest expansion of the middle class the world has ever seen. By 2027, we estimate that 1.2 billion Chinese will be in the middle class, making up one quarter of the world total.[2]

Many of our writers have highlighted how China has benefited hugely from trends in globalization in recent decades. In turn, they have placed a great deal of emphasis on threats to the advance of globalization, due to the challenges facing global governance.

The essays that follow contrast current global governance challenges with the last great world cataclysm—the upheaval caused by World War II between 1939 and 1945—which was also the catalyst that laid the foundations for a 'rules-based world order'. Several writers highlight the 1944 Bretton Woods meeting that played a crucial catalytic role in creating this 'order' or 'system'. At the core of that order was the creation of the United Nations (UN), the World Health Organization (WHO), the World Bank, the International Monetary Fund (IMF) and GATT, which eventually gave birth to the World Trade Organization (WTO). Our essayists explain how the United States led the foundation of this 'rules-based world order' and continues to dominate its operation.

Our writers also present data about global governance trends that provokes serious reflection. For example, when the UN was founded in 1945 the population of the world was around 2.5 billion. By 2021 that total was over 7.8 billion. Of all the people living in the world today, less than 4% live in the USA, while no more than 10% of the global population comes from European nations. This explains why so many of our authors urge that global governance needs to evolve to reflect the views of the 86% of the world's people who, so far, have had a very limited influence on the creation of the rules in today's 'rules-based world order.'

---

[1] https://digitallibrary.un.org/record/1657187?ln=en.

[2] https://www.brookings.edu/research/chinas-influence-on-the-global-middle-class/.

## Think Tanks Add Value by Generating New Governance Policies

Our collaboration as both colleagues and co-editors is built on consensus on many topics. A primary shared belief is in the immense importance of the role of think tanks, which have become even more valuable as the pace of change increases and the world has to deal with exceptional crises like COVID-19. Governments lack the luxury of time to think and reflect as officials deal with the daily demands in an ever fast-moving world. Think tanks like CCG provide the space for careful thought and reflection. In an ideal world, think tanks should support governments by providing a stream of ideas from multiple angles and sources that can be turned into policies to tackle challenges in governance. It is our sincere wish that some of the many ideas in this book may contribute to the genesis of new policies that deliver positive benefits to all of humanity.

As globalization is embedded in the DNA of CCG, we naturally came together as co-editors to reflect both western and Chinese thinking. However, we quickly realized that while there is great clarity in defining China, there is no broad acceptance of the definition of 'western' — as any search of the internet or dictionaries will tell you. Since a definition of 'western' matters for the purposes of this book, we have chosen to interpret 'western' as referring to the regions of Europe and North America.

## A 'Flat, Fused' Globalized World Is Racing Ahead of the 'Rules-Based' Order

Thomas L. Friedman,[3] Pulitzer winner and New York Times columnist, kindly participated in a virtual forum with CCG on March 29, 2021. As co-editors we would like to share his thinking with you, as Friedman embraces the very thoughts and trends that inspired us to create this book.

> The world is fast, fused, deep and open. When I say the world is fast now, what I mean is that there's been a change in the pace of change. Second, the world isn't just flat now, it's fused. We're not just interconnected, we're now interdependent. We're fused by technology and by climate. Third, the world's gotten deep. Deep is the most important word of this era. Because what we've done now is that we have put sensors everywhere. Now our knowledge of that is deep. It's very deep. We had to coin a new adjective—deep state, deep mind, deep medicine, deep research, deep fake—to describe the fact that this is going deep inside of me. I can sit here right now in Washington and look at publicly available satellite pictures of different parts of China from Google Earth. And lastly, the world is getting radically open. With this, every citizen is now a paparazzo, a filmmaker, a journalist, a publisher, with no editor and no filter. So, the world is getting fast, fused, deep and open. That is the central governing

---

[3] Thomas L. Friedman wrote, *The World Is Flat – A Brief History of The 21st Century*. It was published in 2005 and won in that year the Financial Times and McKinsey business book of the year award.

*challenge today. How do you govern the world that is that fast, fused, deep and open? That is our challenge.*

## Policies for Changing the 'Rules-Based World Order'

We gave our eminent writers the task of expressing their views about the options for governance and globalization in the twenty-first century. We challenged them to explain how consensus, rather than conflict, could be a way forward for mankind. As a response, the majority of our writers chose to analyse why the current 'rules-based world order' needs reform. Overall, most authors stressed that the need for change is extremely urgent.

Professor Amitav Acharya, Chair of Transnational Challenges and Governance of UNESCO, suggests that COVID-19 has ushered in a more pluralistic, multiplex world in the form of a "G20+ world" where the main players will not be just big powers or nation-states, but also institutions, corporations and networks, operating at multiple and intersecting levels.

H. E. Shaukat Aziz, former Prime Minister of Pakistan, references his experiences during the worst earthquake in Pakistan's history to suggest the creation of a global one-stop-shop disaster relief unit under the auspices of the UN. He also uses his expertise as a top global banker to argue that the IMF and the World Bank must be restructured for the realities of the revolutionary digital and biosphere age.

The US scholar, economist and currently a China resident, Prof. David Blair, brings an authoritative perspective to the analysis of world governance. He believes the US is and, in the near term, will remain militarily and economically dominant and will use its power to impose a liberal and benevolent international system. However, he warns of the considerable danger of accidental conflict between the USA and China.

Professor Kerry Brown is a former diplomat and eminent Sinologist. In pushing reforms in global governance, both for the US and EU, he writes that, "there needs to be an acceptance that a radical difference in viewpoints with China has to proceed alongside a similarly crucial admission." He stresses that it would be self-defeating not to work with China and that dis-engagement with China is not an option.

A Chinese view comes from Prof. Yafei He, a former Foreign Affairs Vice Minister and now a Distinguished Professor at Peking University. He proposes four points to consider in revising global governance. First, avoid zero-sum geopolitics. Second, defend globalization and free trade. Third, take global poverty alleviation seriously. And fourth, restore the spirit of mutual assistance.

Professor Masahiro Kawai, former Deputy Finance Minister of Japan and now an esteemed scholar, provides the Japanese perspective. He proposes a way in which Japan can play a major role in addressing the reform of the 'rules-based world order'. He contends that Japan could contribute by working with the US, the EU and China to reform the WTO and put it back on the center stage of global rule making for trade and investment.

Former Deputy Prime Minister of Poland, Prof. Grzegorz W. Kołodko, is now a renowned scholar known for creating the concept of "Chinism." Chinism is a syncretic economic system based on multiple forms of ownership with strong macroeconomic policies and limited government control. In the context of China, Chinism has helped eliminate shortages and keep price inflation in check, something that none of the other models of state socialism were able to accomplish.

Pascal Lamy brings exceptional knowledge to reforming global governance as a former WTO Director General. He suggests that the world should not revolutionize the current system, and it is essential that a new order serves not only the established powers, but a greater number of the newly emerging nations. He concludes that globalization can continue to contribute to the betterment of mankind.

As a former Government Minister and now a senior scholar, Dr. Vladimir Yakunin provides a penetrating and authoritative perspective from the point of view of Russia. He emphasizes that "the current crisis is global and systemic in nature. On the one hand, this is an inevitable result of globalization. On the other hand, it is a result of defects in the existing economic model and global political system."

Former Chinese Deputy Finance Minister Guangyao Zhu promotes the G20 and the UN as a means to reform global governance. He writes that, "the importance of multilateral governance systems in the resolution of COVID-19 cannot be overstated. The G20 has the ability to mobilize the resources of the the world. Also, maintaining political order and governance should be centred on the UN."

Co-editor of this book, Huiyao Wang, propounds that, as we emerge from COVID-19, there is a unique opportunity for a long-overdue "Bretton Woods 2.0" moment to rethink global governance. China can help lead this by supporting the strengthening of existing institutions, for example, transforming the Asia Infrastructure Investment Bank into the Global Infrastructure Investment Bank.

## Policies to Create Public Health and Humanitarian Governance Reform

Peter Maurer, as President of the International Committee of the Red Cross, focuses on four key issues in this area. First, reconciling humanitarian, security, stability and peace-building agendas. Second, engaging in quiet but robust dialogues with the armed actors of today's conflicts. Third, breaking cycles of violence, and fourth, striving for diverse partnerships to find a way through political stalemates.

Professor Yuanli Liu, a global public health expert based in Beijing, suggests that the COVID-19 pandemic has revealed to the world both the vulnerability and power of the human community. He focuses on the creation of vaccines in a fraction of the time that was the norm before 2020 to highlight the power of humanity while also warning against the vulnerability of multilateral mechanisms like the WHO that must not be allowed to weaken.

COVID-19 has exposed deep weaknesses in the governance of global health. This is the view of renowned economist Lord Jim O'Neill who created the acronym BRICS.[4] He has urged the world to learn from COVID-19 in order to guide the reform of global public health from the 'Global Review Into Antimicrobial Resistance (AMR)' that was created in 2014. Lord O'Neill chaired the AMR review board that highlighted how antibiotic use is abused around the world.

## Governance to Nurture the Next Generations Through Education, Exchange and Migration

Professor Sir Keith Burnett, the former President of the UK Science Council, stresses that high priority must be given to building personal relationships. Personal experiences can demolish so many of the simplistic notions held by non-Chinese people about China. He contends that without a greater comprehension of China, its history and its language, any understanding of the world is incomplete.

Jeffrey Lehman is the Inaugural Vice Chancellor of New York University in Shanghai. This explains why he has highlighted, in particular the value of the global network of transnational universities. He makes the case for global governance reform to ensure the value of intellectual curiosity, academic freedom and a radical openness to people who hold different worldviews so that they are respected and protected by governments.

Dr. James G. McGann is a global leader in the analysis of think tanks at the Lauder Institute, demonstrating how they play a vital role in education and scholarship. However, he also explains how the general trend of globalization has put think tanks at a disadvantage, requiring them to find new and innovative ways to present information so that they remain relevant in today's world.

Dr. Lu Miao is Secretary-General of CCG and a scholar of migration and education. She explains that while talent migration makes a very significant contribution to global economic development, the global governance of talent migration is sorely neglected when compared to other economic sectors such as international trade and finance. She states that there is an urgent need for a new global infrastructure for talent migration.

Professor Sir Anthony Seldon, former Vice Chancellor of Buckingham University, gives four reasons for prioritising educational links. First, he notes that the deeper the divide between nations the greater the need for cooperation. Shared history is the second reason. Third is shared learning. Finally, he warns that it is folly to not find ways of trading more with China, and befriending it, despite all the difficulties and differences of opinion.

---

[4] **BRICS** is an acronym for Brazil, Russia, India, China and South Africa. Goldman Sachs economist Jim O'Neill coined the term BRIC (without South Africa) in 2001, claiming that by 2050 the four BRIC economies would come to dominate the global economy by 2050.

## Global Governance Trends and Dealing with the Digital and Biosphere Revolutions

Robert D. Atkinson is founder of the Information Technology and Innovation Foundation. He propounds that data governance and the management of global digital data flows pose immense challenges for global governance. International digital data agreements must be embedded in revisions of the global 'rules-based' order and China should revise its restrictive approach so it can play a constructive role.

Dr. Hermann Hauser is Chairman of Amadeus Capital and has played a pivotal role in advancing the global digital revolution since its genesis. He exposes how the revolution in digital and biospheres has created new threats to national sovereignty. He emphasizes that the view of sovereignty built on military strength is outdated and nations are now exposed to economic coercion that is no less severe than military coercion.

Professor Peter Nolan is Director of the China Centre at Jesus College, Cambridge University. His analysis shows that the 'Internet of Things' needs to be considered as a comprehensive whole. The entirety of the 'Internet of Things' is dominated by firms from high-income countries, especially the USA, which has created great potential for conflict in global governance.

Professor Denis F. Simon is a scholar of Chinese business and technology at Duke University. He describes how the twenty-first century has been a dynamic period for international exchanges in science and technology. Globalization has enabled the almost unhindered movement of people, products and services and knowledge across borders, but he also questions if US–China tensions will inhibit these trends.

## Global Governance Perspectives from Africa, Asia, North America and Europe

Jean-Christophe Bas is CEO of The Global Compass. He argues that it is essential to block the drift towards a bi-polar world, calling on European Union foreign policy efforts to take a much more proactive and strategic role in revising the American led 'rules-based world order'. His analysis also examines why Europe is struggling to develop a coherent position towards these challenges.

For many years Wendy Cutler was a leading official in US trade negotiations. She writes, "Twenty years ago, Asia accounted for less than a third of global output. Twenty years from now, Asia will account for more than half the world's total economy. Now there is a serious danger that the US will miss its opportunity to shape trade rules and norms within the largest and most rapidly growing region in the world."

COVID-19 has been a massive test of governance for nearly all nations. In that test, China has scored extremely well and the EU and USA have failed. This is the view of Prof. Martin Jacques, formerly a Senior Fellow at the University of Cambridge.

He provides updates to *When China Rules The World,* which he published in 2009, and projects that the world is now in a period of 'great transition' of power from the west to China.

Opinions about the rise of Asia come from Parag Khanna, who is the founder of Future Map. His analysis stresses core trends: first, imagination and creativity, which will be crucial as the world changes faster and faster with technologies ranging from AI to gene therapy evolving at revolutionary speeds and colliding in novel and unexpected ways. Second, he suggests that complexity must be embraced.

Professor Kishore Mahbubani is a scholar and former diplomat who chaired the UN Security Council. He says the US has made three strategic mistakes. The first mistake was letting the top 1% in the US reap huge rewards from globalization. The second mistake was to weaken governmental institutions. The third mistake was to allow the top 1% to create a functional plutocracy in America.

A voice from Africa comes from Prof. Carlos Lopes from the University of Cape Town. He presents data to show how demography will shape global governance. The current population of Africa is 1.3 billion. Some forecast that will double by 2050. His essay says that narratives about Africa tend to be negative, but Africa will ultimately be home to 2.6 billion people that will make up a full quarter of the world's population.

## Lessons from History for the Next Steps in Global Governance and Trends

Professor Daniel A. Bell is a leading scholar of history and political science based in China. He expounds on the rich legacy of the written world in China that goes back three millennia, where ancient theories can be mined for contemporary insights. One example he gives is how, in classical China, political thinkers developed rich and diverse theories of international politics that was based upon the hierarchy of states.

Ronnie C. Chan, as Chair of Hang Lung Group, has an exceptional business acumen, but in the broader context of world affairs, he turns to historical patterns to make sense of contemporary commercial trends and global governance. He highlights the impact of China's 'reform and opening' up. He reveals patterns in history that illustrate how globalization has always been cyclical. He believes that as the US retreats into isolationism, China has unique opportunities to become a driver of systems of global governance.

The 2005 Nobel economics prize winner, Edmund Phelps, suggests China should learn from history as it transits from a middle-to-high-income country. China has long enjoyed high growth rates as it has worked to catch up to rest of the world. If China is to make the leap from a middle-to-high-income country, then China must develop indigenous innovation and continue improving its institutions.

## 'Soft Power' in Governance, the Burden of Debt and the Crisis of Communications

Former Dean of Harvard's Kennedy School of Government, Prof. Joseph S. Nye Jr. coined the term 'soft power'. He proposes that the US should create a "COVID Marshall Plan" to strengthen global healthcare systems. Such leadership could enhance US 'soft power' and by 2030 have a similarly significant geopolitical effect as the original Marshall Plan.

Sir Martin Sorrell provides perspectives as a member of an elite group of successful founders and leaders of multinational businesses. He says we need to think long and hard about how to pay for the extraordinary amount of necessary debt that has been accrued in the fight against COVID-19 — just as we are having to pay for the investment to tackle climate change, to counter inequalities and re-skill labour forces as a result of the disruption.

A crisis of communication is the proposition of Alistair Michie, Chair of the International Council of CCG. He stresses how the current crisis is corroding cohesion of individual societies. If this erosion persists, it will create even more severe impediments for global society to change and introduce the measures needed to counter challenges such as climate change. He believes that this crisis can be resolved through leadership from China and the US.

## Consensus or Conflict?—Conclusions

Any co-editors tempted to create such a book might benefit from taking heed from our experience. While we are proud of this work, we have been left with a deep regret that we were unable to cover other serious issues and should have gathered a greater variety of writers and perspectives. We regret that none of our essays reflect the rising and serious issues on the topic of nuclear safety and its control and management. There are also serious shared global governance issues in the moral choices, as biosciences charge forward at a revolutionary pace. We are also concerned that we did not give a greater regional balance to the different continents of the world. Finally, we are also frustrated that we were only able to include three women amongst thirty five men. However, regardless of the shortcomings of this work, the process of co-editing has been a pleasurable, if massive task, and publishing deadlines must be met.

As co-editors, we wish to once again express our profound gratitude to all our authors. It is our very sincere wish that all of our readers are inspired by the diverse ideas expressed in this book. We believe our authors have provided the ingredients for a ground-breaking book. We hope that their thoughts will stimulate a fruitful dialogue on the future of global governance, which is so urgent and vital in today's world, to meet the challenges mankind currently faces.

We leave you to consider the many problems the world faces with a few words from Thomas L.Friedman, who so poignantly asked: *"How do you govern a world that is that fast, fused, deep and open?"*

Beijing, PRC and Edinburgh, UK                                    Huiyao Wang
                                                                 Alistair Michie

# Acknowledgements

As co-editors, we have accumulated many debts in the creation of this book. In the Preface section, we have acknowledged our profound appreciation to all the eminent scholars and leaders who have contributed essays.

We now also wish to express our sincere gratitude to our commissioning editors at Springer Nature Group and their team, especially Yingying Zhang and Yan Li. We applaud their vision to publish this very topical book at a time in global history when there is such an urgent need for new thinking, ideas and policies in world governance.

When we started the project, we set a deadline of getting the book to the publishers by the end of April 2021. At the beginning, we could not have predicted the number of essays our invitation would attract. As the total grew to 35 essays, it placed tremendous demands on our brilliant and professional teams within the CCG Publishing Centre. The final outcome of their work is a source of pride for us and we would like to express our warmest thanks and appreciation to Yueyuan Ren, Joshua Dominick, Ruijun Zhang and Yanjie Li.

Co-editor Huiyao Wang wishes to give special thanks to the international council members of Center for China and Globalization (CCG) for exchanging views and sharing thoughts.

Co-editor Alistair Michie also wishes to give special thanks to Tengbo Yang (Chris), with whom he has nurtured a 14-year-long friendship. That rapport has helped Alistair navigate and learn about China; without it, Alistair could not have co-edited this book.

The editors also wish to express thanks for the support provided by Dongyu Globalization Think Tank Foundation.

CCG's previous co-edited volume *Handbook on China and Globalization* (Edward Elgar, 2019) has evoked strong response in the academic community since its publication. However, we believe that this newly co-edited work *Consensus or Conflict?* boasts even more representative and authoritative authors writing about the most relevant global governance issues in the world today. This is why, as co-editors, we would also like to express our gratitude to all those who read this book.

We hope the essays it contains inspire its readers to help create and grow systems of governance that ensure future generations enjoy a peaceful and sustainable world.

Beijing, PRC                                              Huiyao Wang
Edinburgh, UK                                          Alistair Michie

# Contents

# Editors and Contributors

## About the Editors

 **Huiyao Wang** is the Founder and President of Center for China and Globalization (CCG), a think tank ranked among top 100 think tanks in the world. He is also Dean of the Institute of Development Studies of Southwestern University of Finance and Economics of China, Vice Chairman of China Association for International Cooperation and a Director of Chinese People's Institute of Foreign Affairs. He is currently a steering committee member of Paris Peace Forum and an advisory board member of Duke Kunshan University. He served as an expert for World Bank, IOM and ILO. He pursued his Ph.D. studies at University of Western Ontario and University of Manchester. He was a Senior Fellow at Harvard Kennedy School and a Visiting Fellow of Brookings Institute. His books in English include: *Globalizing China* (2012); *China Goes Global* (2016); the *Handbook on China and Globalization* (2019); and the *Globalization of Chinese Enterprises* (2020).

 **Alistair Michie** is the Chair of the International Council of the Center for China and Globalization (CCG). During the last three decades, he has visited and worked in over 28 provinces and regions of China. The focus of his work in China has been on strategic advice that aims to build cross-cultural understanding between the world and China. This has led to a number of advisory roles. His major advisory role is Business and Government Advisor to Hampton Group, which is a global leader in strategic consulting and investment related to China. In 2013, the Chinese government awarded Alistair the 'Friendship Award' Medal.

## Contributors

**Amitav Acharya**  American University, Washington, DC, USA

**Robert D. Atkinson**  Information Technology and Innovation Foundation (ITIF), Washington, DC, USA

**H. E. Shaukat Aziz**  Green Templeton College, Oxford University, Oxford, UK

**Jean-Christophe Bas**  The Global Compass, Paris, France

**Daniel A. Bell**  Shandong University, Jinan, China

**David Blair**  Center for China and Globalization (CCG), Beijing, China

**Kerry Brown**  Lau China Institute, King's College London, London, UK

**Sir Keith Burnett**  St John's College, Oxford University, Oxford, UK

**Ronnie C. Chan**  Asia Society Hong Kong Center, Hong Kong, China

**Nigel Cory**  Information Technology and Innovation Foundation (ITIF), Washington, DC, USA

**Wendy Cutler**  Asia Society Policy Institute (ASPI), Washington, D.C., USA

**Hermann Hauser**  Amadeus Capital Partners, Cambridge, UK

**Yafei He**  Peking University, Beijing, China

**Richard Higgott**  University of Warwick, Coventry, UK

**Martin Jacques**  Department of Politics and International Studies, Cambridge University, Cambridge, UK

**Masahiro Kawai** The Economic Research Institute for Northeast Asia, Niigata, Japan;
University of Tokyo, Tokyo, Japan

**Parag Khanna** FutureMap, Singapore, Singapore

**Grzegorz W. Kołodko** Kozminski University, Warsaw, Poland;
Belt and Road School, Beijing Normal University, Beijing, PRC, China

**Pascal Lamy** Paris Peace Forum, Paris, France

**Jeffrey Lehman** New York University Shanghai, Shanghai, China

**Yuanli Liu** School of Health Policy and Management, Peking Union Medical College, Beijing, China

**Carlos Lopes** Mandela School of Public Governance, University of Cape Town, Rondebosch, South Africa

**Kishore Mahbubani** Asia Research Institute of National University of Singapore, Singapore, Singapore

**Peter Maurer** The International Committee of the Red Cross (ICRC), Geneva, Switzerland

**James G. McGann** Think Tanks and Civil Societies Program, Wharton School and School of Arts and Sciences, Philadelphia, PA, USA;
Fels Institute of Government, University of Pennsylvania, Philadelphia, PA, USA

**Lu Miao** Center for China and Globalization (CCG), Beijing, China

**Alistair Michie** International Council of the Center for China and Globalization (CCG), Beijing, China

**Peter Nolan** China Centre, Jesus College, Cambridge University, Cambridge, UK

**Joseph S. Nye Jr.** Harvard's Kennedy School of Government, Cambridge, USA

**Lord Jim O'Neill** Royal Institute for International Affairs, London, UK

**Edmund Phelps** Columbia University, New York, USA

**Sir Anthony Seldon** University of Buckingham, Buckingham, UK

**Denis F. Simon** Duke's Fuqua School of Business, Duke University, Durham, USA

**Sir Martin Sorrell** S4 Capital, London, UK

**Huiyao Wang** Center for China and Globalization (CCG), Beijing, China

**Pei Wang** Fudan University, Shanghai, China

**Vladimir Yakunin** Faculty of Political Sciences, Lomonosov Moscow State University, Moscow, Russia

**Guangyao Zhu** Counsellor's Office of the State Council, Beijing, China

# List of Figures

# List of Tables

# Policies for Changing the 'Rules-Based World Order'

# Back to the Future or a Brave New World?—Reflections on How the COVID-19 Pandemic is Reshaping Globalization

Amitav Acharya

**Abstract** Many times, *history shows that pandemics kill millions* and disrupt economic activity and linkages on a global level. COVID-19 will not be the *end of globalization* or *global governance*, but, policymakers seem to develop a convenient case of amnesia about the role of globalization as a transmission belt for a whole variety of threats, such as, pandemics, drug trafficking, people smuggling, money laundering, and environmental degradation. It likely that COVID-19 will further push the world beyond the US-dominated *rules-based world order*, and usher in a more *pluralistic multiplex world*. The concept of a multiplex world offers a window into how the emerging world order is likely to take form in the coming decade. This trend toward a multiplex world was already under way well before COVID-19. A multiplex would not be managed or lead by a single power or group, but formed through a *G20 plus world* where its main players would not be just big powers or nation-states but also institutions, corporations, and networks, operating at multiple and intersecting levels. In such a world order, the nature of threats would be increasingly transnational. These *transnational perils* would be beyond the ability of any single nation to address and defeat. There is now an opportunity to rethink and *reinvent globalization* and *global governance* to fit this new reality.

**Keywords** History shows that pandemics kill millions · End of globalization · Global governance · Rules-based world order · Pluralistic multiplex world · G20 plus world · Transnational perils · Reinvent globalization

A. Acharya (✉)
American University, Washington, DC, USA

© The Author(s) 2021
H. Wang and A. Michie (eds.), *Consensus or Conflict?*, China and Globalization,
https://doi.org/10.1007/978-981-16-5391-9_1

# 1 Back to the Future?

Sometime during the late 1320s, a bacterial infection originating in Eurasia[1] spread rapidly through the vast land and maritime trade routes developed by the mighty Mongol empire to the rest of Asia, Europe, and Africa. That pandemic turned out to be bubonic plague (better known as the 'Black Death'), which reduced the world's population by over 100 million[2] and disrupted the process of what some call "oriental globalization," which had reached its peak during the Mongol empire.[3]

After building the largest land empire in world history, the Mongols had linked East Asia, the Middle East and Europe into a vast economic network. They had built roads, bridges, relay stations, and provided security for traders and travelers. At one end of the system was China, the center of the Mongol economic and manufacturing system and the world's largest economy. On the other end was Western Europe, which was in the early stages of developing its modern capitalist economy, with an extensive regional network linking Italy and Flanders, the Nordic countries and the Baltic in the north with Venice and Genoa, Constantinople, Crimea, Alexandria, and Tunis in the south.

As the Black Death spread, these avenues of commerce rapidly turned into conduits of the pandemic. As Jack Weatherford, the biographer of Mongol Empire founder Genghis Khan, writes, "With luxurious fabrics, exotic flavors and opulent jewels, the caravans brought the fleas that spread the plague from one camp to another, one village to another, one city to another, and one continent to another."[4] In a crucial blow to the Mongol system, the plague disrupted the interlocking economic relationship, known as the Khubi system, between the empire's four segments, the Yuan in the East (Beijing), the Chagatai Khanate in the center, the Ilkhanate in Southwest (central Asia and Iran), and the Golden Horde in the northwest on Russia's border. At the same time, European cities closed their borders and turned on the Jews, who as in the past, got blamed for Europe's latest catastrophe. The Black Death cut China off from Europe for centuries. The extent of human misery and social devastation was such that the Renaissance poet Petrarch would write later, "O happy posterity, who will not experience such abysmal woe and will look upon our testimony as a fable."[5]

Thanks to advances in medicine and vaccines, the effects of COVID-19 will not be anywhere as horrific as the Black Death. Moreover, it is too soon to make any

---

[1] While there is no doubt that the fourteenth-century plague had a major impact on the Mongol Empire, its precise place of origin is still debated, with China, northern Iraq (Kurdistan), and southern Russia, suggested by different researchers. See, Byrne (2012); "Scientists Have Traced The Origin Of The 14th-Century Plague That Killed More Than Half Of Europeans", https://www.iflscience.com/editors-blog/14thcentury-black-death-plague-that-killed-more-than-half-of-europeans-traced-back-to-russia/; Black (2019).

[2] All data and quotes about the thirteenth-century Black Death are from Weatherford (2004).

[3] The opening section of this essay draws upon Acharya (2020).

[4] Ibid., 243–4.

[5] Cited in Benedictow (2005).

judgement on the long-term impact of COVID-19 on the future of globalization and world order. But one of the key lessons of the COVID-19 pandemic is how easy it could be for the international community to forget or wish away the dangers of globalization because of the benefits it has unquestionably brought to the world. COVID-19 is not the first pandemic to have killed millions and disrupted economic activity and linkages, and it will surely not be the last.

It has been well known and debated for some time that globalization produces winners and losers in terms of growth and equity. But amid much hubris over its benefits, policymakers have developed a convenient amnesia about the role of globalization as a transmission belt for a whole variety of threats, such as, pandemics, drug trafficking, people smuggling, money laundering, environmental degradation, etc. Looking back, during the SARS pandemic of 2003, I wrote:

> Financial volatility, transnational terror and infectious disease represent a new breed of transnational threats that are likely to become a recurring scourge of globalization in the 21st century… Although the three challenges have different causes, they share some common features. First, they tend to materialise suddenly and rather unexpectedly. Second, they reflect the forces of globalization at work. The manner in which they spread and their contagion effects attest to this. Third, the sources of these dangers are not exclusively external or internal to the region. Rather, they emanate from external forces interacting closely with the internal vulnerabilities of states.[6]

I further argued that, "Because they are rooted in globalization, which is an irreversible trend, such perils cannot be defeated permanently. It is more realistic to think in terms of their management, rather than eradication. This reality is going to define a new international hierarchy and order in the twenty-first century."

The outbreak and effects of COVID-19 not only bear out these remarks but also require us to fundamentally rethink globalization and its related issue of global governance. At the same time, hype about globalization should not be replaced with hype about "deglobalization."

As the pandemic hit the world, some argued that it would effectively put an end to globalization and that we are perhaps entering into an era of de-globalization. In an op-ed for the *Wall Street Journal,* published on April 3, 2020, Henry Kissinger wrote, "The contraction unleashed by the coronavirus is, in its speed and global scale, unlike anything ever known in history…The pandemic has prompted an anachronism, a revival of the walled city in an age when prosperity depends on global trade and movement of people."[7]

My own view was a bit different. In an essay for *The National Interest* published on April 18, 2020, I argued that while the pandemic was "going to undercut support for globalization, which was already weakened by rising populism and the policies of the Trump presidency,… [it] will not end globalization, but hopefully, it will increase demands for making it more humane and regulated."[8]

---

[6] Acharya (2003).

[7] Kissinger (2020).

[8] Acharya, "How the Coronavirus May Reshape the World Order."

There is no question that in some societies, the COVID-19 pandemic has undercut popular support for globalization, at least in the short term. In people's minds, the virus' lightning spread around the world could be blamed on globalization, including tourism and travel. The manner in which countries and even states within countries closed their borders, in a totally unilateral and uncoordinated manner, exposes the myth of a borderless world, and shows the reassertion of national sovereignty, which was supposed to have been tamed by globalization.

But analysts and policymakers should be thinking not about the "end of globalization," but about how it is changing, or taking on a new form, and how it can be made more just, humane, inclusive, and effective in dealing with perils like COVID-19.

## 2 Re-inventing Globalization: Silk Roads and "Nirvana Routes"

To understand its present context and future trends, one needs to revisit the history of globalization. Globalization was not invented by the West. Nor is it an exclusively modern phenomenon. Much of the recent debate over globalization associates it with the rise of the West and Western modernity. This is essentially the Davos (World Economic Forum) view, which holds that "true globalization," or the "first wave of globalization" started only in the nineteenth century.[9]

To be sure, European voyages from the late fourteenth century, the Industrial Revolution in Europe, and lest we forget, European imperialism, linked the Western hemisphere with the rest of the world in a way that had not been done before. But the origins of the overland Silk Roads[10] date back to the second century BCE. Moreover, the Indian Ocean trading network, which is now referred to as the Maritime Silk Roads, carried far greater volumes of trade while also remaining open to all, without monopolies or encumbrances of the kind the Europeans introduced after fifteenth century CE. Then there was the Mongol empire's short-lived but efficient Eurasian trade and transport system. All these networks left enduring legacies, including exchanges of goods, technologies, and ideas (from paper and printing to gunpowder and compasses).[11] In addition, they were governed by principles and customs (such as free and open trade in the Indian Ocean before European arrival), that not only fueled globalization but also contributed to the rise of the West.

---

[9] Peter Vanham, "A Brief History of Globalization," https://www.weforum.org/agenda/2019/01/how-globalization-4-0-fits-into-the-history-of-globalization/. Vanham was writing as the Head of Communications for the Chairman's Office of the WEF.

[10] The term Silk Road is itself a modern name, coined by German geographer and traveler, Ferdinand von Richthofen in 1877 AD, as 'Seidenstrasse' (silk road), or 'Seidenstrassen' (silk routes). But the reality of it having been a major artery of overland commerce since ancient times is indisputable.

[11] For a full analysis of the flow of inventions and ideas from China to Europe, see the 7 volumes in 24 parts in 'Science and Civilisation in China' by Dr. Joseph Needham and published by Cambridge University Press.

Hence, globalization did not begin after 1500 CE, but at least a thousand years before that. As John M. Hobson argues, "after 500 [AD] Persians, Arabs, Africans, Javanese, Jews, Indians and Chinese created and maintained a global economy down to about 1800."[12] This globalization was characterized by a relatively stable environment, low transit taxes, and rational economic institutions to support trade. This globalization was multi-civilizational, featuring Byzantium, the Tang, Song, Yuan and Ming in China, the Islamic empires of the Abbasids, Umayyads and Fatimids, and south Indian Hindu kingdoms (such as Chola and Vijayanagar) and the Islamic Moghuls in India. It was carried by both land and sea trade. More important, "[t]he limits to the effective authority of the state, combined with the powerful presence of universal belief systems, notably Hinduism, Buddhism, Islam and Christianity, encouraged the movement of ideas, and with them people and goods, across regions and continents."[13]

Together, the two Silk Roads, overland and maritime, created commercial, cultural, and political linkages and frameworks across Asia. They became what I have called "the Nirvana Routes,"[14] through which the transmission of two of the world's oldest major religions, Buddhism and Hinduism, spread among the societies of India, Southeast Asia, Central Asia, China, Korea and Japan, with Islam joining later.

Just because the political systems and institutions supporting this globalization were empires, rather than modern nation-states, does not make it less significant as a foundation for modern globalization and world order. On the contrary, the core feature of this classical globalization was its combination of political and cultural diversity on the one hand, and economic inter-connectedness on the other. This is the first known example of a "Multiplex World Order,"[15]and offers a window to how the emerging world order is likely to shape up.

Moreover, it is very important to keep in mind that globalization was already changing before COVID-19, and before the Donald Trump presidency. Trump gave globalization a further push downhill, but he did not cause the slowdown of, and the poplar backlash against, neo-liberal globalization. Instead he exploited and benefited from it to get elected.

Globalization was always hyped, especially by elites around the world, led by vocal and influential champions like the WEF in Davos. The Davos Man's (to use Samuel Huntington's phrase) view of globalization always seemed, to me as well as to many other scholars and activists, as unrealistic, unjust and thus unsustainable. Now ironically, many of the same advocates of globalization are talking about its crisis and reversal. They should have raised the flag much earlier.

---

[12] Hobson (2004). George Modelski, who was among the first to write about globalization, argued that globalization began around 1000 AD, with the rise and spread of Islam and Arabic knowledge. Modelski (1972).

[13] Hopkins (2002).

[14] The founding of the two Silk Roads and the flows of ideas and religions though them are discussed in Acharya (2021).

[15] Acharya (2014, 2018).

There have been demands for "deglobalization" before, especially after the financial shocks of 1997 and 2008, and there are now terms going around that look for "re-globalization," or globalization "2.0", "4.0," etc. But the future of globalization would not be a return to pre-COVID-19 normalcy or "business-as-usual." The past will matter, especially a deeper past, which should make us think about the pluralistic and Eastern-led globalization before the rise of the West. But the future is likely to be a brave new world.

# 3 A Brave New World?

Even before Trump's anti-globalization policies had time to take effect and before COVID-19 hit the world, trends in the future direction of globalization could be anticipated based on available indicators. I summarized those trends in the following words:

> It is wrong to say that globalization is over. Instead it will, and is already taking, a different form. Globalization may become less driven by trade and more by developmental concerns. This might give more space to the initiatives of the emerging powers, which focus more on infrastructure than on free trade. The new globalization could thus well be led less by the West and more by the East, especially China and India, as it had been for a thousand years before European colonialism…Moreover, the new globalization will be anchored more by South-South, rather than North-South linkages….Due to the prominence of China and other emerging powers, the new globalization might be more respectful of sovereignty. It will be more economic and less political or ideological. It could even be less coercive, especially compared to the Western-led globalization during the 19th and 20th centuries.[16]

The above assessment was based on trends that had been apparent for some time. A report by the United Nations Development Program (UNDP) in 2013 had estimated that the Global South had increased its share of the global GDP from one-third in 1990 to about half and increased its share of world merchandise trade from 25% in 1980 to 47% in 2010.[17] And South–South trade increased from less than 8% of world merchandise trade in 1980 to over 26% in 2011.[18] According to UNCTAD, South–South flows in foreign direct investment now constitute over a third of global flows.[19] These trends were already reshaping globalization.

These trends, which I would simply call "New Dynamic of Globalization" (NDG), are now becoming visible as the world recovers from the economic effects of the COVID-19 pandemic. To be sure, the economic impact of the pandemic is still unfolding and it is too early to make any definitive assessments about its long-term economic impact. But there are some revealing early signs. The International Monetary Fund (IMF)'s October 2020 report showed that in 2021, Asia might grow

---

[16] Acharya (2017a).

[17] UNDP (2013).

[18] UNDP, *Human Development Report 2013.* p. 2.

[19] UNCTAD (2015).

at 6.9% in 2021 compared to 5.2% for the world as a whole.[20] The UN Conference on Trade and Development (UNCTAD) estimated that by the end of 2020, a recovery from the global trade slump had begun, and it "was largely driven by the trade of goods from and to developing countries, especially by the very strong performance of East Asian economies."[21]

That Asia's economic recovery has been faster than that of the rest of the world should not be surprising since the region had good economic fundamentals, but it is possibly even more so due to the fact that Asia as a whole has done a better job in controlling the pandemic than other regions and the West.

When the fourteenth-century plague crippled the Mongol world order, it created the basis for a new world order. In the east the Ming rose, the first major Han Chinese Empire since the Tang Dynasty (the Song was a cultural and scientific giant, but not a military one). Central Eurasia saw the rise of the Ottomans. One branch of the Turko-Mongol elite founded the Moghul empire in India. And ultimately, the Black Death might have even contributed to the rise of Western Europe by reducing population and the Mongol threat, thus paving the way for new economic activity.

Just as the fourteenth-century plague contributed to the rise of Europe, it may well be that COVID-19 will hasten the rise of Asia, which was already under way for some time. The pandemic has also rendered Asia-led globalization more likely than ever before.

There is no question that the role of the US and China will be critical in shaping the future of globalization. Before the pandemic, the US under the Trump administration had already expressed its distaste for globalization and taken numerous steps, such as pulling out of the Trans-Pacific Partnership (TPP) and replacing the North American Free Trade Agreement (NAFTA). COVID-19 was seen by the Trump administration as a vindication of its anti-globalization ideology and strategy. As Peter Navarro, Trump's lead economic adviser, put it: "if there's any vindication of the President's buy American to secure borders and a strong manufacturing base philosophy, strategy and belief it is this [pandemic] crisis."[22] Trump himself denounced supply chains, the critical element of current globalization. As he put it, "somebody, years ago, got this crazy idea: Let's build all over the place and let's have parts—let's have a screw for a car delivered and made in a country that's far away, and let's have a fender made someplace else, and let's do this, and let's do that, and let's put it all together."[23]

Upon becoming the US President, Joe Biden has promised to restore elements of the liberal international order, reviving alliances, reengaging with multilateral institutions, and promoting human rights and democracy in the world. The Biden administration's "Interim National Security Strategic Guidance" would like the US to "lead

---

[20] "Asia Still Rises: India, China and ASEAN-5 lead world growth in 2021", https://www.imf.org/en/Publications/WEO/Issues/2020/09/30/world-economic-outlook-october-2020.

[21] "East Asian economies drive global trade recovery", 10 February 2021. https://unctad.org/news/east-asian-economies-drive-global-trade-recovery.

[22] White House Coronavirus Task Force Briefing April 2, 2020. https://www.rev.com/blog/transcripts/donald-trump-coronavirus-task-force-briefing-april-2.

[23] "Remarks at a White House Coronavirus Task Force Press Briefing", April 20, 2020, https://www.govinfo.gov/content/pkg/DCPD-202000278/html/DCPD-202000278.htm.

and sustain a stable and open international system…strong democratic alliances, partnerships, multilateral institutions, and rules."[24] But it does not talk about reviving globalization since that would depend on the strength of the US economy, which remains highly fragile and uncertain. Instead, the Biden administration seeks the return of a world where the US provides leadership and sets the agenda. While Biden's shift from Trump's populist and transactionalist approach, and his quick and humane approach to COVID-19 are welcome and deserve praise from the international community, one should also realize that his goal of reviving US global leadership would not be easy to achieve thanks to the combination of toxic politics at home, with Trumpism still very much alive, and competition abroad.

What about China? China will persist with globalization, as clearly affirmed by President Xi Jinping in his Davos speeches of January 2017 and January 2021 (the latter was delivered virtually).[25] China is seeking new opportunities for itself in leading globalization, especially in areas where it has particular strengths—like infrastructure development—which is a vital ingredient of this new globalization.

Even before COVID-19, China had pledged strong support for free trade and globalization.[26] It has been the force behind institutions that support the new globalization dynamic, like the Belt and Road Initiative (BRI), the Asian Infrastructure Investment Bank (AIIB), and the institutions of BRICS countries (Brazil, Russia, India, China, and South Africa), such as the New Development Bank (NDB), and the Contingent Reserve Arrangement (CRA).

But China also faces daunting challenges in providing leadership in this new globalization dynamic. China is steadily overtaking the US in terms of overall GDP output. But leadership in globalization requires more than material power, or technological and financial resources. It also requires international legitimacy or trustworthiness. Global leadership is very difficult to realize without strong support from within one's own neighborhood in East and Southeast Asia.[27]

---

[24] The White House, "Interim National Security Guidance", March 2021, https://www.whitehouse.gov/wp-content/uploads/2021/03/NSC-1v2.pdf.

[25] "Full text: Xi Jinping's speech at the virtual Davos Agenda event", January 25, 2021, https://news.cgtn.com/news/2021-01-25/Full-text-Xi-Jinping-s-speech-at-the-virtual-Davos-Agenda-event-Xln4hwjO2Q/index.html.

[26] Acharya (2017b).

[27] One signpost of the challenge China faces in ensuring support for its leadership comes from its own neighborhood, especially in Southeast Asia. A recent opinion survey showed that the China's "trust perception" (p. 3) is declining. The percentage of respondents who had "little confidence" and "no confidence" for China "to do the right thing in the interests of the global community", increased from 51.5% in 2019, to 60.4% in 2020 to 63.0% in 2021 (p. 42). For the US the same question showed a marked decline in distrust, from 49.7% in 2020 to 31.3% in 2021 (p. 50). *The State of Southeast Asia 2021 Survey Report* (Singapore: ISEAS-Yusof Ishak Institute, 2021), https://www.iseas.edu.sg/wp-content/uploads/2021/01/The-State-of-SEA-2021-v2.pdf. In my own research, part of the trust gap for China has to do with its handling of the initial outbreak of the pandemic, which was viewed as non-transparent, a concern similar to that of Western countries, despite China's subsequent aid of masks and vaccines to Southeast Asian countries.

# 4  Toward Humane Globalization

While globalization is not ending, in its new form the world should worry more about how to make it more just and humane than how to make it more efficient. This is critical to the future of globalization.

To ensure popular support for globalization, the international community must ensure that it attracts more stakeholders. This means ensuring that the benefits of globalization are more equitable or at least mitigate the inequalities caused by neo-liberal globalization. This means accepting a role for different leaders and various constituencies, instead of having it led by a single nation (be it the US or China) or a bloc (the West).

This is in keeping with the reality of an increasingly Multiplex World. A Multiplex World order is a world without a hegemon. It is culturally and politically diverse yet connected by economic and other transnational linkages. And in such a world, the makers and breakers of order are not just great powers and states but also non-state actors—corporations, social movements, and extremists—interacting at global, regional, and sub-national levels. Last but not the least, challenges to the world order, peace and stability, come from transnational forces, such as climate change, terrorism, and pandemics.

While COVID-19 may see a greater push for national self-reliance, the logic of a Multiplex World and the dangers of globalization dictate that any effective international response system to transnational challenges like COVID-19 must be based on two realities:

> First, exclusionary and inward-looking responses will not work. No region [or nation] can afford to be an island. Second, old attitudes towards sovereignty and non-interference must change. Currency speculators, terrorists and viruses have scant regard for national boundaries. Hence, the old framework of the nation-state is inadequate for responding to transnational perils. Collective action to combat the dangers should be seen not as an abrogation of sovereignty, but rather the pooling of it.[28]

This principle applies as much to the current situation as it did in 2003, when these words were written, and as much to China as to the US, and indeed to the international community at large.

Moreover, the global pandemic calls for a wider and normative view of globalization, not the narrow economistic view. As the late Canadian scholar and my former colleague at York University in Toronto, once wrote, globalization was and will be, "multidimensional: connectedness in politics and the organisation of security, in economics and welfare, in culture, in ecology, in values of all kinds. No area of human activity is isolated; and within each area, no one is untouched by the condition and activities of others."[29]

The key to generating popular support for globalization lies in addressing the human costs of the pandemic in terms of deaths, impoverishment, and inequality.

---

[28] Acharya, "ASEAN Needs New Tools for New Threats."

[29] Cox (1997).

While the exact numbers will take time to unravel, they are already horrendously high, and should be front and center in any attempt to revive globalization. Hence, the foremost challenge for the international community is to make globalization more humane.

To this end, in order to make globalization more just and humane, as well as more effective in addressing repeats of dangers such as the COVID-19 pandemic, the West should listen to the voices of the Rest.

The idea of "Humane Globalization,"[30] requires a shift of focus from national to human security. Contemporary globalization, from the rise of the European balance of power order through to the post-World War II period, has been associated with the concept of national security, meaning protecting sovereignty and territory from external military attack. Human security implies security for the human person, for the individual and for the people. To quote the late Pakistani economist Mahbub ul Haq, who pioneered the ideas of human development and human security in partnership with Indian Nobel Laureate Amartya Sen, "We need to fashion a new concept of human security that is reflected in the lives of our people, not in the weapons of our country."[31]

The ideas of human security and human development suggest that while the traditional understanding of globalization remains obsessed with "power-shift," measured in terms of GDP growth, military and technological power, but an equally visible and ultimately more important trend in world politics is the "idea-shift."[32]

Hence, in remaking globalization, one must not assume the superiority of ideas, norms and institutions of the West. Existing commentaries on globalization and global governance show an abundance of narratives in which the "good" norms and effective institutions of governance, development, security, and justice are supposed have been pioneered in the West. These then are supposed to prevail over the "bad" ideas and inadequate institutions of governance in the non-Western world.

COVID-19 has turned this assumption upside down. The fact that the United States, the world's strongest nation in terms of economic (as yet), military and "soft" power, has also suffered from the highest infection and mortality rate in the entire world, that too by a huge margin, cannot simply be blamed on Trump's poor leadership. But more structurally blame should be directed also on a weak public health system, racial inequality, and a political system led by what Fareed Zakaria, using Alexander Hamilton's words, calls "government ill-executed."[33]

The pandemic has shown that coping with global challenges depends more on governance, rather than ideology. While "pundits will debate whether national

---

[30] I had first proposed the idea of "humane globalization" in a speech to the Youth Peace Conference of the Singapore Soka Association, 30th September 2005. A written version of the speech is Acharya (2006). Later, others including President Barrack Obama have called for humane globalization. See "Obama's call for humane globalization may be too late: Walkom", *Toronto Star*, 1 July 2016, https://www.thestar.com/opinion/commentary/2016/07/01/obamas-call-for-humane-globalization-may-be-too-late-walkom.html?rf.

[31] Cited in Bajpai (2000).

[32] Acharya (2016).

[33] Zakaria (2020).

responses to the crisis put democracies in a more positive light over authoritarian states," it is clear that countries and territories "that have offered reasonably strong responses to the coronavirus include both. The real contest here is about governance, rather than ideology or regime type."[34]

The historian Niall Ferguson has argued that emerging powers such as China and India could not have achieved progress except by "downloading" the ideas and institutions of the West. He calls these "killer apps," and mentions six: competition, science, medicine, property rights, consumer society, and work ethic.[35] My response, made during a debate with Ferguson in March 2017 at Tsinghua University's Schwarzman College, was not only that the West could not have developed these "killer apps," especially science and medicine, without drawing upon the prior advances of the civilizations of the East, China, India and the Islamic world among them. I also argued that the East, now revived, is also "uploading" its own "apps," or ideas and institutions, for the benefit of all humankind, including the West.

Some of the ideas the West should learn from, or "download" are precisely those of human security and human development, although one could think of many more, such as responsible sovereignty, sustainable development and now, humane globalization. Aside from new advances in science and technology, manufacturing, and medicine, especially in China and India, many ideas about peace, humanitarianism, and political pluralism have roots in the non-Western world, including in Hindu, Buddhist, Confucian, and Muslim traditions and writings. It is understandable why the West wants to propagate its "own" ideas and norms to the rest of the world. What is more problematic and increasingly indefensible, is its claim that anything that does not conform to the Western model of governance is not good enough and ought to be rejected.

## 5  Conclusion

To conclude, COVID-19 does not spell the end to either globalization or to global governance. It is more likely that COVID-19 will push the world further beyond the US-dominated world order and usher in a more pluralistic Multiplex World, which was already under way well before COVID-19. It would be culturally and politically diverse, but functionally interconnected. Such a world would not be managed or led by a single power or group, but would be a G-Plus world, with its main players not limited to big powers or nation-states, but also including institutions, corporations, and networks, operating at multiple and intersecting levels. Threats to such a world order would be increasingly transnational in nature and beyond the ability of any single nation to address and defeat.

There is now an opportunity to rethink and reinvent globalization and global governance to fit this new reality. Such an effort should aim for developing greater equity,

---

[34] Acharya, "How the Coronavirus May Reshape the World Order."

[35] Ferguson (2012).

justice, and collective capacity for providing pubic goods, rather than depending on a single nation or a handful of nations.

# References

Acharya A (2003) ASEAN needs new tools for new threats. Yale Global, 4 June 2003. https://yal eglobal.yale.edu/content/asean-needs-new-tools-new-threats

Acharya A (2006) Peace and human security in a globalized world: a perspective on classical, contemporary and humane globalization. In: New thinking on peace. Singapore Soka Association, Singapore, pp 65–85

Acharya A (2014, 2018) The end of American world order. Polity, Cambridge

Acharya A (2016) 'Idea-shif': how ideas from the rest are reshaping global order. Third World Q 37(7):1156–1170

Acharya A (2017a) After liberal hegemony: the advent of a multiplex world. Ethics Intern Aff 31(3):271–285. https://www.ethicsandinternationalaffairs.org/2017/multiplex-world-order/

Acharya A (2017b) Emerging powers can be saviours of the global liberal order. Financial Times, 19 January 2017, p 12. https://www.ft.com/content/f175b378-dd79-11e6-86ac-f253db7791c6

Acharya A (2020) How the coronavirus may reshape the world order. The National Interest, 18 April, 2020. https://nationalinterest.org/feature/how-coronavirus-may-reshape-world-order-145972

Acharya A (2021) The Nirvana Route: how early encounters between India, China and Southeast Asia shaped Asian civilization," Part I: "'Journey to the West': The Buddhist Reimagination of China", January 19, 2021, https://thediplomat.com/2021/01/journey-to-the-west-the-buddhist-reimagination-of-china/. Part II, "Journey to the East: The Hindu-Buddhist Making of Southeast Asia" 15 February, 2021, https://thediplomat.com/2021/02/journey-to-the-east-the-hindu-buddhist-making-of-southeast-asia/

Bajpai K (2000) Human security: concept and measurement. School of International Studies, Jawaharlal Nehru University, New Delhi

Benedictow OJ (2005) The black death: the greatest catastrophe ever. Hist Today 55(3). https://www.historytoday.com/archive/black-death-greatest-catastrophe-ever

Black W (2019) What was the black death?, 12 December, 2019. https://www.livescience.com/what-was-the-black-death.html

Byrne JP (2012) Encyclopedia of the black death, vol 1. ABC-CLIO

Cox R (1997) Economic globalization and the limits to liberal democracy. In: McGrew A (ed) The transformation of democracy?: globalization and territorial democracy. Polity, Cambridge

Ferguson N (2012) Civilization: the six killer apps of western power. Penguin, New York

Hobson JM (2004) The Eastern origins of Western civilization. Cambridge University Press, Cambridge, p 32

Hopkins AG (2002) Introduction: globalization: agenda for historians. In: Hopkins (ed) Globalization in world history. Pimlico, London, p 4

Kissinger H (2020) The coronavirus pandemic will forever alter the world order. Wall Street J. https://www.wsj.com/articles/the-coronavirus-pandemic-will-forever-alter-the-world-order-11585953005

Modelski G (1972) Principles of world politics. Free Press, New York

United Nations Conference on Trade and Development (UNCTAD) (2015) World investment report, 2015. United Nations, Geneva, pp 5, 8–9. http://unctad.org/en/PublicationsLibrary/wir2015_en.pdf

United Nations Development Program (UNDP) (2013) Human development report 2013. The rise of the south: human progress in a diverse world. United Nations Development Program, New York, p 2

Weatherford J (2004) Genghis Khan and the making of the modern World. Three River Press, New York

Zakaria F (2020) The U.S. is still exceptional—but now for its incompetence. The Washington Post, March 26, 2020

**Amitav Acharya** is the UNESCO Chair in Transnational Challenges and Governance and Distinguished Professor at the School of International Service, American University, Washington, DC. Previously he taught at York University, Toronto, University of Bristol, and Nanyang Technological University, Singapore. He also held the inaugural Boeing Company Chair in International Relations at the Schwarzman Scholars Program at Tsinghua University in 2016–2018 and was elected to the Christensen Fellowship at Oxford. His recent books include *The Making of Global International Relations* (2019); *Constructing Global Order* (2018); *The End of American World Order* (2018). He is a two-time recipient of International Studies Association's Distinguished Scholar Award.

**Open Access** This chapter is licensed under the terms of the Creative Commons Attribution-NonCommercial-NoDerivatives 4.0 International License (http://creativecommons.org/licenses/by-nc-nd/4.0/), which permits any noncommercial use, sharing, distribution and reproduction in any medium or format, as long as you give appropriate credit to the original author(s) and the source, provide a link to the Creative Commons license and indicate if you modified the licensed material. You do not have permission under this license to share adapted material derived from this chapter or parts of it.

The images or other third party material in this chapter are included in the chapter's Creative Commons license, unless indicated otherwise in a credit line to the material. If material is not included in the chapter's Creative Commons license and your intended use is not permitted by statutory regulation or exceeds the permitted use, you will need to obtain permission directly from the copyright holder.

# COVID-19 as a Catalyst in the Transition to a Future of Multipolar Global Cooperation

## H. E. Shaukat Aziz

**Abstract** The challenges of an *interconnected globalized world* are more wide reaching than ever. They include the growing need to *tackle climate change*, the *spread of extremism*, the threat of *natural disasters, future pandemics, world cyber-attacks* and the fallout from conflict. These issues mean there is a need for a *global one-stop-shop disaster relief unit*, which should be formed under the auspices of the United Nations (UN). This *UN global disaster relief unit* needs the authority and capacity to help any country around the world—to be able to provide physical help, advance warning and post-disaster management. There is much to be learned from case studies—such as the *2005 Pakistan earthquake*, which was the worst in Asia for decades. In another vein, *outdated Bretton Woods institutions* must be dealt with as they were created for global needs of a world shattered by World War II. These institutions are the multilateral organizations—the United Nations, the International Monetary Fund and the World Bank—and they must be restructured for realities of the *revolutionary digital and biosphere age*. Crucially, there must be a focus on generating inclusive, equitable growth—something the *global technological revolution* makes more attainable than before.

**Keywords** Interconnected globalized world · Climate change · Extremism · Natural disasters · Future pandemics · World cyber-attacks · Global one-stop-shop disaster relief unit · UN global disaster relief unit · 2005 Pakistan earthquake · Bretton Woods · Digital and biosphere age · technology revolution

Even before we faced an unprecedented global shock in the form of COVID-19, the geopolitical norms we had known for decades were making way for a less familiar world.

Three decades after the Berlin Wall fell and Asia gained prominence, the centre of power was no longer automatically weighted towards the West. This was coupled with major countries becoming increasingly siloed, withdrawing from their role on the world stage and turning to increasingly protectionist policies. The role of the old

S. Aziz (✉)
Green Templeton College, Oxford University, Wellington Square, Oxford OX1 2JD, UK

© The Author(s) 2021                                                                                      17
H. Wang and A. Michie (eds.), *Consensus or Conflict?*, China and Globalization,
https://doi.org/10.1007/978-981-16-5391-9_2

multilateral alliances was diminishing as they effectively vacated the pitch. At the same time, some of the old Cold War rivalries began to re-emerge.

The global pandemic has only accelerated this shift. Unlike the crises we are more familiar with, it has affected us in a multitude of ways—in addition to the human cost through mass loss of life, the virus has closed borders, halted freedom of movement, disrupted supply chains and diminished consumer confidence.

However, just as a recession leads to less-viable businesses folding, it can also open the door to exciting innovation, so too must we use this pandemic to discard old practices that no longer work and leverage it as a springboard for growth. The time is now to focus on fresh thinking for the future—how to better equip ourselves for another unplanned catastrophe on this scale, how to react faster and more effectively.

## 1   Reactions to the Challenges of COVID-19

The challenges facing us, in our increasingly interconnected and globalized world, are also more wide reaching than ever. They include the growing need to tackle climate change, the spread of extremism, the threat of natural disasters and future pandemics, cyber-attack and the fallout from conflict. The great challenge of our globalized world is that issues which arise in far-flung countries have the potential to affect us all.

Today, we have a chance to build a prosperous and equitable world—all that is needed is collective will. If we fail to improve how we work together, we risk falling behind and being stuck in the past.

The shockwaves that reverberated globally in 2020, making the pandemic unique in its scale, largely boiled down to the porous nature of modern borders, the ease of travel and interconnectivity that we have become accustomed to. They allowed the COVID-19 pandemic to spread to every corner of the globe to an unprecedented extent and to become a truly worldwide problem.

Today, it is important to carefully study the lessons learned from our collective—as well as individual approaches—and learn how to improve the world's preparedness and capacity to withstand similar pandemics in the future. When we analyse how different governments responded to the challenges of the pandemic, it is hard to generalize about any one country's response, although many have followed similar models of "lockdown" with varying levels of enforcement. But societies have different needs and some were more receptive to the kind of public health measures that have been needed. One universal aspect was that, when such a fundamental and far-reaching crisis happens, people expect their leaders to act, to bring in measures of support and to tackle the crisis head-on.

When a crisis of such proportion hits, governments have to be agile—to disregard old norms, move quickly and do everything they can to save lives, support infrastructure and the fabric of society. It is a race against time and is unlike any normal kind of policy-making.

In 2020, we saw the importance of the "big state" model take hold across Europe and in the United States as well, where government intervention in the economy, as well as in industry, has been exercised on an unprecedented level. The US witnessed rescue packages not seen since the Marshall Plan as well as direct state intervention in the economy.

## 2  Looking Forward to a New Post-pandemic Reconstruction

As we look forward to the worst of the pandemic being over, we need to reflect on mistakes that were made and learn the lessons of the past year. The need for swift, decisive action in such a crisis is paramount. Governments that took decisions quickly to stop the spread of the virus will be praised in the long run. Those that struggled to show leadership are likely to face the heaviest criticism.

The way decisions were communicated with the public is key—it is not enough to decide on a strategy. Being able to relay it clearly, as well as having people on the ground who you rely on to implement it—from local government to police and border patrol—is important for maximum compliance. Whatever strategy you decide to pursue, you must have buy-in from all relevant stakeholders. The military forces, as well as civil society, should be ready to help in the distribution and support of public services.

Governments must be prepared to think outside the box, whether it is in designing new rescue packages or temporarily relaxing regulations to help the national effort. Technology has been a game changer in many ways, but it also creates new challenges for governments in such a crisis. Getting your message across is harder when everyone sees what other countries are doing differently—in real time. This can result in pressure and criticism of a government that is not pursuing a similarly successful strategy.

But the main lesson is that we need to rebuild our capacity—and willingness—to work together and deal with major crises as citizens of the world. Diseases do not recognize borders and all governments must accept that cooperation is the key to dealing with a pandemic—we live in a globalized world, and a crisis like this needs a global response.

Past tensions must be set aside and countries must work together to help each other meet medicine and equipment shortfalls. The pandemic should hopefully serve as a wake-up call to all those who think unilateral action is the answer.

## 3   Globalization in a Multipolar World

I have long argued that a multipolar world is better than a unipolar world. The existence of new world powers could be a source of strength for all nations. The emergence of a new balance of power, which we have been seeing over the past few decades and which will only continue in the 2020s, must be handled maturely by all sides. Instead of seeing each other as rivals, key world players should focus on interacting more closely at the summit level and increasing their use of soft, rather than hard power.

Most importantly, we must not let this crisis—and the economic fallout from it— usher in a world of more protectionist inward-looking policies. We have already seen the damage vaccine nationalism can have and the damage it can cause to trust and relationships between countries. Siloing yourself, looking inward and playing to the domestic audience would be a mistake. It risks delivering poor results and ultimately propping up less competitive, and therefore often unviable, industries. In the long run, it stifles innovation, limits growth and, as a result, it keeps living standards low.

Overall, the path to collective prosperity does not lie in insularity, but through embracing the opportunities of globalization. Through this we can ensure competition, increased productivity and the incentive to innovate—ultimately boosting collective prosperity. The globalized nature of our interactions mean traditional borders lose their relevance, which is particularly as a result of technological breakthroughs. You can be in one country and have something delivered from the other side of the world at the touch of a button. This should not be seen as a threat, but rather as a chance to access completely new markets.

## 4   Tectonic Shifts in Geopolitics

We have spent the past decade concerned about changing global power dynamics, as the tectonic plates shifted away from the West and towards Asia, and in particular towards China. Much has been said and written of the "Thucydides Trap", referring to the Ancient Greek historian who, writing about the conflict between Sparta and Athens at the time, posited that conflict is inevitable when rising powers emerge to rival dominant ones. While today this outcome is far from inevitable, the argument deserves our careful attention to prevent tension from escalating into conflict.

While we have seen some "growing pains" as the established powers struggle to learn how to react to the changing world order, there is enough room for China to play a major role alongside the United States, a nation that has enjoyed hegemonic status since the collapse of the Soviet Union. Also, China has a valuable role to interact more with the other five permanent members (P5) of the UN Security Council. and other P5 countries Raising the number of key powers that are able to help us collectively navigate global challenges can ultimately be beneficial. The struggles that nations—particularly in the developing world—are having with distributing a COVID-19 vaccine only proves this point. The emergence of more than one global center of power will provide balance to the world and act as a vital source of international strength.

## 5    COVID-19 Vaccines as a Bridge to Better Global Cooperation

Questions must be asked about how COVID-19 started and spread and I welcome continued international efforts to assess this. But the pandemic has already brought us positive examples of how global cooperation can—and should—work. For example, Asian countries that had experience in fighting SARS did a great deal to provide the West with much needed protective equipment as well as personnel, equipment and R&D resources.

These same principles should now apply to the global distribution of the vaccine. Scientists working on the Oxford-Astra Zeneca vaccine have pointed out that it is not enough for any individual country to vaccinate its people. The porous nature of our borders—through trade, travel and human connection—means that only once every corner of the world is vaccinated will we finally be able to close the book on COVID-19. The rollout of the vaccine should soon become an automatic occurrence, as we saw with small pox, and will hopefully lead to the eradication of the virus. Countries cannot continue to shut their borders to keep out the virus—this is antithetical to the life and values to which we have become accustomed.

Once the monumental task of the vaccine rollout is complete, and even greater work is done to make sure it is resistant to mutations, governments must take a new look at their approach to international affairs. In recent years, we have seen the major powers of the world growing further and further apart. Cooperation between the P5 (the five permanent members of the UN Security Council) has been a struggle for years and in our hyper interconnected, globalized world, where—as we have seen—disease spreads so quickly—the necessity for governments to be on the same page is greater than ever.

There needs to be a renewed effort to build linkages and inter-dependencies, which will serve us well when the next crisis comes along. When already in place, these connections play a key role in enabling cooperation. Increasing interconnectivity can be accomplished by encouraging trade, investment and people-to-people contact—even if it is by Zoom for the moment. These efforts will help shore up a level of trust, which will be invaluable in the event of any future tension. Connectivity is the true safeguard of peace.

As the economic impact from repeated lockdowns begins to sink in, there will be a renewed need for economic cooperation. Many governments have understandably relied on quantitative easing and record levels of borrowing at cheap interest rates to fund their way through the emergency measures needed to tackle COVID-19. The drawback of this is that it can lead to ever-rising inequality. The solution is almost universally to go for growth—to expand markets and focus on creating opportunity and jobs. The Belt and Road Initiative (BRI), launched by President Xi Jinping, set a new standard for global cooperation, one which can be replicated by countries around the world. Pakistan has already benefited considerably from the BRI, which includes billions of dollars being deployed in our country. More recently, Pakistan has also benefited from support, expertise and vaccine distribution from China during the health crisis. All of this has further contributed to the strength of the relationship between our two nations and demonstrated how countries with more abundant resources can, and should, help their neighbours, creating a win–win for all involved.

## 6 The Role of Multinational Organizations in Fighting COVID-19

It is important to properly define the role of multilateral organizations during the recent pandemic. Over the past year we have seen how poorly prepared they were to face a global crisis of this proportion. The World Health Organization (WHO) has a particularly important role to play in providing accurate information during a pandemic, supporting the global effort to find a vaccine and then driving its equitable distribution. The WHO should have been miles ahead of everyone else, an authoritative voice in the early days of confusion over a new and unknown enemy. It should have been the source of the most authoritative information, a repository of experience for this whole global effort.

Instead, it was largely missing in action. The WHO is uniquely placed to play a vital role in early detection, targeting and then spreading accurate information as soon as it learns a virus has emerged. It should not be waiting for the virus to start spreading before it acts. By then, it is too late. Unfortunately, the organization's response during the critical early stage of the pandemic—before it became an actual pandemic—was a total failure. By all accounts, the WHO was too passive and too slow to take the necessary steps to contain the spread of the virus.

Going forward, we must find ways to reform the WHO, to sharpen its antenna and broaden its scope. The WHO should become a global clearinghouse of information on preventing, managing and providing relief during pandemics that is accessible to all. The WHO should be encouraged to lead from the front and track the world. For example, the WHO should advise what pandemics are currently active, and their causes, so that we can be pre-emptive, timely and effective.

A new paradigm for a global response to such crises is necessary. One that enables us to act faster and to be more nimble. Clear channels of communication within the WHO must be established, so that countries know whom to alert the moment it has concerns—whether it is about a virus or other public health issue. The response must be instant and well prepared with teams of experts ready to assess the situation and draw up recommendations.

The key message is that planning and preparedness are vital. And every country must have the tools in place to handle a crisis—before it starts.

Not all countries have the necessary specialists or infrastructure to tackle a pandemic or to quickly vaccinate its people—particularly in the developing world. Nor do they have manufacturers that can produce the necessary equipment or labs that can manufacture vaccines. Initially, even advanced Western countries such as the United Kingdom did not have the manufacturing capacity to produce vaccines and had to effectively develop them from scratch. Not everyone has the resources to do this at speed, which is why there must be a go-to window in the world where they can get help. A one-stop-shop disaster relief unit.

On the back end of the COVID-19 pandemic, we must ensure there is a proactive, empowered organization that can act as a global repository of expertise, providing the right equipment and specialists to any country in the world that needs them. This organization should have expertise in every type of disaster—from pandemics to floods to earthquakes. It should be formed under the auspices of the United Nations, which has the authority and capacity to help any country around the world—to be able to provide physical help, pre-warning and post-disaster management. No country can stand alone in a crisis in our globalized world. This is why disaster management will only succeed if it is a truly global effort.

The need for reform does not only apply to the WHO. Many multilateral organizations and the Bretton Woods institutions created after the Second World War—the United Nations, the International Monetary Fund and the World Bank are outdated and have needed to be reformed for a long time. The pandemic exposed problems that existed both in their structure and ability to respond. Regrettably, meaningful cross-border cooperation also did not start until later on in the crisis, seeming to do little while we see major powers splintering—and struggling to co-exist harmoniously.

## 7 The Future of Multilateral Cooperation

Today we see an unwillingness between the major powers of the day to work together—more than there has been in recent years. Arguably, this leaves space for the United Nations to take on a bigger global role and be a force for good. This should include the other institutions related to the United Nations. Reforming the United Nations structure and encouraging cohesion and cooperation would be a step towards achieving this objective. These institutions should do more to act as peace brokers, bringing adversaries to the table and encouraging engagement on any level. These multilateral institutions can be a true force for good and have an important role to play, but without reform to bring them up to date with the modern world, they will simply not be able to step up in a crisis and react fast enough.

What we increasingly see, as different security, economic or social threats emerge, is that the world is suffering from a leadership deficit. Politicians and decision-makers lack a global perspective and are too focused on short-term domestic political cycles. Such an absence of global, far-sighted leadership inevitably becomes a barrier to successful cooperation. This can be seen in Europe with divisions that have yet to heal in the wake of Brexit as well as the recent rifts over vaccine procurement failures. It has also been evident in the relationships between the major economic and political superpowers, including the United States, Russia and China.

This comes at a time when the need for clear, effective and strategic leadership is greater than ever. We need leaders to be able to convince their people into taking these unprecedented—and often painful—lockdown steps, rally support and work together with their counterparts across the world. They must be able to effectively coordinate national, state and local government—which, as we know, are not always in sync. All of this must be done against the backdrop of remote working—with some government departments working almost entirely from home while implementing complex new policies.

## 8   First-Hand Experience in Disaster Relief

I had first-hand experience of how a government manages the fallout of a major crisis during my time in office as Prime Minister of Pakistan. The tragedy caused by the devastating earthquake of 2005, which led to 73,000 people losing their lives and three million more being left homeless was the worst humanitarian disaster in Pakistan's history and we could not have undertaken the relief effort without coordinated action on a global scale. The fact that it had struck Pakistan's most mountainous and remote areas created an additional logistical hurdle for the relief efforts.

President Musharraf and I realized the scale of the disaster meant we were in urgent need of extra funds. We held a donors' conference in Islamabad, which raised USD 6.5 billion for the relief effort. In this, we realized personally involving world leaders to galvanize support and raise awareness throughout the world was very important. George H.W. Bush, the former President of the United States, personally visited Pakistan. UN Secretary General Kofi Annan also flew to Pakistan specifically to co-chair the donors' conference in Islamabad—which made a big difference to our fundraising efforts. High-profile visitors also came—including the Hollywood actor Ben Kingsley all helping draw global attention to the scale of the disaster.

Volunteers and medical professionals flew in from across the world—including Saudi Arabia, Jordan, Turkey, the United States, the UK and other European nations. From countries, such as, China, the UAE, Korea, Brazil, Iran, Japan and Malaysia - people from all walks of life came to help out. Some set up field hospitals overnight, others provided vital medical aid and humanitarian assistance on an astonishing scale. Charities like Doctors Without Borders were invaluable, while The World Food Programme and the United Nations provided vital aid and expertise. It was a truly global effort.

We also realized the Government had to be visible on the front line—to show leadership and decisive action. Every day—for months—President Musharraf and I, along with the Cabinet, were active, flying out by helicopter to newly affected areas to view temporary shelters and hospitals. After the earthquake, we set up a specially dedicated agency within the government to deal exclusively with future natural disasters. The key element of any disaster management effort is coordination and knowing whom to access for information and logistics. It is little use having doctors and volunteers who wish to help without knowing where to go in the relief effort and with no clear channel to report to. Countries and governments must try to plan ahead to ensure essential equipment and expertise is available when and where it is needed.

Pakistan's armed forces also played a vital role—we relied heavily on the medical corps, helicopter units and search and rescue teams. The disaster demonstrated vividly how a country's military forces should also be specifically trained to provide emergency aid—this lesson has once again been made clear during the global pandemic. Many countries have found the military support invaluable in coordinating logistical side of the fight against COVID-19 and the subsequent vaccine rollout. That positive experience should be built upon to deliver a permanent benefit for all humanity out of COVID-19. It could be a catalyst to create a global one stop disaster relief unit.

## 9 Threats and Solutions for 2021 and Beyond

Looking towards 2021 and beyond, we are increasingly faced with growing global threats like climate change, terrorism, nuclear proliferation, cyber-attacks and natural disasters that could create problems for the future and disrupt prospects for peace and progress. Even as many countries remain in the grip of the COVID-19 pandemic, we must not let these other pressing issues take a back seat. The more we allow ourselves to look inward and focus on our internal problems, the greater these global challenges will become. These are not issues you can sweep under the rug, or leave for a few years while we focus on other problems—they need to be urgently addressed. And no one country has the ability to resolve them alone.

For successful cooperation, it would help to have a renewed focus on collaborative efforts regarding issues of common interest. For example, climate change threatens our entire planet. Major carbon emitting countries must take joint action to reduce emissions and build a world economy based on green energy. Warm words and high-profile summits are not enough—a comprehensive strategy to achieve environmentally sustainable growth is urgently needed.

The world's population is growing rapidly and developing countries, in particular, are witnessing a demographics boom. Where governments make a concerted effort to invest in the education and health of their peoples, growing populations can contribute to more rapid economic growth and development. Where they do not, growing legions of the poor and jobless can fuel conflict, terrorism and turmoil. It has become essential, therefore, to plan and execute programmes for the inclusive and equal development of all the peoples of the world—with a clear and special priority for the poor.

There needs to be a new architecture for global cooperation—meaning we must also resolve long-standing tensions and differences and manage any potential points of tension through diplomacy and dialogue. In any areas of potential conflict, the method of communication between key countries should be institutionalized to encourage frequent contact, dialogue and discussion to prevent conflict escalating from little more than misunderstanding. Initiatives such as joint production for exploiting undersea hydrocarbons in contested areas could help smooth over tensions.

One of the most serious international challenges that faces us all is the failure to curtail the crisis in the Middle East. The region has been traumatized by decades of conflict and the wounds of unsettled long-standing disputes, military interventions and regime changes. Now the economic damage of the pandemic risks throwing the region into a new wave of instability. There is as yet no overarching design to restore peace and stability in the region. Instead, we see major global powers withdrawing from a mediating role. Instead of withdrawing, we must to develop a sense of collective responsibility. Failure to navigate the changes in the geopolitical world order will not only make it harder for us to collectively face security challenges, it could also open us up to new risks.

As COVID-19 has shown, some of the greatest challenges we face could also be opportunities to build a better, more stable world. No change is easy or painless—it requires a lot of political will, buy-in from the important stakeholders in multiple countries and, above all, strategic leadership. Let us see this as a chance to develop a new vision of the world. One that will reshape the global economy to make the most of the opportunities we are presented with, and that guides us through the challenges. One that will create progress and growth that is equitable and fair for all.

There needs to be informed discussion of bigger picture solutions at the highest levels and how they can be implemented. It is crucial that we focus on generating inclusive, equitable growth—something the technological revolution makes more attainable than ever before. If handled correctly and coupled with prudent policies and regulation, it can help transform society. Unlocking these opportunities will not only help us on our path to a new global order—it will ensure peace, stability and progress for decades to come.

**H. E. Shaukat Aziz** was elected as Prime Minister of Pakistan and served from 2004–2007, following five years as Finance Minister from 1999. Mr. Aziz was the first Prime Minister of Pakistan to complete a full term in office. Prior to public service, Mr. Aziz had a 30-year career in global finance. With Citibank he held several senior management positions followed by Chief Executive of the bank's global wealth management business. Mr. Aziz is a director of several businesses and member of advisory boards of various commercial and non-profit entities around the world. Mr. Aziz's book, *From Banking to the Thorny World of Politics*, was published by Quartet in May 2016.

**Open Access** This chapter is licensed under the terms of the Creative Commons Attribution-NonCommercial-NoDerivatives 4.0 International License (http://creativecommons.org/licenses/by-nc-nd/4.0/), which permits any noncommercial use, sharing, distribution and reproduction in any medium or format, as long as you give appropriate credit to the original author(s) and the source, provide a link to the Creative Commons license and indicate if you modified the licensed material. You do not have permission under this license to share adapted material derived from this chapter or parts of it.

The images or other third party material in this chapter are included in the chapter's Creative Commons license, unless indicated otherwise in a credit line to the material. If material is not included in the chapter's Creative Commons license and your intended use is not permitted by statutory regulation or exceeds the permitted use, you will need to obtain permission directly from the copyright holder.

# Will Liberal Hegemony Lead to a Cold War in Asia?

**David Blair**

**Abstract** The system of liberal US hegemony set up after World War II had very beneficial effects for Western Europe, Japan and some other countries. During this period of Pax Americana, there was no direct great power hot war and prosperity in many countries soared. The peaceful environment in Asia and open trading system in Asia and the open world trading system was also fundamental to China's economic rise over the last 40 years. But, it should not be forgotten that this US-led international order was crafted as a military-strategic counter to the Soviet Union, which was labeled as an evil enemy. The rise of China poses a key challenge to US-dominance in that China's economy is a rival to the US economy in a way that the Soviet economy never was. China's increasing military capabilities also limit the ability of US forces to project power easily in Asia. Nothing in the history or military doctrine of the US suggests that it will recognize that it has few real interests in the region and thus adopt a policy of restraint. More likely, we are entering a dangerous period in which the US focuses on economically and strategically constraining China.

**Keywords** US strategic theory · Liberal hegemony · American leadership · "America as the indispensable nation" · "Rules-based global system" · Liberal benevolent international system · Open trading system in Asia · Power projection · Technological innovation · US - China conflict · Cold war · Pax American · Realism

There are many terms and phrases used to describe the predominant US strategic theory since World War II. These include liberal hegemony, American leadership, "America as the indispensable nation," "rules-based global system," and so forth. There are slightly different implications among these terms, but they all describe a world, or large part of the world, where the US is militarily and economically dominant and uses its power to impose a more or less liberal and benevolent international system.

This American-led system has paid off for the US, its allies, and much of the rest of the world. The transformative economic growth and technological innovation during

D. Blair (✉)
Center for China and Globalization (CCG), Beijing, China

© The Author(s) 2021
H. Wang and A. Michie (eds.), *Consensus or Conflict?*, China and Globalization,
https://doi.org/10.1007/978-981-16-5391-9_3

the so-called "thirty glorious years," roughly from 1945 to 1975, would not have been possible if the US had not provided Western Europe and Japan both military protection and easy access to its markets. Similarly, the peaceful environment in Asia and the open trading system was also fundamental to China's economic rise over the last 40 years.

Yet, there are big questions about whether this system can be maintained over the next decade as China continues to rise economically and militarily. How will the US respond to China's increasing ability to thwart US power projection capabilities? Will there be an arms race combined with US attempts to forge cold-war-style alliances that designate China as the main potential enemy? Or, will the US decide that it has few hard, real interests in the region and is not willing to pay the price of maintaining a US-led international system in the area?

And, how will the US respond to China's continued economic and technological growth? Will the US accept that China may become the largest economy and most advanced technological innovator in the world? Or, will the US see China primarily as a strategic competitor whose economic and tech capabilities must be limited?

There are only two ways to sustain American commitment to a liberal world order regime. One way is to make maintenance of this international regime relatively cheap and easy. Basically, the US becomes the policeman in a not very dangerous world. The other way is to convince the American public and elites that maintaining the liberal world order is part of an overall fight against an enemy, preferably an evil enemy. We don't have any history of something in-between these two extremes. Make no mistake, traditional concepts of a liberal world order depend on American hegemony.

The grand task going forward is to try to find a middle ground between American withdrawal from Asia versus a new economic and military cold war. Unfortunately, post-WWII history gives no precedent for such a system.

# 1 The Pax Americana and the Cold War

The American-led system has secured a long Pax Americana in the sense that there have been no great power wars and both Western Europe and East Asia have been largely peaceful. General public opinion in many countries recognizes the benefits of this system. A Eurasia Group survey published in April 2020 found that across Asian countries, with the exception of China, 77% of respondents agreed that the United States would be preferable as a global leader for their country and 79.1% of respondents said that US leadership was better for the world overall.

In China, almost half the respondents said that US influence in the region was very or somewhat negative with just 6.8% reporting a very positive view.[1]

---

[1] Panda (2020a).

But, Americans themselves are even less favorable to a US-led international order. In another Eurasia Group poll, published November 2019, 57.6% of American respondents said that the US should reduce its military presence in Asia while transitioning regional allies to defend themselves. 47.1% said that the US should refrain from military intervention when Americans are not directly threatened and only 19.4% would support a US-led response to humanitarian abuses abroad.[2]

The US was willing to maintain large military expenditures and economic generosity to allies during the long cold war largely because there was an enemy that was perceived to be evil. In his inaugural address on January 20, 1961, President John Kennedy famously said: "Let every nation know, whether it wishes us well or ill, that we shall pay any price, bear any burden, meet any hardship, support any friend, oppose any foe, in order to assure the survival and the success of liberty."

And, as Kennedy predicted, the Cold War cost the US a lot of blood and treasure. The long wars in Korea, Vietnam, and, after the Cold War, in the Middle East have cost trillions of dollars and many lives. They have also had very damaging effects on US institutions and culture. Are Americans willing to pay a huge price to protect an international system if neither American interests nor core ideals are at risk?

The first Gulf War seemed to confirm the idea that future military intervention by the US and its allies would be quick, easy, and relatively painless. It created the illusion that the US military would be able "to intervene easily, far from our homeland and close to the homeland of our enemies."[3] But, this dream that we were approaching Frank Fukuyama's "end of history" did not last long.[4]

For a while, until roughly 2010, it looked like the ideal international regime might exist in East Asia. The US military in the region was so dominant that intervention was unnecessary and many thought that the nations in the region, especially China, would move toward liberal domestic regimes.

There are some vague ideas that there might be an EU-led system, but that assumes that the world is a very peaceful place. In the early 1990s, there was a brief period where it looked like we might be entering a world system resembling a European Union writ large: (1) where military conflict looked impossible in much of the world, (2) where US and allied military power was so overwhelming that police-like actions could easily manage the rest of the world, (3) where disagreements among nations were settled by multilateral rules-based organizations, and (4) where the US/Western European democratic capitalist system looked so superior that most of the world was expected to converge on this model. None of those conditions holds true today.

In his well-known 2014 book *Restraint: A New Foundation for U.S. Grand Strategy*,[5] Barry Posen of MIT argued that liberal hegemonists believe that "the United States can only be truly safe in a world full of states like us..." In the early 2000s, many Americans believed that China was on an inevitable path to become "like us"

---

[2] Hannah and Gray (2019).

[3] Blair (1996).

[4] Fukuyama (2006).

[5] Posen (2014).

and thus was not an adversary. But, now few American strategists see China on a this path and thus see it as a strategic rival and probable future cold or hot enemy.

The US has no vital interests in Asia in the sense that the long-term livelihoods of average American people would be drastically harmed if current ties with Asia were reduced. As Chinese production has risen over the past 20 years, many Americans have gained from cheaper imports of a large variety of goods, interest rates and inflation rates have probably been reduced, and tech supply chains have been optimized. But, going back to the trade status quo as of 1995 or even 1975 would not be devastating to Americans. Many would gain as factories moved to North America. In the very extreme case that all trade would be cut off, mines in Nevada and other places would need to reopen to supply so-called "rare" earths, raising gadget prices a bit. A rational purely economic calculus of US interests would not find these impacts to be worth fighting, or even risking, a war over.

The major issues at stake in Asia center on the economic interests of US allies and on maintaining American liberal hegemony there, not on direct US economic or homeland-protection interests.

American military strategy has long been based on the idea of force projection— that US forces have the capability to intervene all around the world. For decades, the US could intervene in East Asia with little fear of being countered, except in Korea. As we saw in the 1996 Taiwan Straits incident, the US could intervene without firing a shot, so there was little danger of escalation. In the late 1990s, the US could thus maintain a liberal hegemony regime in East Asia without too much risk or expenditure and did not need an enemy to justify its military expenditures.

Now, US intervention in East Asia would be both highly risky and vastly expensive. Recent Chinese investments in "carrier-killer" missiles seriously weaken the US ability to project power in seas adjacent to China. China often points out that it spends a fraction on defense of what the US does, but that is irrelevant. The strategic goals that each country hopes to achieve with its forces are what is really relevant. To reach its goals, the US has to build and maintain the capability to project power across an ocean and intervene against a Chinese military with rapidly rising power to destroy US Navy ships.

One danger is that we are getting into a spiraling arms race. China is building anti-carrier weapons. Leading the US to build up its forces. Leading to more Chinese arms expenditures and a vicious cycle.

Another danger is that neither side can predict its own behavior or that of the other side if an incident occurs. If some kind of incident occurs at sea, will China shoot at US carriers? What happens if they sink one? Will the US attack missile batteries on Chinese territory? The risks of unwanted war and escalation are very real.

Are these risks and costs worthwhile for the US? Probably not if we are just propping up a vague international trading regime. But, the American people can probably be convinced to support this strategy if they can be convinced they are opposing another evil empire.

Neither side appears to want this outcome. Almost everyone in China recognizes that the country has benefited greatly from US-led liberal hegemony in the region and that American military withdrawal could make the region much more risky. But, most Chinese also support the military buildup that is a factor in changing the system. Would China really benefit from pushing the US out of East Asia? Similarly, few in the US look forward to another cold war or more military misadventures in Asia, but we seem to be adopting policies that lead in that direction.

## 2  What Will Be the Strategic Doctrine of the Biden Administration?

As of this writing in March 2021, we are starting to get confirmations that the new Biden administration is seeking to maintain traditional views of American liberal hegemony in Asia. While maintaining flexibility and seeking to smooth relations with China, Biden appears to be building a Quad (US, Japan, Australia, India) quasi-alliance in preparation for a long cold war.

Many observers in China saw the start of the Biden administration as the start of fundamentally improved US–China relations compared to the Trump era. This was based on the idea that American strategists who support Biden see the role of the US as managing a rules-based world order that would open US markets to Chinese goods and would not be very interested in limiting the economic, technological, or military rise of China.

This is a clear misreading of post-World War II US strategy. That strategy had elements of liberalism in that it promoted trade, primarily among US allies, and sought to impose a rules-based order—though the US was frequently excepted from the rules. The often-ignored part of this strategy was that it was, at its core, an anti-Soviet alliance.

The "Interim National Security Strategic Guidance" issued by the White House on March 3, 2021 (referred to hereafter as the National Security Strategy Document, NSSD) gives little hope to those who believe that US–China relations will move back toward the amity that prevailed during the George W. Bush or Reagan administrations.[6]

The Biden administration is certainly more interested in alliances than was the Trump administration, but the NSSD makes clear that these are primarily seen as alliances against China. The document repeatedly says that it is targeted against "an increasingly assertive China and destabilizing Russia." It states that the key agenda is to "strengthen our enduring advantages, and allow us to prevail in strategic competition with China or any other nation" and to "out-compete a more assertive and authoritarian China over the long-term."

The NSSD also makes clear that President Trump's interest in trade agreements that focus on working-class jobs in the US will continue. It says: "our trade and international economic policies must serve all Americans, not just the privileged few. Trade policy must grow the American middle class, create better jobs, raise wages, and strengthen communities. We will make sure that the rules of the international

---

[6] The White House (2021).

economy are not tilted against the United States. We will enforce existing trade rules and create new ones that promote fairness."

Two key paragraphs of the NSSD lay out the Biden administration's view that China is the main threat to the international system:

> Taken together, this agenda will strengthen our enduring advantages, and allow us to prevail in strategic competition with China or any other nation. The most effective way for America to out-compete a more assertive and authoritarian China over the long-term is to invest in our people, our economy, and our democracy. By restoring U.S. credibility and reasserting forward-looking global leadership, we will ensure that America, not China, sets the international agenda, working alongside others to shape new global norms and agreements that advance our interests and reflect our values. By bolstering and defending our unparalleled network of allies and partners, and making smart defense investments, we will also deter Chinese aggression and counter threats to our collective security, prosperity, and democratic way of life.

> At the same time, revitalizing our core strengths is necessary but not sufficient. In many areas, China's leaders seek unfair advantages, behave aggressively and coercively, and undermine the rules and values at the heart of an open and stable international system. When the Chinese government's behavior directly threatens our interests and values, we will answer Beijing's challenge. We will confront unfair and illegal trade practices, cyber theft, and coercive economic practices that hurt American workers, undercut our advanced and emerging technologies, and seek to erode our strategic advantage and national competitiveness....We will support China's neighbors and commercial partners in defending their rights to make independent political choices free of coercion or undue foreign influence. We will promote locally-led development to combat the manipulation of local priorities. We will support Taiwan, a leading democracy and critical economic and security partner, in line with long-standing American commitments. We will ensure that U.S. companies do not sacrifice American values in doing business in China. And we will stand up for democracy, human rights and human dignity in Hong Kong, Xinjiang, and Tibet.

Notice that this wording is not very different from official documents of the Trump administration. For example, then US Secretary of Defense Jim Mattis at the 2017 Shangri-La Dialogue in Singapore stated: "by further strengthening our alliances, by empowering the region, and by enhancing the US military in support of our larger foreign policy goals, we intend to continue to promote the rules-based order that is in the best interest of the United States, and of all the countries in the region."[7]

It is important not to misconstrue the currently poor state of US–China relations as a partisan issue that started with the Trump presidency. The so-called "pivot to Asia" was an Obama administration initiative, started by Hillary Clinton when she was Secretary of State.

It is often thought, especially after the Vietnam War, that Democrats are less warlike than Republicans. That does seem to be the case among ordinary voters. But, there is little evidence that the Democrat party foreign policy elites are less aggressive than Republican party elites. Foreign countries should be wary of using political party affiliation to predict the international behavior of an American leader.

It is also hard to predict the Biden administration's actions in East Asia from previous actions of the President. He voted for the 2003 authorization of the war with Iraq and reportedly supported air strikes against Bashar Al-Assad's forces in

---

[7] US Department of Defense (2017).

Syria. On the other hand, he claims to have argued strongly in the White House, as Vice-President, against the toppling of Gadaffi in Libya. And, in an interview with Politico, he said the US should not use force unless the interests of the country or its allies are directly threatened, whether it can be done efficaciously, and whether it can be sustained."[8] So, President Biden himself has, at times, adopted somewhat restrained and realist views but has also supported interventionist policies. His administration, like the Obama administration, seems to aim to maintain American-led liberal hegemony in the region and seems to plan to use local allies in a cold-war-like system.

Kurt Campbell, who, as assistant secretary of State for East Asia during the Obama administration, was the principal author of the pivot to Asia, is now the Indo-Pacific Coordinator in the National Security Council under Biden. As far back as the Clinton administration, Campbell captained then Assistant Secretary of Defense Joseph Nye's "Nye Initiative," which strengthened US alliance relations in the region.[9]

In a July 2018 speech at Harvard University, Ashton Carter, who was US Secretary of Defense during the Obama administration, said that the single most important factor in the 70-year history (of prosperity in Asia) has been the pivotal role of American military power in the region. The US aims to keep that going he said. But, he added, "I'm not one of those people who believes war, cold or otherwise, with China is likely. It's certainly not desirable."[10]

From the point of view of the US, these moves are not nefarious and are not necessarily aimed to limit China's growth. This US strategy is certainly not intended to lead to a shooting war with China—it can be argued that military strength and reduced ambiguity reduce the chance of war. A balance of power might stabilize the region. And, it is conceivable that it will not lead to anything that could be characterized as a cold war. But, it is not a big step from an informal military alliance to a cold war. History suggests that the US will not be willing to make the required expenditures unless we can designate an enemy.

The March 12, 2021 virtual meeting between the leaders of the Quad–President Biden and the leaders of Japan, Australia, and India–focused mostly on COVID-19 vaccines and made attempts not to antagonize China. But the White House said the leaders would work toward "a stronger regional architecture through the Quad."[11] Preventing China from becoming dominant in the region is a clear goal of that architecture.

The national security/intelligence state agencies are very influential and powerful in Washington. They win most interagency battles and even Presidents have failed to overcome their interests. Barack Obama came into office as a "peace" President who had opposed the war in Iraq. Donald Trump also opposed the Iraq War, sought to withdraw the US from wars in the Middle East, and, quoting President Eisenhower's farewell address, railed against the national security establishment. But,

---

[8] Valverde (2020).

[9] Ackman (2021).

[10] The Economic Times (India) (2018).

[11] Biden meeting Quad amid own pivot toward Asia (2021).

both achieved little along the lines they promised. So, I fear that the default path will involve more buildup of American forces in East Asia and a new cold war.

If maintaining a liberal order in Asia were a relatively cheap and relatively easy strategy, there would be no reason to worry. But, as China's economy rises to match or exceed that of the US, and as China invests in technology designed to match that of the US and builds more military forces capable of countering US naval and other power projection forces, the Quad-based pivot to Asia in which the US builds up its own forces and tries to maintain military hegemony in the region looks to be neither cheap nor easy.

Nothing in the history of military doctrine of the US suggests that it will recognize that it has few real direct interests in the region and thus adopt a policy of restraint. Instead, we are probably looking at a strategic plan designed to constrain China.

## 3 Managing the Dangerous Decade

Current US public opinion toward China is scary. According to a 2021 Gallup poll, favorable ratings of China among Americans have plummeted to a record low since 1979 of 20% and Pew, the leading US polling organisation, found that 89% of American adults now consider China to be a competitor or enemy rather than a partner.[12]

This is not surprising since current US press reports and government discussions of China are unrelentingly negative. A cynic might fear that the US public is being prepped to see China as a cold war enemy.

Chinese views of the US are a lot less biased, but 2020 still showed a low point. Twenty-eight percent of respondents reported an unfavorable view of the United States, up from 17% a year earlier. The number of respondents reporting a favorable view also fell from 58 to 39%.[13]

I'm often asked in China what I think the probability of war between the two countries is. My reluctant answer is "not zero." But, war is not a random event that can be probabilistically predicted. War can be created only by short-term or long-term decisions of national leaders. How can both sides manage the coming dangerous decade in a way to minimize the chances that they or future leaders will feel obligated to go to war?

Graham Allison's book, *Destined for War: Can America and China Escape Thucydides's Trap?*[14] did a great service to the world by warning us about the danger that a seemingly stable world order can fall apart, even though maintaining it is in everyone's interest. Many have struggled to explain the decisions that led from the apparently globalized, prosperous world of the summer of 1914 to the incredible

---

[12] Niewenhuis (2021).

[13] Panda (2020b).

[14] Allison (2018).

destruction of the first world war, even though Germany and Britain were culturally close and economically interdependent.

This essay is about strategic theories and doctrines, which certainly play a big role, but they are not everything, Thucydides certainly did warn about the dangers inherent in a changing balance of power. But, he also stressed that leaders could have made decisions that led to much better, or worse, outcomes.

One major factor leading to the Peloponnesian Wars was the idea of pride, which could be interpreted as credibility in modern times. The Athenians had many opportunities to make minor face-saving concessions to Sparta, which probably would have headed off the war. But they were afraid they would lose their own credibility with their own allies and subject states, some of whom wanted to break away if they thought Athens was weak.[15] Such factors drive leaders in modern times. For example, it is hard to understand US involvement in the Vietnam War except as an attempt to maintain American credibility.

American and Chinese leaders need to understand that not just hard realist interests drive the decisions of the others. Credibility and pride may cause leaders to make decisions that are apparently not in their interests. One big danger that China may preemptively decide to assert its dominance and that could lead to some kind of conflict, maybe accidental conflict. On the other hand, the US may decide that it has to assert its hegemony to maintain its credibility in Asia. Either of these steps could lead to unthinkable disaster.

The American founding fathers were very familiar with Greek literature and Greek history. So, drawing on Thucydides, George Washington's farewell address warned us against entangling alliances. The US needs allies, but it should be sure that the interests of allies don't drag it into risky situations and a new cold war.

China could go a long way toward reducing the attractiveness of a Quad alliance simply by using kinder diplomacy and gentler rhetoric toward Japan, India, and Australia. The so-called "wolf warriors" have put regional countries on high alert. Strictly following the trading rules in the RCEP and, potentially, the TPP for a long period of time would reduce some of the fears of China's economic domination.

For the foreseeable future, there are unlikely to be fundamental changes in US–China relations. On trade, the Biden administration will seek agreements to create jobs and raise wages in the US. Most of the damage to the US working class has been done by domestic financial reforms and the government's failure to enforce antitrust laws, but it's a lot easier just to blame China. So, it is unlikely that the US and China will be able to reach a wide-scale rules-based trade agreement, but even a continuation of the more transactional Phase One trade agreement would be economically beneficial. More importantly, it would help smooth relations between the two nations.

The US is unlikely to end its campaign to prevent the transfer of technology to China. But, that may not be a bad thing for China in the long term. After all, China is the only country in the world to develop its own software ecosystem because it banned the Silicon Valley oligopolists from its markets. China has a very strong interest in

---

[15] Waldron (2017).

promoting its own indigenous tech capability. It would have that interest regardless of whether the US had put sanctions on it, but those sanctions make China's interests more urgent. Withdrawal of the tech sanctions will not change Chinese behavior because China has now been warned that the US can try to destroy major parts of Chinese tech companies and it will not want to be put in that position again, regardless of the administration in power in Washington.

Domestic factors will be key in the long term. If the Chinese economy continues to grow so that it is able to escape the middle-income trap and become a country with indigenous innovation and a GDP 50–100% higher than the US, then it is hard to believe that the US will be able to maintain anything that looks vaguely like hegemony in Asia regardless of the strategic or military policies it implements now. If China fails at its economic transformation, then the long-term strategic balance won't shift. And, if the US is not able to fix its own economic problems, its adventures and misadventures in Asia will make its domestic problems even worse. I hope that both countries just calm down for the next 10–20 years and see how it works out.

In addition to the liberal hegemony school of strategy, there is an alternative "realist" school of thinking about American strategy. For example, Harvey Sapolsky and his former students at MIT argue for a focus on America's real interests, with a "strong military, just not a large or busy one."[16] And, in a 2014 Council of Foreign Relations-sponsored task force, General David Petraeus and Robert Zoellick argued for prioritizing North America.[17] If China clearly becomes the leading world economy, US strategy will probably move in this more realist direction. Let's hope it doesn't take a war to move us there.

My view is that the best we can hope for is a continuation of the current unsettled status quo. Both sides should seek to muddle through until the long-term balance of power is clear. But just because nothing huge will change does not mean that small steps will not enhance safety. Discussions and seemingly unrelated agreements between the US and China can go a long way to salve the fears driven by the strategic situation. As George H.W. Bush stressed, "goodwill begets goodwill."[18] So any negotiations, confidence building measures, or joint actions could pay off by reassuring both sides.

## References

Allison G (2018) Destined for war: can America and China escape Thucydides's trap? Mariner Books, Boston

Blair D (1996) How to defeat the United States: the operational military effects of the proliferation of weapons of precise destruction. In: Sokolski H (eds) Fighting proliferation: new concerns for the nineties. Air University Press and Federation of American Scientists. https://fas.org/irp/threat/fp/b19ch4.htm

Petraeus DH, Zoellick RB (2014) North America: time for a new focus. Council of Foreign Relations. https://www.cfr.org/report/north-america

[16] Gholz et al. (1997).

[17] Petraeus and Zoellick (2014).

[18] Rome (2021).

US Department of Defense (2017) Remarks by secretary Mattis at Shangri-La Dialogue. https://www.defense.gov/Newsroom/Transcripts/Transcript/Article/1201780/remarks-by-secretary-mattis-at-shangri-la-dialogue/

Waldron A (2017) There is no Thucydides trap. SupChina. https://supchina.com/2017/06/12/no-thucydides-trap/

Ackman S (2021) Obama's pivot to Asia architect will be Biden's China troubleshooter. MSN. https://www.msn.com/en-us/news/politics/obama-s-pivot-to-asia-architect-will-be-biden-s-china-troubleshooter/ar-BB1cIy4M

Rome H (2021) Why Iran keeps quoting George H.W. Bush. Foreign Policy. https://foreignpolicy.com/2021/03/12/why-iran-keeps-quoting-george-h-w-bush/?utm_source=PostUp&utm_medium=email&utm_campaign=31078&utm_term=Editors%20Picks%20OC&?tpcc=31078

Fukuyama F (2006) The end of history and the last man. Simon and Schuster, 2006 digital edition

Gholz E, Press DG, Sapolsky HM (1997) Come home, America: the strategy of restraint in the face of temptation. Int Secur 21(4):5–48

Hannah M, Gray C (2019) Indispensable no more?: how the American public sees U.S. Foreign Policy. Eurasia Group Foundation. https://egfound.org/wp-content/uploads/2019/11/Indispensable-no-more.pdf

The White House (2021) Interim national security strategic guidance. https://www.whitehouse.gov/briefing-room/statements-releases/2021/03/03/interim-national-security-strategic-guidance/

Niewenhuis L (2021) American overall opinions about China hit record low. SupChina. https://supchina.com/2021/03/04/american-overall-opinions-about-china-hit-record-low/

Panda A (2020a) The American political system remains unpopular in China. The Diplomat. https://thediplomat.com/2020/04/survey-chinese-report-less-favorable-views-of-us-democracy/

Panda A (2020b) Survey: Chinese report less favorable views of US democracy. The Diplomat. https://thediplomat.com/2020/04/survey-chinese-report-less-favorable-views-of-us-democracy/

Posen BR (2014) Restraint: a new foundation for U.S. grand strategy. Cornell

The Economic Times (India) (2018) US seeks rise of China and India: defence secretary Ashton carter. https://economictimes.indiatimes.com/news/defence/us-seeks-rise-of-china-and-india-defence-secretary-ashton-carter/articleshow/50006312.cms

Valverde M (2020) Fact check: did Biden support wars in Iraq, Serbia, Syria, and Libya? WRAL.com. https://www.wral.com/fact-check-did-biden-support-wars-in-iraq-serbia-syria-and-libya/19257083/

https://thefrontierpost.com/biden-meeting-quad-amid-own-pivot-toward-asia/

**David Blair** is an economist specializing in macroeconomics, monetary policy and entrepreneurship. He has also held numerous positions related to foreign policy. He retired in 2016 as professor of economics and finance from the Eisenhower School of National Defense University in Washington, where he also served as chairman of the economics department. Previously, he was a senior columnist at China Daily. He holds a Ph.D. in economics from UCLA and was a MacArthur Foundation Avoiding Nuclear War Fellow at Harvard University. He has led projects and consulted in Italy, Tajikistan, India, Bulgaria and Ethiopia.

**Open Access** This chapter is licensed under the terms of the Creative Commons Attribution-NonCommercial-NoDerivatives 4.0 International License (http://creativecommons.org/licenses/by-nc-nd/4.0/), which permits any noncommercial use, sharing, distribution and reproduction in any medium or format, as long as you give appropriate credit to the original author(s) and the source, provide a link to the Creative Commons license and indicate if you modified the licensed material. You do not have permission under this license to share adapted material derived from this chapter or parts of it.

The images or other third party material in this chapter are included in the chapter's Creative Commons license, unless indicated otherwise in a credit line to the material. If material is not included in the chapter's Creative Commons license and your intended use is not permitted by statutory regulation or exceeds the permitted use, you will need to obtain permission directly from the copyright holder.

# Forging a Partnership Between the China and the World in an Era of Division: Finding Common Ground in Climate Change and Health

**Kerry Brown**

**Abstract** *Public perceptions about China on social media outside of China* often resemble a field of battle, but in words. Some users and groups produce endless statements bolstering their conviction that *China is the epitome of wickedness*. Others push out equivalent amounts that look remarkably like *Chinese propaganda* saying nothing but good things about the People's Republic. The crucial space for neutrality seems to be closing down. This acknowledges, both for the US and EU, the acceptance that a *radical difference in viewpoints on China* has to proceed alongside a similarly crucial admission that it would be *self-defeating not to work with China. Comprehensive dis-engagement with China is not an option.* Whatever the problems with China, those involving human impact on the environment causing climate change and combating global public health issues are far more serious. The first poses, in the longer term, an *existential threat to humanity*. The stark reality is that a solution to this issue will not happen without partners like China, and it is likely that China will be a huge part of whatever ultimate solution must be found.

**Keywords** Social media and China · China is the epitome of wickedness · Chinese propaganda · Radical difference in viewpoints on China · Self-defeating not to work with China · Comprehensive dis-engagement with China is not an option · Existential threat to humanity

If anyone wanted to check the temperature gauge in early 2021 on public perceptions on China and its relations with the outside world, all they needed to do is to scroll through Twitter. Debates about issues relating to China often resembled a civil war in words unfolding on social media. Some users and groups produced endless statements and pieces of evidence bolstering their conviction that the current government and political system in China is the epitome of wickedness. Others pushed out equivalent amounts that look remarkably like propaganda saying that nothing but good emanates from the People's Republic. Finding an island of peace between these fiercely clashing forces is getting harder. The crucial space for neutrality seems to be closing down.

K. Brown (✉)
Lau China Institute, King's College London, London, UK

© The Author(s) 2021

H. Wang and A. Michie (eds.), *Consensus or Conflict?*, China and Globalization,
https://doi.org/10.1007/978-981-16-5391-9_4

41

Public opinion in the UK is a useful barometer for this. Surveys in the period before 2020 were sparse. They mostly showed either indifference on the part of the UK towards China, or a focus simply on economic matters. Even during the 'golden age', as the Chinese labelled this, during Chinese President Xi Jinping's visit to Britain in late 2015, the dial did not seem to shift much. As someone from Britain who dealt with China as a diplomat and then academic since 1994, I was also struck by this strange incongruity—visits to China showed a place over this period that was transforming almost by the second. But the China story in the UK was best characterised as a very static one. It was broadly split, at least in the media, between 'China is a human rights hell hole' on the one hand, and on the other 'this place is getting wealthier by the minute—let's go make money from them'! This remained the default for almost the entire period from the mid-1990s onwards.

The prominence given to the first cases of COVID-19 being observed in China in late 2019 and the spread of the pandemic across the world have changed this, though it is an interesting question about how deep and enduring that change will prove to be. In Europe and the US politicians, who never showed great interest in the place that a fifth of humanity call home and by 2020 accounted for a similar proportion of global GDP, suddenly had strong opinions about the world's largest country still practicing communism. China figured as a suitable object of anger, blame and, in the more extreme cases, hate. Ex-President Donald Trump declared on his Twitter that COVID-19 was 'the China virus'. Even the populist politician in the UK, Nigel Farage,[1] stated that, having dealt with the European Union (EU) issue through Brexit in the UK, he was now going to focus on the threat from China. The shift from a sort of complacent indifference, to active antipathy seemed sharp and dramatic.

## 1   Moderate Places

What is striking over this time, however, from someone who had to observe this issue of China's relations with the world almost every day, was the acknowledgement away from the noisy platforms on which figures had to posture publicly to get attention, that the issue humanity was facing was far more complex that this almost Manichean mentality being deployed towards China indicated. Officials and public opinion formers (even if they were self-appointed!) were more than happy to concede this crucial fact, albeit in private. The tone of their remarks was often far more questioning and circumspect. This was backed up by one reasonably good quality survey undertaken by the British Foreign Policy Group towards the end of 2020 and published in 2021. It showed that on the whole, while those over 55 in the UK had a measurably dimmer view of China than in previous years, younger people were more positive.[2] There was, even now, no straightforward consensus.

---

[1] https://www.dailymail.co.uk/debate/article-9282657/NIGEL-FARAGE-Communist-takeover-schools-Britain-end-once.html published 21 February 2021.

[2] Gaston and Aspinall (2021).

This complexity was reflected in the ruling Conservative Party's evolving position on China. The Prime Minister, Boris Johnson, deployed the word 'sinophile' a number of times in 2020. His government continued to declare that there were rich opportunities in doing business with China. After all, in the era of 'Global Britain', after the UK formally left the EU and the Customs Union in 2020, it was natural to look at the fastest growing, major economy, and one that, according to official data, the UK was doing more and more business with—and had potential to do far more.[3] Alongside this, however, were important factions in the Conservative Party who established a 'China Research Group'[4] in mid-2020 which, in effect, operated as a lobbying group for a far harder line on China because of issues in Hong Kong, reports of repression in Xinjiang, and elsewhere. The imposition of the National Security Law in Hong Kong in July 2020 was a particular trigger for harsh words from the Foreign Secretary, Dominic Raab, about the Chinese government. There were plenty of other cases of this manifestation of sometimes furious antagonism between the two governments as the year proceeded.

That there was even a small moderate middle space, even as these arguments intensified for Britain, Europe and the US, in particular, which was important for the very simple reason that for all the legitimate concerns about the places where China increasingly didn't align to Western interests and expectations, and in some of the most important (perhaps the most important) areas, there was plenty to work together on. Of these, areas concerning climate change, sustainability, public health and economic recovery after the pandemic were at the front. In all of these, China figured as a largely collaborative partner—even if this was more about potential than actuality. The key thing was that the possibility was there. That meant that those figuring about the best approach to China, once they steered clear of the extremes alluded to above, had to somehow craft a policy which recognised the real issues between much of the world and China, but also balanced these with the equally large areas of common interest and necessary cooperation.

## 2    Outline of the Issue

One of the crucial things to accept, when contemplating this imperative of seeking balance and finding a meaningful middle space to work from, was to have consensus on the nature of the problem in the first place. One issue about US or European views on China was that it was haunted by a frustration verging on anger that, despite decades of 'engagement' on the economic front, there had been no political returns on this. China continued with its one-party system, with the Communist Party under Xi seeking to make this sustainable and permanent. The fundamental issue for the most critical groups in the West was that it seemed this ambition was proceeding well in China. Speculation about the stability and security of the regime abounded.

---

[3] Ward (2020).

[4] https://chinaresearchgroup.org.

Maybe there were deep fault lines that external observers just weren't seeing, but a sober assessment had to admit that, for all the issue about how the pandemic was first handled when it appeared in China over 2019, and into 2020, compared to many in developed countries, some of whom were its fiercest critics, the Xi government had ended up managing the crisis well. By the time of the National People's Congress in March 2021, economic growth had been restored, and, as far as anyone could tell, the health crisis had been largely dealt with. This had all ended up reinforcing Xi's dominance, rather than eroding it. That too was antagonising to the most implacable of his critics.

In the era when economic engagement with the goal of political change by actors from the US outwards had clearly ended up simply not delivering in the case of China, and regardless of the complex reasons behind this, it was clear that some of the fundamental assumptions about both the global order and about China's role, in particular, in it needed to be rethought. There were a few factors by which to undertake this exercise.

The first was simply to accept that the People's Republic of China's accrual of vast amounts of material wealth in the last few decades would inevitably and increasingly translate into geopolitical influence. This was not to claim that all of this accrual had happened as something designed by anyone. China might not have intended to have this much new power, and might not even want it, but the fact was that simply being as large as it was economically meant that this was a fact regardless of whether China or anyone else liked it.

The second was to understand that there was no easy model for the outside world to use to understand how best to interpret China's intentions and strategies. This is a good antidote to the group that like to employ moral absolutes towards China and demand it be ethically condemned for what it is in and of itself. We have dealt with a Communist run superpower—the USSR—but not with a Communist run superpower that is also a supremely successful practitioner of capitalism. China's hybridity, whereby it mixes political, cultural and economic elements that often seem incompatible, disorientates the outside world, meaning that there is no easy single-track response that will wholly work. Perhaps the 'frenemy' term coined a decade or so go—neither a friend nor an enemy—captures this situation the best. In this situation, bringing in some existing template to understand and manage things won't work. We have to create something fresh. That at least explains some of the messiness of the current moment.

The third was to stress the need for some strategic caution. Commitment to one image of what China currently is (an ideological and values competitor seeking to change the outside world to look like it), and one notion of what it is up to (military dominance) means that the other options (of China being ideologically exceptionalist and largely driven by self-interest while not wanting the responsibility of dominance) get pushed into the background, even though this might, in some areas, and in some ways, have validity. China operates on different layers, some of which fit the first response, and in others by the others. The desire to commit wholly to one attitude and one approach, which easier and more straightforward for American and European policy making mores, means that attempts to 'manage' or 'deal' with the challenge end up being partial and sometimes self-defeating.

All of this makes it easy to see why China's challenge is such a tricky one. The dominant mindset in the most powerful blocs in the world (the US, EU) is to operate in terms of universals, to be seeking a singular 'truth' and to feel that behind complexity there must ultimately like some foundational, unitary reality. That probably hails from the positivist understanding of the world that served so well during the scientific revolution and into the industrial revolution in Europe, since the 17th century. China's challenge in the end is not military, economic or as a human rights actor. The principal issue is its ontological complexity. This lies at the root of all the other issues. It is multiple things—capitalist and communist, old (as a culture) and new (as a state), Confucian and Marxist. That means that dealing with a complex issue in simple ways, when that problem is small, might work. China today is so large as an issue that it demands to be dealt with on its own terms. That necessitates a hybrid response. For lovers of uniformity and unity, this is almost heretical. But if we want to come to terms with how to view China, heresy is what we need to embrace and practice.

We can maintain the current dominant mindset that China is to be transformed, or conquered, or utterly eschewed. China has been on a transformation path for 40 years and it is clear that whatever transformation China might experience, it will not end up aligning with models that have emerged elsewhere. The USSR's collapse should make us less blithely confident we can know what we will end up with, and worried that it will be far worse than what we had! Conquering is also beyond the bounds of reason. China is a nuclear power and contains a fifth of the human race. Any attempts at forcing decisions on it will end up in conflict that will almost certainly be catastrophic for everyone. Eschewing China by decoupling might be the only vaguely viable option. But even here, climate change, public health and other global issues means that willingly or not, China is a partner that has to be worked with, if for no other reason than the outside world's self-interest. All this means that one change that might work is to lay down the activist and proselytising proclivities of the US and Europe, and simply adopt a more pragmatic attitude of acceptance towards China. It is as it is, with the values and the system it currently has. The main thing is to seek common ground, where at least some changes at a more local level might happen (to both, if we are being even handed about this) rather than place unilateral, comprehensive change in the country right at the start, and at the head of everything else. This might seem just a matter of change of attitude—but attitudes are hugely important, and at least in this case, the agency is with those outside China to change their own minds and frameworks.

We do have to accord some sympathy to the outside world in view of all of this. It is easy to understand why the current predicament is a hard one for Western policy-makers and politicians. Communicating a hybrid response to a public which often has little knowledge or background of this vast new, and very different, partner is a huge challenge. This is especially the case when that partner also has a way of operating that is perpetually ambiguous on key issues, and often highly antagonistic on matters like Hong Kong, Xinjiang and Taiwan. The outcome for those trying to communicate means they are often left being daubed with crude labels like 'appeaser', 'apologist' or 'cold war warrior'.

The events of 2020 and into 2021, however, have made one thing clear—the fact of China. For example, of China being a fifth of global GDP and likely increases to this after the impact of COVID-19 on other major economies, of its geographical vastness and key strategic position, and of its decisive impact on environmental and other global common issues—these facts do not change. What needs to change is the response to this. Mindsets and frameworks are key. So is intellectual and conceptual clarity about spelling out with precision where China is a problem, why it is a problem and how that problem can be managed. We cannot solve the issue of China. We can, however, manage it. At the moment, too many are striving for the former task, which is probably impossible, and meaning that we have less and less time to focus on the latter, which is possible.

## 3   The Change Is Starting

In a lucid discussion of the various divisions and arguments in democratic societies, author Ian Leslie[5] outlines the genesis of some of the most intractable and problematic disputes. These, he shows, usually blow up from a refusal by one party to see any validity in that of the other, which has the toxic result of then causing them to stick even more closely to their own view. The issue is the threat to their status and identity, rather than anything the argument might, on the surface at least, be about.

Of course, the number of actors and the complexity of issues between China and its main international interlocutors means that the parallels between individual arguments and national, geopolitical ones, shouldn't be overstretched. Leslie, however, does show that even in the most violent clashes of view and opinion, there are pathways that can be created where people can be guided, or guide themselves, back to the middle ground, and do so with a recognition of mutual self-interest foremost in their minds.

In some ways, the world in early 2021, after the economic and health ravages of the pandemic, looks like it is a place where, geopolitically, some kind of extra-terrestrial mediator needs to arrive to carry out the sort of work that Leslie describes is undertaken by earthly counsellors and negotiators. Despite the gloomy feelings around the current moment, however, there should be two things that at least provide a little light at the end of the tunnel—at least as far as China's relations with the outside world go.

The first is that with the arrival of the Biden Administration from January 2021, and the EU's position over 2020, embedded in their position is an implicit acknowledgement that rather than a single policy framework by which to understand and work with (or against) China, there is a multi-level approach. This at least goes some way to capturing the complexity referred to in the section above. Anthony Blinken,

---

[5] Leslie (2020).

the US Secretary of State, in a speech on foreign policy in March 2021, delivered shortly after his appointment, used the phrase '*Our relationship with China will be competitive when it should be, collaborative when it can be, and adversarial when it must be*'.[6] This strangely echoed the trilateral division the European Union who, in a strategic paper issued in March 2019, had presciently stated that:

> *China is, simultaneously, in different policy areas, a cooperation partner with whom the EU has closely aligned objectives, a negotiating partner with whom the EU needs to find a balance of interests, an economic competitor in the pursuit of technological leadership, and a systemic rival promoting alternative models of governance. This requires a flexible and pragmatic whole-of-EU approach.*[7]

This acknowledges, both for the US and EU, the acceptance that a radical difference in viewpoints with China has to proceed alongside a similarly crucial admission that it would be self-defeating not to work with China. Comprehensive disengagement therefore, despite the language used in some quarters, was not and could not be an option.

There was a simple reason for this, which brings us to the second structural factor. Whatever the problems with China, and however significant they were, those involving human impact on the environment causing climate change, and combating global public health issues (as COVID-19 showed), were far more serious. The first posed, in the longer term, an existential threat to humanity. Indeed, Toby Ord, in a fascinating study of the greatest calamities that might face humankind in the coming decades, put the threat from Artificial Intelligence even higher.[8] In all these issues, China stood in the same critical position as everyone else. Indeed, on climate change, the deterioration of water and air quality in China had been an increasingly important concern for citizens since the turn of the millennium. Unlike the US, it had stayed committed to the Paris Agreement of 2015, rather than temporarily withdrawing. The Climate Change Conference (COP26) in November 2021 only underlines this, with China a key attendee. The stark reality is that a solution to this issue will not happen without partners like China, and, more positively, it is likely that China will be a huge part of whatever ultimate solution must be found.

These areas of common interest and alignment act as the basis for cooperation. They are acknowledged in the language used by the US and EU about common areas where there is strategic alignment, as quoted above. The political reality is that no government acting rationally and responsibly would, or could, jeopardise working together on these global issues for those which are more local, no matter how important they are. This is not to denigrate or deny the concerns about Hong Kong, Xinjiang and other issues, but it does place them in a crucial context. However

---

[6] Clarissa Yong, 'Biden Administration Establishes China Competition as Key Strategic Focus', March 4, Strait Times, https://www.straitstimes.com/world/united-states/us-secretary-of-state-antony-blinken-calls-china-biggest-test-vows-us-strength.

[7] European Commission and HR/VP contribution to the European Council, 'EU-China – A strategic outlook', March 2019, https://ec.europa.eu/info/sites/info/files/communication-eu-china-a-strategic-outlook.pdf, page 1.

[8] Ord (2020).

strong feelings are on these, there has to be a pragmatic framing. Granting the illusion of choice is for solipsists and daydreamers. All contact and discussion with China now have to happen in a framework that acknowledges the parameters supplied by global, common problems that threaten the very future of the human race, and where China and the rest of the world stand in the same place.

This means that it is not a matter of choice to live with the multi-level, multi-dimensional approach to China that the US and EU have had to adopt since 2019. This will be a feature of diplomacy for the foreseeable future. It is not elegant, and it certainly violates the usual desire to have a neat, holistic framework by which to deal with things. But in many areas, we are used to speaking the language of spectrums, where there are no orderly boundaries dividing issues. That sort of spectrum framework with China is the new normal. And for all its complexity, at least it makes things workable and manageable. Not win–win, for sure, but at the very least not lose either, which is something at least to celebrate in a world often looking overwhelmed by its own sense of divisions and strife.

# References

Gaston S, Aspinall E (2021) UK foreign policy and global affairs: annual survey 2021, issued 2021. https://bfpg.co.uk/wp-content/uploads/2021/02/BFPG-Annual-Survey-2021.pdf

Leslie I (2020) Conflicted XE "Leslie, Ian" : why arguments are tearing us apart and how they can bring us together. Faber, London

Ord T (2020) The precipice XE "Ord, Toby" : existential risk and the future of humanity. Bloomsbury, London

Ward M (2020) Statistics on UK Trade with China, UK Parliament, House of Commons Library, 14 July 2020, https://commonslibrary.parliament.uk/research-briefings/cbp-7379/#:~:text=In%202019%3A,deficit%20of%20%2D%C2%A318.3%20billion.&text=China%20accounted%20for%204.4%25%20of,fourth%20largest%20source%20of%20imports.

**Kerry Brown** is a Professor of Chinese Studies and Director of the Lau China Institute, King's College London. From 2012 to 2015, he was Professor of Chinese Politics and Director of the China Studies Centre at the University of Sydney, Australia. Prior to this, he worked at Chatham House (2006 to 2012) as Senior Fellow and then Head of the Asia Programme. From 1998 to 2005, he worked at the British Foreign and Commonwealth Office, and as First Secretary at the British Embassy in Beijing. He is the author of over ten books on modern Chinese politics, history and language.

**Open Access** This chapter is licensed under the terms of the Creative Commons Attribution-NonCommercial-NoDerivatives 4.0 International License (http://creativecommons.org/licenses/by-nc-nd/4.0/), which permits any noncommercial use, sharing, distribution and reproduction in any medium or format, as long as you give appropriate credit to the original author(s) and the source, provide a link to the Creative Commons license and indicate if you modified the licensed material. You do not have permission under this license to share adapted material derived from this chapter or parts of it.

The images or other third party material in this chapter are included in the chapter's Creative Commons license, unless indicated otherwise in a credit line to the material. If material is not included in the chapter's Creative Commons license and your intended use is not permitted by statutory regulation or exceeds the permitted use, you will need to obtain permission directly from the copyright holder.

# Challenges and Reconstruction of the International Order in the Post COVID-19 Era

**Yafei He**

**Abstract** Living in *a period of historic transition*, countries around the world need to rethink their own position and that of their counterparts in the context of the world as a whole. As this pandemic continues to disrupt the world order, it will play a crucial role in global history, marking a change in the *"rules-based world order."* There are four major points that should guide the course of *developing a new world order*. First, is to *be vigilant against the pitfalls of the zero-sum geopolitical game*, and to avoid any form of cold or hot war. Second, is to staunchly *defend economic globalization and free trade*, and oppose protectionism while carrying out reforms to institutions like the WTO. Third, is to *take global poverty alleviation and poverty relief seriously*, making concerted efforts to *bridge North–South gaps*. Fourth. is to *restore the spirit of mutual assistance* in the face of common threats and a sense of community with a shared future for humanity facing common existential crises. Under the threat of a raging pandemic, *climate change*, *cybersecurity risks*, collapse of the *nuclear non-proliferation* regime, and the *grain crisis*, there is no more important, pressing challenge than preserving the environment for human existence.

**Keywords** A period of historic transition · "Rules-based world order" · A new world order · Zero-sum geopolitical games · Defend economic globalization and free trade · Global poverty alleviation and poverty relief · North–South gaps · Mutual assistance · Climate change · Cybersecurity risks · Nuclear non-proliferation · Grain crisis

The impact of COVID-19 on the current international order is unprecedented and to some extent recalls the stress test that major banks weathered after the 2008 global financial crisis. As this pandemic continues to disrupt the world order, it will play a crucial role in world history, marking a change in the "rules of the game" and a test of current systems of governance and administration in all countries.

As of early 2021, China was the only country that had been able to contain the virus and claim victory over the pandemic. The considerable uncertainties and bottomless

Y. He (✉)
Peking University, Beijing, China

© The Author(s) 2021
H. Wang and A. Michie (eds.), *Consensus or Conflict?*, China and Globalization,
https://doi.org/10.1007/978-981-16-5391-9_5

traps that lie ahead create tremendous concern over issues that urgently need solutions, which include not only the pandemic, but also economic recovery and social
stability. Emerging complicated global issues necessitate a fundamental rethinking of
the challenges to the current international order and questions regarding its structure,
which will ultimately lead to new approaches confronting a post-pandemic world.

## 1 The Challenge of the United States

Other than the COVID-19 pandemic, the toughest challenge facing the world comes
from domestic problems in the United States—worsening social division, political
polarization, and a resurgence of "America First" populism—which not only reflects
public opinion, but also shapes US domestic and foreign policies. Following President
Joe Biden and the Democratic Party taking office in January 2021, the previous high
level of unpredictability in US politics will hopefully subside to some extent. The
withdrawal of the United States from international organizations will also be reversed,
which means that these international institutions may regain some of their influence.
Nevertheless, the fundamental conflicts that are inherent to US society will no doubt
persist over the long term and grave crises, like the damage to capitalism, will become
more serious than ever before. The US is clearly not what it used to be.

The biggest variable affecting global political and economic orientation in the US
was summed up by the American scholar Francis Fukuyama as early as 2014 when
he described what he called "political decay" that had been growing in recent years
due to the control of a powerful elite group.[1] Political chaos and disorder in the US
are rooted in inequality resulting from a widening wealth gap, which has to do with
globalization but is more closely related to US political and economic institutions.

The norms of US politics dictate that after coming to power, the new administration will reassess the policies of the previous administration, including foreign
relations (particularly with China and Europe) as well as responses to challenges
to global governance challenges like climate change. Political trajectories preferred
by the Democrats and Biden mean that related policies will very likely see realign-
ment. Some of them will likely to undergo strategic and short-term changes, while
comprehensive adjustments will require sufficient time and public support. However,
the polarization of US politics means that strong sentiments of anti-globalization,
the appeal of populism, and narrow-minded nationalism will continue to direct much
of US foreign policy.

---

[1] "Political Order and Political Decay: From the Industrial Revolution to the Globalisation of
Democracy" by Francis Fukuyama, published by Polity Press, 2014.

## 2  Restructuring the International Order

The current international order and system of global governance is fragmented and is in dire need of reconstruction. The reshuffling of the global power structure and the redistribution of interests are also beset by mounting risks and crises. The US still represents the greatest uncertainty, while China could be an important player in driving the restructuring of the international order.

The most serious challenge facing the international order is that traditional and non-traditional security threats overlap and exacerbate each other. A shared awareness of the need to work together when facing global challenges, which was demonstrated in the close cooperation among countries during the 2008 financial crisis, has unfortunately diminished and a consensus on cooperation is absent in the interactions among great powers. In its place is suspicion and confrontation that overshadow relations and exacerbate geopolitical and ideological conflicts. However, no country can completely isolate itself in this age of information and globalization, which is characterized by mutual interdependence. Whether it's climate change or cybersecurity, no individual state can solve these global challenges alone.

The United States, major European countries, and many others are drowned in a flood tide of populism and anti-globalization characterized by outright unilateralism and narrow-minded nationalism that has gradually galvanized mass support in their societies. Issues of illegal immigrants, free trade, and racial conflicts fill the domestic agenda and have become systematic ills that pervade capitalist societies. Doubts of the credibility of American "liberal democracy" have been raised even among major American allies such as Germany.

The double whammy of COVID-19 and the cyclical recession of the world economy, which in early 2021 has yet to hit bottom, has the potential to slide the world into a global depression on the scale of the Great Depression of the 1930s. It is hard to say how long the economy will remain in such a depressed state before seeing an uptick, but history shows us that the recovery period for the global economy after a financial crisis can be 7 to 8 years. However, it is possible that this can be avoided if the Chinese economy, as the only global economy showing positive growth, continues to evolve steadily, while at the same time implementing new reforms. In contrast, other major economies like the United States will remain at zero or negative growth until 2022 at the earliest. The subsequent financial risks associated with the uncapped liquidity and negative interest rates implemented by many central banks since the onset of COVID-19 are also starting to appear.

Against a background of unique international environment and historical events, the world order will inevitably experience fundamental change, which will also require corresponding adjustments to the system of global governance. Originally, to counter the incalculable damage pandemics could do to humanity, an array of multilateral institutions and treaties was put in place after World War II as part of the global governance framework. So, it's ironic and regrettable, that despite the tremendous efforts made so far this seemingly impeccable system did not live up to expectations—though one might note that the system itself is not to blame so much as its members, who are the decision-makers. To the extent the global public health system functions, it is the member states, and especially the major powers, that are the real governors. The negative and dismissive attitude of the US toward the World Health Organization (WHO), in particular, is quite revealing of this chilling reality.

In addition to negative externalities like the pandemic, the current technological revolution, while bringing the world tremendous wealth and new opportunities, like other revolutions, is yet another challenge to the current world order, as it will also profoundly change society and its structure. According to estimates by international organizations, 50% of current jobs will be taken over by automation and robots using artificial intelligence by 2030, and global supply chains will undergo adjustments and reorganization. This process will inevitably lead to another round of turbulence in society.

Cascades of non-traditional security threats including the COVID-19 crisis, climate change, environmental security, energy crises, food crises, technological advances, and even space security, interplay with geopolitical competition and consequently complicate global challenges. However, the fragmentation and disorder in global governance has pushed the system itself to the edge of collapse. The unpredictability, uncertainty, and instability that fill the future threaten the survival of mankind as a community with common destiny. Hence, finding a solution to the challenges facing global governance requires that China, the United States, Europe, and other countries quickly resume discussion and cooperation. Governments must turn away from unilateralism and return to multilateralism to address international affairs and rebuild the international order.

## 3   International Institutions and Global Governance

The United Nations and the system of global governance built around it are the cornerstone for the reconstruction of an international order and should be carefully preserved. Naturally, these institutions also have to undergo necessary adjustments and reforms; in this context, the World Trade Organization (WTO) could be a litmus test. We hope that with the Biden administration in place that the United States will commit to a system of free trade that is based on a reformed WTO. We must also consolidate and improve the global health system that the WHO represents. In turn, the WHO must effectively coordinate the distribution of vaccines and to contain the COVID-19 pandemic, while at the same time strengthening global public health emergency response mechanisms to better contain future epidemics.

Common sense dictates that the two most important issues in global governance are security and economics, both of which are in jeopardy because of the current pandemic. "Lives or livelihoods" is today's version of "to be or not to be," as the pandemic has taken so many lives and the livelihoods people rely on for survival. In many developing countries, there are large cities in which poor people live in cramped quarters, with scarce or nonexistent sanitation, providing fertile ground for the spread of infectious diseases. This is unacceptable.

Given the highly connected world we live in, the global village is a reality, and a community of nations with a shared future is no mere slogan. It is a statement of fact. Naive isolationism that means closing borders and severing all connections to outside world is not going to work in the long term. It is no real solution at all. In times of calamity, helping others is helping oneself, simply because it is impossible to live in total isolation in the age of globalization.

Globalization is not the enemy; it is the solution. Just look at how scientists and medical communities have worked together across borders day and night since the coronavirus outbreak to find and produce vaccines for it, even as politicians bicker over things that only serve their short-term interests, such as elections.

In this context, reaching a fundamental consensus and conviction to maintain international peace and promote economic development among great powers, in particular, China and the United States, is the basis for a restructuring of the world order. It is neither realistic nor possible to adopt a "G2" model in which China and the US rule the world. However, the fact that these global powers are the world's largest economies and have considerable international influence means that their combined roles are crucial to addressing international affairs and confronting traditional or non-traditional security threats.

Europe has also been very active in global governance, especially in combating climate change and promoting the proper functioning of a rules-based system of global governance such as in the operation of the 'World Wide Web' or the internet. The different attitudes in Europe and the United States on issues like the WTO, the WHO, and the Iran nuclear deal demonstrate the pivotal role of Europe in the development, maintenance, and consolidation of global governance. If the Biden administration is able to re-engage with the world in multilateral actions including the Paris Agreement on climate change, the Iran nuclear deal framework, the WHO, the WTO, and its reform, there will be more room for cooperation between China, Europe, and the United States. It is from this kind of collaboration that consensus can emerge and solidify a basis for the joint provision of public goods in the global sphere.

Emerging economies like Russia, India, Brazil, Indonesia, Turkey, and Argentina as well as a large group of developing countries all have their own views on the future development of a new international system, but they all share some common ground. The "internationality" of the international order represents a universality, which means that such a system should be recognized and followed by all members of the international community, rather than being imposed by one or two great powers. History shows us that crucial principles in modern world history originated from the treaty signed in 1648 called the Peace of Westphalia that ended the 30-year war. The treaty proposed sovereignty and non-interference in the domestic affairs of individual nations. The rise of the British Empire, which resulted from competition among the great powers of Europe, created a world dominated by the British, which was later taken over by the consolidated superpower of the United States after World War II and has lasted until the present day. Now, we are witnessing a new round of changes and a reshuffling of power. The world is becoming "a world for all countries" with no single country maintaining hegemony over the rest of the international community.

Global governance is also transitioning from "Western predominance" to "East-West co-governance."

## 4 New Challenges Facing a New World Order

In this era of digital revolution, continuously emerging technological breakthroughs are key elements and driving forces that are spurring on changes to the global order. Part and parcel with the information age, interpenetration, and integration of virtual and real spaces through big data, AI, biotechnology, space, and deep-sea exploration as well as cyberspace have created a new world with new challenges. The new international order, therefore, must also catch up with these technological advancements. Otherwise, obsolete ideas and structures that are incompatible with these new technologies will quickly become unsustainable. We need to seriously consider the impact of technologies when restructuring the world order and system of global governance.

The mountain of domestic problems facing the United States and many other countries as well as widening inequalities between rich and poor are the root of the social disintegration, political polarization, and growing populism and pose the greatest challenge for human development. Continued efforts to alleviate absolute poverty in recent decades have seen phenomenal success in China and laid a solid foundation for political stability, economic development, and social harmony. Arguably, the ability to effectively address domestic problems, in particular, the balance between economic development and social equality, will be a deciding factor in a country's relative competitiveness. A future international order will be decided by how countries deal with social inequality and the gap between rich and poor, which ultimately lead to social divisiveness.

When discussing a vision for the global community as a shared future for mankind, it is important to point out that this future should be a future of all people. The key to finding pathways and solutions for the challenges we now face lies in universal acceptance and recognition of new thoughts and concepts by governments as well as individual citizens, which are produced by the creation of a global community, a sense of the individual as a global citizen, global partnerships, and building a community with a shared future.

There are four major points that we should keep in mind in the course of developing a new world order.

First is to be vigilant against the pitfalls of the zero-sum geopolitical game, and to avoid any form of cold or hot war. Competition between the largest countries in the world is normal, but there must be order, bottom lines, and rules. And competition must be kept in check in the search for peaceful coexistence.

Second is to staunchly defend economic globalization and free trade, and oppose protectionism while carrying out reforms to the WTO. As the world enters a period of increased availability of knowledge and a digital economy, new rules have to be made to adapt to the technological revolution and changes in global supply chains. Green, sustainable development must be promoted.

Third is to take global poverty alleviation and poverty relief seriously, making concerted efforts to bridge North–South gaps. Advanced countries should assume appropriate responsibilities, and take global development as a whole instead of the interests of only a small number of countries. The UN 2030 Agenda for Sustainable Development is a fine platform. China's achievements in poverty alleviation and its Belt and Road Initiative have similar goals.

Fourth is to restore the spirit of mutual assistance in the face of common threats and a sense of community with a shared future for humanity facing common existential crises. Under the threat of a raging pandemic, climate change, cybersecurity risks, collapse of the nuclear non-proliferation regime, and the grain crisis, there is no more important, pressing challenge than preserving the environment for human existence. Fragmentation of the global governance regime and a state of anarchy are unsustainable. Humanity won't be able to overcome the extreme difficulties posed by the confluence and simultaneous outbreak of traditional and non-traditional security threats.

Living in a period of historic transition, countries around the world need to rethink their own position and that of their counterparts in the context of the world as a whole. The time of "one country dominating all" is over, but the paradigm of competition and coexistence of different political systems has not ended as claimed by Professor Fukuyama.[2] Rather, the changing balance of power requires governments to reconsider their domestic and foreign policies based on a new status quo. Furthermore, international and regional organizations should participate in or even direct the remaking of international rules and the restructuring of the global order. Safeguarding world peace, accelerating economic development, and promoting cultural integration are still the main themes for this new era and new international order. It is only by these means that we can facilitate the building of a better world that is founded upon stability, peace, prosperity, affluence, equality, and justice.

**Yafei He** is the Former Vice Minister of Ministry of Foreign Affairs of China and the Former Vice Minister of Overseas Chinese Affairs Office of the State Council. He graduated from Beijing Foreign Studies University, and later studied at the Geneva Graduate Institute of International and Development Studies. He currently serves as the Secretary General of International Mountain Tourism Alliance, and Distinguished Professor of Yenching Academy of Peking University. He has rich experiences in diplomatic practices, and in-depth research and studies on global governance and China's foreign policy, on which he has published several books, of which the latest is *China and Global Governance* (2019).

---

[2] Professor Francis Fukuyama is an American political scientist best known for his book published in 1992 called "The End Of History And The Last Man"(Free Press).

**Open Access** This chapter is licensed under the terms of the Creative Commons Attribution-NonCommercial-NoDerivatives 4.0 International License (http://creativecommons.org/licenses/by-nc-nd/4.0/), which permits any noncommercial use, sharing, distribution and reproduction in any medium or format, as long as you give appropriate credit to the original author(s) and the source, provide a link to the Creative Commons license and indicate if you modified the licensed material. You do not have permission under this license to share adapted material derived from this chapter or parts of it.

The images or other third party material in this chapter are included in the chapter's Creative Commons license, unless indicated otherwise in a credit line to the material. If material is not included in the chapter's Creative Commons license and your intended use is not permitted by statutory regulation or exceeds the permitted use, you will need to obtain permission directly from the copyright holder.

# Japan's Role in Improving Global Economic Governance in the Era of US–China Strategic Competition

Masahiro Kawai

**Abstract** This essay provides an analysis of *global economic governance from a Japanese perspective.* There is an analysis of the *"rules based world order" in the context of changing trends,* such as the *relative decline of the US economy* and a *rapid rise of the Chinaese economy.* The essay focuses on the *state of global economic governance* from the perspectives of international forums—such as the *G7* and the G20 - and international organizations such as the *IMF, World Bank and the WTO* It tackles key questions: Can the international community build a new rules-based, liberal, multilateral economic governance order? If so, what needs to be done and what role can Japan play as a strong supporter of such an order? How *can Japan work with China* for this purpose? The essay argues that Japan can play a major role in addressing such challenges. It also urges Japan to work with not only the US and the EU but also China and other major emerging economies in order to reform the WTO, and put it back on the center stage of global rule-making for twenty-first-century trade and investment.

**Keywords** Global economic governance from a Japanese perspective ·
Rules-based world order · Relative decline of the US · Rapid rise of the Chinese
economy · State of global economic governance · G7 and G20 · The IMF ·
The World Bank and the WTO · Japan - China cooperation · Reform of the WTO

## 1 Introduction

COVID-19 has severely affected most economies in the world. For any return to sustained economic growth, a rules-based, liberal global economic order is vital. At the same time, US–China strategic competition has expanded from trade to technology, security, and state governance issues. So, it is unclear if, or how, the international community can deal with the urgent need to strengthen global economic governance.

M. Kawai (✉)
The Economic Research Institute for Northeast Asia, Niigata, Japan

University of Tokyo, Tokyo, Japan

© The Author(s) 2021                                                   59
H. Wang and A. Michie (eds.), *Consensus or Conflict?*, China and Globalization,
https://doi.org/10.1007/978-981-16-5391-9_6

The administration in the US, under Joe Biden, is returning to multilateralism and global cooperation through the UN-led Paris Agreement on global warming; the World Health Organization (WHO); the UN Human Rights Council; the UN Educational, Scientific and Cultural Organization and possibly the UN Educational, Scientific and Cultural Organisation (UNESCO) the Iran. Whether the US under Biden will rejoin the Trans-Pacific Partnership (TPP) is not clear, but if it does, it may take a few years. The Biden administration continues to regard China as the "strategic competitor" of the US and describes China as the "most serious competitor" to the US. The Biden team has adopted a tough policy stance against China on issues including human rights, Hong Kong's autonomy, and Taiwan. In facing China, the Biden administration has been acting together with its allies, such as the EU, the UK, Japan, Australia, and Canada rather than acting alone. At the same time, Biden favors cooperating with China on common global issues such as climate change, anti-terrorism, cybersecurity, and arms control.

Given this background, this essay asks the following questions: What is the structure of the global economy that characterizes recent changes such as the relative decline of the US and a rapid rise of the Chinese economy? What is the state of global economic governance from the perspectives of international forums like the G7 and the G20, and international organizations like the International Monetary Fund (IMF), World Bank and the World Trade Organization (WTO)? Can the international community return to a rules-based, liberal, multilateral economic governance order, which has benefited many countries, including China and Japan enormously in the post-WWII period? If so, what needs to be done and what role can Japan play as a strong supporter of such an order? How can Japan work with China toward this goal?

## 2   Structural Changes in the World Economy and the Evolution of the G20

One of the most fundamental structural changes in the world economy over the last 30 years is the relative decline of the US and other advanced economies such as the G7 and the rapid rise of the Chinese and other emerging and developing economies such as the BRICS countries (Brazil, Russia, India, China, and South Africa). As a result, the latter economies have begun to demand a greater voice for global economic management. A core catalyst for this structural change was the 2007-09 global financial crisis (GFC), which led to the G20 assuming a leading role in navigating global economic recovery.

## 2.1 Structural Shift in the World Economy

Emerging and developing economies had made their voices heard for rule-making in global economic governance well before the GFC. During negotiations for the WTO's Doha Development Round (DDR), they placed priorities on their own socio-economic development needs, which were different from those of advanced economies, thereby complicating global trade negotiations. They also wanted to have a greater voice in the IMF, but this took much longer to realize than expected. China launched the Belt and Road Initiative (BRI) and took leadership in 2016 in establishing the Asian Infrastructure Investment Bank (AIIB).

As an outcome of this structural change, particularly the rapid growth of the Chinese economy achieved since its accession to the WTO in 2001, the US has come to view China as having "exploit(ed) the free and open rules-based order" supported by the WTO, IMF, and the World Bank, as well as attempting to "reshape the international system in its favor" through the BRI and other related frameworks.[1] The US has begun to view the rise of China's economic, technological, and military capabilities as a threat to its global hegemonic dominance.

Projecting world economic growth over the next 50 years or so, China's economy will continue to expand, exceeding the size of the US economy (measured by nominal GDP at market exchange rates) around 2030, and becoming by far the largest in the world by 2050. This is a major concern for the US and its allies.

However, the sum of the US and EU GDPs would remain larger than China's GDP for the next 50 years and beyond. This suggests that it would be in the interest of the US to work with the EU and other like-minded advanced democracies (such as Australia, Canada, Japan, and the UK), if it wanted to maintain economic dominance and national security against a rising China, as the US would remain the leader among these democracies. The Trump administration ignored and the Biden administration recognizes this fact. India will also grow rapidly and will likely work with Western democracies, making China's economic dominance even more difficult. The rise of China and India would also mean that the Indo-Pacific will be one of the most dynamic regions of the world.

Thus, for the US, cooperation with allies rather than the "America-first" approach is the way to assure global leadership and national security, as economic size is a key determinant of military capabilities. At the same time, if China achieves a peaceful, harmonious rise without major friction with the US and other advanced economies, and provides an increasing volume of genuine international public goods, the country can legitimately claim a greater voice in the high table of global economic governance.

---

[1] US National Security Council (2020) .

## 2.2   Evolution of the G20 Summit

The G20 summit, upgraded from a process for finance ministers and central bank governors to that for leaders, played a crucial role to resolve the GFC. Each member of the G20 was identified as a "systemically significant economy" that should be at the G20 table to help overcome global economic challenges for the benefit of all. This meant a major shift in global economic governance from the G7 to a broader group, encompassing large emerging and developing economies, with not only greater voice but also greater responsibilities for global economic management.

The G20 leader process was needed because cooperation by the rising economic power of emerging and developing economies was considered essential to tackle the severe negative impact of the GFC, as the G7's ability to manage the GFC by themselves was limited. Indeed, emerging and developing economies grew much faster than the G7 economies and thus greatly contributed to world economic recovery.

For a few years after the 2008 Lehman shock, the G20 Summit focused on tackling the GFC jointly, strengthening the resource bases and functions of international financial institutions (particularly the IMF, the World Bank, and regional multilateral development banks), and stepping up financial sector regulation to avoid another financial crisis. The Summit was called "the premier forum for international economic cooperation" in Pittsburgh in September 2009. Once global economic recovery took hold, the summit shifted its focus to various macroeconomic, financial, structural, and developmental issues of global relevance, with support from major international organizations (such as the UN, IMF, World Bank, WTO, Organisation for Economic Co-operation and Development [OECD], and more recently WHO) as an integral part of global economic governance.

## 3   The Bretton Woods System

The Bretton Woods System (BWS)[2] played a critical role in supporting the rules-based, liberal, multilateral economic order in the post-WWII era. The IMF and the World Bank, which had evolved from the Bretton Woods Conference, responded to the negative impact of the 2007-09 GFC and have been dealing with economic difficulties arising from the recent COVID-19 pandemic. The WTO complements the BWS by setting rules for, and promoting free, non-discriminatory and multilateral trade.

---

[2] See Sandra Kollen Ghizoni, "Creation of the Bretton Woods System," Federal Reserve History (November 22, 2013). https://www.federalreservehistory.org/essays/bretton-woods-created.

## 3.1 The IMF

The IMF began significant reform to augment its crisis response capacity and streamline lending conditions after the Asian financial crisis of 1997-98. The IMF was required to respond to the GFC with a quota increase and adjustment of voting shares in favor of emerging and developing economies (agreed to in 2010 and implemented in 2016). The US is the largest shareholder in the IMF and holds veto power, followed by Japan, China, Germany, France, and the UK . Reflecting the rising importance of the Chinese yuan for global use, the currency was included in the Special Drawing Rights (SDR) basket in October 2016. However, the next quota increase, which would accompany voting power shifts, is not scheduled to take place until the end of 2023.

Facing the COVID-19 pandemic, the IMF, headed currently by Kristalina Georgieva, has responded to its negative impact with support for vulnerable developing countries. For example, it has provided emergency assistance to developing countries with high levels of debt, weak medical systems, and severely impacted commodity sectors. It has temporarily doubled the member countries' access to emergency facilities, such as the Rapid Credit Facility and Rapid Financing Instrument, without the need to have a full-fledged program in place. It has also extended debt service relief through the Catastrophe Containment and Relief Trust (CCRT) to 29 of its poorest and most vulnerable member countries to cover their IMF debt obligations falling due to the IMF for the period between April 2020 and April 2021. Adopting the joint proposal made by the IMF and the World Bank, the G20 countries agreed in April 2020 to suspend repayment of official bilateral credit from the 73 low and lower middle-income countries initially until the end of 2020 and later until the end of June 2021 under the Debt Service Suspension Initiative (DSSI). In November 2020, the G20 countries agreed on a framework of debt reduction for these developing countries, which the IMF supports together with the World Bank.

It is likely that more financial assistance will be needed for not only low and lower middle-income countries but also for emerging economies severely hit by the pandemic. The IMF has about USD 1 trillion available for new lending. Although this is sufficient at the moment, the institution has been exploring ways to expand resources to support its more vulnerable members. The proposed new allocation of SDRs—as much as USD 650 billion—to provide flexibility to countries with liquidity shortages, which had been opposed by the Trump administration, gained support from the Biden administration, on the condition that new resources should benefit those developing countries truly in need of support, and not countries like China. This new allocation of SDRs was finally approved by the IMF Governors in the summer of 2021.

## 3.2   The World Bank

The World Bank has been transforming itself from an organization using a one-size-fits-all "Washington Consensus"[3] to one that respects members' ownership and country-driven institutional and governance reforms to improve the business climate. As in the case of the IMF, the US, Japan, China, Germany, France, and the UK are the top six shareholding members in the International Bank for Reconstruction and Development (IBRD), and these countries with the exception of China are the top five contributors to the International Development Association (IDA), with China being the tenth largest contributor.

The World Bank has maintained relatively good relations with China by supporting its economic reform and market opening, although most experts view these reforms to have stalled in recent years. The Bank has also cooperated with China on the BRI (Belt and Road Initiative) and jointly financed projects. Even though David Malpass, a China "hawk" and a critic of the BRI, assumed Bank presidency in April 2019, the Bank has not cut its lending to China drastically and has maintained joint projects with the AIIB.

In response to the COVID-19 pandemic, the World Bank announced in May 2020 that it would provide up to USD 160 billion to most of its developing member countries over the following 15 months through the Fast-Track Facility to address their health, economic, and social difficulties. This would include funding of USD 50 billion from IDA resources as grants and highly concessional loans. By February 2021, a total of 84 countries had benefited from the dedicated COVID-19 Fast-Track Facility, and 87 countries (with overlap with the above) had been under other financing programs.[4]

The IMF and the World Bank have been fully backed by the US government, and even the Trump administration never criticized the IMF or the Bank. The reason for this is that the US is the number one shareholder for both institutions with veto power and that these sister institutions are located in Washington, DC. Although the managing director (MD) of the IMF has always been a European, the US has played a key role by ensuring that the first deputy MD is always an American. The president of the World Bank has always been an American.

---

[3] The "Washington Consensus" is a set of economic policies prescribed for developing countries by Washington, D.C.-based institutions such as the IMF, World Bank, and the US Treasury Department.

[4] See World Bank Group's Operational Response to COVID-19 (coronavirus)—Project List. https://www.worldbank.org/en/about/what-we-do/brief/world-bank-group-operational-response-covid-19-coronavirus-projects-list#fasttrack.

## 3.3   The WTO (World Trade Organisation)

The world trading system under the General Agreement on Tariffs and Trade (GATT), and the subsequent WTO, worked well until the turn of the millennium.[5] The WTO has faced the most serious challenges as its function has been severely damaged in recent years.

The WTO, established in 1995, was expected to strengthen the global trading system by stepping up existing trade rules, introducing new rules, and upgrading the dispute settlement procedure. China's accession to the WTO in December 2001 was considered a boost to global trade and investment. However, the failure of the DDR to deliver comprehensive agreements and the Trump administration's engagement in a US–China trade war in 2018–19 have put the WTO in a crisis situation in all of its three functions: providing a forum to negotiate new trade rules; monitoring members' trade policies; and resolving trade disputes among members.

It is difficult for the WTO's diverse members to reach agreements on further trade liberalization, new trade rules, and changes in member obligations because such agreements require full consensus among them. This was evident in DDR (Doha Development Round) negotiations, where the interests of developed and developing members collided and, as a result, comprehensive agreements were not reached.

Many developing countries, including China and India, have not complied with notification and transparency obligations with regard to changes in such trade policies as subsidies and regulations. Although the US, the EU, and Japan have called for new rules that would penalize members for not complying with their notification obligations,[6] it is unlikely that such rules would be agreed upon by all members, especially developing countries.

In addition, the US has long criticized the function of the Appellate Body (AB), a standing body that can uphold, modify, or reverse the legal findings and conclusions of a panel after hearing appeals brought by WTO members, for its excessively interpretative decisions and overreach.[7] There is a major philosophical difference between the US and the EU on the role of the dispute settlement mechanism. The issue is whether it is permissible for the AB to articulate rules and develop a set of international common laws without the consensus of all members.[8] The EU supports this idea while the US rejects it. The US has claimed that the AB has repeatedly exercised its authority beyond its original mandate by reinterpreting WTO agreements and has treated AB reports as precedent against the Dispute Settlement Understanding. As

---

[5] See VanGrassteck (2013).

[6] WTO General Council, "Procedures to Enhance Transparency and Strengthen Notification Requirements under WTO Agreements." Communication from Argentina, Australia, Canada, Costa Rica, the European Union, Israel, Japan, New Zealand, Taiwan, United Kingdom, and the United States, JOB/GC/204/Rev.4, JOB/CTG/14/Rev.4 (24 November 2020). www.wto.org.

[7] The Office of the United States Trade Representative, *2020 Trade Policy Agenda and 2019 Annual Report* (February 2020). https://ustr.gov/sites/default/files/2020_Trade_Policy_Agenda_and_2019_Annual_Report.pdf.

[8] Willems (2020).

a result, the US government, since the Barack Obama administration, has blocked new appointments of judges to fill vacancies and refused their reappointments after their terms, eventually leaving the AB with only one judge in December 2019. With a minimum of three judges required for it to function, the WTO has become unable to fully resolve trade disputes among members.

Furthermore, the US government has had bipartisan concerns over China's "non-market" policies and practices, forced technology transfers, its "developing country" status, and the special and differential (S&D) treatment enjoyed by China. The US, together with the EU and Japan, has argued that "non-market-oriented" policies and practices, as well as forced technology transfers, have created unfair competitive advantages and undermined the proper functioning of international trade.[9] The US has urged "non-market" economies, such as China, to move toward greater market openness and competition by reforming state-owned enterprises (SOEs) and eliminating state subsidies. The US has also argued that entitlement to S&D treatment should not be granted to countries classified as "high income" by the World Bank, OECD members or its acceding ones, G20 members, or any country accounting for 0.5% or more of world trade.[10]

The new Director-General of WTO, Ngozi Okonjo-Iweala, faces daunting challenges as, under the consensus requirement, these fundamental reforms are unlikely to be achieved soon, even though most members believe some reform is necessary.

# 4 Japan's Approach

Japan strongly supports the IMF, the World Bank and the WTO because she has benefited enormously from a rules-based liberal international economic order. Japan delivered productive outcomes at the Osaka G20 summit in June 2019[11] and is now pushing forward the Free and Open Indo-Pacific (FOIP) vision to forge trade in the region that is rules-based, free, and open, and designed to have positive implications for global economic governance. At the same time, Japan has been working with China with a view to encouraging it to be a responsible player in the global community.

---

[9] See the joint statements by the trade ministers of Japan, the US, and the EU, particularly from the 4th (September 2018) through the 7th trilateral meeting (January 2020). The most recent statement is available from: https://www.meti.go.jp/press/2019/01/20200114007/20200114007-2.pdf.

[10] WTO General Council, "Draft General Council Decision: Procedures to Strengthen the Negotiating Function of the WTO." Communication circulated at the request of the delegation of the United States, WT/GC/W/764/Rev.1 (November 25, 2019). https://www.mofa.go.jp/policy/economy/g20_summit/osaka19/en/documents/final_g20_osaka_leaders_declaration.html.

[11] The most recent G20 summit was held in Riyadh, Saudi Arabia in November 2020, which was limited to a virtual meeting due to the COVID-19 pandemic.

## 4.1   Japan's Presidency of the Osaka G20 Summit

The Osaka G20 summit in June 2019 was a big success for Japan, assisted by ministerial processes, particularly by ministers of finance, foreign, trade, digital, and economics along with central bank governors.[12] All provided key inputs to the G20 leaders.

On the trade and investment agenda, the G20 leaders strove to realize a free, fair, non-discriminatory, transparent, predictable, and stable trade and investment environment, and to keep their markets open. In addition, they supported necessary reforms of the WTO and recognized the complementary roles of bilateral and regional free trade agreements (FTAs) that are WTO-consistent. During this period, when the WTO had become severely dysfunctional, it was considered important for economies to explore trade and investment liberalization and new rule-making through bilateral and regional FTAs.

Japan indeed has been promoting regional trade and investment through two mega-regional FTAs, namely the Comprehensive and Progressive Agreement for Trans-Pacific Partnership (CPTPP), which took effect in December 2018, and the Regional Comprehensive Economic Partnership (RCEP), which was signed in November 2020. Japan supports the vision to forge a Free Trade Area in the Asia–Pacific region among Asia-Pacific Economic Cooperation (APEC) member economies. To connect itself with Western Europe, Japan has also implemented two major FTAs, including the Japan-EU Economic Partnership Agreement (EPA). That became effective  in February 2019, and the Japan-UK Comprehensive Economic Partnership Agreement (CEPA), which came into force in January 2021. Japan's aim has consistently been to achieve high-standard, WTO-consistent FTAs.

The G20 leaders also declared that the cross-border flow of data, information, ideas, and knowledge would stimulate productivity, innovation, and sustainable development, and recommended "data free flow with trust" (DFFT), recognizing the challenges of protecting privacy, data, intellectual property rights (IPR), and security. This concept reflected the Osaka Track, which Japan promoted as one of the priorities set for the summit to encourage collective efforts to realize governance of global data flows and unleash the benefits of cross-border flows of trusted data. The "free" part of DFFT does not mean a world without appropriate rules or safeguards, but it meant a world where the security of data flows and IPR protection are ensured to avoid damaging public trust in digital technologies and data management. So "trust" is crucial and designed to coexist with freedom (or openness) in symbiosis.[13] It should be noted that the e-commerce chapter of the CPTPP is consistent with the DFFT concept, while close to 90 WTO members have also been pursuing new negotiations on rule-making for digital trade or e-commerce.

---

[12] See G20 Osaka Leaders' Declaration, June 2019. G20 Osaka Leaders' Declaration I Documents and Materials I G20 Osaka Summit 2019 (mofa.go.jp).

[13] See World Economic Forum, *Data Free Flow with Trust (DFFT): Paths toward Free and Trusted Data Flow*, White Paper (May 2020). hhttp://www3.weforum.org/docs/WEF_Paths_Towards_Free_and_Trusted_Data%20_Flows_2020.pdf.

The leaders also endorsed the "G20 Principles for Quality Infrastructure Investment," which was recognized as a common strategic direction and high-level goal. Japan has been promoting the concept of "quality infrastructure investment" for some time and in May 2015 issued a document titled Partnership for Quality Infrastructure, and pushed forward the "G7 Ise-Shima Principles for Promoting Quality Infrastructure" at the Ise-Shima G7 summit hosted by Japan in May 2016.[14]

The G20 principles adopted in Osaka are a streamlined version of the previous ones and describe a set of voluntary, non-binding principles that include maximizing the positive impact of infrastructure to achieve sustainable growth and development (job creation, transfer of expertise, enhancing connectivity); raising economic efficiency in view of life-cycle cost; integrating environmental considerations into infrastructure investments; building resilience against natural disasters and other risks; integrating social considerations in infrastructure investment (open access to infrastructure services, safety, respect for gender, and the socially vulnerable); and strengthening infrastructure governance (openness and transparency of procurement, and debt sustainability).

## 4.2 Support for the Bretton Woods System and WTO Reform

Japan is a staunch supporter of the IMF and the World Bank as their number two shareholder. Following the GFC, Japan provided USD 100 billion to the IMF, which had only USD 200 billion available for lending at the time, and encouraged other member countries to provide similar funding. In response to the COVID-19 pandemic in April 2020, Japan provided an additional USD 100 million to the IMF's CCRT (Catastrophe Containment and Relief Trust) as immediately available resources to support grant-based debt service relief for the poorest and most vulnerable countries, and also announced it would double its contribution to the poverty reduction and growth trust from the existing SDR 3.6 billion, with an additional SDR 1.8 billion immediately available and a subsequent SDR 1.8 billion to be provided once other member countries made their contributions.

While supporting the IMF and the World Bank, Japan has taken leadership in developing regional arrangements, such as the Asian Development Bank (ADB) to provide regional public goods as well as the Chiang Mai Initiative Multilateralization (CMIM) and the ASEAN+3 Macroeconomic Research Office (AMRO) to promote regional financial stability. The creation and management of CMIM and AMRO were made possible by working with other East Asian countries, particularly China. If the World Bank does not provide sufficient financial resources for Asia's development needs, Japan can increase its assistance bilaterally and multilaterally through the

---

[14] The G7 principles focused on: life-cycle cost including maintenance, repair and management; social and environmental consideration; local job creation, technology transfer, and human resource development; consistency with the borrowing country's development strategy and effective resource mobilization.

ADB. If the IMF does not respond to the needs of Asian countries in the case of a liquidity shortage, Japan is also willing to extend liquidity support through bilateral currency swaps and via the CMIM financial safety net supported by AMRO's surveillance services.

Japan is an active defender of the WTO and works with the US, EU, and other like-minded countries on WTO reform to introduce and/or strengthen disciplines on the protection of IPR and the avoidance of "non-market" policies and practices, improve notification and transparency obligations, clarify "developing country" status, and restore an effective dispute settlement mechanism.

Among the WTO reform agendas, the most urgent priority would be to restore an effectively functioning AB for dispute settlement. For this, the US and the EU have to reconcile their differences in the dispute settlement system.[15] Japan's view of dispute settlement embraces that of the US, considering its negative experience with disputes with the Republic of Korea regarding the latter's import ban on fishery products introduced after the Great East Japan Earthquake, tsunami, and nuclear power plant accidents, while also recognizing the importance of accumulating a set of effective rules through the WTO's "court." Being more flexible, Japan can make efforts, together with the Ottawa Group,[16] to narrow the gap between the US and the EU.

It will be more difficult for WTO members to come to consensus agreements on other contentious issues, such as new trade disciplines on "non-market" policies and practices; notification and transparency obligations; "developing country" status; and S&D treatment.

Given the wide division between developed and developing members, not just between the US and China, a long-term approach is advised to narrow the gap between the two. To tackle these issues, Japan, together with the US and the EU, should hold an intensive dialogue with China to narrow these differences. On the issue of "non-market" policies and practices, the two sides should focus on the fundamental role of the WTO, namely whether and how the institution should promote market-based economic practices, openness, and competition through reducing members' anti-competitive policies and practices (including "non-market" ones such as state subsidies and SOEs). On the issues of notification obligations and "developing country" status, they should discuss the importance of S&D treatment for countries truly in need of it and in justifiable areas as well as the role of capacity development programs to support developing countries, particularly low-income ones, in implementing agreed notification and transparency obligations.

Given the current constrained role of the WTO, Japan has been engaged in negotiations for plurilateral agreements. These are an important tool for liberalization

---

[15] A draft decision paper circulated at the WTO by Ambassador David Walker of New Zealand, who was the Facilitator of the Informal Process on Matters related to the Functioning of the Appellate Body, in November 2019, WT/GC/W/791, was a good starting point for agreement but was reportedly rejected by the US delegation. https://docs.wto.org/dol2fe/Pages/SS/directdoc.aspx?filename=q:/WT/GC/W791.pdf&Open=True.

[16] https://www.canada.ca/en/global-affairs/news/2019/05/ottawa-group-and-wto-reform.html.

and rule-making among like-minded members, given the requirement of consensus-based decision-making at the WTO and the difficulties of "single undertaking" principles that failed during DDR negotiations. Plurilateral agreements allow a group of WTO members to address specific issues and areas on a MFN (Most Favoured Nation) basis, benefiting non-signatories as well. This lays the foundation for WTO-wide rule-making in the future, thereby supporting a multilateral trading system. These include the Agreement of Government Procurement (GPA; 1981, revised in 1996, further revised in 2012, and applied to all WTO members in 2021); the Information Technology Agreement (ITA; 1997, expanded in 2014); the Environmental Goods Agreement (EGA—to be concluded); the Trade in Services Agreement (TiSA—to be concluded) and more recently an agreement on e-commerce (under negotiation).

## 4.3   Cooperation—Japan and China

Given the expanding market size of China and deep economic interdependence through trade and investment, it is in Japan's interest to cooperate with China in mutually beneficial areas, even in the era of US–China strategic competition. Japan's approach has been to balance security and economic interests and encourage China to transform itself into an internationally harmonious, open market economy so that it becomes, and acts as, a responsible global player. Key instruments to achieve these aims are high-standard FTA negotiations, high-quality infrastructure cooperation in third-party countries, and bilateral and regional financial cooperation.

First, while Japan would welcome the US to return to TPP, Japan also welcomes President Xi Jinping's indication that China is seriously considering participation in CPTPP. The reason is that Japan wants to see China's shift from "state capitalism" to a "market-oriented" economy through trade and investment reforms and associated changes in domestic legal and regulatory systems. This would enable China to return to "reform and opening up," redefine the role of government consistent with an open market economy, substantially reduce subsidies for "Made-in-China 2025," and restructure and ultimately privatize SOEs and state-owned commercial banks.

However, joining CPTPP is a significant challenge for China and would require much greater IPR protection; further opening of the services sector; a more open internet; much freer flows of data across borders than RCEP; addressing the distortion of market competition created by SOEs and government subsidies. Most significantly, the chapter on SOEs would require China to share information on its SOEs and expressly restrict preferential treatment for them. The Japanese government does not seem to have a clear strategy of how to encourage China to carry out domestic reforms to prepare for CPTPP negotiations, but a useful avenue would be to build on RCEP agreements and pursue negotiations for a high-standard China-Japan-ROK (CJK) FTA, which would address provisions included in CPTPP. If China makes efforts to agree on a high-standard CJK FTA, the country would be in the position to move to formal discussions for CPTPP participation.

Second, there is scope for greater cooperation between Japan and China to support high-quality infrastructure development and connectivity in third countries. If the two countries were to agree to pursue joint projects in third countries by their firms under the four conditions of economic viability, openness, transparency, and fiscal sustainability, this would create synergies in supporting developing countries in need of infrastructure investment.[17]

The BRI has been useful in augmenting infrastructure investment and connectivity for many developing countries. But at the same time the BRI has encountered various international criticisms in recent years, such as non-transparency of project details and procurements; disregard for borrowing countries' economic, environmental, and social interests; lack of considerations for economic feasibility and debt sustainability, etc. Partly as a response, in the "2nd BRI Forum for International Cooperation" (April 2019), President Xi Jinping underlined the need for developing high-quality BRI projects, stressing transparency, clean governance, green projects, widely accepted rules and standards, and commercial and fiscal sustainability. In addition, China agreed to the "G20 Principles of Quality Infrastructure Investment" adopted at the G20 Osaka Summit (June 2019). Thus, Japan–China cooperation in third-party countries for high-quality projects can help China to enhance the quality of BRI projects. This will contribute to the convergence between the BRI and the economic pillar of the FOIP (Free and Open Info-Pacific) vision.[18]

Although not an AIIB (Asian Infrastructure Investment Bank) member, Japan together with the US has encouraged the World Bank, ADB and other existing multilateral development banks to work with AIIB. The aim has been to enable AIIB to follow international standards on environmental and social safeguards, avoid economically non-viable projects, and maintain debt sustainability in borrowing countries. Partly as a result, AIIB has been performing better than initially expected as it has avoided projects with low environmental and social standards and potential debt distress.

---

[17] There are similarities and differences between Japan's and China's approaches to development assistance. Japan's assistance has been focusing on the trinity combination of ODA for infrastructure development, trade expansion and foreign direct investment (FDI) inflows, thereby supporting recipient countries' industrialization and economic development. China also supports recipient countries' economic development through infrastructure investment. One of the major differences between the two countries' approaches is that Japan has provided grants and technical assistance to support low-income countries and yen-loans to support middle-income countries because of debt sustainability concerns, while China provides loans even for low-income countries which may lack loan repayment capacities.

[18] Japan's FOIP vision is now shared by the US, Australia, India, and ASEAN and has attracted the interests of the UK and the EU. The FOIP vision includes both security and economic pillars. The economic pillar includes trade and investment as well as infrastructure connectivity. The RCEP and CPTPP are key arrangements for trade and investment, and participation by India and the US in the respective arrangements would strengthen the initiative. High-quality infrastructure connectivity in transport, energy, and digital sectors, guided by the "G20 Principles for Quality Infrastructure Investment," is another element. It is designed to be inclusive and open to any country sharing the vision and thus does not exclude China.

In addition, as the two largest official bilateral creditors to these low- and lower middle-income countries, Japan's and China's participation in the G20 DSSI (Debt Service Suspension Fund) has been useful in assisting indebted countries affected by COVID-19 to alleviate their fiscal constraints.

Third, Japan and China have been pursuing bilateral and regional financial cooperation. Bilateral financial cooperation (agreed to in October 2018) includes China's provision of CNY 200 billion Renminbi Qualified Foreign Institutional Investor (RQFII) status for Japanese investors; China's setting up of an RMB clearing bank in Tokyo; an arrangement of bilateral yen-yuan currency swaps; China's issuance of licenses to Japanese financial firms to conduct securities businesses in China; and mutual listing of exchange-traded funds (ETFs) in the respective markets. Other types of bilateral financial cooperation include the use of yen and yuan for trade, finance, and reserve holdings, issuance of RMB bonds in Tokyo, and making yen–yuan direct exchange active in their foreign exchange markets.

More importantly, the two countries have been cooperating to promote regional financial stability in East Asia: creating CMIM for ASEAN + 3 economies, supplemented by bilateral currency swap arrangements, to prepare for a financial crisis or the risk of such a crisis; establishing AMRO for effective regional economic surveillance; and participating in IMF programs in other countries, an example being Mongolia, where China, Japan, and the ROK jointly provided financial assistance. One remarkable fact is that Japan–China regional financial cooperation remained intact even at the height of extreme bilateral tension in 2012–13 when Japan nationalized the Senkaku Islands, which set off large-scale anti-Japan demonstrations in various cities in China and the suspension of official bilateral dialogues and cooperation programs.

## 5   Conclusion

The current global structural shift, which is characterized by the relative decline of the US and other advanced economies, and the rapid rise of the Chinese and other emerging and developing economies, will continue in the decades to come. This means that global economic governance must accommodate such a structural shift if it is to be sustained over the long term.

Even though China is projected to become the number one economy in the world in around 2030, the US can still preserve its global leadership and security by closely coordinating with the EU, Japan, and other like-minded democracies. By uniting democracies and retaining a rules-based liberal economic order, the US would be able to deter China's ambition (if any) to challenge and replace it as the next global hegemon. Thus, the return of the US to multilateralism and international cooperation is essential to global peace and stability. This will allow the US and its allies to craft a strategy of how to get China and other emerging and developing economies engaged more deeply in the existing international order. Their challenge is to design a framework to accommodate the global structural shift, allow the coexistence of different systems, and induce convergence toward a rules-based market economy, openness, and transparency.

Japan can play a major role in addressing such challenges. Its tasks include retaining a rules-based, liberal, multilateral economic order; making global forums (such as the G7 and G20) and Bretton Woods Systems more effective; and engaging China so it becomes a responsible global player. Japan needs to work with not only the US and the EU, but also China and other major emerging economies, to reform the WTO and put it back on the center stage of global rule-making in twenty-first-century trade and investment.

At the same time, Japan has been developing regional arrangements in a way consistent with global precedent, implementing high-standard FTAs, such as the CPTPP, Japan-EU EPA, and Japan-UK CEPA, which help to preserve a liberal trading system given the constrained role of the WTO today. Japan's approach of promoting the FOIP vision and encouraging domestic and external reforms in China through a high-quality BRI and a high-standard CJK FTA would also contribute to stronger global economic governance. Lastly, the return of the US to TPP and China's participation in CPTPP would ultimately prove to be a big plus in strengthening global economic governance.

# References

US National Security Council (2020)United States Strategic Approach to the People's Republic of China. https://www.whitehouse.gov/wp-content/uploads/2020/05/US-Strategic-Approach-to-The-Peoples-Republic-of-China-Report-5.20.20.pdf.
VanGrassteck C (2013) The history and future of the world trade organization. WTO Publications, Geneva. www.wto.org/english/res_e/booksp_e/historywto_e.pdf
Willems C (2020) Revitalizing the world trade organization. Atlantic Council, Washington, DC. https://www.atlanticcouncil.org/wp-content/uploads/2020/11/Revitalizing-the-WTO-Report_Version-11.6.pdf

**Masahiro Kawai** is the Representative Director of the Economic Research Institute for Northeast Asia (ERINA) in Niigata, Japan. He teaches Asian finance at the University of Tokyo as Professor Emeritus; he also serves as a Councilor of the Bank of Japan; a Senior Fellow of the Policy Research Institute of Japan's Finance Ministry and he is a distinguished Research Fellow of the Japan Forum on International Relations. Previously, Dr. Kawai held positions as Dean of the Asian Development Bank (ADB) Institute and Chief Economist for the World Bank's East Asia and the Pacific Region. He holds a BA in economics from the University of Tokyo and a Ph.D. in economics from Stanford University.

**Open Access** This chapter is licensed under the terms of the Creative Commons Attribution-NonCommercial-NoDerivatives 4.0 International License (http://creativecommons.org/licenses/by-nc-nd/4.0/), which permits any noncommercial use, sharing, distribution and reproduction in any medium or format, as long as you give appropriate credit to the original author(s) and the source, provide a link to the Creative Commons license and indicate if you modified the licensed material. You do not have permission under this license to share adapted material derived from this chapter or parts of it.

The images or other third party material in this chapter are included in the chapter's Creative Commons license, unless indicated otherwise in a credit line to the material. If material is not included in the chapter's Creative Commons license and your intended use is not permitted by statutory regulation or exceeds the permitted use, you will need to obtain permission directly from the copyright holder.

# Chinism and the Irreversibility of Globalization: Implications for Global Governance

**Grzegorz W. Kołodko**

**Abstract**  *Global governance trends from an East European perspective* are the focal point of this analysis. The study suggests that in the future, none of the world's great problems can be solved without China. *Irreversible globalization* requires proper *reinstitutionalization of global governance*, which cannot happen without China's active participation. Understanding China will be key. The author coined the term 'Chinism' to advance understanding and he defines *Chinism as a syncretic economic system* based on multiple forms of ownership with strong macroeconomic policies and limited government control. Under this system, deregulation is subordinated to maintaining enterprises' activities on a course that is in line with the social and political goals set by the Communist Party of China. The policy of the government and the central bank, and to a lesser extent local authorities, use *classic instruments of market intervention*. At the same time, Chinism has helped eliminate shortages and effectively keeps price inflation in check. This is a feat none of the former models of state socialism, including the *Soviet Union and CEE economies*, were able to accomplish, which was the main reason behind their economic and, consequently, political demise.

**Keywords**  Global governance trends from an East European perspective ·
Irreversible globalization · Reinstitutionalization of global governance · Chinism
as a syncretic economic system · Classic instruments of market intervention ·
Soviet Union and CEE economies

## 1  Introduction

Recently, opinions have been quite often expressed that a new era is inevitably coming in which Asia and especially China will dominate the world. This is not necessarily true as certain parts of the world, specifically the European Union and United States

---

G. W. Kołodko (✉)
Kozminski University, Warsaw, Poland

Belt and Road School, Beijing Normal University, Beijing, People's Republic Of China

© The Author(s) 2021                                                                 75
H. Wang and A. Michie (eds.), *Consensus or Conflict?*, China and Globalization,
https://doi.org/10.1007/978-981-16-5391-9_7

will still play a significant role. However, certainly the relative importance of China—due to the enormity of its still burgeoning economy and population—will continue to grow. It will not only have obvious economic but also political implications. In the future, none of the world's great problems will be able to be solved without China. It is, therefore, necessary not only to compete with China but also to cooperate with her in a creative manner. The sooner a culture and practice of cooperation develops, the sooner support institutions can be developed, which will be better equipped to drive the development of the global economy. Irreversible globalization requires proper reinstitutionalization of global governance, which cannot happen without China's active participation.

In the world of the future, human capital and technology will be key to the competitiveness of knowledge-based economies. However, it may not be enough to promote sustainable development. A political and economic system that favors the formation of capital and its efficient allocation will also be indispensable. In such context, a question arises: to what extent will the evolving Chinese system be able to contribute new impetus to global governance in the twenty-first century.

## 2  Population and Human Capital

The time of quantity will never end, but now the time has come for a new generation of quality. Today, and even more so in the future, economic success will depend less and less on the possession of natural resources, tangible and financial assets, and increasingly on human capital. Since the dawn of time, the economy has relied on knowledge but never has so much depended on knowledge resources as it does now. It is knowledge and the skills in leveraging it in production and trade that will determine which economy is at the leading edge. The competitiveness of economies increasingly depends on knowledge. China is fully aware of this and has accordingly invested increasing amounts of time and money in knowledge and technology.

While education and skills are of great importance, the size of each country's population should also be taken into account. China's population will soon stop growing and begin aging (Table 1).

According to United Nations projections, China's population will start to decline after 2030. In India, this turning point will not be reached until a generation later, after 2060. It is of significance in this context that India—unlike China and other countries with a quickly aging population—can leverage its demographic dividend in the form of a relatively young population, which is a contributing factor for a dynamic economy. While the median age in India is around 28 years, China's is over 37 (the global average is 30). Hence, in this respect, China's situation is already unfavorable and will continue to deteriorate.

The state of a society and the well-being of the people, especially the financial situation of individual households and the assessment of individual economic situations are not determined by economic size or by the nation's population. Being "the largest country" or "having more people" counts for something—more in political

**Table 1** Population growth forecasts, 2020–2060 (in millions)

| Country | Year | | |
|---|---|---|---|
| | 2020 | 2060 | % change ± |
| China | 1,439 | 1,333 | −7.4 |
| India | 1,380 | 1,651 | 19.6 |
| United States | 331 | 391 | 18.1 |
| Russia | 146 | 133 | −8.9 |
| Japan | 126 | 98 | −22.2 |
| World | 7,795 | 10,151 | 30.2 |

*Source* UN (2019)

than in psychological terms—but the welfare and the subjective sense thereof has not improved as much as in China simply due to the fact that China still has the world's largest population[1] and that they produce the most (based on PPP). In China, the average lifespan is only two years shorter than in the United States (77 compared to 79) and while most people see a rapidly rising average income, it still represents only 30% of the average American income, which stood at USD 62,000 per capita in 2019. These are reasons why a broader range of information is needed, rather than simple measures of per capita income. Criteria that assess the level of human capital are highly useful from this perspective.

Another key issue is the dynamic of change and global shifts that reflect differences in the level and quality of human capital. In a period of just three decades, since 1990, the average HDI (Human Development and Inequality) for the world as a whole has risen from 0.598 to 0.731, whereas in the United States it has risen from 0.860 to 0.920 and in China from 0.501 to 0.758. This means that 30 years ago, China was below the global average and has since risen above it. While the quality of human capital measured this way has been rising globally by 0.72% a year, the pace of growth in the United States was three times as slow (0.24%), while in China it was twice as fast (1.48%). Naturally, it is much easier to work your way up the ladder when you start farther down, but this is getting increasingly difficult (Table 2).

In terms of HDI, the United States ranks 15th, between New Zealand and the United Kingdom, and Belgium and Japan,[2] and China, 85th, between North Macedonia and Peru above and Ecuador and Azerbaijan below.[3] Norway tops the list (HDI of 0.954) and Niger is at the bottom (HDI 0.377). Taking income distribution inequality into account, which is very high in both the United States and China, with a Gini index (a measure of income inequality) of 41.5 and 38.6, respectively, the United States goes down 13 spots to number 28, while China moves up by four to

---

[1] The UN estimates that India will become the most populous country in the beginning of the fourth decade of twenty-first century. In 2035, it will have a population of 1.504 billion, while 1.464 billion people will inhabit China (UN 2019).

[2] In the ranking, Belgium and Japan sandwich Lichtenstein, which I omit in those comparisons.

[3] The ranking includes Hong Kong, which with a HDI of 0.939 ranks fourth ex equo with Germany.

**Table 2** Human Development and Inequality adjusted human development indices

| Country | HDI ranking | HDI | IHDI | Overall loss (%) | Change in HDI ranking |
|---------|-------------|-------|-------|------------------|-----------------------|
| Norway | 1 | 0.954 | 0.889 | 6.8 | 0 |
| United States | 15 | 0.920 | 0.797 | 13.4 | −13 |
| Japan | 19 | 0.915 | 0.882 | 3.6 | 15 |
| Russia | 49 | 0.824 | 0.743 | 9.9 | 1 |
| China | 85 | 0.758 | 0.636 | 16.1 | 4 |
| India | 129 | 0.647 | 0.477 | 26.3 | 1 |
| World | – | 0.731 | 0.584 | 20.2 | – |

*Note* Overall loss: percentage difference between the IHDI value and the HDI value
*Source* UNDP (2019), pp. 308–311

81st place (UNDP 2019), which means that the distance between them is slightly smaller than if only income is considered (Table 2).

## 3  Chinism

To solve the dilemma of choosing socialism/communism (yet) or capitalism (already), often the single criterion of the ratio of state to private ownership in the economy is used. Kornai (2008) uses this principle to claim that capitalism has existed in China since the turn of the century because as of 1998 the private sector was already delivering a larger proportion of national income. Capital markets have also been gradually developing since the beginning of market reforms. *Inter alia*, treasury bonds were offered for the first time in 1981, in 1984 stocks and company bonds were already being been issued and circulated, and in 1990 the Shanghai and Shenzhen Stock Exchanges—now very important on the global capital market—were established.

State-owned enterprises are particularly visible among China's largest companies. These include those in which the state has full or majority ownership as well as those in which, although there is no majority participation, it has a sufficiently large block of shares to control the company. In 2018, state-owned companies owned 88.2% of assets and took in 84.2% of revenues from a group of China's 100 largest enterprises. Of the ten largest Chinese firms, four were in the oil and gas sectors, four were in construction and two were in manufacturing; nine were state-owned. To put this in perspective, this is radically different compared with other major economies, including Germany and Japan. While state-owned enterprises dominate in China, only a few appear in Germany and Japan, mainly in infrastructure (roads, railways and post office). However, it is worth noting that, while the change is small, the number of state-owned companies in China's 100 largest companies is decreasing—from 87 in 2009 to 81 in 2018.

China differs in terms of quality and it would be too far-fetched to classify it according to routine models. This is neither a case of communism, as some would still have it, nor of capitalism, even one adorned with this adjective or another, but that of a different quality. It is a political/social/economic system in its own right, which I refer to as Chinism (Kolodko 2018, 2020a). This is not a *Beijing Consensus* laden with statism and centralized bureaucracy, which some attempted to hail for a time as the antithesis for the neoliberal *Washington Consensus* (Halper 2010). Though one can see some analogies between those concepts, there are definitely more significant differences (Lin 2013). Neither is it a simple period of transition from a centrally planned economy to a market economy, even in the form of state capitalism (Lardy 2014).

Chinism, sui generis, is a syncretic economic system based on multiple forms of ownership of the means of production, with strong macroeconomic policies and limited government control with respect to microeconomic management. Deregulation is subordinated to maintaining enterprises' activities on a course that is in line with the social and political goals set by the Communist Party. Widely used, flexible but generally far-reaching economic interventionism uses both indicative planning that addresses the business sphere and command planning with respect to some state-owned enterprises and infrastructure. The policy of the government and the central bank, and to a lesser extent local authorities, use classic instruments of market intervention. The pricing system is essentially decentralized, which, despite a lack of fully hardened budget constraints with respect to public enterprises, guarantees that a money market equilibrium is maintained.

At the same time, Chinism has helped eliminate shortages and effectively keep price inflation in check (Kolodko 2020c). This is a feat none of the former models of state socialism, including the Soviet Union and CEE economies, were able to accomplish, which was the main reason behind their economic and, consequently, political demise (Kolodko and Rutkowski 1991; Csaba 1996).

Such a hybrid economic system comes hand in hand with a state wielding centralized power that is essentially based on meritocracy, where rational people do rational things in a rational way. The policy implemented by the state is competent and responsible. At the same time, it is oriented to fulfilling long-term strategic goals, to which medium-term and immediate goals are subordinated. The authorities also use traditional and modern social impact methods. For example, they resort to enforcing social compliance through behavior based on the general direction of development set by the Party as well as legislative and executive powers.

Chinism does not represent a turning away from the path of market reforms and to the omnipotence of the state sector in the economy; this is an overly simplified image of a highly complex reality. The state plays a major role—most of all as a regulator and also as the owner of some means of production—but it does not crowd out nor replace the market but rather corrects and supports it and creates a synergy with its forces (Huang 2017). One should not overestimate isolated events nor hastily generalize individual observations. The fact that in 2008, the prestigious post of Chief Economist and Senior Vice President of Development Economics at the World Bank was assigned to the eminent Chinese economist, Justin Yifu Lin, is very meaningful. This was not an empty gesture directed at China in recognition of the country's achievements from those who in fact decided it—the United States in consultation with Japan, the United Kingdom, Germany and France. It was a sign, especially to economically less developed countries, that valuable conclusions can be drawn from China's experience in creating policies on development that may be worth adopting elsewhere. Lin's term of office, 2008–2012, did not revolutionize Washington's technocratic way of thinking or the World Bank's activities, but it undoubtedly contributed to the organization's further departure from neoliberal orthodoxy.

## 4 Relative Attractiveness of Chinism

Certainly, Chinism will not be adopted by countries with liberal capitalism, but, in turn, it can be—and already is—an inspiring offer, or at least an option worth contemplating, for many developing countries that are attempting to catch up with richer ones. This is not an option for countries whose leaders believe that their strong political power and a large state sector in the economy are enough to replicate China's boom. Chinism, deeply rooted in China's unique history and culture, is much more than that.

There are several indicators typical to Chinism that already exist in the economic systems of some countries. Particular attention should be paid to large proportions of state ownership, including monopolies in strategic industries (in this case, "strategic" implies much more than in Western market economies), central planning, control of the exchange rate regime and a central bank that reports to the government. There are also certain similarities with regard to economic policy methods, especially state intervention as a means for setting industrial and trade policies, protectionism of vital sectors, state subsidies for export-oriented firms, and government influence over major inbound and outbound foreign direct investments. In the case of more technologically advanced sectors, there is often protection and state financial support to increase the international competitiveness of these companies.

Countries with liberal democracies, in the face of looming crisis, must look for ways to protect themselves against a new wave of nationalism and the crisis-generating potential of neoliberalism (Galbraith 2018), but they will surely not follow the Chinese model. This may be done, though in very different ways, by emancipating economies and societies, especially those thrown into the category of so-called emerging markets as defined by neoliberalism (Kolodko 2014b). One important thing to note here is that two significant processes overlap: the huge economic success of Chinism and the structural crisis of liberal capitalism.

Countries that look for a lighthouse in this turbulent ocean that is the global economy may find that the light coming from Beijing is brighter than that coming from Washington and can be seen more clearly from the Pearl River Delta and Guangzhou than from New York and Manhattan. This is also supported by China's strong foreign policy. Beijing has more diplomatic posts scattered around the world than the United States. Its political impact cannot be underestimated, but at the same time one should not expect it to eclipse the West, including Anglo-American influence when it comes to soft power. The opening of more than a hundred Confucius Institutes in various countries, which promote China and Chinese values is a good thing. This is not a threat. On the contrary, an increased number of Mandarin speakers will also contribute to expanding international exchange in areas like education, science, culture and sports. The next round in the soft power clash will be the 24th Winter Olympic Games in Beijing in 2022, especially after the postponement of the 2020 Summer Olympics in Tokyo to 2021, due to the calamity of the COVID-19 pandemic.

China's external expansion—irrespective of its strictly economic goals, which are mainly to export major surpluses in infrastructure construction, develop outlets for increasingly competitive industries and gain access to deposits of raw materials and inputs—is pursued on a spectacular scale by means of the Belt and Road Initiative (BRI), which is often referred to as the new Silk Road (Maçães 2018). The principal purpose of the BRI is not to conquer other countries by making them economically dependent—though this, too, can happen if the recipient country is reckless and relies too much on borrowed money, so caution should be exercised—but to maintain an internal economic dynamism. Despite China's considerable size, this cannot be achieved without having recourse to external factors and further tapping into globalization for quick growth in domestic production and consumption. Over the last couple of decades, nobody has leveraged globalization so well for its own growth as China has. No wonder that it wishes to continue to do so. The Chinese are better positioned to do that, because unlike Western representatives, who tell the locals how the world should be organized on their visits to China when visiting a country the Chinese look around for solutions that may prove useful to themselves as well. No doubt, China has learned more from the West over the last few decades than the West has from China, though quite a lot of things could be learned there too.

## 5  The Battle for Tomorrow: The Imperative of Inclusive Globalization

The COVID-19 pandemic—with its psychological and political side effects, such as growing xenophobia and mutual hostility—highlights the symptoms of protectionism and naïve mercantilism that could already be felt before (Kolodko 2020b). The financial and economic crises of 2008, driven by neoliberalism, led to a wave of new nationalist sentiment. Neoliberalism intended to help a few get rich at the expense of the majority and the public enemy was the government as the regulator and income redistribution policymaker, whereas in populism and new nationalism, the role of such a foe is reserved for globalization. This clash both weakens the capacity of countries, which may already be impaired, to focus policymaking on a multinational scale and is conducive to throwing political, social and economic relations into anarchy.

Adding to the crisis of mishandled economic liberalization—it being improperly deregulated from the point of view of social cohesion and economic equilibrium— is the crisis of liberal democracy. There are those who believe that liberalism has already collapsed (Deneen 2018). This crisis is taking different, sometimes surprising forms—one in the United States following the election of President Donald Trump and another one in Poland under the Law and Justice Party. Yet another example can be seen in Australia with its nationalist government under Prime Minister Scott Morrison and a different one in Brazil with the populist right-wing President Jair Bolsonaro. In every case, these trends harm supranational social cohesion and make it difficult for globalization to maintain a reasonable course.

This course must be based on non-orthodox economic thought, with particular importance being placed on new structural economics (Lin 2012), economics for the common good (Tirole 2017) and new pragmatism—a sort of interface between descriptive and prescriptive economics indicating the ways to integrate economic, social and environmental development into an economy of moderation (Kolodko 2014a). Economists of various contemporary theoretical schools (Galbraith 2014; Phelps 2013; Rodrik 2015; Stiglitz 2019) voice the conviction that it is possible to create a good economy.

China—the greatest beneficiary of globalization—fully grasps that, which is why (though above all, because it has its own interests at heart) is its great advocate. To save globalization and make it truly irreversible, it must become inclusive. Letting it continue in its neoliberal variety preferred by special interest groups and selfish economic and political lobbies, coinciding with adverse megatrends in the form of changes in the natural environment, global warming, uncontrollable large migrations and the COVID-19 pandemic, which has led to what I call a Yet Greater Crisis, YGC (Kolodko 2011, 2021), is not an option.

This is not only just inclusive globalization and there is no form of globalization whatsoever that can be maintained without the necessary degree of harmony between the world's two largest economies—that of China and the United States (Kissinger 2011). The hope for the development of *pro publico mundiale bono* cooperation and friendly rivalry as part of the so-called G2 concept—or Chimerica—was replaced with Cold War 2.0. The reason why this is so dangerous is that in addition to former President Donald Trump's extreme Sinophobia, Republicans' Democratic opponents are not fully devoid of similar sentiments. Even under President Joe Biden, it will take some time before better pragmatism-driven relations will be re-established.

A harmonized global order requires a strong and united European entity, but unfortunately, this is also being weakened due to financial and migration crises and the growing wave of new nationalism and devolutionary tendencies. Brexit is further undermining the EU, reducing its economy by around 15%. Unfortunately, the European Union is becoming weaker at a time when it should gain strength to co-govern globalization's reset. The EU is both China's leading partner and strategic rival, which is not a contradiction, but a sort of dialectic.

Against such a background, another complication to this already complex equation should also be recognized: the triangle formed by China, Russia and the EU, most notably Germany. The latter wants a strong, more deeply integrated European Union.

It also wants good, pragmatic relations with both Russia and China. To both, China is a vast market outlet; to Germany, for high-tech industrial products, to Russia, for raw materials, which are scattered across its vast territory, sprawls over eleven time zones with larger underground deposits than any other country. Geopolitical games played between these three countries have had a major impact on the geoeconomic state of the world.

China, which cares about developing cooperation with other countries and regions, at the same time is engaging them further in the globalization process. While the United States has over 200 military installations in 120 countries, China has one—a small naval base in the Horn of Africa, in Djibouti—but in contrast, is the largest trade partner for 130 countries.

Since globalization can no longer be stopped, there will be an incessant debate on what is good and bad for the world. Yes, there are good and bad economies (Kolodko 2011; Sedlacek 2011), there are systems that are more and less effective in terms of meeting their objectives, there are progressive and backward ideologies and political systems that follow them. This makes it all the more important to learn as much as possible from one another and draw on the experience of others in a creative way. Anti-examples are also useful; if only to know what not to do. China has learned a lot from others while showing a unique capacity for approaching its problems from a pragmatic standpoint rather than an ideological one—the way it used to do. Nevertheless, it still needs to learn a lot. One should hope that it would be willing and able to do so.

The British historian Ian Morris suggested one of the most interesting comparative analyses of history. He developed an original Social Development Index, which takes particular account of the energy capture, a given social culture's capacity for organization, measured with the size of its largest urban areas, war-making capacity and the advancement of information technology, determined by the speed and extent of the spread of the written word and telecommunications (Morris 2010). Using those metrics, he reaches the conclusion that the West will continue to dominate the world for only a couple of generations, after which, in the first decade of the twenty-second century, the world will be dominated by the East, the most important part being, of course, the Middle Country—China. Well, only time will tell…

A long, long time ago—the Mediterranean world knew almost nothing of Chinese civilization, but even then the smoothest silk was arriving from China. It was once said that *omnes viae Romam ducunt*—all roads lead to Rome. Is now the time that *omnes viae Pekinam ducunt?*

# 6 Conclusions

The huge leap forward made over the past four decades by the Chinese economy as a result of market reforms and openness to the world is awe-inspiring for some and creates anxiety for others. Questions arise as to whether the foundations of China's economic success are sustainable and whether economic growth will be followed by political expansion. China has made great use of globalization and is therefore interested in its continuation. At the same time, China wants to give it new features, specific Chinese characteristics. This is met with reluctance by the current global hegemon, the United States, even more so as fears arise that China may promote abroad its uniquely original political and economic system—Chinism. However, the world is still big enough to fit us all in. What we need to make this happen is a proper policy, which, in the future, must also involve better coordination of governance at a supranational level. I believe that China can and, let us hope, will contribute to this end significantly.

# References

Csaba L (1996) The political economy of the reform strategy: China and Eastern Europe compared. Communist Econ Econ Transform 8(1):53–65
Deneen PJ (2018) Why liberalism failed. Yale University Press, New Haven and London
Galbraith JK (2014) The end of normal: the great crisis and the future of growth. Simon and Schuster, New York
Galbraith JK (2018) Backwater economics and new pragmatism: institutions and evolution in the search for a sustainable economics. TIGER Working Papers Series, No. 138. Kozminski University, Warsaw. http://www.tiger.edu.pl/TWP%20No.%20138%20--%20Galbraith.pdf. Accessed 12 May 2020
Halper S (2010) The Beijing consensus: how China's authoritarian model will dominate the twenty-first century. Basic Books, New York
Huang Y (2017) Cracking the China conundrum: why conventional economic wisdom is wrong. Oxford University Press, New York
Kissinger H (2011) On China. Penguin Press, New York
Kolodko GW (2011) Truth, errors and lies: politics and economics in a volatile world. Columbia University Press, New York
Kolodko GW (2014a) Whither the world: the political economy of the future. Palgrave-Macmillan, Houndmills, Basingstoke, Hampshire
Kolodko GW (2014b) The New Pragmatism, or economics and policy for the future. Acta Oeconomica 64(2):139–160
Kolodko GW (2018) Socialism, capitalism, or Chinism? Communist Post-Communist Stud 51(4):285–298
Kolodko GW (2020a) China and the future of globalization: the political economy of China's rise. Bloomsbury I.B. Tauris, London, New York
Kolodko GW (2020b) After the calamity: economics and politics of the post-pandemic world. Polish Sociol Rev 2(210):137–155
Kolodko GW (2020c) The Great Chinese transformation: from the third to the first world. Acta Oeconomica 70(Spec Iss)71–83

Kolodko GW (2021) The quest for development success: bridging theoretical reasoning with economic practice. Rowman & Littlefield, Lanham, Maryland

Kolodko GW, Rutkowski M (1991) The problem of transition from a socialist to a free market economy: the case of Poland. J Soc Polit Econ Stud 16(2):159–179

Kornai J (2008) From socialism to capitalism. Central European University Press, Budapest

Lardy NR (2014) Markets over Mao: the rise of private business in China. Peterson Institute of International Economies, Washington, DC

Lin JY (2012) New structural economics: a framework for rethinking development and policy. The World Bank, Washington DC

Lin YJ (2013) Against the consensus. Reflections on the great recession. Cambridge University Press, New York

Maçães B (2018) Belt and road: a Chinese world order. Hurts, London

Morris I (2010) Why the west rules—for now: the patterns of history and what they reveal about the future. Profile Books, London

Phelps ES (2013) Mass flourishing: how grassroots innovation created jobs, challenge, and change. Princeton University Press, New York

Rodrik D (2015) Economics rules: why economics works, when it fails, and how to tell the difference. Oxford University Press, Oxford

Sedlacek T (2011) Economics of good and evil: the quest for economic meaning from Gilgamesh to Wall Street. Oxford University Press, Oxford, New York

Stiglitz JE (2019) People, power, and profits: progressive capitalism for an age of discontent W.W. Norton, New York, London

Tirole J (2017) Economics of the common good. Princeton University Press, Princeton, New Jersey

UN (2019) World population prospects 2019. United Nations, Department of Economic and Social Affairs, Populations Dynamic, New York. (https://population.un.org/wpp/Download/Probabili stic/Population/. Accessed 08 May 2020

UNDP (2019) Human development report: beyond income, beyond averages, beyond today: inequal-ities in human development in the 21st century. United Nations Development Programme, New York. http://www.hdr.undp.org/sites/default/files/hdr2019.pdf. Accessed 09 May 2020

**Grzegorz W. Kolodko** is a professor of economics, public intellectual and politician and a key architect of Polish economic reforms. He served as Deputy Prime Minister and Minister of Finance, 1994–97 and 2002–03. He is a member of the European Academy of Arts, Sciences and Humanities as well as a Honorary Doctor and Professor of dozen foreign universities. He is Founder and Director of Transformation, Integration and Globalization Economic Research, TIGER at Kozminski University in Warsaw as well as Distinguished Professor at the Belt and Road School, Beijing Normal University. He is also the author of research papers and books published in 26 languages and the world's most quoted Polish economist. He is also a marathon runner and globetrotter who has explored 170 countries and Antarctica.

**Open Access** This chapter is licensed under the terms of the Creative Commons Attribution-NonCommercial-NoDerivatives 4.0 International License (http://creativecommons.org/licenses/by-nc-nd/4.0/), which permits any noncommercial use, sharing, distribution and reproduction in any medium or format, as long as you give appropriate credit to the original author(s) and the source, provide a link to the Creative Commons license and indicate if you modified the licensed material. You do not have permission under this license to share adapted material derived from this chapter or parts of it.

The images or other third party material in this chapter are included in the chapter's Creative Commons license, unless indicated otherwise in a credit line to the material. If material is not included in the chapter's Creative Commons license and your intended use is not permitted by statutory regulation or exceeds the permitted use, you will need to obtain permission directly from the copyright holder.

# The Pitfalls, Principles and Priorities of Establishing a New Global Economic Order

**Pascal Lamy**

**Abstract**  Some scholars call it the *world legal economic order*, while others describe it as the *'rules-based' global order*. This essay contends that the world urgently needs a *new economic order*. While the world cannot, and should not, revolutionize the system that is currently in place, it does need to consider how it should be reorganized and subsequently replaced by a new order. It is essential that a new order serves not only the established world powers but a greater number of the newly *emerging economies and nations*. The development of this new order must ensure that it is representative of a world that is markedly different from the post Second World War 'legal economic order'. Those creating the new order are dealing with new challenges that could not even be imagined at the end of the Second World War. Humanity now inhabits a *world that is more interconnected*, more interdependent and, in a word, more 'global'. This connectivity is part and parcel of the process of globalization, which at this point cannot be avoided. China and other emerging powers will be greater contributors to the process of globalization if they follow fundamental principles that benefit all of mankind.

**Keywords**  World legal economic order · 'Rules-based' global order · New economic order · Established world powers · Emerging economies and nations · Interconnected

## 1  Genesis of the Current Global 'Economic Order'

An 'economic order' or system is, in my view, the superstructure of an infrastructure of production systems, the purpose of which is to create value for people. It cannot be understood, nor established, without a deep comprehension of the economic infrastructure. In turn, it requires a grasp of the principles and structural framework of any economy. This is true for domestic economics as well as at the global level. In this essay, I will attempt to explain why, in my view, a new global economic order is needed.

P. Lamy (✉)
Paris Peace Forum, Paris, France

© The Author(s) 2021  87
H. Wang and A. Michie (eds.), *Consensus or Conflict?*, China and Globalization,
https://doi.org/10.1007/978-981-16-5391-9_8

The current economic order is a legacy of Western capitalism that has developed since the sixteenth century following successive waves of globalization. The ideology underpinning this development is based on liberalism, markets and free enterprise, while science, technology and competition are seen as the main sources of innovation and economic growth.

This order has to be organized by a rules-based system, represented in the notion of 'ordoliberalism'.[1] The theoretical foundation of this system was established by Adam Smith, David Ricardo and Joseph Schumpeter, who developed concepts such as the 'invisible hand', 'comparative advantage' and 'creative destruction'. This ultimately resulted in two different schools of thought stemming from this common trunk: Hayek's analysis of laissez-faire capitalism and Keynes' emphasis on the importance of the state in macroeconomic management.

These principles were then enshrined in treaties and multilateral institutions. The catalyst for the core gatherings that laid the foundations of this global 'legal economic order' was the Second World War. For example, the 1944 Bretton Woods System Conference and the 1948 Havana Charter Conference. These meetings led to the creation of the International Monetary Fund (IMF), the World Bank and the General Agreement on Tariffs and Trade (GATT). In turn, GATT evolved into the World Trade Organization (WTO) in 1994.

The purpose underpinning this system, later labelled as the 'Washington Consensus',[2] was to promote private enterprise, open trade and investment, and ensure financial and monetary stability. This system successfully competed during the 'Cold War' with the so-called 'non-market economies' such as the state-run centrally planned communist economies like the Soviet Union. It was considered unrivalled after the fall of the Berlin Wall in 1989. As John Ruggie argued, it represented a system of 'embedded liberalism'—a global balance between openness and regulation, capital and labour, markets and society.[3]

This global economic order generally delivered steady economic growth, in both developed and developing countries, for a period of roughly 60 years following the end of the Second World War in 1945. However, it has run into trouble for the last 20 years. The problems came into sharp focus as an outcome of the 2008 global financial crisis. This system is now being questioned for several reasons. The foremost questions focus on financial instability, an increase in inequality; negative

---

[1] First developed around and during the Second World War, ordoliberalism grew out of the work of economists and legal theorists associated with the Freiburg School, such as Walter Eucken and Franz Böhm. At its core, the ordoliberal tradition converges around the idea of an economic constitution. Recognizing the contingencies borne out of the free market, ordoliberals are committed to robust state intervention in the form of a concrete set of rules directing socio-economic activity.

[2] The term Washington Consensus usually refers to a level of agreement between the International Monetary Fund (IMF), World Bank and U.S. Department of the Treasury that the operation of the free market and the reduction of state involvement were crucial to economic development.

[3] In a widely cited 1982 article, John Ruggie identified the normative framework of the Bretton Woods System as 'embedded liberalism' and pointed to its enduring legacy in international economic governance through the 1970s.

environmental externalities; a deficit in global governance and a geopolitical shift brought about by China's increasingly prominent status.

## 2 Global Systemic Flaws in Finance, Trade and Inequality

Financial instability, a well-known feature of capitalism, was one of the main factors that led to the 2008 world economic crisis. The root of the crisis was mainly due to insufficient regulation of a financial industry which had rapidly globalized.

The close links that had been established after the Second World War between economic development, trade and investment and monetary stability, were built on a foundation of fixed currency exchange rates. This principle was abandoned in 1973. The outcome was a movement that created excessive financial deregulation of many economies.

The sheer scale of the economic outcome and financial deregulation has been to embed great complexity into the system. Another serious outcome has been the creation of exotic financial instruments and where they are now packaged and repackaged into ever more complex products. This makes it increasingly hard to understand the international financial system, let alone regulate it.

Even more challenging is the need to match an increasingly open world trading system with greater international fiscal and monetary coordination. Global macroeconomic imbalances were a major cause of the recent financial crisis. But the macroeconomic adjustment, which conventional wisdom says is needed to reduce surpluses in Asia, and reduce deficits in America—has barely begun.

Meanwhile, the successive waves of globalization also promoted the growth of inequalities. While market-based capitalist globalization was efficient in reshuffling capital and labour in a more productive way, it was, as expected, painful for the losers. Even if, on a global scale, the benefits of efficiency outweighed the negative impact of the pain caused, local distribution of these benefits has become increasingly unbalanced, resulting in growing criticism over unfairness. This in turn led to people questioning the previous consensus, which stated that the playing field between developed and developing countries could only be levelled gradually in order to preserve necessary policy space for weaker economies.

## 3 Globalization—The Future

However, despite this negative side-effect, we should be careful to not dismiss globalization itself. Some think that COVID-19 spells the end of globalization and this may be true to some (limited, in my view) extent from the perspective of the US or Europe, but look at the rest of the world: Asia wants to resume the process as quickly as possible, and the same commitment comes for Africa. For most of the world, globalization is the way to get out of poverty and may entail for some time, an increase in inequality. I would caution that the globalization of fear is not the same as the fear of globalization.

## 4 The Environment and COVID-19

Another result of this rapid expansion of market capitalism was the rapid growth of negative environmental externalities, starting with carbon emissions, which have led to global warming. A consensus is slowly emerging that states the current 'economic order' model is not sustainable and has to be reformed, starting with the way growth is measured. The COVID-19 pandemic, which has resulted in enormous global damage, unprecedented since the Second World War, is likely to reinforce the trend towards preventing future environmental crises.

Geopolitically, COVID-19 has made the triangle of the EU, US and China even more fragmented and more difficult to manage. Bilateral relationships within this triangle have also been severely damaged by the COVID-19 crisis. That's the bad news. However, the good news is that, while Joe Biden does not have a magic wand, there is a good reason to believe that the US has come back to the table of international cooperation. That trend will be beneficial for moving things forward.

The most urgent and short-term matter for bringing COVID-19 under control is vaccines. We know that China, the US and the EU are covered regardless of which vaccine comes first and the citizens of those countries will be vaccinated. The real problem is what do we do with parts of the world that do not have effective access to a vaccine. This makes up roughly more than half of the world's population and is a major issue of international cooperation in times to come.

## 5 The Deficit in Global Governance

This challenge of international cooperation, and a number of other problems, stem from a fourth issue arising from the current 'economic order': a deficit in global governance.

Globalization produced a number of new common challenges, but arrangements between sovereign nation-states did not rise to these challenges. This was despite the existence of the very international fora meant to coordinate them such as the G7, which had its genesis in 1973, or the G20 that evolved with the financial crisis. The mediocre level of international cooperation during the COVID-19 crisis is a clear manifestation of this deficit.

The drive towards globalization has presented immense opportunities and huge economic and social benefits, but it has also resulted in concomitant inequalities, instability, contagion and stresses to humanity and the earth. This combination represents an issue for global governance in how to harness globalization in order to maximize its benefits and minimize its costs. It has become painfully clear that the current global governance system is insufficient to address borderless challenges like reducing carbon emissions, combating protectionism, currency volatility, tax evasion or cyber criminality. These and other problems can only be addressed with a new form of global governance.

The emergence of the current collection of international organizations has been an arduous and painful process. But it has emerged, underpinned by the treaties through which state entities have gradually agreed to renounce portions of their sovereignty. However, today, the pace at which global governance is being advanced by dominant players in the world has stalled to a near standstill due to a sequence of geotechnical, geoeconomic and geopolitical developments that have intensified existing obstacles.

The emergence of developing economies in the wake of globalization has also fundamentally reoriented the global balance of power between North and South, East and West. These emerging powers have leveraged market capitalism and information technologies to realize economic and social development at astonishing speeds.

# 6 Unlocking The Global Governance Gridlock

These complications and recent crises have caused international governance itself to also enter a sort of crisis phase, seemingly incapable of adapting to the new global balance or creating new common ground on which to cooperate. We currently find ourselves in a context of global governance gridlock.

However, despite these difficult circumstances, I believe that there are some avenues that could allow us to bridge the gap. In order to do so, it is important that we abandon the idea of a 'big bang' in global governance—the likes of which would only result from a major global conflict, which fortunately, I think we can avoid.

I believe the way forward to unlock the global governance gridlock requires improvements of the existing international framework. This is the triangle formed by the G20, the United Nations system and specialized international organizations. But for this approach to work, greater effort must be made to introduce the tools and benchmarks necessary to monitor organizational and institutional activities and to measure their successes, thereby improving their overall accountability.

In addition to this, there are also opportunities for advances in governance that are outside of the current global framework. For example, continued regional integration has led to different models of 'mini-global governance' in Europe. These, in their own way, are moving in the same direction in Asia, Africa and Central America.

## 7   The Impact of the Rise of China on the Current 'Legal Economic Order'

There is fifth development leading to a questioning of the viability of the current global 'economic order'. This stems from the geoeconomic and geopolitical shift brought by China regaining the status of a major economic power.

It is obvious that some of the Chinese specificities are not in line with some of the underlying principles of the dominant global 'economic order'. This starts with the driving role of the state-owned sector in the economy. As already mentioned, following the fall of the Berlin Wall in 1989, there was a clear underlying assumption according to which the 'Washington Consensus' was to be the future point of convergence of economic and social systems in a globalized world. Events over the past 20 years have proven these assumptions erroneous.

Perhaps the biggest change is globalization's impact on the geopolitical landscape. This is uniquely exemplified in China's increasingly active presence on the global stage. Globalization has both enabled—and rewarded—a shift in production, investment and technology to emerging economies.

The result—as Martin Wolf wrote—is that the periphery is becoming the core and the core is becoming the periphery.[4] The US remains a key player but it is no longer dominant. Fast-rising powers, like China, India, Indonesia and Brazil, play a role that was unimaginable even 20 years ago—while smaller developing countries want a say in a system in which they have a growing stake.

The simple—even simplistic—North–South divide has given way to a more complex world of many different Souths and many different Norths. Arguably, this multipolar system is much more 'democratic' than the previous 'economic order' which is manifested in the outmoded and redundant old post Second World War order. The days when a single or a few countries could design and direct the international system are gone. Yet the old powers are cautious to share the centre stage—and worried about decline—while the new powers are timid in sharing responsibility or designing a new, different 'order'.

China has the potential to play a real role in the formation of a new global order both political and economic. But the emphasis in the short term will be decidedly economic. The reason is that China has built strong economic credentials worldwide drawn from its track record in manufacturing and trade. On the political influence, and outside of China, the Chinese governance system engenders much caution and concern. The creation of a new world order is an opportunity that China should take very seriously and not squander. It will not mean China following the rules established by the US and Europe, but agreeing to a better level-playing field with them and others in order to keep benefiting from the benefits of globalization.

---

[4] "In the past few centuries, what was once the European and then American periphery became the core of the world economy. Now, the economies that became the periphery are re-emerging as the core. This is transforming the entire world." Martin Wolf, Financial Times, January 4, 2011.

# 8 A New Global Economic Order—Principles and Priorities

A new global economic order must then be shaped in order to address the aforementioned limitations, and pitfalls of the existing one. This new order should be based on four principles, the recognition of which should bring about a number of changes:

The first principle should be the establishment of sustainability in three inseparable dimensions: economic, social and environmental as a collective goal. The first step in this direction would be to base these objectives on the United Nations Sustainable Development Goals as they currently exist.

The second principle would aim at rebalancing competition and cooperation. While market systems promote competition and produce efficiencies, the cost is a host of negative externalities imposed on both humans and nature that are becoming excessively stressed and must be corrected. Market systems could be reformed either by changes of relative prices, or by appropriate regulatory cooperation, or by new arrangements between capital and labour. The WTO would be one of the platforms for reaching this balance, but it is based on a triangle of the US, EU and China agreeing or disagreeing. This is not to say that the rest of the membership does not matter, but an agreement between the US, China and Europe is essential for any step forward in global competition, trade and investment.

The third principle has to do with changing preconceptions of convergence in economic and social systems. That means accepting coexistence as the new normal and recognizing that economic globalization and political globalization may not follow the same paths. Also, that a new global economic order should be compatible with different collective preferences, be they cognitive, cultural, religious or political as long as they recognize the dignity of each human person as enshrined in the UN Charter.

The fourth principle is about acknowledging that for international cooperation to deliver more global public goods, it cannot be left only in the hand of sovereigns and diplomats. Delivery of global public goods must be open to the participation and engagement of non-state entities, such as businesses, non-governmental organizations, big cities or even key academic and scientific research entities. Their proven ability to coalesce around impact-driven initiatives must be further put to the test if they are to contribute to these goals.

On the foundation of these principles, I believe that there are three priorities that the nations involved in the creation of this new world order should adhere to:

The first of these priorities is the reorganization of the above-mentioned coexistence, which will ensure a proper, level-playing field between different economic systems in order to ensure fair competition. This implies a reform of global rules based on a multilateral trading system. This is necessary in order to strengthen disciplines on state aid as well as a reform of the international monetary system in order to address the dominance of the dollar.

The second priority is to ensure that the new global economic order does better to deliver on global public goods such as the environment, health, social inclusion and security. This implies a transformation of the present model of capitalism. Examples of the transformation needed are a repricing of carbon in order to accelerate the decarbonization of economies or a standard for wages and collective social security that is higher than current levels. It also implies reforms of classical international organizations in order to strengthen global rules. This includes the WTO, which the US tried to weaken under Trump and the WHO, the limits of which were evidenced by the COVID-19 crisis. Then there are the IMF and the World Bank, which need to be rebalanced to address ingrained Western supremacy in these institutions. The same intention of refitting international cooperation and revitalizing multilateralism is behind the creation and the development of the Paris Peace Forum as a new collaborative global platform for state and non-state actors to deliver results more rapidly.

The final priority is to recognize that this new global economic order will also be a digital one as value creation migrates from tangible to intangible. This raises many new questions about how to ensure market transparency, competition as the value of data keeps growing with progress in artificial intelligence. This is a complex challenge as it aims to reconcile the benefits of openness of data flows on the one side and different precautionary systems for data localization, accessibility, security and privacy on the other. Such profound structural transformations of the dominant global economic order necessitate major adaptations of legal superstructures.

## 9   Conclusion

In this essay, a number of elements have been described indicating that the current global 'economic order', and the institutions that accompany, are not up to the task of delivering the necessary global public goods nor the benefits of cooperation.

While we cannot, and should not, revolutionize the system that is currently in place, we do need to consider how it should be reorganized and subsequently replaced by a new order. It is essential that the new order serves not only the established powers of the world but a greater number of the newly emerging economies and nations. The different principles and systems that they represent will be fundamental to this new order. The development of this new order must ensure that it is representative of a world that is markedly different from the post Second World War legacy. Those creating the new order are dealing with new challenges that could not even be imagined 70 years ago.

Humanity now inhabits a world that is more interconnected, more interdependent and in a word, more 'global'. This connectivity is part and parcel of the process of globalization which is not to be pushed back but better harnessed.

China and other emerging powers should embrace an ambition and strive to be greater contributors to shaping a new, more sustainable and fairer version of globalization: a new open and cooperative 'global economic order'.

**Pascal Lamy** is the President of the Paris Peace Forum and coordinator of the Jacques Delors think tanks (Paris, Berlin, Brussels). He was the longest serving World Trade Organisation (WTO) Director-General so far (2005–2013). Between 1999 and 2004 he was the EU Trade Commissioner. He holds degrees from the Paris based École des Hautes Études Commerciales, the Institut d'Études Politiques and the École Nationale d'Administration. He began his career in the French civil service at the Inspection Générale des Finances and at the Treasury, then became an advisor to the Finance Minister Jacques Delors and subsequently to Prime Minister Pierre Mauroy. He served as Chief of Staff to EU President, Jacques Delors between 1984 and 1999.

**Open Access** This chapter is licensed under the terms of the Creative Commons Attribution-NonCommercial-NoDerivatives 4.0 International License (http://creativecommons.org/licenses/by-nc-nd/4.0/), which permits any noncommercial use, sharing, distribution and reproduction in any medium or format, as long as you give appropriate credit to the original author(s) and the source, provide a link to the Creative Commons license and indicate if you modified the licensed material. You do not have permission under this license to share adapted material derived from this chapter or parts of it.

The images or other third party material in this chapter are included in the chapter's Creative Commons license, unless indicated otherwise in a credit line to the material. If material is not included in the chapter's Creative Commons license and your intended use is not permitted by statutory regulation or exceeds the permitted use, you will need to obtain permission directly from the copyright holder.

# Demand for Responsible Leadership in a Chaotic World

Vladimir Yakunin

**Abstract** There is *a need to find new mechanisms that will allow nations and civilisations to cooperate better* on specific issues despite their ideological differences. The *current crisis is global and systemic in nature.* On the one hand, this is an inevitable result of globalisation. On the other hand, it is a result of *defects in the existing economic model and global political system.* In the context of the global order and governance crisis, the *roles and responsibilities of states are strengthening* and *a new type of global leadership is required.* The emergence of a global threat, or catastrophe, should motivate states to put aside ideological differences and economic and political competition in *search of a joint solution in the name of survival of human civilisation.* The most recent threat has been the danger of new diseases in the form of global pandemics. To combat such threats effectively, we need to cooperate within the paradigm of *"a community for the shared future of mankind"* that combines the positive human potential of diverse civilisational identities, state structures, social and economic features, as well as cultural and historical diversity. By working together, we can bring order to the existing global disorder and find a way to secure the greater prosperity of humanity.

**Keywords** A need to find new mechanisms that will allow nations and civilisations to cooperate better · Global systemic crisis · Defects in the existing economic model and global political system · Roles and responsibilities of states are strengthening · A new type of global leadership is required · Search of a joint solution in the name of survival of human civilization · "A community for the shared future of mankind"

## 1 A New Type of Global Leadership is Required

Whenever humanity experiences challenges, those challenges are seen as unique. But this is only our perception. History in fact gives us many lessons of global crisis survival, whether it be future pandemics, cyber threats, poverty or the biggest threat

V. Yakunin (✉)
Faculty of Political Sciences, Lomonosov Moscow State University, Moscow, Russia

© The Author(s) 2021
H. Wang and A. Michie (eds.), *Consensus or Conflict?*, China and Globalization,
https://doi.org/10.1007/978-981-16-5391-9_9

of all—climate change. We need to find new mechanisms that will allow nations and civilisations to cooperate better on specific issues, despite their ideological differences.

The current crisis is global and systemic in nature. On the one hand, this is an inevitable result of globalisation. On the other hand, it is a result of defects in the existing economic model and global political system. In the context of the global order and governance crisis, the roles and responsibilities of states are strengthening and a new type of global leadership is required.

The demand for a new model of leadership that provides global solidarity is growing sharply. Combating the current pandemic and similar global challenges should become the foundation for this sort of development. The question is what country or group of countries can initiate such a project and involve the rest of the world in its implementation, thereby demonstrating responsible leadership.

This is an ideal challenge and an excellent opportunity to take the initiative and make a bid for a new format of world development. If this model of responsible leadership in a multilateral world is successful, an evolutionary transition to new models of sustainable development will be quite possible.

In the last few years, more and more major powers have put their own national interests first. This raises the question of what kind of "leadership" the world actually needs. The problem with what we are seeing today is that we have so-called leaders who follow ideologies of exclusivity and superiority.

Adopting a zero-sum perspective is an over-simplified way of understanding international relations. A multilateral world should be based on equal cooperation, not necessarily in the military or even economic terms, but with equal opportunity and ability to engage in global dialogue. In the context of the crisis in global order and governance, state systems are faced with the need to form anti-crisis and post-crisis policies that can ensure public dialogue and consensual decision-making to reduce inequality and social tension. Political systems should be adjusted to ensure broader and more effective public representation in order to mitigate against irresponsible populists rising to power. It is possible that we may see new forms of political participation, as well as an expanded space for the digitalisation of public policy and management to address these issues. There is demand for an adequate level of international cooperation, particularly in economic and humanitarian spheres, in order to prevent the worsening of socio-economic crises. Ensuring this will require that relevant international institutions have maximum stability.

Over the past decades, the main drivers of globalisation and key participants in international processes have been the countries of the developed world—mainly representing the so-called Western world. The social, economic and political structure of these countries was a model for almost all other states. At the heart of the universal measurement of national well-being was the economic indicator of Gross Domestic Product (GDP), which endorsed the advantages of the chosen development models of Western countries compared to the rest of the world. As a result, the processes of globalisation have been based on technologies, values and a way of life inherent to Western societies.

## 2   The Emergence of a 'Financialised' World Economy

It is no secret that the crisis of 2007–2008 began with the subprime mortgage collapse in the United States. This was due to low quality financial instruments—'derivatives'—that created a financial bubble such that the real value of goods was substantially overvalued due to a 'frenzied demand' based on incorrect information about economic realities. In practical terms, the world economy became 'financialised'; i.e., the financial sector of the economy increasingly dominated the real sector. This uncontrolled imbalance eventually led to the financial crisis and later to the global systemic crisis.

The financial crisis of 2008 led to a lower level of investment in infrastructure projects globally. On the one hand, governments reduced investment in long-term infrastructure because this was less painful than cutting other budgets at a time when it was essential to secure the provision of basic necessities. On the other hand, private investors also turned away from infrastructure projects and towards more liquid assets and projects with quick returns.

Numerous studies conducted after the crisis demonstrated a positive correlation between investment in infrastructure and economic growth. More importantly, it was also shown that infrastructure projects play a positive role in short-term outcomes as well, due to their creation of new jobs and their development of local enterprises, which support long-term regional development. Another conclusion voiced by many prominent economists over the last ten years has been the need to develop a new economic model to replace the existing neoliberal system, because neoliberalism no longer meets the needs of many states. Such statements were difficult to imagine before the crisis, but now seem obvious.

## 3   Creating New Integrated Global Values

This crisis shows that the world needs a new protocol for international relations and new responsible leadership if it is to be better prepared for future crises of this scale. So far, development has been based on values such as market capitalism, GDP growth and competition. We should be very careful when speaking about poverty and see this metric only in financial terms, as is the case today among key international organisations. We must follow human development through an integrated approach that takes into account access to healthcare, education and basic living standards. Going forward, I am convinced we need to be driven by values of solidarity, responsibility and a shared commitment to overcoming poverty and inequality. We must offer a new platform and paradigm for global powers to work together, including global North–South and South-South cooperation.

Taking into account the scale of the Belt and Road Initiative and the amount of investment China has put into it through newly founded multilateral financial institutions like the Asian Infrastructure Investment Bank, the New Development

Bank and the Silk Road Fund, it is not surprising that major powers including the European Union and the US are expressing significant concerns.

On the one hand, this is due to an inherent Western scepticism about any initiative offered by the non-Western world. On the other hand, as the geography of the project expands and its support grows across the developing world, Western countries are beginning to worry that their long-dominant positions are becoming untenable. This is also a consequence of the fact that, for a long time, traditional international development institutions did not provide the necessary weight for developing countries to participate in the global financial system, given their real contribution to global economic development alongside their institutional voting power and roles.

At the same time, the core concept of the Belt and Road initiative—'equal and mutually beneficial cooperation without imposing any political conditions'—clearly contradicts the currently dominant thesis in contemporary world politics. This new approach could change the very essence of geopolitics and geoeconomics by altering the outdated Cold War mentality of the past. Geopolitical theory has always been articulated through a lens of conflict, dividing the world into 'us' and 'them'. The pervading instability of ongoing trade wars and sanctions contribute their own limitations, which will need to be overcome and are mainly derived from economic relations between the US and other countries, primarily China. The Belt and Road Initiative could be the source of a future model of solidarity-driven global development.

Today, with the countries of Asia and Africa developing rapidly, we are observing the emergence of new leaders on the global stage, and a corresponding decrease in Western representation. As a result, we can conclude that the international architecture is currently undergoing a transition from a dominant Western-centric model to a new model that should take into account the needs of the developing world and its cultural diversity. An essential factor in determining the effectiveness of international relations in the modern multilateral world is deep knowledge about the different cultures, mentalities and values that underpin the formation of state policies in different countries. It is incorrect to view the developing world through the standards of the Western world.

# 4  Creating Solidarity-Driven Development

The key here is the impossibility of returning to a unipolar or bipolar world, which can be seen today in global trends towards development of a truly multilateral world. The change towards solidarity-driven development, which we see in the Belt and Road Initiative, provides a very different perspective. This enables consideration of external geopolitical and geoeconomic zones not as sources of danger, but as parts of a planet-wide life-support mechanism for development at local, regional and global levels.

Critical issues for the development of global initiatives include deficits of leadership, practical skills and knowledge to manage and support dialogue-based international cooperation towards human-centric development goals. Experts within and beyond the policymaking community should foster serious scholarly and practical efforts to support the research and development of new socio-economic models, based around solidarity-driven development, in which cooperative multilateral mechanisms are used. The question is which country or group of countries can put forward such a project and involve the rest of the world in its implementation, demonstrating 'value leadership'. This is a good challenge and an opportunity to take the initiative and make a bid for a new format of world development. If such a model of 'cooperative leadership' is successful, an evolutionary transition to new models of economic development will be quite possible.

Since the start of the pandemic and the ensuing crisis, politicians, government officials and experts across the globe have become increasingly aware of the magnitude and systemic nature of the problems at hand. This has created grounds for cautious optimism. That said, much remains to be done, and it will require collaboration between the state, the private sector and the public, as well as cooperation between governments at different levels and across different platforms.

Any form of dialogue—bilateral, trilateral, multilateral—is better for inclusive international development and peace than geopolitical competition. From this perspective, trilateral dialogue between the US, China and Russia is a necessary condition for future prosperous development. If we are talking about the possibility of trilateral dialogue, we need to answer three questions:

(1)   Do the parties have the motivation to engage in joint dialogue?
(2)   Is there a risk that dialogue among these three states could develop into a situation in which two participants compete or "team up" against the third one?
(3)   Will cooperation among the three become a conspiracy of the three against the rest of the world?

Today we have more grounds for drawing negative conclusions in response to these issues. This is undoubtedly a matter of serious concern. We need to concentrate our intellectual efforts on researching and defining the theoretical foundations for overcoming this tension, and provide practical recommendations on how to re-establish international cooperation based on the values of dialogue, inclusion and solidary development.

A key trend in global affairs is that developing countries are accounting for a greater share of global economic output. This clearly illustrates that when speaking about international development we must take into account new centres of political and economic growth and interactions among these centres. In this time of crisis, only solidarity among nations can help us to weather the storm. It is time to address critical global issues together. We should not let historical baggage and cultural biases prevent us from moving forward. We need to offer a new system and principles and build a new type of international leadership that will take into account the interests of the emerging world in Asia, Latin America and Africa, and help to avoid future global threats.

## 5    The Demand for New Leadership

Modern international leadership requires a number of qualities that are currently missing:

• The ability to see the global picture;
• The ability to see pathways to long-term sustainable global development, without being limited by considerations of electoral cycles or short-term political gain;
• The ability to unite people in the face of global threats.

The demand for new leadership is being met through specific actions and initiatives. A good example of maintaining such policies is China, whose government provides active assistance to countries across all continents by using China's manufacturing and technological capacities. The launch of projects such as the Health Silk Road and the Digital Silk Road is a great example of a country responding to the ongoing crisis appropriately and in a flexible manner. We can also observe the pragmatic policies of several European countries, which in times of bureaucratic uncertainty, are making independent decisions related to the need for economic development or the provision of medical goods.

We should remember that every crisis is also an opportunity. Humanity is now aware that it is facing new global challenges—such as climate change, for example. By properly reacting to these new challenges, we have a chance to undergo technological modernisation—and emerge from the crisis as a renewed society, more sustainable than before. But the only way for these changes to be successful is to first ensure social and economic sustainability—to make sure that interests of businesses and communities are not ignored at a national level, and that the interests of individual countries are respected on a global level. Securing this type of balanced development is a goal that all of us share.

Geopolitics is a kind of geographically construed politics, an intermediate science that focuses on political events and endeavours to provide them with a geographical interpretation within state borders. In contrast, the geographical boundaries of civilisations determine the natural boundaries of influence of great powers and remove any limitation and artificiality from geopolitics, supplementing it with essential and substantial value.

By defining China and Russia as independent civilisations, and the United States as the leader of Western civilisation, we can determine actual boundaries and spaces of interaction. We can easily observe that interaction in these spaces is far from positive. Most regions are filled with political and economic instability, and many of them are engulfed in military conflict. One of the most dangerous factors of this confrontation is that the religious and cultural foundations of local societies are becoming radicalised, which leads to a degradation and possibly the loss of traditional ways of life, and dependence on external resources.

The idea of a geopolitical division of the world between a limited group of states—whether two, three, five or some other number—is not new from a historical perspective. One look at the twentieth century and we can see the dangerous consequences of this, when a country or group of countries choose a strategy of exclusivity over others. During the Cold War, geopolitical games included not only containment strategies, but also the purposeful strengthening of other states or local groups to confront geopolitical opponents. Today, we see new mechanisms of influence outside the norms of international law. One example of such external influence is sanctions, which have become part and parcel of achieving economic and political goals in different countries. The possibility of using such instruments, as well as a tacit lack of action to give developing countries a corresponding role or vote weight in international institutions, are clear signals of the need to reform existing institutions of international cooperation such as the International Monetary Fund (IMF), World Bank and its related bodies.

## 6   The Impact of the Digital Revolution

Modern civilisational analysis cannot be complete without evaluating a new factor—the development of information technologies and social networks—which is becoming a comprehensive element of geopolitics itself. Russia, China and the US represent major players in this field among global powers.

I would like to touch upon a new phenomenon that we have termed 'the madness of the digital crowd'. Sociology provides a lot of information on the effect of irrationality and destructive behaviour caused by the influence of crowd forces. We realise from geopolitics that hidden manipulative crowd control is one of the most common techniques of indirect external influence. In addition to this, algorithms create an echo-chamber effect, which leads to polarisation of views and reduces opportunities for forming a comprehensive and fact-based understanding of events. Combined with modern informational systems and algorithms, we can see a new level of control and manipulation of the daily news agenda at both the individual and global levels. Under these conditions, any person or organisation can be rendered defenceless in the face of an attack by a 'digital crowd', which could be transitioned into the real world on the same scale. At the same time, there is a new phenomenon called 'deplatforming', whereby a person or organisation is denied the opportunity to express their opinion by private actors. This threat should also be the subject of research as part of the development of new foundations for international cooperation towards peace and inclusive development.

## 7   Towards a Dialogue of Civilisations

The emergence of some kind of global threat or catastrophe should motivate states to put aside ideological differences and economic and political competition in search of a joint solution in the name of survival of human civilisation. Such a threat can be seen in the danger of new diseases in the form of global pandemics as with COVID-19. To combat these threats effectively we need to cooperate within the paradigm of "a community for the shared future of mankind". In this situation, we will be able to rely on the common value of human life for all, while preserving life for future generations.

The concept of a dialogue of civilisations is in fact a way of building a global community. It combines the positive human potential of civilisational identities, state structures, social and economic features, as well as cultural and historical diversity. By working together, we can bring order to the existing global disorder and find a way to secure greater prosperity for humanity.

**Vladimir Yakunin** is a Russian public figure and academic. Currently, he serves as the Head of the State Policy Department at Lomonosov Moscow State University and as a Visiting Professor at Peking University. He occupied various positions in business and public service, including in the Presidential Administration of the Russian Federation and was Deputy Minister of Transport. In 2005–2015, Dr. Yakunin served as President of Russian Railways. In 2003, Dr. Yakunin co-founded the World Public Forum—Dialogue of Civilizations, which brings together diverse perspectives from the developed and developing states in a non-confrontational, equal, inclusive and collaborative way. In Russia, he also leads a number of public, philanthropic, social and educational initiatives.

**Open Access** This chapter is licensed under the terms of the Creative Commons Attribution-NonCommercial-NoDerivatives 4.0 International License (http://creativecommons.org/licenses/by-nc-nd/4.0/), which permits any noncommercial use, sharing, distribution and reproduction in any medium or format, as long as you give appropriate credit to the original author(s) and the source, provide a link to the Creative Commons license and indicate if you modified the licensed material. You do not have permission under this license to share adapted material derived from this chapter or parts of it.

The images or other third party material in this chapter are included in the chapter's Creative Commons license, unless indicated otherwise in a credit line to the material. If material is not included in the chapter's Creative Commons license and your intended use is not permitted by statutory regulation or exceeds the permitted use, you will need to obtain permission directly from the copyright holder.

# Re-energizing the G20 to Thwart a Global Systemic Crisis

**Guangyao Zhu**

**Abstract** *Maintainingpolitical order and governance on a global level should be centered on theUnited Nations*, follow the principles in the UN charter and be supported by the IMF, World Bank and WTO. *The role of China could potentially be key in global recovery as mankind conquers COVID-19.* China's ability to keep the virus under control, restart its economy and maintain growth, while, as of early 2021, much of the rest of the world continued to flounder, positions China as a driver for future economic development and trade growth. *The importance of multilateral governance systems in the resolution of COVID-19 cannot be overstated.* This is especially true of the G20 system. *The G20 has the ability to mobilize the resources of the most influential and powerful countries in the world.* G20 members, potentially in concert with China, have the power to put the world back on a path of multilateralism that emphasizes cooperation and consensus. *COVID-19 transcends borders, nationalities and political systems.* All nations must put aside pride and biases and replace them with more mutual respect, exchange suspicion for understanding and accusations with action. *If nations are united, mankind can overcome the COVID-19 pandemic* and work toward the continued development of economies and better manage the global community.

**Keywords** UN centered political order and governance · The role of China could potentially be key in global recovery from COVID-19 · The importance of multilateral governance systems in the resolution of COVID-19 cannot be overstated · The G20 has the ability to mobilize the resources of the most influential and powerful countries in the world · COVID-19 is a borderless threat · If nations are united, mankind can overcome the COVID-19 pandemic

The COVID-19 pandemic that is currently sweeping the world is a systemic crisis of global proportions on a scale that hasn't been seen since World War II. It is also the biggest global public health crisis since the 1918 flu,[1] which infected over 500 million and claimed the lives of over 50 million people around the world.

---

G. Zhu (✉)
Counsellor's Office of the State Council, Beijing, China

[1] www.cdc.gov/flu/pandemic-resources/1918-pandemic-h1n1.html.

© The Author(s) 2021

H. Wang and A. Michie (eds.), *Consensus or Conflict?*, China and Globalization, https://doi.org/10.1007/978-981-16-5391-9_10

105

COVID-19 has also spawned the biggest economic crisis since the 2008 financial crisis as well as a crisis in global governance that has impeded world peace and global development. However, there is little doubt that humanity will overcome this pandemic and that the current era of peaceful global development will not come to an end because of COVID-19.

The most important response to a pandemic like COVID-19 is for the world to communicate and work together to overcome the massive uncertainties that come with such a crisis. Specific actions required to tackle these uncertainties fall in four main areas—first, tracking the course of the pandemic; second, forecasting its impact on the global economy; third, ensuring the stability of industry and supply chains and fourth, assessing the impact of the pandemic on systems of global governance.

As of April 2021, this global pandemic has affected the health of over 130 million people and taken nearly three million lives. As a common enemy of all of humanity, the rise and fall in the number of cases, the emergence of new variants and the unequal distribution of vaccines throughout the world only add to the uncertainties about what the future will bring.

# 1 The Financial Impact of COVID-19

COVID-19 continues to impact the global economy, and the economic crisis that we face will last for years. The IMF estimates that global growth contracted at 3.5% in 2020. This is much worse than the 0.1% negative growth that the world saw in 2009 after Lehman Brothers went bankrupt on September 15, 2008, which led to the 2008 global financial crisis. In early 2021, and 12 months after COVID-19 was identified, the impact that this pandemic will have on the global economy has only begun to manifest itself.

The United Nations estimates that global direct investment dropped by 30–40% in 2020, higher than the 35% drop that was seen in 2009 after the global financial crisis. The WTO estimates that global trade dropped somewhere between 13 and 32% in 2020, which is also much higher than the drop that was seen in 2009 following the financial crisis. If we compare this with 1933, when global trade fell 30% due to the Great Depression, we can see just how big a challenge this presents for the world economy. Some say that the impact of the COVID-19 pandemic has affected only supply and demand. These comments suggest COVID-19 hasn't dramatically influenced the financial sector. However, in the coming years, we need to be prepared for rapid falls in the price of assets, a drastic increase in defaults on loans and the potential of bankruptcy of financial institutions.

Newly emerging markets should also be watched. The liquidation of USD 100 billion over the course of three months, by various countries, was four times the amount that bled from newly emerging markets during the 2008 global financial crisis. Argentina was one of the earliest countries to submit loan restructuring requests to the IMF and private lenders. This indicates that both developed countries and emerging economies have both felt the financial pressure caused by the COVID-19 pandemic. In March 2020, the G20 leaders reached an agreement to commit USD 50 billion to the fight against COVID-19. This amount was based on recommendations from international economic organizations, but only a month later the situation became increasingly worse and by May 2020 the United States alone had allotted USD 90 billion in financial support.

By the end of 2020, the US Federal Reserve amassed fiscal debt of USD 90 billion, while also providing USD 40 billion in the form of loans to support American businesses. Desperate times call for desperate measures and coordination between fiscal and monetary policies is critical. At the time, the Federal Reserve provided financial support to small and medium businesses without collateral, but it demanded that the Treasury Department provide guarantees for the loans. Clearly, this unique challenge has required innovative macroeconomic ideas that can only be achieved through cooperation and coordination.

Today's supply and industry chains are the result of many years of work by multinational companies that have followed trends in economic globalization, characterized by relative advantage, division of labor across borders and goals of efficiency and profit. They also reflect the nature of resources, labor and market conditions in different countries as well as the return on investment and operating environment in various countries.

## 2   Challenges Facing Industries and Systems

The pressure of the COVID-19 pandemic has caused some people to question existing industry and supply chains, expressing a desire to "bring home" certain industries, but this is not something that can be accomplished overnight. We must listen to business people in various countries and the opinions of multinational companies in particular. We should also be aware that these industry and supply chains may also need to be adjusted in the wake of COVID-19. These are a few of the main areas in which I believe they should be adjusted:

The first is in terms of security. Multinationals will naturally emphasize the concentration of industry chains and make both supply and industry chains as simple as possible, because they wish to make them as secure as possible, especially in unusual circumstances.

The second is the impact of certain policies on industry and supply chains. This includes bringing back the pharmaceutical industry to the United States, which has led to similar calls for the return of a wider range of manufacturing sectors. This has been discussed for a number of years, but in the context of the pandemic, pharmaceuticals have been a special focus. However, what can be done is ultimately limited because of the allocation of resources and issues of market demand, which includes the supply of raw materials and cannot be accomplished overnight.

The third is a more rapid restructuring of regional industry and supply lines in the context of COVID-19. Whether it is geographic proximity or similarities in systems, regulations and standards, or even better integration, new changes will likely come to regional industry and supply chains.

The fourth element is the impact of the digital economy on industry and supply chains. This was first seen in the digitalization of industries, in which I believe China has a unique advantage. This gain comes from extremely convenient infrastructural supports that ensure massive logistical capabilities as well as the world's most extensive mobile telephony base station coverage, which enables huge volumes of data to be exchanged. China also leads in the use of convenient forms of payment and electronic payment systems. With all of these digital advantages, it is likely that China will be one of the most efficient places in the world in terms of the digitalization of industry and supply chains.

Ultimately, stable industry and supply chains are in the interest of all countries and we should strengthen communication and coordination on policies to ensure that they remain stable.

# 3 China's Role in Recovery After COVID-19

The world is changing, and China, currently the world's largest developing country and the second-largest economy, has turned its sights to taking care of business at home. President Xi Jinping has placed the physical and economic recovery of the country's 1.4 billion people at the top of his list of priorities. This means that China is in a position to potentially help much of the world, especially the developing world, to recover more quickly from the devastating effects of the pandemic. Similar to the United States after World War II, China could potentially work to help countries recover economically, reform systems of global governance and ensure that globalization trends in a direction that is beneficial for all countries.

The International Monetary Fund (IMF) predicts that data will confirm that China will be the only major economy to maintain positive growth in 2020, growing at a rate of 1.9% overall (Q1 6.8%, Q2 3.2%, Q3 4.9%, Q4 ~6%). The IMF's forecast for China's economic growth is 8.2% for 2021. While this will enable China to maintain confidence and optimism on economic growth, it must also be very prudent and ensure that development is both healthy and sustainable, which is one of the goals of its current "dual circulation" policy that will balance domestic and international production and trade.

One specific way in which China is maintaining this trend of growth is the start of a large number of new infrastructure projects, which is a key element in the "six priorities"[2] as laid out by the central government. To accomplish this, the central government has arranged for a fiscal deficit of 3.6%, an increase of RMB 1 trillion, as well as RMB 1 trillion in special treasury bonds and RMB 3.75 trillion in local special treasury bonds for a total of nearly RMB 8 trillion. RMB 2 trillion of this is

---

[2] 1. Job security; 2. basic living needs; 3. operations of market entities; 4. food and energy security; 5. stable industrial and supply chains; and 6. normal functioning of primary-level governments.

allocated exclusively for local governments to support employment, market players and basic livelihood with a special focus on the welfare of small and medium-sized enterprises, which is seen as key to China's economic resilience and vitality.

In early 2021, the "14th Five-Year Plan" and the "Long-Range Objectives Through the Year 2035" were adopted at the fifth plenary session of the 19th CPC Central Committee and by all accounts mark a new trend in development objectives that will no doubt affect how China interacts with the world. The overall size of China's economy is already something that can't be ignored, but the purchasing power of its people is also something that should be watched more closely. China's gross national product (GNP) was USD 14.3 trillion in 2019, while per capita GNP reached USD 10,261. According to the latest adjusted data from the World Bank, China is not far from the threshold for high-income countries, which is currently set at USD 12,535 per capita of GNP.

As the world's two largest economies, China and the United States should adhere to the principles of non-conflict, non-confrontation, mutual respect, cooperation and win–win, which are in the interests of both their peoples and peaceful global development. Objective economic development has resulted in a narrowing of the gap between the Chinese and US economies, but we must remain acutely aware that the GDP per capita in 2019 in the United States was USD 66,000, over six times that of China. This clear difference points out that while China is in a position as a country to impact and even possibly guide the world, it cannot ignore the overwhelming economic heft of the United States. This is why it has always been China's position that each country should make its own contribution in the process of building a community that focuses on shared prosperity for mankind.

## 4   Three Points for Moving Forward

To overcome the current crisis, there must be a systematic, holistic, strategic thinking that enables the countries of the world, especially key players, to return to a spirit of unity and collaboration. Unfortunately, the United States, as the world's largest economy and the largest developed country, inflicted severe damage to the global governance system by withdrawing from the multilateral institutions and agreements in 2020. It is essential that the United States return to multilateralism and a path of peaceful global development, which is ultimately in line with the interests of the United States.

There is an urgency and importance to restoring and strengthening the functions of the G20. The global public health crisis, the global economic recession and the issues in global governance triggered by the COVID-19 pandemic compounded existing problems, which created a serious systemic crisis that humanity has not seen since World War II. However, the international community failed to work together to effectively respond as it did when it responded to the global financial crisis in 2008. As of the early months of 2021, and a full year into the COVID-19 pandemic, the G20 was still basically at a standstill.

"Conflict reduction" under the leadership of the G20 can only be regarded as a part of the overall function of the G20. Its most important function is actually to foster cohesion and solidarity and cooperation of major countries in times of crisis, focusing on coordinating macroeconomic policies and other policy issues. The G20 should take immediate action and coordinate policy to achieve the following three goals.

First, we need to coordinate macroeconomic policies, including both fiscal policy and monetary policy. By early 2021, countries around the world had already invested USD 15 trillion to ensure economic stability, support employment and efforts to counter economic depression. However, the results have not been encouraging. In terms of monetary policy, major economies have implemented negative interest rate policies. The European Central Bank currently has an interest rate of $-0.5\%$, and the Bank of Japan has an interest rate of $-0.1\%$. The US Federal Reserve (The Fed) has kept interest rates at zero since March and despite the 10-year dollar bond yield being set at $0.7\%$, after taking inflation into account, the rate is actually negative. The Fed also stated that it will not normalize interest rates (i.e. change its zero interest rate policy), until 2023. International coordination is urgently needed in this regard.

Second, the G20 needs to reach a policy consensus on digital taxation and digital currency, effective supervision of digital platforms and prevention of a "New Cold War" as soon as possible. Progress had already been made in terms of digital taxation prior to the pandemic, with the G20 reaching a consensus and taking actual steps, but momentum has been lost and there is an urgent need to restore the functions of the G20 in this area.

Third is trade policy. The WTO is now at a standstill, mainly due to the actions of the United States, which even went so far as to challenge the 2020 election of the WTO Director-General. In order to ensure the survival of the WTO, the G20 member states urgently need to rally to form an effective policy consensus. Some in the United States have called for decoupling, which would be unlikely and incredibly difficult, but at the same time not too long ago, the US representative had asked to establish a mechanism by which China could join the G20 under the format of the China-US Strategic Economic Dialogue.

This tells us that while things have stagnated, there is still room for discussion and functionality to return to the G20. This is why maintaining close coordination between China and the United States is not only in the interest of China and the United States but also in the interest of the world. In the field of global cooperation, it is time to return to the multilateral framework and strengthen the role of the G20.

# 5 Conclusion

Ideally, maintaining political order and governance on a global level should be something ensured through the United Nations, following the principles in its charter with support from the IMF, World Bank and WTO. As a specialized arm of the UN, the WHO should shoulder the responsibility of setting health policies and monitoring their execution. This is a massive burden as the COVID-19 pandemic continues to ravage the world, made even more difficult by the Trump administration and its lack of interaction and threat to leave the WHO entirely, which severely damaged its ability to tackle this challenge.

The role of China could potentially be key in global recovery as we come out of the worst of the COVID-19 pandemic. China's ability to keep the virus under control, restart its economy and maintain growth, while much of the rest of the world continued to flounder, positions China as a driver for future economic development and trade growth. This economic stability, underpinned in 2021 by the launching of its most recent five-year plan and other development goals, as well as rising income levels, makes China a key part of any plan for global economic recovery.

The importance of multilateral governance systems in the resolution of the negative impact of COVID-19 cannot be overstated. This is especially true of the G20, which has the ability to mobilize the resources of the most influential and powerful countries in the world, coordinating them to effectively resolve the core challenges that the world faces. In a post-Trump world, the G20 member countries, potentially in concert with China, have the power to put the world back on a path of multilateralism that emphasizes cooperation, coordination and consensus, which is essential.

The fight against COVID-19 is something that transcends borders, nationalities and political systems. What's more, there is no aspect of life that it has not affected. It has impacted our health, our economies and our futures. We must unite against this common challenge and cooperate to overcome it. I recommend that we put aside our pride and biases and replace them with more mutual respect, exchange suspicion for understanding and accusations with action. If we are united, we can overcome the COVID-19 pandemic. We can, and must, work toward the continued development of our economies and better manage our global community.

**Guangyao Zhu** is a former Vice Minister of Finance of China (2010–2018). He previously worked in the World Bank as a Senior Advisor, Alternate Executive Director and Executive Director for China. He currently serves as a Counsellor of the State Council of China. He graduated from Finance Science Research Institute of the Finance Ministry of the PRC with a Masters Degree in Economics. He has rich experience in dealing with international economic and financial affairs. With his deep knowledge of the development of the International Financial Reporting Standards (IFRS) and the international convergence of Chinese accounting standards, he also plays a vital role in promoting the research in accounting theory in China.

**Open Access** This chapter is licensed under the terms of the Creative Commons Attribution-NonCommercial-NoDerivatives 4.0 International License (http://creativecommons.org/licenses/by-nc-nd/4.0/), which permits any noncommercial use, sharing, distribution and reproduction in any medium or format, as long as you give appropriate credit to the original author(s) and the source, provide a link to the Creative Commons license and indicate if you modified the licensed material. You do not have permission under this license to share adapted material derived from this chapter or parts of it.

The images or other third party material in this chapter are included in the chapter's Creative Commons license, unless indicated otherwise in a credit line to the material. If material is not included in the chapter's Creative Commons license and your intended use is not permitted by statutory regulation or exceeds the permitted use, you will need to obtain permission directly from the copyright holder.

# Bretton Woods 2.0? Rebuilding Global Governance for the Post-pandemic Era

**Huiyao Wang**

**Abstract**  In the first half of the twentieth century, in *the absence of effective global governance mechanisms,* unchecked forces of fragmentation, economic hardship, and polarization led to two devastating world wars. To prevent this from happening again, after the Second World War, countries from around *the world came together at Bretton Woods* and other landmark conferences *to build a new system of global governance* that would *promote international cooperation, stability, and peace and prosperity.* Today, like after the Second World War, the world faces major challenges, not only in the short term to recover from the pandemic but also in the long term to overcome *global threats like climate change, which no country can solve alone.* As we emerge from COVID-19, there is a unique opportunity for *a long-overdue "Bretton Woods 2.0" moment* to rethink global governance and forge multilateral institutions that better reflect the realities of the post-pandemic world. China can, and should, help lead by supporting the update and strengthening of existing institutions. For example, the *Asia Infrastructure Investment Bank should be transformed into the Global Infrastructure Investment Bank.* Overall, China should be drawing on its knowledge as *the longest continuous civilization in the world* and using these strengths to propose its own solutions to pressing global issues.

**Keywords**  The absence of effective global governance mechanisms · The world came together at Bretton Woods · To build a new system of global governance · Promote international cooperation, stability and peace and prosperity · Global threats like climate change, which no country can solve alone · A long-overdue "Bretton Woods 2.0" moment

Global governance can have a significant impact on how the world recovers from a major catastrophe. After the twin tragedies of the First World War and the Spanish Flu pandemic of 1918–19, the newly formed League of Nations was unable to prevent a vicious cycle of nationalism, protectionism, and economic hardship that would wipe out two-thirds of international trade, plunge the world into the Great Depression, and ultimately sow the seeds of the Second World War.

H. Wang (✉)
Center for China and Globalization (CCG), Beijing, China

© The Author(s) 2021
H. Wang and A. Michie (eds.), *Consensus or Conflict?*, China and Globalization,
https://doi.org/10.1007/978-981-16-5391-9_11

The contrast with the aftermath of the Second World War is striking. Even before the war ended, allied leaders were putting together pieces of a new system of global governance to support a more constructive economic and international order. In 1944, delegates from 45 nations descended on New Hampshire for the Bretton Woods conference to devise institutions that would govern the post-war international monetary system, including the International Monetary Fund (IMF) and the World Bank. Just under a year later, delegates from around the world met in San Francisco to create the United Nations Charter, which established the purposes, governing structure, and framework of the UN system. This was followed by the signing of the General Agreement on Tariffs and Trade (GATT), the forerunner of the World Trade Organization (WTO), in Geneva in October 1947.

Assembled in just a few short years, these institutions became the building blocks of "Global Governance 1.0"—the international system that remains to this day. While far from perfect, the system of global governance based on the UN and Bretton Woods institutions succeeded in preventing the world from sliding into another all-out global conflict in the challenging conditions that followed two devastating wars. Economic arrangements that grew out of Bretton Woods helped feed a virtuous cycle of openness, trade, prosperity, and stability. Trade barriers fell and global foreign direct investment grew eight times from 1950 to 1970. At the same time, governments took a long-term perspective and made sustained investments in human and physical infrastructure, most famously the Marshall Plan, which helped to rebuild and modernize economies in Europe.

As the world struggles to get back on its feet after COVID-19, such divergent outcomes after the two world wars provide valuable lessons for our times. The first is that major external shocks like a war—or a pandemic—can be a catalyst for sweeping reforms of global governance. The second is that the ability of global governance to adapt to a new post-crisis environment and perform crucial functions can have a major long-term impact on geopolitics and the trajectory of the global economy.

Like a global conflict, the pandemic has claimed millions of lives and caused untold disruption to people's lives and economies around the world. Its effects will linger for many years and the UN is warning of a "lost decade" for development. But the pandemic has also triggered a serious discussion about globalization and global governance, and broadened the spectrum of possibilities for what comes next. Kristalina Georgieva, IMF Managing Director, has declared that we face a new "Bretton Woods moment" and may need to reorient global institutions to the demands of our times. UN Secretary-General António Guterres has called for a fundamental rethink and reform of global governance to bring about a stronger and more inclusive multilateralism.

The architects of the post-war world recognized that global problems need global attention. COVID-19 has led to a similar consensus that global governance must be reformed to meet the challenges of the post-pandemic era. But what should this new system of "Global Governance 2.0" look like? Building on an analysis of the key features and trends shaping the post-pandemic world and the challenges and the implications this has for global governance, this essay sketches some contours of what Bretton Woods 2.0, or better still Global Governance 2.0, might look like. Also proposed are the five steps China could take to contribute to its emergence.

# 1 Key Trends Shaping the Post-pandemic Global Landscape

COVID-19 should have been a chance for global governance to shine. Pandemics are a prime example of a transnational threat that no country can solve alone. Unfortunately, rather than show the enduring relevance of multilateralism, the pandemic and our failure to mount an effective international response did more to expose the fractures and fragilities in our current system of global governance.

Multilateralism had been under increasing strain long before the outbreak. In part, this is due to long-term structural shifts which the system has failed to adapt to. As we start to imagine a renewed system of global governance, it is important to understand five "megatrends" that have strained global governance 1.0 and that any new international system will have to accommodate and adapt to. As discussed below, this is particularly so as, in many ways, the pandemic will only serve to strengthen and accelerate these trends, creating a post-pandemic world that is more multipolar, interdependent, digital, and marked by rising regionalism and geoeconomics.

## 1.1 A More Multipolar World

The first reality that any new system of global governance must accommodate is that we live in an increasingly multipolar world. The existing US-led system was designed for a world where power was highly concentrated. However, long-term structural trends, in particular the rise of developing countries, mean that in the post-pandemic era, no single power will be able to dictate global norms and rules by itself.

Nowhere is the shift to multipolarity more evident than in the rise of Asia. By many measures, Asia's economy is now bigger than the rest of the world combined, for the first time since the nineteenth century. Post-pandemic recovery trajectories will likely reinforce this shift. While there are significant differences between individual countries, overall, Asia suffered less and is coming out of the pandemic earlier compared to Europe and America, meaning economic recovery will also be faster. China is at the heart of this story. The country will continue to be the leading engine for global growth for many years to come. 2020 was a milestone in the shift of economic gravity as China attracted more foreign investment than the USA for the first time and the number of Chinese companies on the Fortune Global 500 (124) overtook the USA (121).

It is not only between states that this gradual diffusion of power is occurring. Non-state actors from multinational corporations and philanthropists to civic groups and terrorist networks play an increasingly important role in global affairs, with the power to both create international problems and solve them. While the initial stages of the pandemic seemed to reassert the importance of states as the only agents with the power to take major steps such as close borders and enforce lockdowns, later stages have highlighted the importance of non-state actors. Transnational networks of research institutes, businesses, and foundations played a crucial role in vaccine development and distribution. Technology companies, whose tools played a crucial role in containment efforts and adaptations during the pandemic, have seen their wealth soar. The five leading US tech giants now have a combined market capitalization of roughly USD 7 trillion—greater than the GDP of every country except China and the USA.

Given the trends outlined above, in the post-pandemic era, our global governance framework must adapt to give developing countries a stronger voice in decision making, while harnessing the combined strengths of non-state actors to work on global challenges.

## 1.2 A More Interdependent World

Interdependence is the next feature that Global Governance 2.0 must be equipped for. It might surprise some to talk of rising interdependence when globalization and long cross-border supply chains are increasingly being questioned. Yet the fates of different countries are more entwined than at any point in human history, and this is only becoming more so.

Rising interdependence stems from two related sources. The first is cross-border flows of people, goods, capital, ideas, and data, which are broader and deeper than ever. These flows tie the interests of different countries together through global supply chains, cultural flows, and global finance. While the movement of goods and people was severely disrupted during the pandemic, global trade has recovered faster than expected, dispelling speculation that COVID-19 would be the death knell for global supply chains. International travel remains curtailed for the time being, but in the meantime, other cross-border flows such as data have accelerated, as discussed below.

Dense cross-border linkages contributed to the rapid global spread of COVID-19, which brings us to the other driver of interdependence: the rise of transnational challenges. In the twenty-first century, the most serious existential threats faced by humanity—such as climate change, infectious disease, and nuclear weapons—share an important commonality; they pay no heed to national boundaries and can only be addressed through global, multilateral efforts.

What's more, transnational threats intersect in myriad ways. For example, climate change could also increase the risk of future pandemics by damaging natural habitats and raising the risk of zoonotic transmission. Climate change can also act as a destabilizing "risk multiplier" for geopolitics. It will aggravate stress on societies and institutions by exacerbating demographic pressures from climate migration and open new areas for rivalry.

Our current system of global governance was designed in an age when the most salient security threats that countries faced were those emanating from other states. But deepening cross-border linkages and shared global threats mean that no country is an island in the post-pandemic era. The purpose of Global Governance 2.0 will perhaps be less about preventing conflict between states, though that remains a crucial function and more about facilitating collective responses to the myriad shared threats we face.

## 1.3  A More Digital World

Staying with the theme of growing interconnectedness, perhaps nowhere is more evident than in the rise of transnational data flows and the global digital economy. Just as oil opened new possibilities for commerce and trade in the last century, data has become the lifeblood of global growth in the twenty-first century. Trade in digital services is booming. Data flows increasingly underpin trade in physical goods, too, supporting complex global value chains and emerging technologies such as blockchain, artificial intelligence, and the Internet of Things.

The pandemic has only served to accelerate digitalization. Data flows soared in 2020 as work, play, and education shifted online. International internet traffic surged 48% from mid-2019 to mid-2020 according to data from TeleGeography.[1] One study found that cross-border e-commerce sales of discretionary goods spiked 53% in the second quarter of 2020.[2] Many businesses and organizations have had to adopt digitized models amidst the pandemic, including my own thinktank which has shifted to virtual event formats that allow people anywhere on earth to participate or watch.

While the full implications of digitalization for global governance have yet to become clear, they are sure to be profound and manifold.

First, the digital economy is arguably the area where global economic governance is weakest at present. As cross-border data flows soar, our global trade rules have barely changed since the 1990s. In the absence of shared global norms on how data flows should be governed, domestic policymakers everywhere are developing their own "patches" to regulate data and protect national security and their citizens' privacy. According to the OECD, the number of data regulations has risen from around 50 worldwide in the early 2000s to just under 250 in 2019. The patchwork nature of these rules is making things more complex for firms and stifling the potential of the global digital economy, which should be a bright spot in the post-pandemic economic recovery. These gaps in global data governance are also creating friction between nations.

---

[1] https://blog.telegeography.com/internet-traffic-and-capacity-in-covid-adjusted-terms.
[2] DHL Global Connectedness Index 2020.

Second, digitalization will have wide-reaching impacts on the real economy and societies around the world. Change will accelerate as production is dematerialized. Machines that drove earlier waves of globalization had to be made and shipped before use. Upgrading took time and considerable expense. Today, algorithms that overturn industries can be updated instantly at zero marginal cost. Digitalization and the associated technologies of the Fourth Industrial Revolution, such as AI, Internet of Things, and robotics, have the potential to drive inclusive global growth, but will also have a destabilizing effect on many communities and industries. If not addressed, these disruptions and the continuing digital divide may worsen inequality between and within countries.

Digitalization has caused strains on our current global governance framework, but it also creates new imperatives for cooperation—in particular, to develop a new framework that can support the safe and healthy growth of the global digital economy, and to build out digital infrastructure so that all can benefit from this growth.

## 1.4 The Rise of Regionalism

In recent years, the strains on global governance—such as the weakening of the UN, failure to reform Bretton Woods institutions, and breakdown of WTO negotiations—have led to a proliferation of multilateral initiatives at regional levels.

As global trade rules fray, a patchwork of regional deals has emerged as vehicles for deeper liberalization. The new free trade pact between the USA, Mexico, and Canada (USMCA) came into force in 2020, followed by the African Continental Free Trade Area (AfCFTA), which started trading at the start of 2021. Asia in particular is a locus for regional multilateralism. After it was abandoned by the USA, the reformed Trans-Pacific Partnership (TPP) (also known as the Comprehensive and Progressive Agreement for Trans-Pacific Partnership or CPTPP) was revived and came into force at the start of 2019. The Regional Comprehensive Economic Partnership (RCEP), set to be the world's largest Free Trade Agreement (FTA), was signed in November 2020. These living agreements will continue to evolve and will likely attract new members, offering a flexible, multitrack path to economic integration in Asia. For example, the more rigorous CPTPP may help to set standards for future trade for advanced economies, while the less-demanding RCEP will offer a way for developing countries to participate in free trade.

Some of these new regional multilateral initiatives address existing gaps in global governance. For example, the CPTPP includes rules on e-commerce. The Asian Infrastructure Investment Bank (AIIB), launched in 2014, aims to help close the yawning infrastructure gap, which existing multilateral development banks such as the World Bank have not been able to resolve. One of the tasks for Global Governance 2.0 is to accommodate these regional arrangements, exploit synergies with them, and help to coordinate so that they work together harmoniously.

## 1.5   The Age of Geoeconomics

The fifth megatrend that Global Governance 2.0 must deal with is the rising specter of "geoeconomics"—the use of economic tools to advance geopolitical objectives.

Until relatively recently, economic cooperation served as a ballast for the international system. Global institutions underpinned a virtuous cycle of cooperation and prosperity, providing powerful incentives to follow rules and avoid confrontation with other countries. However, in our present times, economic relations are increasingly a source of friction that undermines international cooperation and global governance. The use of sanctions is rising and struggles over strategic technologies are a growing flashpoint in international relations. States are increasingly willing to weaponize global networks for finance or critical inputs for their own strategic ends.

The rise of economic statecraft began to cast a shadow over the global economy even before the pandemic dealt it another blow. COVID-19 has increased calls to "reshore" production and some governments are intervening to draw supply chains home. Even the distribution of vaccines and critical medical equipment has been caught up in politics.

As Pascal Lamy, former WTO director-general, has pointed out, in the aftermath of the pandemic, a certain degree of "precautionism"—legitimate safeguarding of citizen needs—is to be expected.[3] But mechanisms are needed to ensure this is done in a transparent, coordinated manner and does not slide into more sticky and harmful forms of protectionism.

The WTO is the obvious solution to push back against protectionism and the weaponization of economic policy. But like other global institutions, it has been weakened by years of deadlock and fallen far behind the realities of the twenty-first century global economy. Our new system of global governance must find ways to contain dangerous tendencies toward economic statecraft and ensure that competition between great powers remains healthy, to ensure that the global economy remains open and inclusive, and remains a force for peace and prosperity.

## 2   A Vision for Global Governance 2.0

Global Governance 1.0 was designed for a world in which a few powerful countries called the shots; a world in which national boundaries were all important and the most pressing problems arose within or between states. As described above, we now live in an increasingly digital and multipolar world linked by cross-border flows and global challenges. Economic relations have grown fractious and regional institutions have become some of the most dynamic vehicles of multilateralism.

To adapt to these realities, Global Governance 2.0 will need to embody three principles. First, it needs to be more inclusive. That means better representing voices

---

[3] https://www.afr.com/world/europe/trade-s-new-bogeyman-isn-t-protectionism-it-s-precautio nism-20200516-p54tj2.

and interests of emerging economies and mobilizing a new set of actors to work on global problems, including both developing countries and non-state actors.

The second principle is that global governance needs to be more integrated. Complex, cross-cutting challenges, such as climate change, need to be addressed in an integrated manner, accounting for links between different sectors and issues, based on strong links between global and regional organizations, international financial institutions, and other global alliances and institutions.

Third, our post-pandemic world calls for global institutions that are more flexible. Network science has shown the importance of both strong and weak ties. Small groups are good at getting things done, while large ones maximize participation and the flow of information and innovation. Rather than sticking to large, unwieldy member-driven formats for all purposes, global mechanisms should be tailored to the job at hand. For some purposes, such as kickstarting the process to reform key global institutions, a smaller group of key powers may be preferable. For other tasks, it may be more suitable to forge a broad and inclusive group of nations and other stakeholders such as businesses, cities, and universities.

There is a growing consensus that the next iteration of global governance needs to embody the guiding principles of being inclusive, integrated, and flexible. UN Secretary-General António Guterres advocates a "networked multilateralism" that better links various global and regional institutions.[4] Thomas Friedman, New York Times columnist, and fellow contributor to this volume, says that the only way to govern our twenty-first-century world is through "global complex adaptive coalitions."[5] Writing in *Foreign Affairs*, Anne-Marie Slaughter and Gordon LaForge call for a more participatory order that is rationalized around what they call "impact hubs"—issue-specific organizations that sit at the center of important actors working on a particular problem, coordinating their collective work toward common goals and outcomes.[6]

As for what a more inclusive, flexible, and integrated Global Governance 2.0 would look like in practice, there are three areas to think about. First, existing global institutions such as the UN, IMF, World Bank, and WTO would remain at the core, updated to give developing countries more of a say and to better focus on twenty-first-century issues like climate change and the digital economy. Second, underneath this global framework, new regional multilateral initiatives made up of smaller, more dynamic groupings of countries would be allowed to develop and explore new pathways for cooperation that could eventually also feedback to the global level. Third, new global institutions could be created, tailored to niches and problems not adequately covered by the present system, designed to complement the existing system and harness the power of diverse stakeholders, including non-state actors, to work on a common problem. The next and final section of this essay looks ahead to China's role in rebuilding post-pandemic global governance. Included in

---

[4] https://www.un.org/press/en/2020/sgsm20264.doc.htm.

[5] https://global.chinadaily.com.cn/a/202104/14/WS60764ba2a31024ad0bab5670.html.

[6] https://www.foreignaffairs.com/articles/world/2021-02-16/opening-order.

these thoughts are outlines of some proposals for steps China could take to boost governance in these three areas.

## 3   China's Role in Global Governance 2.0

China has benefited enormously from participating in the current system of Global Governance 1.0. Embracing globalization and its institutions such as the WTO, IMF and World Bank spurred development and helped to transform the country. After several decades of rapid growth, China is now the second-largest economy and poised to be the largest in the not-too-distant future.

As its influence grows, China has growing capabilities, and indeed a growing responsibility, to help address gaps in global governance and increase its contribution to global public goods. For many years, the reform of global governance has been held back by a lack of global leadership and consensus. China is well placed to help overcome this gridlock and galvanize international cooperation. As it transitions from being a developing nation into a developed one, China can help bridge the divides that have stalled reform. China is also well placed to propose new global governance solutions for the post-pandemic era. The rest of this essay is devoted to five ways China could do this in the three areas outlined above, namely promoting the reform of existing institutions, participating in next-generation regional agreements, and finally proposing new solutions for global governance.

### 3.1   Create a Dedicated UN Body for Climate Change

Despite its weaknesses, the UN continues to play an irreplaceable role in the international system. China should work to reinvigorate the UN to serve as the linchpin of a new overlapping system of institutions and coalitions that make up Global Governance 2.0.

The structure that is most obviously outdated is the UN Security Council, whose five permanent veto members reflect the outcomes of the Second World War rather than contemporary realities. However, reforming this body has long proved an intractable problem and for now there are no ideal solutions and no easy way forward.

In the short term, green issues may offer a more promising field to forge consensus and meaningful reform. In particular, China could work with other partners to promote the creation of a dedicated UN institution focused on climate change as a unique crisis that affects many areas of global cooperation. The UN already plays a leading role in addressing climate change through the UN Environmental Program (UNEP) and UN Framework Convention on Climate Change (UNFCCC). However, the former's work spans many other environmental issues, and the UNFCCC is limited by its need for universal consensus via infrequent moments of agreement between members. A permanent and dedicated UN climate change body could serve to build continuous momentum for climate governance and foster collaboration between various stakeholders—not just states, but also firms and other organizations at the local, regional, and global level—to nurture long-term policy and technological solutions.

## 3.2 Promote WTO Reform

Reviving the WTO is another priority in the course of post-pandemic recovery. The aftermath of the Second World War and the Global Financial Crisis of 2007–2008 shows that trade can support economic recovery after a major global calamity. As the world emerges from the COVID-19 crisis, the steps we take to limit or liberalize trade can profoundly affect the world's economic trajectory. The WTO is the obvious vehicle to manage this process, but unfortunately, the institution has failed to keep up with important developments in the global economy and its dispute settlement mechanism remains paralyzed.

A plan is needed to breathe life back into the WTO. The WTO secretariat could play a bigger role in driving change and adjustments like using more flexible plurilateral agreements would also help. However, ultimately the WTO remains a membership-driven organization and real change requires that major powers play ball. This has proved challenging in recent years, but COVID-19 and the change of administration in Washington have widened the realms of political possibility. China should work with leading powers—the USA and EU in particular—to kick-start the WTO reform process so that it can be an institutional catalyst for post-pandemic economic recovery. Completing the WTO's e-commerce negotiations has also become a priority as billions go online to shop, study, work, or seek health care.

## 3.3 Join the CPTPP

While working to revive the global free trade agenda, China should also be an active participant in FTAs developing at the regional level. In years to come, membership in the RCEP will boost China's growth and solidify the nation's place at the heart of regional supply chains. Looking ahead, China should move toward joining the CPTPP, a higher standard FTA geared to advanced economies.

Joining the 11-member CPTPP agreement would push back against decoupling and protectionism and give China better access to one of the world's most dynamic regional markets. It would also provide an external impetus for the next phase of reform and opening—just as WTO entry did two decades ago. In particular, CPTPP principles are well aligned with China's goals to improve IPR protection and reform state-owned enterprises.

In the long term, an enlarged CPTPP could provide a blueprint for reforming the WTO and getting the global free-trade agenda back on track. Given that President

Biden has said he is open to rejoining the pact, there is even a chance that China and the USA could one day come under the CPTPP's common umbrella. Regardless of the course Washington takes, Chinese membership could help reduce friction and the rise of geoeconomics by aligning China closer with progressive global trade norms.

## 3.4 Multilateralize the Belt and Road

Moving on to ways in which China can propose and develop new innovations for global governance, the fourth suggestion is to reconfigure the Belt and Road Initiative (BRI) as a multilateral endeavor for global governance and development.

Since it was launched in 2013, the BRI has become a vector of globalization, growth, and investment in many regions. Belt and Road projects have created nearly 300,000 jobs. The World Bank estimates that host countries have reduced shipping times by up to 3.2%, and trade costs by up to 2.8%.[7] In addition, the initiative has helped build up the so-called "soft" infrastructure such as education, healthcare, and other services.

However, two factors contribute to a more challenging environment ahead for the BRI in the post-pandemic era. First, the BRI has evolved beyond expectations and become truly global, with over 130 countries having signed cooperation agreements. As the initiative links diverse geographies, it also needs to engage with a more complex group of stakeholders, who have their own interests and development plans. Second, a shift in the geopolitical climate has cast a shadow of suspicion over the BRI. Ironically, the problems that call for a global vision—economic uncertainty, protectionism, and mistrust—have created headwinds for the very initiative that could be part of the solution. At the international and local levels, some have politicized and misrepresented the initiative to serve their own interests.

Given these conditions, concrete steps must be taken to ensure that the BRI can fulfill its long-term potential to contribute to global governance and development in the post-pandemic era.

First, an international cooperation committee could be created to help the Belt and Road plan transition from a bilateral to a more multilateral approach. This committee would comprise a selection of representatives from key international organizations. Embedding a broad spectrum of experiences and perspectives into the advisory apparatus of the initiative would enhance its multilateral nature and help address concerns over its sinocentric approach.

Second, the initiative needs deeper engagement with international organizations, 29 of which have come on board. Working closely with established institutions, such as the World Bank, brings in additional expertise and resources, and helps ensure BRI projects meet the highest international standards.

---

[7] https://documents.worldbank.org/en/publication/documents-reports/documentdetail/592771539 630482582/how-much-will-the-belt-and-road-initiative-reduce-trade-costs.

Third, other mechanisms for multilateralizing the plan could be extended. For example, an overseas Belt and Road arbitration center could be set up, as a counterpart to the BRI courts in Shenzhen and Xi'an. There could even be an arbitration agency in Geneva. This would build transparency and trust in the trade plan's institutional framework. To increase transparency around the plan, additional platforms could be set up, such as an open online system for project bidding worldwide.

## 3.5  Upgrade the AIIB into a Global Infrastructure Bank

Continuing the theme of multilateralizing the BRI, to date, the Asian Infrastructure Investment Bank (AIIB) provides the most compelling model for how this might be achieved. Over the last six years, the AIIB has established itself as an effective multilateral development bank (MDB) and successfully integrated into the international financial architecture. Having attracted advanced economies as voting members and adopted the high standards of other MDBs, it has gained recognition from multilateral organizations like the UN and AAA ratings from leading rating agencies.

With a fresh capital injection and expanded membership, the bank would be well placed to expand its remit and become the Global Infrastructure Investment Bank (GIIB). This would involve inviting new members to play major roles—notably the USA and Japan—as well as getting more countries in other regions such as Africa and Latin America to join. In addition, the GIIB could form a special body for multilateral actors including MDBs and regional organizations to enhance coordination between existing infrastructure initiatives around the world.

To succeed, the GIIB would need a clearly defined mission. One priority would be sustainable infrastructure. Making the wrong investments during post-pandemic recovery could lock countries into carbon-intensive development paths for decades to come. Aligning investment with climate goals would also be a key task for the new bank.

Another top priority would be inclusive connectivity, in particular, closing the "digital divide." As discussed above, the pandemic has spurred digitalization and online forms of work, study, and business. However, 3.7 billion people still lack Internet access.[8] The GIIB could take a lead in digital infrastructure financing—an area that accounts for only around 1% of total Multilateral Development Bank (MDB) commitments at present.[9]

The third priority would be mobilizing private capital. With public finances limited in the wake of COVID-19, innovative financing models are needed to incentivize private sector involvement. This is something the AIIB is already focusing on, with a goal to boost the share of private financing to 50% by 2030.

---

[8] https://www.weforum.org/agenda/2020/04/coronavirus-covid-19-pandemic-digital-divide-int ernet-data-broadband-mobbile/.

[9] https://www.aiib.org/en/policies-strategies/operational-policies/digital-infrastructure-strategy/. content/_download/Full-DISA-Report_final-with-Appendix-2020-01-10.pdf.

The new GIIB could play an important role in the "networked multilateralism" of Global Governance 2.0 and would be designed to complement existing MDBs, not compete with them. The AIIB has pursued a collaborative model and most of its projects have been co-financed with other MDBs. As a global bank, it could further develop this model and find new ways to co-finance, share expertise, and tap synergies with other organizations. This collaborative role has grown more important with the proliferation of integration arrangements at the national and regional levels. At present, these don't always join up well. The GIIB could serve as a multilateral platform to enable long-term planning and coordination so that intra- and inter-regional connectivity can be enhanced more efficiently.

# 4  Conclusion

In the first half of the twentieth century, in the absence of effective global governance mechanisms, unchecked forces of fragmentation, economic hardship, and polarization led to two devastating world wars. To prevent this from happening again, after the Second World War, countries from around the world came together at Bretton Woods and other landmark conferences to build a new system of global governance that would promote international cooperation, stability, and peace and prosperity.

Today, like after the Second World War, the world faces major challenges, not only in the short-term to recover from the pandemic but also in the long-term to overcome global threats like climate change, which no country can solve alone. As we emerge from COVID-19, there is a unique opportunity for a long-overdue "Bretton Woods 2.0" moment to rethink global governance and forge multilateral institutions that better reflect realities of the post-pandemic world.

Global Governance 2.0 needs to be more inclusive and geared to twenty-first-century problems like climate change, infectious diseases, and addressing inequality by boosting free trade, overcoming the global infrastructure gap, and closing the digital divide. China too faces challenges, with pressures at home as well as questions about how other countries will respond to its rise. But it is in the interest of both China and other countries that the world's most populous country, and soon-to-be largest economy, play a leading role in shaping the next iteration of global governance. China can, and should, help lead by supporting the update and strengthening of existing institutions. In addition, China should be proactively participating in forward-looking regional initiatives. And in an even broader sense, China should be drawing on its knowledge as the longest continuous civilization in the world and using these strengths to propose its own solutions to pressing global issues.

**Huiyao Wang** is the Founder and President of Center for China and Globalization (CCG), a think tank ranked among top 100 think tanks in the world. He is also Dean of the Institute of Development Studies of Southwestern University of Finance and Economics of China, Vice Chairman of China Association for International Cooperation and a Director of Chinese People's Institute of

Foreign Affairs. He is currently a steering committee member of Paris Peace Forum and an advisory board member of Duke Kunshan University. He served as an expert for World Bank, IOM and ILO. He pursued his Ph.D. studies at University of Western Ontario and University of Manchester. He was a Senior Fellow at Harvard Kennedy School and a Visiting Fellow of Brookings Institute. His books in English include: *Globalizing China* (2012); *China Goes Global* (2016); the *Handbook on China and Globalization* (2019); and the *Globalization of Chinese Enterprises* (2020).

**Open Access** This chapter is licensed under the terms of the Creative Commons Attribution-NonCommercial-NoDerivatives 4.0 International License (http://creativecommons.org/licenses/by-nc-nd/4.0/), which permits any noncommercial use, sharing, distribution and reproduction in any medium or format, as long as you give appropriate credit to the original author(s) and the source, provide a link to the Creative Commons license and indicate if you modified the licensed material. You do not have permission under this license to share adapted material derived from this chapter or parts of it.

The images or other third party material in this chapter are included in the chapter's Creative Commons license, unless indicated otherwise in a credit line to the material. If material is not included in the chapter's Creative Commons license and your intended use is not permitted by statutory regulation or exceeds the permitted use, you will need to obtain permission directly from the copyright holder.

# Policies to Create Public Health and Humanitarian Governance Reform

# Our Conflict-Ridden Globe and How to Win a Better Future for a Globalized World

Peter Maurer

**Abstract** Nearly *160 years ago, the International Committee for the Red Cross (ICRC) was founded.* Together with the *Red Crescent Movement*, both have wanted to combine mitigating measures for victims with respect for norms, principles and policies protecting civilians. *All the signs today point to global chronic instability.* This is driven by *unresolved global and regional power competition; fragmentation and proliferation of nations; marginalization and stigmatization of populations in the aftermath of wars* and slow, or *non-existent, post-war reconstruction.* In early 2021 the *ICRC has identified around 90 ongoing armed conflicts.* There is an urgent need to build on the experiences of the past few decades and forge innovative responses: (1) *Putting human security at the center of our concerns* and reconciling humanitarian, security, stability and peace-building agendas. (2) *Engaging in quiet but robust dialogue with the armed actors* of today's conflicts. (3) *Identifying humanitarian issues that can build minimal trust between the parties to break cycles of violence.* And (4) *striving for new forms of diverse partnerships to find a way through political stalemates.* When discussing the political, security and strategic issues of concern to the world, it is urgent to keep human security as our focus. Without human security, we risk chronic instability and cycles of violence without end.

**Keywords** International Committee for the Red Cross (ICRC) · Red Crescent Movement · Global chronic instability · Unresolved global and regional power competition · Fragmentation and proliferation of nations · Marginalization and stigmatization of populations · Non-existent post-war reconstruction · ICRC has identified around 90 ongoing armed conflicts · Putting human security at the center · Engaging in quiet but robust dialogue with the armed actors · Humanitarian issues can build minimal trust between the parties to break cycles of violence · Striving for new forms of diverse partnerships to find a way through political stalemates

P. Maurer (✉)
The International Committee of the Red Cross (ICRC), Geneva, Switzerland

© The Author(s) 2021
H. Wang and A. Michie (eds.), *Consensus or Conflict?*, China and Globalization,
https://doi.org/10.1007/978-981-16-5391-9_12

# 1   COVID-19 Has Been a Catalyst for a More Fragile World

As the President of ICRC, the question I am most often asked in interviews is: "What are the concerns that keep you up at night?"

My greatest concern is not one single issue or place, but the "death by a thousand cuts" inflicted upon too many people in conflict zones over too many years.

All the signs today point to chronic instability. This is driven by global and regional power competitions; fragmentation and proliferation of actors; marginalization and stigmatization of populations in the aftermath of wars and slow; or non-existent, reconstruction after wars.

In early 2021, ICRC identified around 90 ongoing armed conflicts. Some have lasted for decades without political solutions, such as Afghanistan. Other conflicts feature more intensified forms of asymmetric violence such as in Burkina Faso. Some of the trends we are observing include:

- Wars are lasting longer than they did two decades ago. The ICRC's early work focused on short-term emergency situations. However, over the years our involvement has become more long term. ICRC's ten largest operations are in protracted armed conflicts, some lasting for decades.
- Wars are increasingly fought in densely populated urban areas, such as the Gaza Strip, Mogadishu, Mosul or Idlib. However, the weapons used are often designed for open battlefields. Weapons with explosive charges and large blast areas, such as artillery and rocket launchers, can mean the risk of civilian casualties is high. Urban conflicts inflict long-term damage, or entirely destroy, the basic infrastructure including the water and electricity supply along with markets, workplaces and schools.
- The root causes of conflicts are becoming increasingly complex and difficult to tackle—they are often a tangled web of politically motivated violence, terrorism, social violence and white-collar crime.
- Armed groups have become more numerous and radical but are also more fragmented. Today, only a third of all conflicts involve two sides, while more than a fifth involves ten or more parties. This makes our core work—namely promoting respect for international humanitarian law and negotiating access to victims—far more complicated.
- These developments are taking place on a stage where longstanding social problems are creating a perfect storm: developmental deficits and injustice, climate change and failed governance at all levels are an expression of these multi-layered threats. You can see the fragility, the deep inequalities and desire for political change in many societies right now through the wave of protests around the globe.

The global pandemic has been an additional accelerating force of existing fragilities.

Health systems, like those in Yemen, were already operating at less than 50% capacity of what was needed. As countries shifted their focus to address COVID-19, other health issues were neglected—from childhood vaccinations to the treatment of chronic diseases and mental health services.

The three pieces of preventative advice—"wash your hands; keep your distance from others; stay at home"—was irreconcilable in the displacement camps and the prisons where the ICRC works, places where clean water is scarce, overcrowding a way of life and home a distant memory for the millions of long-term displaced.

As economic crises hit communities, those on the edges are pushed further behind. Discrimination and ostracization are daily realities for millions of people. Exclusion occurs at multiple levels:

- People are locked out of economic participation, or education.
- Others are excluded in the name of punishment—those accused of committing terrorist acts, detained without judicial process, those perceived to be affiliated with the enemy, including families of foreign fighters.

A desire for revenge may be understandable when years of conflict and atrocities have divided communities, but history shows that policies and practices that are driven by short-term considerations and stigmatize parts of the population work against long-term stability.

## 2   A Renewed Partnership for Respect

It is clear that we need to do things differently.

Our decades of experience tell us that a focus on security without a focus on the human dimension of conflict is in fact no security at all.

The ICRC was founded almost 160 years ago, and from the very beginning, the ICRC has been about much more than the delivery of emergency aid. Humanitarian assistance is necessary to help people survive, but not enough to break a vicious cycle: changing belligerents' behavior to prevent further violence and violations of norms and to bring normality back to societies is essential.

This is not wishful thinking. Policies and behaviors that accord with International Humanitarian Law (IHL) and humanitarian action are practical ways to leave vicious cycles behind and take pathways to peace. Civilian populations must not become the hostages of political and security disagreements.

That's why I am proposing today a renewed and re-energized partnership of engagement through which we can work together to turn the tide.

What would such a partnership look like?

# 3 Neutral, Independent and Impartial Humanitarian

Neutral, independent and impartial humanitarian work and its contribution to stability is a critical building block for such a partnership.

For centuries, societies have known that there must be limits to the violence that is inflicted on another side because of the lasting divisions that can be difficult to heal. International humanitarian law is built on longstanding customary norms and rules to ensure there is a minimum of humanity.

Even in the deadliest of conflicts the ICRC, as a neutral intermediary, sees how shared humanitarian objectives can help parties find common ground, whether through exchanges of prisoners, evacuation of the wounded, cross-line humanitarian activities or the respectful exchange of human remains.

The ICRC is called on to facilitate these mutual trust-building measures. In October 2020, in what UN Special Envoy Martin Griffiths described as an "air-lift of hope", we facilitated the return of more than 1,000 people detained in relation to the conflict in Yemen. The release operation was the result of two years of talks and many years of trust-building with the parties, building on the Stockholm Agreement of late 2018. There is hope that with enough confidence-building measures such as this could pave the way for progress on a wider peace agreement.

Front-line humanitarian action can be a stabilizing factor to hold back development losses. For example, in Syria, as the war shifted into a new phase, we adopted a two-track approach—providing food and shelter to displaced populations while also working in more stable areas to repair water and electricity infrastructure so that people will have basic services when they return. We also ramped up our microeconomic initiatives to prepare the way for a return to regular economic life.

Let there be no doubt that professional humanitarian work extends far beyond delivering bags of food. There are critical skills involved in negotiating access and acceptance and navigating political and societal tensions. The principle of impartiality means we must first look at those who are most in need, most vulnerable and hardest to reach.

It is difficult to imagine former enemies living as neighbors. But we must ask ourselves: what can be done so that people, often women and children, have hopes for the future rather than wait to be molded into the fighters of tomorrow? Boys, without education, health or a chance in life can—and have—grown up to become men with guns.

For instance, with approval from Iraqi authorities, the ICRC is taking steps to help groups of women and children return to their communities. The process is as important as the result. Through community mediation, we work with community leaders to help foster acceptance of their return. We help both the returnees and the existing community to rebuild and to set up microeconomic initiatives. This broad approach is vital for social repair: a small income can protect returnees falling into destitution or homelessness that could lead to further ostracization. Our aims, always, are to reduce points of friction, in the absence of which, communities can begin to heal themselves.

The ICRC is also working hard in many contexts to find answers for families of missing people who are desperately searching for news. The issue of missing people haunts many regions—and is one of the most critical for reconciliation. We estimate that it affects millions: our staff are overwhelmed by mothers asking for their sons, husbands searching for their wives.

It is an issue that can leave deep scars in communities, but it is also one where parties can reach mutual agreements on humanitarian grounds to share information or allow the return of remains.

Despite the clear contribution of humanitarians to alleviating suffering, laying the groundwork for stabilization, humanitarian work remains severely underfunded. This is compounded today as the COVID-19 pandemic sees some donor states reallocate funds to domestic issues. The truth is that this year, for ICRC's many operations, like those in Iraq and Afghanistan, are underfunded. These shortfalls come at a time when we see people's needs skyrocketing and economic crises looming.

## 4 New Pathways for Humanitarian Action

Conflict dynamics over the last few decades have severely destabilized whole regions, and it seems unlikely that humanitarian action can be financed in the future by transferring money from only a few states to humanitarian organizations.

While serious discussions on burden-sharing, enlarging the donor base and strengthening local actors are necessary, we need a re-imagined approach.

Given the huge financial and innovative capacity in regions like Asia, new and more innovative forms of assisting people should start here:

- Today, it is better to help affected populations through income-generating activities than by making them "beneficiaries", dependent on traditional aid.
- In many places, it is better to replace aid delivered by trucks with cash transfers to those in need, thereby also preserving people's independence and agency.
- It is more important to build on the potential of the digital economy to do needs assessments for people than to design humanitarian action as the low-tech and low-quality end of assistance. Telemedicine can help reach remote areas; big data analysis allows for sharper assessment of needs; virtual training can teach soldiers how to comply with IHL in real combat situations and science enables us to deliver better orthotic and prosthetic services to those affected by violence and conflict.
- Creating new financial instruments based on impact philanthropy and impact investment can fill an important gap today, which will not be addressed by traditional forms of finance.

In all these areas, we have taken a leading role in the humanitarian sector over the past few years. It is also our hope to bring high-tech solutions to low-tech and unstable countries to achieve greater stability for individuals and whole communities.

## 5 Innovation for Improved Action Scale

There is also a need for increased innovation in the ways in which we deliver humanitarian service. While the ICRC may not have labeled it as "innovation", throughout its 156-year history, ICRC delegates have sought to diagnose problems creatively and improve practice and methods; for example, over a century ago, by creating new treaties in response to the first aerial bombings and chemical weapons attacks in the First World War, or by running international competitions to source the best ideas to perfect the design of stretchers and field hospitals.

Today, digital technologies have the potential to revolutionize the way we work, such as using big data for analysis of people's needs. This initiative allows us to better anticipate conflict dynamics, migratory flows and people's needs, and therefore to deliver a more targeted response.

This is done with full knowledge and awareness of the risks. This is crucial as our mandate to protect victims means that we handle more sensitive data than other organizations. We are currently working with private companies and governments to future-proof and ensure the security of our databases, which contain extremely sensitive data.

At the same time, we are building our own data protection mechanisms, and ICRC is the only humanitarian organization that is a member of the Center for Digital Trust at the Ecole Polytechnique Fédérale de Lausanne (EPFL).

The ICRC is also investing heavily in digitizing our humanitarian services: high-tech facial recognition software is helping us to put more families separated by war back in touch. Credit Suisse, as a member of our Corporate Support Group, financially supports the digitalization of family reunification services.

We also need innovative approaches to produce humanitarian products. In cooperation with EPFL, we have developed a new prosthesis for amputees that are not only functionally better but also more cost-efficient.

For the ICRC, cooperation is a crucial aspect of preparing for future challenges. We know that humanitarian solutions are often more effective when they draw on different sectors, approaches and skills, and involve private and public authorities, state bodies and civil society, as well as scientific and practice-oriented organizations. We, therefore, strive to cooperate in numerous areas, including health, biomedicine, energy, water, construction, the logistics supply chain, environmental issues, IT and communications.

The humanitarian challenges that lie ahead are enormous as needs are spiking and capacities to deliver are not matching. Improving what we do by harnessing new technologies and embracing digital transformation is only one thing. We are undoubtedly at the beginning of a new area, in which we will need to adapt our approach in response to people's shifting needs. It will be a long journey for which we need many partners to join us.

## 6 Response of the International System

The complexity of the issues requires a functioning international system: a system in which states, rather than making empty promises, work together to agree on rules and practical steps forward.

We should also recognize that the future for consensus-building must be not only multi-lateral but also multi-stakeholder, with actors from across sectors coming together to address social issues, rather than to secure political wins.

We are seeing what new platforms can achieve, such as the COVAX alliance, which is bringing together actors from across sectors to work on equitable vaccine delivery.

New forms of partnerships will be critical if we hope to end political stalemates both regionally and globally.

Over the last few decades, we have seen that what happens in a region has an impact on global affairs, and vice versa. From the Israeli–Palestinian conflict and controversial interpretations of the Geneva Conventions over occupation, use of force or terrorism, to the treatment of detainees, the use of chemical weapons or the special cruelty of the fighting in Syria and Iraq—the interplay between regional and global issues is obvious.

It is also true on a more positive note: as recently as last year, the decades-old search for tens of thousands of people who went missing in the Iran–Iraq War and the Gulf War brought—under the leadership of Kuwait—a consensual resolution before the Security Council. Moreover, the resolution recognized IHL, as a key instrument for healing the wounds of war and making pathways to reconciliation.

## 7 Engaging with Actors of Influence

Across the world, the ICRC works hard to build relations with all parties to armed conflicts and those who influence them. Our dialogue aims to secure respect for the laws protecting people in conflict and acceptance for neutral and independent humanitarian action. We also explore opportunities to act as a neutral intermediary and to build belligerents' trust.

Across the world, the ICRC is reaching out to religious circles and schools of thought to better understand the compatibility of the rules governing war and the use of force with religious laws. We are sharing best practices regarding the laws of military operations and the decision-making process in combat and law enforcement operations.

Our lessons learned from working with more than 130 armed forces around the world bring together best practices for protecting and assisting civilians. They are there to be discussed and incorporated into armed forces' training, doctrine, ground rules and practice.

We have identified several key challenges critical for humanitarian action, in particular: how to deal with security and terrorism, how to engage with non-state armed groups, and how to carry out humanitarian action in the context of partnered, proxy or alliance warfare.

## 8  Support Relationships in Armed Conflict

Today, over a third of non-international armed conflicts involve coalitions of states and/or non-state armed groups. The ICRC has launched a global initiative to work with armed forces and other stakeholders to identify practical measures that will improve the protection of civilians and those *hors de combat*.

We are collecting and decontextualizing these lessons so that they can be usefully shared with others.

## 9  Non-state Armed Groups

The ICRC also strives to engage with non-state armed groups. The imperative is clear with the rising number of groups: in fact, more armed groups have emerged in the last seven years than in the previous seven decades. This means there is a significant population—tens of millions of people—living outside the reach of state services and in need of humanitarian aid and protection. The ICRC's dialogue with armed groups is therefore critical.

We engage with more armed groups than any other humanitarian organization in the world, both in terms of the number of groups and the extent of our interaction. In a recent study, we identified 614 armed groups of relevance to our operations around the world. Around half of these groups (296) are located in Africa, while 132 are in the Middle East.

These newly emerging armed groups are for the most part decentralized, with less top-down control, but they collaborate with one another and with states within broader strategic alliances. We follow as closely as possible these coalitions, trying to understand their organizational structure as well, to identify decision-makers and the levers of influence on their behavior.

For example, in 2018, after four years of patient work involving intensive consultation with weapon bearers, the ICRC team in Lebanon managed to persuade 27 armed groups active in the refugee camp of Ein el Helweh to sign commitments to protect health care, which resulted in better access for the refugees to treatment.

In other countries, our knowledge and engagement with armed groups are critical to negotiating access to populations in need, ensuring security for communities and our operations, preparing the ground for exchanges of detainees, and in the search for missing people or access to detention facilities.

## 10    Security and Terrorism

The ICRC is increasingly involved in legal, policy and operational dialogue on finding the acceptable balance between military and security necessities and ensuring people are properly protected under international humanitarian law.

IHL does not pose an undue obstacle to state security. Rather, it offers a framework on dilemmas between humanity and military necessity.

In this regard, the discourse on terrorism deserves a special mention.

The ICRC of course condemns acts of terrorism, whether committed in or outside an armed conflict. Terrorism is anti-humanitarianism. It negates the basic principle of humanity, it goes against the underlying principles and core objectives of IHL.

But in responding to terrorism, IHL strikes a balance between military necessity and considerations of humanity when pursuing a state's security interest.

IHL is there to protect civilian populations affected by terrorism.

Counter-terrorism laws adopted at national, regional and international levels can coexist with IHL and they complement each other, as long as these laws do not generate conflicts of norms and legal confusions, and do not criminalize or unduly restrict humanitarian action.

We realize that in practice there are challenges, which are present in many conflicts and not just in counter-terrorism situations—for instance, distinguishing between fighters and civilians when fighters are hiding among the civilian population. The ICRC has discussions with states around the world on these challenges and seeks to give advice that is as precise as possible and seeks as large as possible a consensus around how to handle some of the difficulties at strategic, tactical and operational levels.

We try to be a pragmatic partner of governments and armed forces, who are confronted with such challenges, rather than a rigid, prescriptive guide. It is through conversation, between weapon bearers and the ICRC, that best practices can be determined and better protection for people affected by conflict and violence can be found.

## 11    China's Potential Contribution in Humanitarianism: A Case for the Belt and Road Initiative

In recent years, China has been championing the Belt and Road Initiative (BRI) as an international public good for many nations that choose to embrace the BRI. In turn, the BRI is equally a platform for China to participate in international governance.

The BRI is about development, and development requires stability and peace. Humanitarian action is contributing to stabilizing societies in some of the most difficult circumstances; it prevents violence to destroy development gains.

That is why I am deeply convinced the BRI should add a humanitarian dimension, which will be an important building-block to deliver on the UN's Sustainable Development Goals (SDGs). I am also certain and know that the ICRC can share its experience and knowledge and bring added value. For instance, the ICRC provides guidance and shares good practices with Chinese companies operating overseas in fragile environments with the aim of strengthening their corporate social responsibility and mitigating the risk of increased instability.

Humanitarian organizations are investing in building systems and vital infrastructure mostly in the most remote and dangerous places. There is clearly a real prospect in engaging with international financial institutions, such as the World Bank, but also with relevant Chinese stakeholders where, for security reasons, development actors are not in a position to invest in infrastructure.

In the BRI context, it is important to recognize the contribution of humanitarian organizations to:

- Uphold the basic humanitarian principles of neutrality, impartiality and independence through their relations with states and non-state actors.
- Contribute, through short and long-term humanitarian assistance, to the stabilization of countries or regions affected by protracted conflicts and therefore provide the conditions for future development.

In today's complex world, more than ever, China has a role to play and will be a part of the search for solutions, especially through innovative infrastructure, digitalization and information technologies.


# 12   Conclusion

Nearly 160 years ago, the ICRC was founded to make professional humanitarianism a force in the service of modern statehood. Instead of handouts for the poor, the International Red Cross and Red Crescent Movements, throughout their histories have wanted to combine mitigating measures for victims with respect to norms, principles and policies protecting civilians.

This remains key to dealing with the complexities of modern, asymmetric and protracted conflicts, but we need to build on the experiences of the past few decades and forge innovative responses, such as:

- Putting human security at the centre of our concerns and reconciling humanitarian, security, stability and peace-building agendas;
- Engaging in quiet but robust dialogue with the armed actors of today's conflict in order to ensure better respect for laws and principles through practical and pragmatic cooperation;
- Identifying humanitarian issues that can build minimal trust between the parties to break cycles of violence

- And striving for new forms of diverse partnerships to find a way through political stalemates.

When discussing the political, security and strategic issues of concern to the world, it is urgent to keep human security as our focus.

Without human security, we risk chronic instability and cycles of violence without end.

**Peter Maurer** is the President of the International Committee of the Red Cross (ICRC). He studied history and international law in Bern, where he was awarded a doctorate. In 2000, he was appointed ambassador and head of the human security division in the political directorate of the Swiss Department of Foreign Affairs in Bern. He was appointed ambassador and permanent representative of Switzerland to the United Nations in New York (2004), Chairman of the Fifth Committee (2009) and Secretary of State for foreign affairs in Bern. Under his leadership, the ICRC carries out humanitarian work in over 80 countries.

**Open Access** This chapter is licensed under the terms of the Creative Commons Attribution-NonCommercial-NoDerivatives 4.0 International License (http://creativecommons.org/licenses/by-nc-nd/4.0/), which permits any noncommercial use, sharing, distribution and reproduction in any medium or format, as long as you give appropriate credit to the original author(s) and the source, provide a link to the Creative Commons license and indicate if you modified the licensed material. You do not have permission under this license to share adapted material derived from this chapter or parts of it.

The images or other third party material in this chapter are included in the chapter's Creative Commons license, unless indicated otherwise in a credit line to the material. If material is not included in the chapter's Creative Commons license and your intended use is not permitted by statutory regulation or exceeds the permitted use, you will need to obtain permission directly from the copyright holder.

# Global Public Health Security: Three Vital Lessons

Yuanli Liu

**Abstract**  Public health and its management have come into very sharp focus due to COVID-19. In this analysis the writer suggests that the COVID-19 pandemic has taught the world both *the vulnerability and power of the human community*. The power is symbolised by the *creation of vaccines in a fraction of the time* that was the norm before 2020. This essay also describes three major lessons that may have important implications for better protecting *global public health security* today and tomorrow. Any open-minded analysis, and serious reflection, on the world's responses to COVID-19 should draw these vital conclusions. In order for the world to stand a better chance of preventing the next public health emergency, such as a new pandemic, all nations must learn how to work together and in the most effective manner. This must include important issues such as *reforms of international health regulations* and *updating of international organisational structures*. It also means we must learn how to *strengthen (not weaken) multilateral mechanisms such as the UN and the WHO*. Of course, any new cooperative spirit must be built on the keen recognition that we are really in this together. That realisation must be extended to *how mankind interacts with all-natural life* in our shared home—the Earth.

**Keywords**  The vulnerability and power of the human communities · Creation of vaccines in a fraction of the time · Global public health security · Reforms of international health regulations · Updating of international organisational structures · Strengthen (not weaken) multilateral mechanisms such as the UN and the WHO · How mankind interacts with all-natural life

Y. Liu (✉)
School of Health Policy and Management, Peking Union Medical College, Beijing, China

© The Author(s) 2021                                                                                                    141
H. Wang and A. Michie (eds.), *Consensus or Conflict?*, China and Globalization,
https://doi.org/10.1007/978-981-16-5391-9_13

# 1 Mankind's Power and Vulnerability

COVID-19 provides a unique collective learning opportunity for all mankind about global public health security. History may very well remember COVID-19 as the pandemic of the twenty-first century.

The spread of viruses does not respect national boundaries and, in a pandemic, no nation is safe until everyone is safe. Therefore, by its very nature, dealing with infectious diseases is always a global issue. In other words, actions or inaction by any one country in a pandemic is bound to have global consequences. In turn, responses to a pandemic by nations in public health terms will have impacts across a range of issues. The bigger the country's relative role in world affairs, the bigger the consequences to international trade.

Moreover, like any other global issue, such as climate change, resolving global public health security issues requires integrated global action. Before well-coordinated global action can be achieved, important issues need to be grasped and a fundamental consensus needs to be built.

As of early 2021, and 12 months since the outbreak of COVID-19, this public health crisis is far from being resolved and has yet to be brought under control in many parts of the world. But, in only one year this pandemic has taught us both how vulnerable and how powerful the human community has become. This essay tries to draw some major lessons that may have important implications for better protecting global public health security today and tomorrow.

# 2 Lesson One: We Are Vulnerable

Wuhan is my hometown. In early January 2020, I was making plans to join my ageing mother for the Chinese Lunar New Year. When this city of 11 million people was locked down on January 23, 2020, I, like many other people, felt uneasy and uncertain. Our concern revolved around thoughts about whether or not the lockdown policy was overkill. After all, descriptions of the illness causing the Wuhan lockdown sounded like a flu-like disease and the total number of confirmed cases amounted to only a little over 400. Nobody at the time, not in our wildest dreams, would have expected this novel disease would turn out to be such a vicious pandemic. The rapid spread of COVID-19 had a huge impact, disrupting the global economy at an unprecedented speed and scale and infecting over 123 million people globally, with a death toll of over 2.7 million and counting.[1] This outcome certainly serves as vivid testimony to the existential threat posted by this novel virus to the whole human community.

The biosecurity issues caused by microbes, such as a virus, possess several important characteristics. First, a virus is not a threat to all life on a global scale. The reality is that the virus creates an inter-species war on the planet, which is a different threat than that posed by 'world wars' of the past. This is not a war that is fought over

---

[1] WHO Coronavirus (COVID-19) Dashboard (n.d.).

national borders, but a battle in which all the countries of the world are faced with the same enemy.

Second, this threat is not a small probability event. Our world has witnessed an increasing number of novel infectious diseases in recent decades.[2] There is compelling evidence that the increasing invasion of human activity into the natural world is connected to the rise of infectious diseases. The result is that animals, like bats, whose habitats had remained apart from humans for millennia, or even millions of years, now have direct contact with people. Viruses that have no effect on bats, or other species, have proven deadly when entering the bodies of humans. This trend provides a vital lesson in the vulnerability of mankind. When COVID-19 is finally over, which is possible with the rapid rollout of vaccination programmes around the world and the emergence of 'herd immunity', the world should, and must be, better prepared for the next novel infectious disease.

There is a big risk that global leaders may shy away from this need for vital preparation once there is 'herd immunity'. One reason for this is the natural human reaction to bury the pain of COVID-19 in the past. People will want messages of hope that promise a return to economic prosperity; they will not welcome messages that project fear of the threat of another pandemic and the need to prepare. This brings back memories of the challenge faced by President Roosevelt in the USA in 1933 when there was widespread fear about the continuous bouts of economic depression. As Roosevelt spelt out his plan for recovery he won support by saying it best—'the only thing we have to fear is fear itself'.[3]

## 3   Lesson Two: We Are Powerful

In his seminal book *Social Conquest of the Earth*, E.O. Wilson suggested that the fundamental factor affecting the chance of a particular species such as ants and humans to successfully survive and thrive lies in the capability to work together.[4] It follows, then, we are powerful because humans are a collaborative bunch. Paradoxically, COVID-19 unveiled both the best and worst sides of human beings. As an example, let us compare the public health performance of the world's two largest economies (Fig. 1).

No nation in modern times has the experience of dealing with a disease like COVID-19, but despite being an inexperienced first responder, China managed to bring COVID-19 under control within two months after the outbreak. As of March

---

[2] Bloom and Cadarette (2019).

[3] World Affairs (1933).

[4] Liveright (2012).

29, 2021, out of China's 1.4 billion people, there were 90,159 confirmed cases and 4,636 deaths. These numbers are in stark contrast to the data in the USA, which despite having a smaller population and bigger economy, has had far more deaths and infections (Fig. 1).

How can this happen and what are the underlying reasons for this paradox? Between 16th February 2020 and 24th February 2020 a survey was conducted in China by a WHO-China Joint Mission. It consisted of 25 national and international experts from China, Germany, Japan, Korea, Nigeria, Russia, Singapore, the USA and the World Health Organisation (WHO). The Joint Mission was headed by Dr. Bruce Aylward of the WHO and Dr. Liang Wannian of the People's Republic of China. In its published report, the Joint Mission described China's response to COVID-19 as consisting of three phases (see Fig. 2).

After the detection of a cluster of pneumonia cases of unknown aetiology in Wuhan, the Chinese government launched a national emergency response. Prevention and control measures were implemented rapidly in three main phases, with two important events defining those phases.

First, COVID-19 was included in the statutory report of Class B infectious diseases and border health quarantine infectious diseases on January 20, 2020. This marked the transition from the initial partial control approach to the comprehensive adoption of various control measures in accordance with the law.

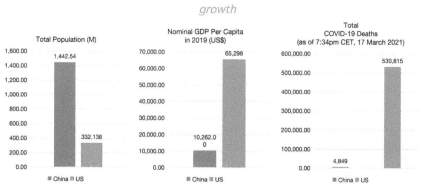

Fig. 1 The public health performance of the world's two largest economies during COVID-19[5,6,7]

---

[5] WHO Coronavirus (COVID-19) Dashboard (n.d.).

[6] United Nations Population Division (n.d.).

[7] GDP per capita (current US$) (n.d.).

The second event was the State Council's issuing, on the 8th of February 2020, of 'The Notice on Orderly Resumption of Production and Resuming Production in Enterprises'. This indicated that China's national epidemic control work had entered a stage of general prevention and control together with the restoration of normal social and economic operations. The main reason why China was able to bring this public health crisis quickly under control was that China vigorously implemented traditional public health measures such as social distancing. This was the first key lesson China learned.

Traditional public health measures for controlling infectious diseases include isolation and quarantine, which are far easier said than done, especially at the early stage of an epidemic. On January 23, 2020, for the first time in the human history of epidemics, a mega city like Wuhan, with more than 11 million residents, was locked down. This lockdown was the most extreme form of social distancing in both scale and speed. When this unprecedentedly strict lockdown policy was implemented, many people started questioning the necessity of taking such an action because the number of confirmed cases in Wuhan, at the time of the lockdown was only a little over 400. In addition, the lockdown decision was taken prior to any scientific understanding of the transmissive power of this new virus. But the Wuhan lockdown turned out to be the most visionary and courageous decision in the fight against the COVID-19 pandemic, not only in China but also in the world at large. The fact is that Wuhan was the epicentre of COVID-19. If Wuhan, with its population of 11 million people, had not been locked down on January 23, 2020, it could have been the catalyst for

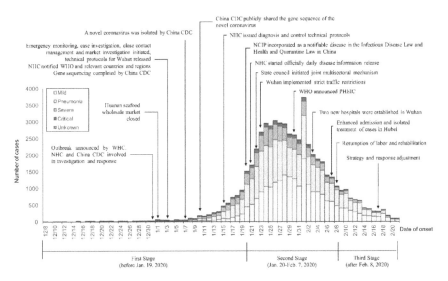

**Fig. 2** Three phases of China's response to COVID-19[8]

---

[8] World Health Organization (2020).

a catastrophe. The reason for this is that January 24 was the day before the Chinese Lunar New Year holiday. In China, millions of people travel during this period to be reunited with their families. If Wuhan had not been locked down, the massive movement of people would have triggered a vast and rapid spread of the virus with disastrous consequences. Out of the total 90,000+ confirmed cases of COVID-19 in China, around 63% were found and treated in Wuhan.

According to research studies published in international peer-reviewed journals, the Wuhan lockdown helped avert millions of infections and hundreds of thousands of deaths. Based in part on data drawn from Wuhan, an Imperial College London Team published estimates of the impact of the lockdown in Wuhan. The analysis showed that a combination of home isolation of suspected cases, home quarantine of those living in the same household as people with suspected cases, and social distancing of the elderly and other high-risk groups may have reduced peak healthcare demand by two-thirds and deaths by half.

Looking back, the world owes Wuhan a debt of gratitude for its sacrifice during the lockdown. The cooperation of the 11 million residents of Wuhan and the thousands of people who rushed there to help greatly reduce the spread of COVID-19 in China and to the rest of the world. The people of Wuhan, and those that helped them get through this difficult time, made enormous sacrifices during the lockdown. But the greatest contribution was that it gave more time to other regions and countries to get ready. In turn, that offered the potential to minimise the global impact of COVID-19.

China also learned that solidarity is essential.

Infectious diseases do not respect geographic boundaries, and thus with any pandemic like COVID-19, we are all in this together. Helping others, especially the emerging epicentres of the crisis, is helping ourselves. Lessons also were learned in other nations. A characteristic of a virus like COVID-19 is that the outbreak comes in waves. In response to this pattern, the Governor of New York State, Andrew Cuomo, called for a rolling deployment strategy,[9] which was exactly what China did, and it was done early and well. Soon after the lockdown in Wuhan, there was a rolling programme of vigorous testing and tracing. This was done by over 1,800 epidemic teams. They found that the number of confirmed cases in Wuhan increased rapidly, which quickly overwhelmed the local healthcare system. As a reaction to these trends, the Chinese government sent over 300 medical teams to Wuhan, including more than 42,000 doctors and nurses. In addition, 16 temporary hospitals were built within a matter of weeks. The objective was to admit all patients with mild symptoms and asymptomatic patients of COVID-19 so they would not spread the virus in their homes and communities. During the next stage, patients who became severely ill could then be quickly transferred to designated hospitals equipped with ICUs. When Wuhan was reopened on April 8, 2020, more than 60,000 patients had already been treated and recovered. This kind of achievement could not have been possible without a nationally coordinated strategy, national mobilisation of resources and aid that came from around China and abroad.

---

[9] Gov. Cuomo: Feds need to consider 'rolling deployment' focused on NY first (2020).

Last but not the least, China, as well as other countries, learned a crucial lesson about the power of humanity during the COVID-19 pandemic and how science can help and save humanity.

When SARS hit China in 2002 it took more than two months to identify the pathogen. In 2020, with COVID-19, just two weeks after the central health authority in China was alerted, the novel coronavirus COVID-19 was identified by Chinese scientists. The information on the complete genetic sequence of the virus was shared with the world on January 10, 2020.

In addition to virology, new scientific knowledge and the power of technology is constantly being developed and implemented, including testing and tracing, treatment guidelines as well as in drugs and vaccines development. Scientists in different countries have developed COVID-19 vaccines at unprecedented speeds. This included scientists from the USA, China, the UK and Russia, and this scientific endeavour serves as another reminder of how powerful we as a human community can be if the best minds are put to work.

## 4   Lesson Three: We Are Vulnerable Because We Are Powerful

While China was engrossed fighting to stem the spread of the COVID-19 virus, the WHO sounded its highest alarm on January 30, 2020, declaring a 'public health emergency of international concern', or PHEIC. This alerted the world that a pandemic might be imminent.[10] With each PHEIC, the WHO advises governments on how to deal with the emergency.

Most importantly, on January 30, 2020, the WHO Director-General Tedros Adhanom Ghebreyesus stressed that, 'It is still possible to interrupt the virus spread, provided that countries put in place strong measures to detect the disease early, isolate and treat cases, trace contacts and promote social-distancing measures'. But governments around the world chose to ignore this piece of vital advice from the WHO and looking back the human cost of this ignorance has been horrendous and incalculable.

On March 28, 2020, Richard Horton, editor of the well-known medical journal *Lancet* criticised the UK government for its failure to heed the advice of the WHO writing, 'The scale of anger and frustration is unprecedented, and COVID-19 is the cause. The UK Government's Contain-Delay-Mitigate-Research strategy failed. It failed, in part, because Ministers did not follow the WHO's advice to 'test, test, test' every suspected case. They did not isolate or quarantine. They did not contact trace. These basic principles of public health and infectious disease control were ignored, for reasons that remain opaque.'

In the USA, the government failed to roll out testing nationwide until late February and it only banned some travel from China. There was a similar approach by many nations outside of China. By mid-March, the virus had spread around the world.

---

[10] World Health Organization News (2020).

As an example of best practices, China's response to novel infectious diseases like COVID-19 shows that no matter how infectious and vicious, they can be effectively controlled—even in the absence of pharmaceutical solutions. Had the USA been equally decisive and successful, it could have saved more than 500,000 lives (Fig. 1).

Some segments of the human community have proven to be powerful leaders in confronting this global public health crisis of COVID-19 head-on and are sharing important lessons learned. It is deeply unfortunate that others turned out to be powerful saboteurs; they became spreaders of a social virus that spread misinformation, discrimination and dirty politics.[11] The result was that powerful destructive human forces were unleashed, the opportunity costs of which can be measured by the excessive and avoidable human loss and serious socioeconomic setbacks for all of mankind.

Any open-minded analysis and serious reflection on global responses to COVID-19 draw these vital conclusions. In order for the world to stand a better chance of preventing the next public health emergency, such as a new pandemic, all nations must learn how to work together and in the most effective manner. This must include important issues such as reforms of international health regulations and the structure of international organisations. That means we must learn how to strengthen (not weaken) multilateral mechanisms such as the UN and the WHO. Of course, any new cooperative spirit must be built on the keen recognition that we are really in this together. That realisation must be extended to how mankind interacts with the natural world on this planet, which is our shared home.

The evolution of the Earth is divided by geologists according to marked shifts in the state of the planet. Recent global environmental changes suggest that Earth may have entered a new human-dominated geological epoch, known as the Anthropocene Epoch. Since the 1950s the influence of human activity on the Earth system has increased markedly. This period of 'great acceleration' is marked by a major expansion in the impact of mankind on the planet. For example, the human population in 1950 was 2.5 billion, but by 2020 that figure had more than tripled to 7.7 billion. In that same time period, there have been large changes in natural processes, the development of new materials from minerals to plastics to persistent organic pollutants and inorganic compounds. It is little wonder that the impact of humans on the Earth has been the catalyst for global climate change.[12]

An increasing body of literature points out that as the Arctic warms, 'zombie' viruses and microbes are rising from the thawing ground. The frozen earth that covers much of the Arctic is home to growing microbial communities. For centuries, they have lain dormant, barely active or completely suspended, subsisting on minuscule pockets of water squeezed between the ice. With the Arctic warming at two to five times the global average, those pockets are becoming pools, rivulets, rivers, puddles and ponds. The Arctic is waking up, and the microscopic organisms embedded in the land might be coming back to life.[13]

---

[11] World Health Organization (2020).

[12] Nature (2015).

[13] The Narwhal (2020).

These trends are just one example of why there is an urgent need for global collaboration to embrace evidence-based etiological modelling of novel infectious diseases. In turn, this would have important implications for expanding our horizons in our global effort for better predicting, preventing and controlling epidemics in the future. Moreover, adopting the Anthropocene perspective may help break the pernicious cycle that asserts that humans are just passive observers of Earth's functioning.

To a large extent, the future of the only place where life is known to exist is being determined by the actions of humans. Global public health security depends on well-coordinated global actions. Divided, we are vulnerable. United, we are powerful and hopeful.

## References

Bloom DE, Cadarette D (2019) Infectious disease threats in the 21st century: strengthening the global response. Front Immunol 10:549

GDP per capita (current US$) (n.d.) Data. https://data.worldbank.org/indicator/NY.GDP.PCAP.CD. Accessed 18 Mar 2021

Gov. Cuomo: Feds need to consider 'rolling deployment' focused on NY first (2020), March 26. https://shelterislandreporter.timesreview.com/2020/03/26/gov-cuomo-feds-need-to-consider-rolling-deployment-focused-on-ny-first/. Accessed 18 Mar 2021

Liveright (2012) The social conquest of earth. Accessed 18 Mar 2021

Nature (2015) Defining the Anthropocene, March 11. https://www.nature.com/articles/nature14258. Accessed 18 Mar 2021

The Narwhal (2020) Will the next great pandemic come from the permafrost?, Apr 10. https://the narwhal.ca/next-great-pandemic-permafrost/. Accessed 18 Mar 2021

United Nations Population Division (n.d.) Department of Economic and Social Affairs https://www.un.org/en/development/desa/population/publications/database/index.asp. Accessed 18 Mar 2021

WHO Coronavirus (COVID-19) Dashboard (n.d.) https://covid19.who.int. Accessed 18 Mar 2021

World Affairs (1933) Inaugural address, March 4. http://www.jstor.org/stable/20662229. Accessed 18 Mar 2021

World Health Organization (2020) Report of the WHO China joint mission on coronavirus disease 2019 (COVID-19), 16–24 February. https://www.who.int/docs/default-source/coronavir use/who-china-joint-mission-on-covid-19-final-report.pdf. Accessed 18 Mar 2021

World Health Organization News (2020) Statement on the second meeting of the International Health Regulations (2005) Emergency Committee regarding the outbreak of novel coronavirus (2019-nCoV), January 30. https://www.who.int/news/item/30-01-2020-statement-on-the-sec ond-meeting-of-the-international-health-regulations-(2005)-emergency-committee-regarding-the-outbreak-of-novel-coronavirus-(2019-ncov). Accessed 18 Mar 2021

**Yuanli Liu** is Professor and Founding Dean of the School of Health Policy and Management at Peking Union Medical College. From 2013 to 2020, Dr. Liu served as founding Dean of the School of Public Health at the Chinese Academy of Medical Sciences & Peking Union Medical College. Dr. Liu has been closely involved in China's major healthcare reforms and development initiatives as an applied health policy researcher since 1993. He currently also serves as a member of the State Councilor' Office, the State Council Healthcare Reform Expert Committee. He is also President of the Chinese Aging Well Association, Vice Chairman of the National

Commission on Health Promotion and Education. From 1993 to 2013, Dr. Liu worked at Harvard University in the area of global health. He has consulted for many international organisations including the WHO, the World Bank and Fortune 500 companies.

**Open Access** This chapter is licensed under the terms of the Creative Commons Attribution-NonCommercial-NoDerivatives 4.0 International License (http://creativecommons.org/licenses/by-nc-nd/4.0/), which permits any noncommercial use, sharing, distribution and reproduction in any medium or format, as long as you give appropriate credit to the original author(s) and the source, provide a link to the Creative Commons license and indicate if you modified the licensed material. You do not have permission under this license to share adapted material derived from this chapter or parts of it.

The images or other third party material in this chapter are included in the chapter's Creative Commons license, unless indicated otherwise in a credit line to the material. If material is not included in the chapter's Creative Commons license and your intended use is not permitted by statutory regulation or exceeds the permitted use, you will need to obtain permission directly from the copyright holder.

# What Is the Right Way to Structure Global Health? The Case for Radical New Organisations and Thinking

Lord Jim O'Neill

**Abstract** *COVID-19 has exposed deep weakness in the governance of global health.* Lessons can be learned for the reform of global public health from the *'Global Review Into Antimicrobial Resistance (AMR)'* that was created by Prime Minister David Cameron in the UK in 2014. The core problem of AMR is both a supply and demand problem. From a supply perspective, *there is a lack of development of new useful antimicrobials.* Fundamentally, the financial returns are not perceived to be suitably high for complex path of bringing new antibiotics to market. From a demand perspective, *modern society has an excessive use of existing antibiotics*, which is causing many of them to lose their ability to work as the microbes adapt and mutate to evade the effectiveness of treatments. The abuse is not just in humans. In many parts of the world, most definitely within the US, *the use of antibiotics in animals is higher than in humans.* If a solution to antibiotic abuse cannot be found, then by 2050, there could be as many *as 10 million people a year dying from AMR-related illnesses.* The COVID-19 pandemic has proved that there are *massive economic and financial costs from global health threats* when not met by fast robust actions.

**Keywords** COVID-19 has exposed deep weakness in the governance of global health · 'Global Review Into Antimicrobial Resistance (AMR)' · There is a lack of development of new useful antimicrobials · Modern society has an excessive use of existing antibiotics · The use of antibiotics in animals is higher than in humans · 10 million people a year could die from AMR-related illnesses · Massive economic and financial costs from global health threats

## 1 What Is the Right Way to Structure Global Health?

In trying to answer this question, I immediately think it is important to recall that frequently, future major challenges are often different than the one we are trying to deal with at the moment. In this regard, while it seems quite likely that COVID-19 will not be the last pandemic the world faces, it might well be that through all the

J. O'Neill (✉)
Royal Institute for International Affairs, London, UK

© The Author(s) 2021
H. Wang and A. Michie (eds.), *Consensus or Conflict?*, China and Globalization,
https://doi.org/10.1007/978-981-16-5391-9_14

151

reactive responses to this crisis, it will stand the world, and many parts of it, in much better shape the next time we do face a major global health challenge.

## 2 Lessons Learned from Antibiotic Abuse

However, notwithstanding this observation, I reflect on my own experience of chairing the independent 'Global Review Into Antimicrobial Resistance (AMR)'. I was invited to chair the AMR Review by Prime Minister David Cameron for the government in the UK in 2014. Out of the AMR Review experience, I have a number of ideas that might allow the world to be better placed, especially from an economic and financial perspective.

When I was asked to lead the AMR Review, many observers, not least me, were somewhat surprised that an economist with little formal training in health or science was asked to lead it. By the time I had spent a couple of months in the role, I quickly realised why it had been an imaginative idea, and one that would at least allow the issues to be considered in a different, probably broader framework.

I recall joking with the then UK Chief Medical Officer, Dame Sally Davies, that the specialist health scientists knew so much about AMR—and so it was not clear why anyone was needed to bring more ideas. I did this partially to make it clear that I was going to stick to my own experience and training and analyse the issues from an economic perspective, especially an international one. Which I did, and this is how I will reflect on COVID-19 in this essay.

The core problem of AMR is both a supply and demand problem, when considered in economic terms. From a supply perspective, there is a lack of development of new useful antimicrobials in existence, or useful alternatives such as relevant vaccines or other alternative treatments.

Fundamentally, the financial returns are not perceived to be suitably high for the long and often complex path of bringing new antimicrobials, especially antibiotics to market. Potential producers, usually major pharmaceutical companies, have higher returns on offer from a variety of other products.

From a demand perspective, modern society has an excessive use of existing antibiotics, which is causing many of them to lose their ability to work as the microbes adapt and mutate to evade the effectiveness of treatments. As I have often said, society has to stop wanting to treat antibiotics like sweets or candy. The outcome is that antibiotics are often misused.

One example is in treating viral infections, with sore throats being a particularly good illustration. The abuse is not just in humans. In many parts of the world, most definitely within the USA, and probably China, the use of antibiotics in animals is higher than in humans, and often in the case of animals, the use of antibiotics is inappropriate. It has become a belief that antibiotics are useful for growth promotion and as a health preserving tool in intensive animal farming. The problem has become so acute in some areas, that so-called last in line antibiotics, critical for helping humans fight illness when other antibiotics would not work, are losing their power.

The example of Colistin, and its overuse in cows in China, is a much-discussed recent example. There is a great deal to be done—but, I was glad to note an analytical paper in the *Lancet* in October 2020 titled, 'How China is getting its farmers to kick their antibiotic habit'.

To solve the problem of AMR, we need to try and boost the supply of useful antimicrobials while at the same time reducing the demand. Of course, this simultaneous challenge adds to the complexity, because the potential producers, as in most areas of business, are naturally attracted to selling as much of a product as possible at the highest attainable prices. But what society needs is precisely the contrary when it comes to the role of antimicrobials. What the world needs is a lot of potential supply, but at affordable prices—and not an overuse.

In the middle of this challenge is the reality that in many parts of the developing world there remains a huge challenge of any access, never mind excess. Many of these challenges are pertinent to the current pandemic, which I shall turn to shortly.

One of the major reasons why our AMR Review became so well known is our predictions of millions of human deaths. We suggested that, if a solution to antibiotic abuse could not be found, that by 2050 there could be as many as 10 million people a year dying from AMR-related illnesses. That number was up from around 700,000 deaths we discovered could be identified in 2015. Around a third of these deaths alone would be in the emerging world as a result of drug-resistant TB.

Indeed, this research taught me that one of the major shared threats that Brazil, Russia, India, China and South Africa, the so-called BRICS countries, face is that they all had a major challenge with TB, and therefore drug-resistant TB. This means it would be in the shared interests of the BRICS nations to find new useful drugs or vaccines.

In other spheres of life, illnesses like sepsis and gonorrhoea are already major problems, and if we do not solve this problem, then many treatments that have become common place in our lifetimes, such as hip replacements or eye cataract surgery will become impossible. We simply will not have antibiotics to treat the infections that are a side consequence of such routine operations. Because of all of this, we also showed that the potential accumulated loss of economic activity for the world could be a colossal USD 100 trillion from 2015 through 2050.

Our AMR Review became known for these two numbers alone, potentially 10 million deaths a year and a USD 100 trillion in foregone economic output. We derived 29 different interventions for the world that would ensure this problem would be solved.

A few observers commented that the likely cost of our AMR Review forecasts would not be anything as high as this. We responded by saying that yes, these and similar forecasts are merely forecasts, but it was equally possible that the costs could be higher, potentially much higher.

## 3 The Massive Economic and Financial Costs from Global Health Threats—New Ideas to Offset

One thing that this COVID-19 pandemic has surely proved is that there are massive economic and financial costs from global health threats when not met with fast, robust actions. It is probably the case that global real GDP declined somewhere in the vicinity of 4% in 2020, which is more than four times larger than the decline in 2008.

I think many people now realise the challenges of health are embedded in our economic and financial lives. Because of this reality, here are the major ideas that I consider necessary—although I repeat my opening comment that some aspects of this crisis will probably automatically lead to a more robust system in the future.

One of the biggest economic and financial challenges the world now faces is, apparently, the huge size of debt, especially that of many governments, and with it, what, if anything, to do about it. Most conventional thinkers believe that as soon as our economies are robust enough, governments will have to start tightening fiscal policy through either spending cuts or tax increases, or a combination of both. This might be, indeed, necessary.

But an alternative, more radical and imaginative way of thinking about this, could be a revamp of how we account for government spending. In particular, I believe we might want to split total government spending—past, present and future—into investment spending and consumption, or maintenance and spending.

Investment spending should create future growth especially for the private sector, often with a large multiplier impact. Consumption spending, especially when it is used to maintain systems, does not and should be treated differently. If we want the latter, maybe tax-payers should be prepared to pay more, whereas the former would create growth in the future and might not need to be paid for now.

This is all hugely relevant for a better domestic health system. Too often, and generally from an accounting perspective, health spending is budgeted as one overall system. But how can government investing in support of new antibiotics, vaccines, or diagnostics, or genomics and so on, be regarded as the same as paying the wages and salaries of more doctors and nurses? The former may be central to stopping any future major diseases, while the latter is primarily done to respond to ongoing health management. It is crazy to treat them as the same from an accounting perspective, and this is often why crucial investments that only pay off in the future get postponed, delayed, cancelled or often not approved at all, especially in democracies.

## 4 Reform of Global Agencies—The IMF

Another obvious issue that became clear to me after our AMR Review finished, and is dramatically clearer even now post COVID-19, is the role of the IMF. Generally, since its creation after World War Two, the IMF has sat at the heart of global economic management and for much of the time focused on traditional macroeconomic goals, including the classic macroeconomic challenges of economic growth, inflation, unemployment, and especially, balance of payments stability. It was not until the Asian financial crisis in 1997 that the IMF began to focus on financial sector stability. Of course, as a result of the 2008 financial crisis, and its consequences, the IMF now regards financial stability as a major part of its remit and usefulness.

In more recent years, the IMF has started to engage on aspects of the battle against climate change, not least of which is because of the potential consequences for macroeconomic stability. But talk to senior people at the IMF before this pandemic, about the need for them to opine more about health systems, and they quickly shy away, saying they have neither expertise nor remit. Surely this is ridiculous. If a global pandemic has been responsible for the loss of circa USD 10 trillion to the world economy, how can the IMF not only want, but avoid the need to understand global health? I had previously articulated the need for the IMF to start offering judgement on member country health systems as part of their Article IV series, and I now believe it is unavoidable. The IMF's Article IV is something that financial markets respect, not least because it is also something ratings agencies respect, and by incorporating an opinion about member country health systems would make it a lot more likely that countries would want to start investing more to improve health systems. In this regard, what about how specific decisions might be made about health spending, both within and across countries?

## 5 Government Health Spending—The Need to Revamp Accounting Principles

Once more, thinking as an economist, I default immediately to the distinction between investments and consumption. During the period just prior to accepting the role of chairing the AMR Review from 2014 through 2020, the UK proudly showed that the risks of pandemics and AMR were prominent in its national risk register, something that the country appeared to be admired for around the world.

When it came to the crunch, and walking the walk, as opposed to talking the talk, it did not seem to be especially useful. As is well known, at least during the 2020 period of the pandemic, the UK suffered more than most when it came to lives lost and the economic consequences. There are many reasons, some of which we still are yet to learn, but chief amongst them is that Public Health England (PHE), the body established to identify best practices, was clearly not up to scratch when it came to the vital role of testing our citizens for COVID-19 and the whole test and trace system failed dramatically to help ward off the spread in early 2020, which on many levels the UK has been trying to make up for ever since.

And while the UK has seemingly excelled so far in both the discovery of new vaccines and based on early 2021 evidence, their rollout, the financing that the UK commits to these vital aspects of the solution are generally stuck in the same bucket of finance as spending on hospitals. It is also the case that the UK's contribution to treatments, diagnostics and vaccines for lower income countries was part of its, only just recently, dismantled Department for International Development (DFID). Why would it not be seen as part of overall health investment spending for the world, alongside its investment spending on health internally?

Then below this set of prioritisations on health investments, what financial tools are being supported to offer as incentives? For example, to universities, the private commercial health sector and others, so that they have an ongoing motivation for the development of new useful vaccines, antibiotics and such. It is crucial that when the next global shock hits, we are in a position to escalate this research immediately.

In the parlance of the health incentives, have we got the appropriate portfolio of push and pull incentives in place? As it happens, the UK appears to have probably been in a better position than most, partly because of its leading universities, and the coincidence that it is home to two major international pharmaceutical companies. But certainly, for example, as it relates to antibiotics and AMR today in 2021, the UK does not have the right set of tools to ensure confidence of its future antibiotic supply.

## 6 Matching the Role and Responsibilities of the World Health Organisation (WHO) with Global Reality

Returning to the international arena and systems of governance, we should address the question of whether the much criticised WHO is fit for its purpose? As part of any fair answer to this question, I find myself quickly thinking, is it set up for modern effective purpose? Do its members really allow for the WHO to call out its member countries about the quality of their health systems?

Moreover, while it has rightly become the parlance to think in terms of 'One Health' which includes all animals, plants and the natural world, as well as humans, why do we have separate entities to preside over each of these?

How can the WHO realistically be expected to stop the threat of AMR or future pandemics, if the responsibilities for animals rests with the Food and Agriculture Organisation (FAO) and not the WHO? While it is fashionable in some quarters to call out the WHO about the source of the COVID-19 pandemic in China, what powers did they really have, since, as most experts seem to believe, it originated in a live animal food market?

Such thinking leads immediately to the idea that perhaps we need a 'One Health' organisation in which the WHO, the FAO and the World Organisation for Animal Health (OIE) are all merged into one. This has a compelling logic if we are going to genuinely have a better global system to cope with future threats. Of course, such an idea raises all sorts of fears about bumbling bureaucracies, but this should not automatically equate to having the best framework. I, for one, believe this is something that needs to be given serious consideration. Post the high level UN agreement that was successfully achieved to combat AMR in September 2016, it was agreed also to proceed with an interagency agreement between the WHO, FAO and OIE about cooperation on AMR, but as far as I have observed, nothing specific has been achieved. Nothing has been done to embed some new ideas or principles as to how, in practise, this relates to managing our planet better in terms of health and prosperity. Of course, some might say, if this step of cooperation is proving to be too challenging what chance would there be of success to a whole new organisation, tasked with such ambition? My answer to this is, do we want to have positive ambition or not?

Obviously, it is very clear the WHO needs to work better regardless of the future institutional arrangements and a number of functions in this regard are equally vital. But unless the WHO is itself is tasked to have a chance of dealing with the threats we face, even this would not mean much.

# 7   Lessons for Global Healthcare Reforms from the 2008 Global Financial Crisis

Another idea I have been influenced about comes also from learning from the 2008 crisis—including the policy response to that crisis. One of the major, albeit, less discussed consequences was the establishment of the Financial Stability Board (FSB) under the auspices of the Group of 20 (G20). The awakening of the G20 in itself was a major positive consequence of the crisis in my view, not least because it brought to the centre of world economic policymaking a stronger legitimate representative group of the world than others that preceded it. This was not least because of the inclusion of China, the other BRICS countries, as well as other emerging economies that matter for tackling truly global challenges. This should not be forgotten in the current times where a mood of us versus them seems to frequently dominate many people's thinking.

Under the G20, the FSB has played a solid role, sometimes below the radar, in ensuring a stronger global financial system that allows for better capitalisation of major global financial institutions, amongst other things. Judging by—at least so far—the stability of the major financial sectors through this pandemic, this has been quite a successful achievement.

# 8   Creating a Global Stability Structure to Focus on Global Public Goods

In this context, I am minded to propose an additional or broader body to the FSB, to be specific, one that is tasked with a focus on global public goods, one central part of which is health.

Just as in the 2008 crisis, COVID-19 has demonstrated the centrality of global finance to the lives of all seven billion of us, and the establishment of the FSB has seemingly made the system more resilient. The reality is we need the same body to protect the interests of even broader societal goals, including combating climate change, health and perhaps education. And certainly, within the focus on health, the early monitoring of pandemics and other global disease threats including AMR must be treated with the same respect we now treat the threat of financial disruption.

## 9  Harmonising the Objectives of Business with the Needs of Global Public Goods

Above all of this, I have one remaining overall observation and takeaway from this crisis, which concerns the state of global capitalism, including the circumstances in which this crisis occurred.

I have often said that leading the AMR Review has perhaps been the most stimulating professional experience I have been lucky enough to have had. Amongst the many reasons I say this is that it taught me that the way the international economic system has evolved during my lifetime has, if not directly created, certainly contributed to considerable global societal challenges.

However, many of the actors in the system do not seem to regard it being their responsibility to help solve global societal challenges. I fundamentally disagree with this avoidance of responsibility. I believe all of us get our licence to operate in our business lives from the societies we inhabit.

In this regard, I believe the sometimes apparent near obsession with profit maximisation has to evolve to an era where the role of business is to optimise its objectives, of which profit attainment is crucial, but not the only one.

Without such a shift in mentality, I fear that once we have beaten this COVID-19 crisis, we may default back to a usual way of life and forget some of the powerful moments of thought this crisis has forced upon us.

**Lord Jim O'Neill** was Chairman of the Royal Institute International Affairs (Chatham House) for three years up until July 2021. Jim worked for Goldman Sachs from 1995 until 2013, spending most of his time there as chief economist. Jim is also the creator of the acronym 'BRIC' and has conducted much research about these and other emerging economies and published various books on the topic. Between 2015 and 2016, he was Commercial Secretary in the British Government working with Chancellor George Osborne. He also led an independent review into antimicrobial resistance (AMR) for UK Prime Minister David Cameron from 2014 to 2016, and remains focused on this challenge.

**Open Access** This chapter is licensed under the terms of the Creative Commons Attribution-NonCommercial-NoDerivatives 4.0 International License (http://creativecommons.org/licenses/by-nc-nd/4.0/), which permits any noncommercial use, sharing, distribution and reproduction in any medium or format, as long as you give appropriate credit to the original author(s) and the source, provide a link to the Creative Commons license and indicate if you modified the licensed material. You do not have permission under this license to share adapted material derived from this chapter or parts of it.

The images or other third party material in this chapter are included in the chapter's Creative Commons license, unless indicated otherwise in a credit line to the material. If material is not included in the chapter's Creative Commons license and your intended use is not permitted by statutory regulation or exceeds the permitted use, you will need to obtain permission directly from the copyright holder.

# Governance to Nurture the Next Generations Through Education, Exchange and Migration

# Addressing the Scientific Challenges of Our Age Begins with Human Connection

**Sir Keith Burnett**

**Abstract** Chinese 'people to people' links as an international strategy are deeply embedded in *Chinese culture*. Facilitating bonds between countries begins by creating connections between people. This essay describes the compelling need for nations and China to come together for mutual benefit to consider the economic and institutional frameworks that will make this possible. Case studies citing the value of *links in science between UK and China* are given here, but in this process, high priority must be given to building personal relationships. Personal experiences can demolish so many of the simplistic notions held by non-Chinese people about China. Often outside of China, *Chinese stereotypes* are mostly drawn from films and photographs of the old China—think Bruce Lee, the land of the bicycle and pastoral images of rice paddies farmed by hand. Through personal relations, visitors to China can discover a developing nation made up of millions of families keen to embrace technology and a better life for their children. China has opened up, and with it has a sense of possibility of trade, exchange and shared scholarship. Yet without a *greater comprehension of China*, its history and its language, any understanding of the world is incomplete.

**Keywords** Chinese 'people to people' links · Chinese culture · Links in science between UK and China · Chinese stereotypes · Greater comprehension of China

As a scientist, my life and work have been marked by international connection and exchange, and my scientific forefathers and teachers reflect a global story. It is one in which China plays a vital role.

I first travelled to China in 2004 as a physicist working at The University of Oxford. I was accompanying the then Vice-Chancellor Sir Colin Lucas and the eminent historian Dame Jessica Rawson, an expert on China's artistic treasures who was securing materials on loan from the Forbidden City for the first major exhibition of these artifacts to be held at the Royal Academy in London.

Yet, it was not just the treasures of ancient China which caught my attention. This was my first experience of a vast nation of 1.4 billion people, and I was simply captivated by this place and the Chinese people I saw and met.

K. Burnett (✉)
Schmidt Science Fellows, Oxford University, Oxford, UK

© The Author(s) 2021
H. Wang and A. Michie (eds.), *Consensus or Conflict?*, China and Globalization,
https://doi.org/10.1007/978-981-16-5391-9_15

My personal experiences also demolished so many of the simplistic notions I had of China. My stereotypes were mostly drawn from films and photographs of the old China—think Bruce Lee, the land of the bicycle and pastoral images of rice paddies farmed by hand.

Instead, I discovered a developing nation made up of millions of families keen to embrace technology and a better life for their children. China was opening and with it came a sense of possibility for trade, exchange and shared scholarship. Yet, it was clear to me that without a greater comprehension of this astonishing country and its language, my understanding of the world was incomplete.

Through my work, I met both dear Chinese colleagues and students and been deeply impressed by their insights and commitment. Chinese scholarship has too long been underestimated in the West by those ignorant of the dedication of those working across many friends of study, but my own experience showed me this was wrong. The challenges of the future would require a global effort and many brilliant minds were to be found in the great universities of the East. It was equally clear that China would be heavily investing in them and their research to build up the potential of the country to move beyond a low-wage economy to a highly skilled future as an innovative global power. Yet most of all, I was struck by the people I met, and I travelled home to Oxford changed by what I had seen.

I first began to learn Chinese using simple tapes on my Sony Walkman and later on an iPod as I walked between my home and my office as Chairman of Physics in Oxford. I had more Chinese students now and my research group was genuinely international. I also read books and stories and practised writing Chinese characters, my fascination growing along with further opportunities to visit this extraordinary land.

My connection with China later became more personal in a surprising way. My son was studying in London and met a wonderful young woman from Guangzhou who later became his wife. China was no longer just somewhere I visited professionally, we had family there. At my son's Chinese wedding, I met generations of warm and loving people who cared deeply for my daughter-in-law. There was laughter and joy. It was apparent to everyone that the love of our families and fervent hope for their happiness knew no linguistic or geographic bounds.

In 2007, I became a university President, and suddenly, I acquired an even larger Chinese family of several thousand undergraduate and postgraduate students, as well as gifted Chinese colleagues across a host of disciplines. These young people had travelled to the UK from China in search of an excellent education, and it was my sacred duty as a teacher to honour the investment in money, time and love made by their families. I did my very best to do so.

In turn, their investment blessed our adopted city of Sheffield. A stunning new home for Engineering and many other students was built largely thanks to the investment of Chinese families in UK education. Chinese students directly benefitted, as did their British peers and the community around us. The impressive building was opened by the first ever UK astronaut Helen Sharman, a graduate of the university who reminded us of our global connections as common citizens of our remarkable blue planet. Now, China itself has a space programme, and in 2020, it planted its flag on the moon, only the second nation to do so. Having visited the Chinese Space Academy in Shanghai, I have no doubt this is just the beginning.

Throughout my time as a University President and Vice-Chancellor, I continued to study Chinese and travelled to China often, visiting scientists in Beijing and Shanghai, and our partners at Nanjing University. There, language became a bridge across which ideas flowed and which allowed friendships to deepen—we shared ideas about the way our work on materials or battery technologies might reduce pollution and a reliance on fossil fuels, and recognised a common need to ensure research that fed into our manufacturing sectors, renewing outdated industries and creating opportunities for the young.

In doing so, we met one another with respect and affection, and realised we had more in common than originally thought. Back in the UK, Chinese language teachers gave their full efforts and commitments to teaching children, students, health workers and business leaders the Chinese languages skills to make connections of their own. I was hopeful that we might indeed be entering a new golden era of cooperation, while recognising the rise of forces of separatism and nationalism which had once again emerged across the world.

I completed my service as a University President in 2018, and shortly thereafter, my son and Chinese daughter-in-law had their own son, Jacob, or in Chinese, 梁爽. He is the beneficiary of the love and cultural richness of two nations. He speaks to his mother and grandparents in Cantonese, and to us in English. He is a living bridge, as his name implies, and a source of hope and joy for us all.

I also found myself part of a group of scientists and leaders in education who were recognising an ever-greater need for high-level exchange as technologies rapidly advanced and our common problems revealed their urgency and complexity.

# 1 Global Problems Require Global Solutions

As a Fellow of the Royal Society in the UK, my colleagues and I met with our scientific peers from the Chinese Academy of Sciences. While our political leaders addressed issues of ideology, our focus remained on the pursuit of knowledge and its power to benefit the peoples of both our countries.

A number of Royal Society Fellows—members of the world's oldest independent scientific academy, dedicated to promoting excellence in science—have worked for decades with colleagues in China, particularly in areas such as medicine. While we spoke the common language of Science, the different cultural contexts in which we undertook our work revealed questions and insights which challenged each of us to think more carefully.

As Chair of the Nuffield Foundation—an independent charitable trust with a mission to advance educational opportunity and social well-being—I also discovered ways in which it was vital we work together.

One established example of this was the globally respected Nuffield Council on Bioethics. The Council informs policy and public debate through timely consideration of the ethical questions raised by biological and medical research. Established by the Trustees of the Nuffield Foundation in 1991, it seeks to provide independent and balanced advice to policy-makers and stimulating debate in bioethics. Recommendations are backed by a thorough process of consultation, engagement and deliberation with a wide range of people and organisations. The Council's work is informed by engaging a range of public, professional, political and policy stakeholders to ensure that the Council is aware of, and responsive to, the major issues of interest and concern to them. And, it draws on a broad range of expertise and opinion to develop a range of high-quality outputs and activities, supported in this endeavour by the charitable research funder Wellcome and the UK Medical Research Council.

Yet, this vital work would clearly be incomplete if it did not draw on international insights and experience. The ethical underpinnings of biosciences and medicine have very practical consequences. So, the Nuffield Council on Bioethics had for example published collaborative research on the scientific and ethical aspects of ageing. There are currently more than 220 million elderly people in China. By 2050, more than 40% of the population will be over the age of 60. Although Chinese governmental expenditures on healthcare and eldercare have been growing, the challenge of how to support an ageing population is as familiar in the East as it is in the West. What factors should we consider as we address this challenge?

And in China there are distinct challenges. The common '4-2-1' family structure of four grandparents, two parents and one child make eldercare in China one of the most pressing social issues of the time. The traditional Confucian value of 'filial piety' and concerns about dignity and agency for older people in their own care touch on everything from inter-generational attitudes to medicines and housing—an issue also at the heart of policy concern in the UK. A process of urbanisation and changing patterns of employment meant many older people now lived far away from a generation who would have traditionally offered support. Seeking an understanding of a balance between cure and care led to deep academic collaboration between the Nuffield Council of Bioethics and the Xiamen University.

And it is not just medicine. New technologies present new ethical challenges, and it has become clear in recent years that the world is in urgent need of a common ethical framework for artificial intelligence. Yet, how to balance a western focus on individual freedom with eastern philosophical focus on the collective? Only by speaking together could we reveal our assumptions and question our thinking.

I took advice on this work from my academic colleague at The University of Cambridge, Professor Huw Price, who is a Bertrand Russell Professor of Philosophy and Academic Director of the Leverhulme Centre for the Future of Intelligence. Together with Professor Yi Zeng of the Chinese Academy of Sciences, Huw directs the China–UK Research Centre for AI Ethics and Governance, a cross-cultural and trans-disciplinary Centre. Through linking Eastern and Western wisdom, the Centre is aimed at bridging scholarship in China and the UK to share, interact and complement efforts about AI Ethics and Governance, with an aim of putting AI development at the service of humanity and social good. So, we convened honest discussions between leading Chinese and British philosophers to open up our thinking to one another, realising in the process that we would need to work hard not to misunderstand one another.

This work is long-term in nature, and that is its strength. The Nuffield Council for Bioethics has been seeking understanding and offering expert advice for 20 years. It is motivated by rigour and insight, not headlines. The ethical questions raised by caring for an ageing population or, of the beneficial societal uses of artificial intelligence, are likely to concern policy-makers and wider society for a generation to come. But without a thoughtful analysis of the issues involved in a truly global context, the opportunity for misunderstanding and inadvertent damage is clear. It was clear to the founders of the Nuffield Council on Bioethics that common purpose required greater understanding not only of technologies but of the cultural priorities and assumptions which guide their use. This meant being willing to challenge ourselves in the interests of the many millions of people who will feel the consequences of the decisions we make, whether in the UK or China.

## 2 The Need for Mutual Understanding

A great English author, sadly lost to us in 2020, John Le Carré, once wrote that: 'Learning a language is an act of friendship'. He was right. A language is much more than a currency that allows us to exchange thoughts and ideas. A language carries within it the stories and culture of a people.

To know another people, you must understand their fears and hopes, and often those are wrapped up in their language. It is how we recognise one another's common humanity, our hopes and dreams for the future. And understanding these is a precondition for peace.

The philosopher Ludwig Wittgenstein wrote, 'The limits of my language mean the limits of my world', and this is as true for those of us who explore the Sciences and the Arts. Sometimes, the challenges we face will require an interdisciplinary approach, while others an international one that draws on the experiences of our different cultures and traditions. It is by meeting one another, virtually and in person, that we expand our vocabulary and with it our comprehension.

For Science, a failure to meet and work together could carry a heavy price in misunderstanding. Certainly, the developing world must have its input into the solutions to the great social and ecological challenges of global health and climate change, and here, China speaks with authority. China has lifted 800 million people out of poverty and a significant portion of our global progress on this issue is due to this fact. How was this possible? On this, as so much else, I know my country has a lot to learn from my Chinese colleagues.

# 3   The Global Challenge of COVID-19

The need to work together as a global scientific community has perhaps never been as starkly apparent as in response to the devastating pandemic of COVID-19. At the end of my road in Oxford are the laboratories of the University's Medical Division and the Jenner Institute where teams of scientists from around the world developed the Oxford Astra Zeneca vaccine, which has recently been approved in the UK and will be made available on a not-for-profit basis for the duration of the pandemic across the world, and in perpetuity to low- and middle-income countries. This scientific triumph will potentially save millions of lives, and give us back so many of the freedoms that have been curtailed during this pandemic.

Oxford University is, in fact, home to many scientists from China, both students and leaders in research. A few weeks ago, I shared a cup of tea in my garden in Oxford with a colleague and friend, Professor Zhanfeng Cui. At our socially distanced, but scientifically warm, meeting we talked about his Oxford Laboratory which is also just around the corner from my home.

Professor Cui is a distinguished Biomedical Engineer with a track record of bringing cutting-edge science to bear on important medical issues. Professor Cui is the Founding Director of Oxford's research laboratory in Suzhou. The institute, named OSCAR, will bring the combined expertise of Chinese and British scientists to solve problems of joint and global significance.

A recent example of the importance of such a joint lab is the development of techniques needed to fight the pandemic. He and his international team are working on COVID-19 detection in a joint project with scientists and medics from across the world. As we discussed the personal and the global, we were each keenly aware of the importance of his work for our own health, for our loved ones and all our neighbours and fellow citizens in China, the UK and the world.

# 4   Learning from Scientific Colleagues in China

On the wall of my office in Oxford are two framed prints, personal gifts from one of my brothers-in-Science Professor Xu. He is a Professor of the Academy of Arts and Design at Tsinghua University in Beijing China and Director of the Future Lab. His teaching and research focus on user experience in computer design and e-heritage. Before joining Tsinghua University, he was a Lead Researcher for Microsoft Research in Asia. But the pictures remind me of his deep love for Chinese culture and our common humanity.

The images he gave me are of his digitisation for conservation purposes of ancient Buddhist cave paintings from Dunhuang in China which is an artistic and cultural wonder of the world. Yet, I also think of the very modern and universal applications of his work.

Deeply committed to accessibility, Professor Xu and his Beijing team have also developed a prototype tactile display system that allows blind people to handle visual information from computers, hoping they can benefit more from the Internet age of booming graphic information. Named 'Graille', the display is comprised of a pin-matrix with 7,200 small tactile dots that can be raised and retracted. The computer controls the pin-matrix of the display to show graphic information in raised tactile dots, which can be read by touch by the blind users.

The idea started in 2009 when Professor Xu, an expert in computer vision and interaction design, was working on a digitalisation project for cultural heritage. He noticed that blind visitors can only absorb information through voice introduction converted from texts. The lack of visual information makes it hard for them to appreciate museum exhibits. Professor Xu's team also worked with the Beijing School for the Blind to learn more about blind people's needs when handling visual information. The team is cooperating with major Internet companies to benefit blind users across China and the world.

## 5  Building Understanding Is Personal

These are just two personal examples of Chinese colleagues whose work I deeply admire, but I cite them for a reason. When we speak of the need for the UK and China to come together for our mutual benefit, we certainly need to consider the economic and institutional frameworks that will make this possible, but we should not forget the personal.

When I think of Chinese scholars and students, scientists and thinkers, I see individual faces and hear their stories. I do not think in terms of stereotypes but of people, colleagues and in many cases friends with whom I can work and think. As my school motto put it: 'He who would be a leader must be a bridge'. In my experience, facilitating bonds between countries begins by facilitating connections between people, it is personal.

When we speak on the phone, Professor Xu and I share stories of our grandchildren and hope that our work might in some way enhance their lives and worlds. Recently I told him: 'I hope for my family and yours that, whether the challenge is COVID-19 or climate change, we will continue to meet one another in a spirit of friendship and that our world will not be constrained by misunderstanding.' I believe it is our duty to work together to ensure that this is so.

**Sir Keith Burnett** is Chair of the Academic Council for Schmidt Science Fellows at Oxford University. He was President of the UK Science Council between 2016 and 2021 and is Chairman of the Nuffield Foundation, a charity which funds research, analysis and student programmes. He is also well-known as an advocate for international students and is widely published in the UK and globally. Sir Keith retired as President and Vice-Chancellor of the University of Sheffield in 2018. He took on the position in 2007 and before he was Head of the Division of Mathematical, Physical and Life Sciences at the University of Oxford.

**Open Access** This chapter is licensed under the terms of the Creative Commons Attribution-NonCommercial-NoDerivatives 4.0 International License (http://creativecommons.org/licenses/by-nc-nd/4.0/), which permits any noncommercial use, sharing, distribution and reproduction in any medium or format, as long as you give appropriate credit to the original author(s) and the source, provide a link to the Creative Commons license and indicate if you modified the licensed material. You do not have permission under this license to share adapted material derived from this chapter or parts of it.

The images or other third party material in this chapter are included in the chapter's Creative Commons license, unless indicated otherwise in a credit line to the material. If material is not included in the chapter's Creative Commons license and your intended use is not permitted by statutory regulation or exceeds the permitted use, you will need to obtain permission directly from the copyright holder.

# Sustaining Transnational Universities as Temples of Cosmopolitan Exploration

Jeffrey Lehman

**Abstract** A lesser known aspect of globalization has been the creation of a *network of transnational universities*. In this essay, there is an analysis for their value. *Intellectual curiosity, academic freedom*, and *a radical openness to people* who hold different worldviews—those norms are vital to humanity's efforts to meet challenges like infectious disease, climate change, and social injustice. It is vital that governments work together to recognize the benefits that follow when they refrain from trying as governments to *micromanage university life*. Governments are right to punish spies and thieves, people who steal military technologies, and people who hack into businesses. But they are wrong to *criminalize scholars' normal contributions to, and withdrawals from, the global intellectual commons*. Even more, governments must affirmatively encourage their citizens, who travel abroad as students and professors, to honor the norms of the university that is hosting them. I hope they will encourage their citizens to encounter other cultures with humility, recognizing that *universal norms* can express themselves in a wide variety of ways. If we are fortunate, the story of China and globalization in the year 2021 will feature the emergence of a stronger global consensus in support of the *unique mission of transnational research universities*.

**Keywords** Network of transnational universities · Intellectual curiosity · Academic freedom · A radical openness to people · Micromanage university life · Criminalize scholars · Universal norms · Unique mission of transnational research universities

The University of Bologna, often described as the oldest continuously operating university, was founded in 1088. Early in its life, foreign scholars who came there to study were granted legal protections by Emperor Frederick Barbarossa. Those protections included a formal right to travel as well as immunity from responsibility for the misdeeds of their countrymen.

Across the centuries, the term "university" has been applied to many different types of institutions of higher learning, including about 25,000 today. The most

J. Lehman (✉)
New York University Shanghai, Shanghai, China

© The Author(s) 2021  171
H. Wang and A. Michie (eds.), *Consensus or Conflict?*, China and Globalization,
https://doi.org/10.1007/978-981-16-5391-9_16

widely influential, however, continue to express a certain spirit of Bologna. They welcome students from other lands to come and join with local students in a quest for insight and understanding.

The transnational quality of great universities supports both the research and the teaching dimensions of their missions. Some "indexical" academic domains (such as the humanities) concern themselves with understanding local cultures, and a diverse scholarly community helps to produce comparative insights. Other, less indexical domains (such as the natural sciences) also benefit from a more heterogeneous community, because students raised in different cultures hold different perspectives on what is salient and may even perceive the same object differently.

During the closing decades of the twentieth century and the first decade of the twenty-first, there was a broad consensus worldwide driving forward a spirit of globalization. Despite sometimes dramatic cultural, political, and economic differences among countries, each found the benefits of expanding interdependence to far outweigh the costs.

Universities embodied this spirit. Academic mobility increased at an accelerating pace, as technological progress made travel safer, swifter, and less expensive. No longer an exclusive privilege of the well-to-do, "study abroad" became normalized for a broad cross-section of students and their families around the world. According to UNESCO's Institute for Statistics, more than 30 million students pursued degrees in countries where they were not citizens in 2018. Mainland China was a key participant in this expansion of academic mobility, sending about 1 million students to study at overseas universities while hosting about 200,000 visiting students from other countries at its own universities.

Professors increased their own movement just as much as students did. Research collaborations exploded, and the norm became for scientific publications to include coauthors who had grown up in more than one country.

The accelerating academic mobility in turn helped to sustain a deepening spirit of humanism and cosmopolitanism that held up, despite trends towards increasing inequality within and among countries after 1975. Even though elites often retained strong patriotic allegiance to their nation of citizenship, they also often presented themselves as "globalists" or "internationalists," people whose loyalties transcended national borders. That phenomenon became even more visible after the end of the Cold War in 1991.

At the dawn of the twenty-first century, some universities took this transnational philosophy to new levels, establishing campus presences outside the countries of their founding. Two areas that were especially welcoming of such extensions were the Persian/Arabian Gulf and China.

In the Gulf region, one of the most ambitious early initiatives was by "Education City," established by the Qatar Foundation in Doha. Opened in 1997, the project now includes degree-granting campuses of eight universities from the United States, the United Kingdom, and France. Early in the 2000s, the United Arab Emirates recruited other American, British, and French universities to open campuses in Abu Dhabi.

Many of these campus projects created a new school devoted to only one or a small set of disciplines, such as the Weill Cornell Medical College in Qatar and INSEAD Abu Dhabi. A few, however, created more comprehensive research university campuses, such as NYU Abu Dhabi and Sorbonne University Abu Dhabi.

In China, an early important development was the launch of the Hopkins-Nanjing Center in 1986, a program that continues today and offers both, a two-year master's program in international studies and a one-year certificate program, in Chinese and American studies. During the 1990s and early 2000s, hundreds of new cooperative programs were set up under which foreign universities established teaching "institutes" and "programs" within traditional Chinese universities.

In 2003, China embraced an even more ambitious model, that of the Sino-Foreign Cooperative University ("SFCU"). Rather than being components of traditional Chinese universities, SFCU's are new legal entities, each created through a partnership between a traditional Chinese university and a non-Chinese university.

The first SFCU's were created through partnerships between Chinese universities and the University of Nottingham, Hong Kong Baptist University and the University of Liverpool. The next three involved partnerships with American Universities: NYU Shanghai, Wenzhou-Kean University and Duke Kunshan University. Since then, three more SFCU's have been established through partnerships with the Chinese University of Hong Kong, the Technion Israel Institute of Technology, and Moscow State University.

The SFCU's are, by design, experimental. Rather than being stamped from a single mold, each of the nine pursues its own vision of what a contemporary transnational university should be.

Among the nine, NYU Shanghai has received the most widespread attention within China. Since its doors opened in 2013, NYU Shanghai students have pursued undergraduate, graduate, and doctoral degrees across a wide range of disciplines in the natural sciences, social sciences, humanities, engineering, and business. From the beginning, it has been distinguished by a commitment to prepare its students to be creative cosmopolitans who can be effective participants in multicultural teams.

NYU Shanghai has pursued that commitment in several ways. As a matter of structure, half of each class of undergraduate students are Chinese; the half that come from outside China are presently drawn from more than 80 different countries. Faculty are selected through competitive global searches and hail from about 25 different countries.

First-year students must live in the residence halls, where each is assigned a roommate from another country. All classes are taught in English, but all non-Chinese students must learn Mandarin in order to graduate. Students spend their first two years on the Shanghai campus, but all are expected to spend their junior year studying in other countries.

As a matter of content, all students must complete an intellectually diverse core curriculum that immerses them in cosmopolitan philosophical values, while experiencing an active-learning pedagogy that promotes critical and creative thinking. They are, moreover, subjected to an ongoing barrage of messaging that stresses the expectation that they will function as a single, integrated student body where every student spends at least two hours every day with someone from another culture.

From my observations, the combination of structure and content leads NYU Shanghai students to change in different ways from the changes of their counterparts at more traditional universities. When they first begin, NYU Shanghai students (whatever their nationality) are rather typical of their generation. Most have grown up in environments that nurture negative, ill-informed stereotypes about people from other countries. Moreover, in discussions about their own countries, many are quite defensive, displaying a fragile patriotism that causes them to treat others' differences in perspective and civil disagreements as micro-aggressions, causing them to miss valuable opportunities for respectful and thoughtful conversation.

After four years of intense, mandatory engagement—in the classroom and in the dorms—with classmates who come from all over the world, almost all NYU Shanghai students change dramatically. They relinquish the false stereotypes that they brought with them, and they develop a truly mature appreciation for their own countries. They no longer feel a need to see their nation as perfect and all others as defective. They understand that every country, including their own, has characteristic weaknesses and characteristic strengths. They understand that they love their own country not because it is superior but rather because it is theirs.

It is reasonable to see NYU Shanghai as an archetype of a spirit of global academic integration that was, until recently, accelerating. That spirit was sustained by three key technological and sociological features of life during that period.

The first feature was *well-defined personal location*. It made sense to say that, at any instant, a person was situated in a well-defined place on the planet that could be specified by longitude and latitude. Countries, in turn, were defined by mostly uncontested non-overlapping geographic boundaries. As a result, it made sense to say that a person was situated "in" only one country at a time, and the government of that country was entitled to have legal jurisdiction over them at that moment.

The second feature was *well-defined military technology*. Many different items in everyday use could, conceivably, be used as weapons, and many intellectual insights could, conceivably, be used both for benign purposes and also to invent more powerful weapons. Nonetheless, the nature of warfare and the pace of military technological innovation were such that it was not thought especially difficult or problematic to define "military research" clearly and narrowly.

The third feature was the *non-proprietary nature of academic ideas*. The insights developed at universities were global public goods. A scholar was deemed to have been productive only when their work was published—given away to the world. The human quest for understanding was understood to proceed at the level of the species, rather than at the level of the individual, the university, or the nation-state. In this regard, universities were very different from the two most important types of organization that conducted non-public research: businesses (which conducted proprietary commercial research) and armies (which conducted military research).

In those happy times, students and professors roamed the world, and the norms that governed them were clear. When in Rome, students and professors who were visiting from the University of Toronto followed Italian rules. Neither Canada's government nor the University of Toronto tried to control their behavior. Italy, for its part, did not perceive the visitors as threats. It welcomed them to participate fully in the life of its temples of cosmopolitanism. It fully expected that during their time as visitors they would encounter new ideas that they would bring back home and build upon in Canada.

Today, those three features no longer hold.

First, thanks to the internet, social media, and videoconference technology, people are no longer situated at discrete point-locations within the singular jurisdiction of a single country. A single classroom discussion will often include a teacher sitting in one country, talking with students who are sitting in several other countries. And even when teachers and students are physically overseas, their home governments are much less hesitant to dictate how they should behave. As a result, students frequently find themselves facing mutually inconsistent expectations—from their home government, from their fellow overseas classmates, and from the university where they are studying.

Second, the concept of "dual-use technology" has been dramatically broadened and pushed much farther upstream. As a result, a much larger percentage of the research and teaching that takes place on campus risks being perceived as "sensitive" or "secret" by cautious government officials. They, in turn, are much more likely to demand that universities prohibit non-citizens from participating in the schools' intellectual life in those domains. And they are much more likely to prohibit professors from participating in multinational research teams working in those domains.

Third, much more of the research that takes place on university campuses is being treated as proprietary. In the United States, for example, the Bayh-Dole Act of 1980 gave universities much greater responsibility and authority to commercialize inventions that were funded with government grants. Thereafter, universities rushed to set up "technology transfer offices" which, in turn, have nurtured a perception of universities as producers of commercial "intellectual property" that requires protection against unauthorized exploitation by outsiders. In an era when universities are expected to produce profitable "IP," it seems much more natural to talk about ideas being "owned" by a university, a company, and even a country.

These three shifts have coincided with the rise of nationalistic movements all around the world. Heads of state have revived modes of speech that draw strong differences between their own citizens and those from other countries. Those leaders have portrayed foreign citizens as holding different interests, often antithetical to those of domestic citizens, and insisted that foreign cultures should be viewed with suspicion. Cooperation has become tolerable only if it can be done in a manner that poses no conceivable risk to "sovereignty."

In 2020, the set of countertrends seemed to come to a head. The COVID-19 pandemic closed international borders. The language of disagreement between the governments of China and other countries—especially that of the United States— took on a degree of overt mutual hostility that had not been seen in decades. Discussions of "decoupling" spread rapidly.

This new mindset led some government officials to insist that universities should understand themselves in national rather than transnational terms. They decried as naïve those university leaders who promote cultures of openness where scholars gather together to investigate topics about which they are curious and where knowledge is a public good. Instead, those officials argued that universities are *national resources*, with special duties to resist both corruption and exploitation at the hands of rival nations.

When NYU Shanghai was established, its American and Chinese founders believed they were early participants in an educational project that would become more and more common in the decades to come. Today, the very idea of launching a new SFCU feels somehow out of step with the nationalistic worldview that has taken hold, and it has been four years since the last SFCU was created.

My claim here is that it would be tragic for that nationalistic worldview to change the character of universities. The well-being of people and of nations calls for a thoughtful but vigorous defense of transnational universities as temples of cosmopolitan exploration.

To be sure, some of the new pressures on universities are understandable. The past few decades have intensified ideological tensions and mistrust between nations. Even more importantly, the abject failure of governments to ensure that the benefits of international cooperation are shared fairly by all their citizens has weakened the sense of common purpose. Liberalized trade in goods, services, capital, and ideas, unaccompanied by aggressive protections for those who are made worse off by such trade, has triggered exploding inequality and a dramatic diminution in quality of life for the disadvantaged.

Nevertheless, those pressures must be resisted. Undermining the identity of universities would provide no assistance whatsoever to those who were hurt by hyper-globalization. To the contrary, it would deprive humanity of resources that we very much need if we are to change course.

Universities that function as temples of cosmopolitan exploration help to sustain the flow of essential information across borders. They preserve the interaction of competing perspectives that fuels creative discovery. They maintain the personal relationships that are most effective in refuting the prejudices that inhibit human flourishing.

Such universities promote the quest for knowledge and insight in three different domains, each of which is profoundly important to the quality of human life. First, they explore the material world of natural science and technology, helping people to enjoy ever-better and ever-more-abundant food, shelter, tangible goods, physical power, and sensory delight. Second, they explore the nonmaterial world of philosophy, mathematics, history, literature, art, music, and dance, enriching "the life of the mind and spirit." Third, they explore the social world of government, economy, and interpersonal interaction, advancing the values of peace, order, and harmony.

In none of these domains, in absolutely no discipline, is it beneficial to obstruct interaction among people from different nations. Progress results from disagreement. From respectful, serious consideration of alternative ideas. From sympathetic engagement with counterargument. In order to sustain a culture of innovation, a society must find a way to ensure that its brightest minds have the habit of critical engagement with conventional wisdom. They must be able to consider how that conventional wisdom might be correct and how it might be incorrect. And they must have developed what the poet John Keats called "negative capability"—the capacity to hold both those considerations in mind at the same time, "without irritable reaching after fact and reason."

The historian Carl Becker memorably explained that an academic is expected to "think otherwise." That habit of mind is what allowed the world to benefit from non-Euclidean geometries, notwithstanding the genius of Euclid. It is what allowed the world to benefit from non-Newtonian physics, notwithstanding the genius of Newton. It is what allowed the world to benefit from a non-Biblical understanding of the origin of species, notwithstanding the genius of the Bible.

A temple of cosmopolitan exploration stands on the pillars of intellectual curiosity, academic freedom, and a radical openness to people who hold different worldviews. Those norms are vital to humanity's efforts to meet challenges like infectious disease, climate change and social injustice. Those same norms are equally vital to humanity's efforts to develop opportunities for all people to prosper during their lifetimes.

In this decade, I hope that governments will, together, recognize the benefits that follow when they refrain from trying to micromanage university life. Governments are right to punish spies and thieves, people who steal military technologies, and people who hack into businesses. But they are wrong to criminalize scholars' normal contributions to, and withdrawals from, the global intellectual commons.

Even more, I hope that governments will affirmatively encourage their citizens who travel abroad as students and professors to honor the norms of the university that is hosting them. I hope governments will encourage their citizens to engage respectfully with all ideas, even wrongheaded ideas. I hope they will encourage their citizens to explore critically, ideas that might be "politically incorrect," without fear of being ostracized or punished. I hope they will encourage their citizens to encounter other cultures with humility, recognizing that universal norms can express themselves in a wide variety of ways.

The story of China and globalization in the twenty-first century is not a simple story of linear progress. It is, rather, a complex story of oscillations and cycles, sometimes operating in different ways in different domains. If we are fortunate, the story of China and globalization in the year 2021 will feature the emergence of a stronger global consensus in support of the unique mission of transnational research universities.

**Jeffrey Lehman** is the inaugural Vice-Chancellor of NYU Shanghai and chairs the board of the American Chamber of Commerce in Shanghai. He is an internationally acclaimed leader in higher education, having served as President of Cornell University, Dean of the University of Michigan Law School, and founding Dean of the Peking University School of Transnational Law. He received MPP and JD degrees from the University of Michigan. His many honors include the NAACP Legal Defense Fund's Equal Justice Award, an honorary doctorate from Peking University, and the People's Republic of China's Friendship Award.

**Open Access**  This chapter is licensed under the terms of the Creative Commons Attribution-NonCommercial-NoDerivatives 4.0 International License (http://creativecommons.org/licenses/by-nc-nd/4.0/), which permits any noncommercial use, sharing, distribution and reproduction in any medium or format, as long as you give appropriate credit to the original author(s) and the source, provide a link to the Creative Commons license and indicate if you modified the licensed material. You do not have permission under this license to share adapted material derived from this chapter or parts of it.

The images or other third party material in this chapter are included in the chapter's Creative Commons license, unless indicated otherwise in a credit line to the material. If material is not included in the chapter's Creative Commons license and your intended use is not permitted by statutory regulation or exceeds the permitted use, you will need to obtain permission directly from the copyright holder.

# Global Trends and Transitions in Think Tanks, Politics, and Policy Advice in the Age of Policy Dilemmas and Disruptions

James G. McGann

**Abstract** Throughout the twentieth century *think tanks stood at the forefront of academic work examining global developments*, collecting and analyzing information to provide important insights that form and guide policy- and decision-making. However, the general trend of globalization, as well as digitalization, informatization, and changes in how information is obtained and consumed, has placed *think tanks at a disadvantage*. These trends are *undermining the authoritative position of think tanks* and requiring them to find new and innovative ways to present information so that they remain relevant in today's world. *Think tanks are uniquely equipped to provide policy suggestions* that governments and business need to make correct and effective decisions. However, crises like COVID-19 also present new obstacles for think tanks in terms of how to communicate information and promote engagement to ensure that they remain relevant and valuable. *Over the last decade, forces have redefined the strategy and structure of many think tanks*. This momentum is primarily driven by changes in politics, how think tanks are funded, and advances in technology and communications. During this period, there have been *five key trends originating in the fourth industrial revolution* that will transform jobs and lives over the next 10 years.

**Keywords** Think tanks stood at the forefront of academic work examining global developments · Think tanks at a disadvantage · Undermining the authoritative position of think tanks · Think tanks are uniquely equipped to provide policy suggestions · Over the last decade, forces have redefined the strategy and structure of many think tanks · Five key trends originating in the fourth industrial revolution

J. G. McGann (✉)
Think Tanks and Civil Societies Program, Wharton School and School of Arts and Sciences, Philadelphia, PA, USA

Fels Institute of Government, University of Pennsylvania, Philadelphia, PA, USA

© The Author(s) 2021
H. Wang and A. Michie (eds.), *Consensus or Conflict?*, China and Globalization,
https://doi.org/10.1007/978-981-16-5391-9_17

# 1 Revitalizing Think Tanks to Meet Unprecedented Global Threats

Recent years have seen changes in the international order and economics that are reshaping the world. Trends away from multinationalism in developed countries, like the United States and Europe, the rise of China, and unavoidable changes in the status and function of international organizations, ranging from NATO to the UN and WHO, are forcing governments, organizations, and societies to rethink their approach to global issues.

Throughout the twentieth century, especially after World War II, think tanks have stood at the forefront in examining global developments, collecting and analyzing information to provide important insights that form and guide policy- and decision-making. However, the general trend of globalization, as well as digitalization, informatization, and changes in how information is obtained and consumed, has placed think tanks at a disadvantage. These trends are undermining think tanks' authoritative position and requiring them to find new and innovative ways to present information so that they remain relevant in today's world.

Global crises, like COVID-19 in particular, have been both a blessing and a curse for think tanks. The challenges that these crises present require the careful and insightful analysis that think tanks are uniquely equipped to provide and that governments and businesses need to make correct and effective decisions. However, these crises also present new obstacles for think tanks in terms of how to communicate this information and promote engagement to ensure that they remain relevant and valuable.

# 2 What Is a Think Tank?

First of all, I would like to revisit what think tanks are and what functions they serve. Think tanks are public policy research analysis and engagement organizations that generate policy-oriented research, analysis, and advice on domestic and international issues, thereby enabling policy-makers and the public to make informed decisions about public policy. Think tanks may be affiliated or independent institutions that are structured as permanent bodies, not ad hoc commissions. These institutions often act as a bridge between the academic and policy-making communities and between states and civil society, serving in the public interest as an independent voice that translates applied and basic research into a language that is understandable, reliable, and accessible for policy-makers and the public.

Over the last 90 years, several distinct organizational forms of think tanks have emerged. These differentiate themselves in terms of their operating styles, patterns of recruitment and aspirations, to academic standards of objectivity and completeness in research. It should be noted that alternate typologies of think tanks have been offered by other analysts. In the global context, most think tanks tend to fall into the following broad categories:

1. Autonomous and independent, enjoying significant independence from any one interest group or donor, and autonomous in its operation and funding from the government.
2. Quasi-independent, autonomous from government, but controlled by an interest group, donor, or contracting agency that provides most of the funding and has significant influence over operations of the think tank
3. Government-affiliated, or a part of the formal structure of government.
4. Quasi-governmental, which means that it is funded exclusively by government grants and contracts but not a part of the formal structure of government.
5. University-affiliated, which are mostly policy research centers at universities.
6. Political party-affiliated, which are formally affiliated with a political party.
7. Corporate, which are for-profit public policy research organizations, affiliated with a corporation or merely operating on a for-profit basis.

The end of the Post-World War II consensus and challenge to the welfare state contributed to the growth of think tanks on the left and the right of the political spectrum. There are currently 2,397 think tanks in North America (Mexico, Canada, and the United States) of which 2,203 are in the United States, while Europe contains 2,932 think tanks. These two regions contain over 47% of the world's think tanks. The number of think tanks in the United States has more than doubled since 1980 and most of these that have come into existence since the 1970s are specialized for a particular regional or functional area.

Asia, Latin America, Africa, the Middle East, and North Africa continue to see an expansion in the number and type of think tanks established, experiencing dramatic growth since the mid-2000s. University and government-affiliated/funded think tanks remain the dominant model and are dependent on government funding along with gifts, grants, and contracts from international public and private donors.

Generally, the growth of think tanks in the twentieth and into the twenty-first centuries can be attributed to these factors: industrial and technological revolution; the end of government monopolies on information and a crisis of confidence in the government itself, and elected officials, as well as the increasing complexity in and technical nature of policy problems. However, in recent years, the number of think tanks worldwide has begun to see a decline. This is mainly due to a failure to understand and respond to non-traditional competition and adopt new technologies and marketing strategies. There has also been a decrease in funding by both public and private donors, who have become more focused on short-term funding projects as opposed to research and institutions. Finally, increased competition from advocacy organizations, for-profit consulting firms, and 24/7 electronic media has also affected the flow of information and its consumption. All these trends have challenged the traditional position and model of the think tank.

As think tanks, we must face the reality that there will be no new normal, only a series of extraordinary events that will create a world where disruptions and the abnormal will be the norm. Big ships turn slowly and think quickly in storms. So only the innovative and agile will survive this most recent COVID storm. The imperative is now more urgent since the winds of change have intensified and accelerated the trends. Only those think thanks that are smarter, better, faster, tech-savvy, and agile will be able to weather the storm.

## 3   The Function of Think Tanks in Global Crises like COVID-19

From April through July 2020, the Think Tank and Civil Societies Program (TTCSP) of the Lauder Institute at the University of Pennsylvania hosted a series of virtual "Global Think Tank Town Halls to Save Lives and Livelihoods." The aim was to respond rapidly and proactively as a global think tank community to the novel corona virus (COVID-19). The pandemic has proven to be an unprecedented threat to the health, economic well-being, and general livelihood of people all over the globe. TTCSP has recognized the value that the think tank community can provide to policy-makers, and the public, as they work toward mitigating the consequences of COVID-19. The Global Think Tank Town Halls served as space for the community to convene and mobilize. 1,226 think tank executives, scholars, and policy-makers from over 540 institutions in over 87 countries met over the course of the three Town Halls to produce actionable responses and solutions to the devastating consequences of the virus.

The first Global Think Tank Town Hall made note that think tanks must become stronger, smarter, and faster in response to COVID-19 and create effective policy recommendations to support vulnerable and impacted sectors around the world.

The second Global Think Tank Town Hall saw the creation of five Working Groups that focused on (1) the public health crisis; (2) preparing national and international strategies for economic recovery and revitalization; (3) identifying innovative and inclusive public and private intervention strategies to help vulnerable groups; (4) fostering international cooperation by creating rapid, responsive, and resilient systems to respond to future crises; and (5) new operating models for think tanks—research, communications, and funding.

The third and final Global Think Tank Town Hall saw each Working Group present their recommendations and key proposals. Each Working Group conducted their analyses and formulated strategic and actionable recommendations within 45 days, reflecting the ability of the think tank community to convene from all corners of the world and produce tangible results in a short span of time. Below are the key recommendations from each Working Group on the five key issues analyzed.

### 3.1   Public Health Crisis

Working Group 1 analyzed the impact of increased globalization, which has not only integrated nations and economies but has also led to the internationalization of infectious diseases. One focal point was knowledge and information sharing, focusing on the importance of collecting consistent, reliable, and disaggregated data; investing in collaboration, innovation, and distribution; and streamlining the regulatory environment and reforming legal regimes to allow innovations.

The Working Group additionally gave recommendations for best practices in managing the public health crisis, which included sharing experiences and simulation models to inform policy. They also discussed the need for research-based solutions and policies, which think tanks can play a role in. The think tank community has the potential to necessitate the augmentation of state capacity, during a pandemic and otherwise. The importance of accelerating progress toward universal health coverage was emphasized, as was the need for the equitable distribution of vaccines, medicines, and capabilities.

## 3.2 Preparing National and International Strategies

Working Group 2 focused on targeting sustainable and broader-based economic recovery, focusing on shaping free-market policies that empower a circular economy and science-based target initiative tools. The Working Group laid out a handful of basic principles that governments should adhere to in order to rebuild national and global economies. These included prioritizing green recovery, international cooperation, democracy and inclusive free markets, market-driven responses to infectious diseases, and dynamic and flexible policies.

The Working Group also noted the importance of prioritizing digitization moving forward. Think tanks can be pivotal in encouraging governments to promote digital transformation and inclusion, as well as support the international community in accelerating talks to reduce the risk of privacy invasion and cyberthreats with greater technological regulation. Finally, they highlighted the importance of shaping the informal economy into an agent of recovery by focusing on three key pillars: building updated databases, making formal employment the easiest and most desired solution, and adopting a comprehensive reform approach to the informal economy. Think tanks can play a key role in shaping policy in this direction.

## 3.3 Innovative and Inclusive Public and Private Strategies to Help Vulnerable Groups

Working Group 3 focused on five particular vulnerable groups: children and youth, the elderly, women in vulnerable conditions, migrants, and racial and ethnic minorities. Regarding children and youth, key recommendations include monitoring the functioning of institutions responsible for the protection of children, ensuring working parents have sufficient time to care for children, and equitable access to safe medical services to all families and youth. For the elderly, it must be ensured that WHO and CDC guidelines for long-term care facilities are effectively implemented, as well as access to phone and video call technology for those in long-term care facilities that require sufficient funding. Regarding women in vulnerable conditions, think tanks should advocate for the development of economic empowerment tools so women are better equipped to be financially independent; furthermore, think tanks can also help shape policy that creates better awareness regarding what constitutes violence against women.

For migrants, it is imperative that states implement protective measures to ensure migrants' rights to personal security and access to basic rights such as food and healthcare; furthermore, the Working Group recommends eliminating custodial detention methods. Finally, for racial and ethnic minorities, recommended policies include localizing and diversifying service and supply chains to support minority-owned businesses; assuring basic items of consumption in minority neighborhoods; improved local government to support housing and employment stability; and prioritizing public health programming with stronger consideration of the social determinants of health.

## 3.4 Fostering International Cooperation: Creating Rapid, Responsive, and Resilient Systems to Respond to Future Crisis

Working Group 4 looked at how to better shape resilient policies and systems to respond not only to COVID-19 but also future crises by focusing on strategies that can be adopted at the local, regional, and global levels. On the local level, technology should be used to effectively control and distribute resources; direct assistance via managing commercial and supply chains, financial relief, and tax exemptions is vital; and unified programs to administer tests throughout the pandemic should be developed.

Regionally, efforts should focus on strengthening regional multilateral organizations and coordinating initiatives and consensual operational protocols between countries. Globally, the Working Group proposes that the international community should prioritize strengthening global multilateral organizations; creating new multilateral cooperation and crisis committees; sharing information systems and technologies for pandemic detection and control; internationally coordinating fiscal and monetary policies; and, finally, creating new sustainability and debt financing framework for low-income countries.

## 3.5 Being Fit for an Uncertain Future: New Operating Models for Think Tanks—Research, Communications, and Funding

Working Group 5 focused on four key areas in which think tanks can strengthen their operating models moving forward: communications, events, fundraising, and research priorities. Regarding communication, think tanks should work in niche intersections of COVID-19 and specific issues in which think tanks have the expertise, focus on highly visible communications and stakeholder outreach initiatives, and invest in new and diverse online formats of communications. Think tanks should also reimagine events in the digital sphere, recognizing the potential for widening one's audience base while reducing the environmental impact of events.

Moving forward with fundraising, think tanks should engage with the private sector as partners in research projects, rather than solely as donors, and think tanks should build partnerships with other think tanks. Think tanks should also redirect and widen research priorities to break thematic silos culture and find new policy intersections, as well as develop thematic partnerships with other think tanks focused on long-term research projects.

A global crisis like COVID-19 highlights both the strengths and weaknesses of think tanks. Their ability to analyze crises and provide practical, objective policy direction for governments and organizations can help mitigate their negative impact on global economies and welfare. However, maintaining their professional and authoritative position in the face of a flood of information from social media and other sources is a serious challenge. That digital information tsunami will decide where think tanks go from here on out and how they allocate funding and support.

## 4 The Future of Think Tanks and Policy Advice

Over the past 10 years, I've been examining the forces that have transformed the policy environment in which think tanks operated and have forced them to redefine their strategy and structure. These forces are primarily driven by changes in politics, how think tanks are funded, and advances in technology and communication.

Over the last decade, there are four key trends that flow from the fourth industrial revolution that will transform all our jobs and lives over the next 10 years. It is these forces that are also driving the digital and political disruptions that are sweeping across the globe. They are:

- The dramatic increase in the rate of technological change.
- The disruptive and transformative power of social media, social networks, artificial intelligence, and big data.
- The increased velocity of information and policy flows.
- Information interdependence.

Digital and social networks are constantly being ended by new strategies and technologies which in turn increase the volume and velocity of information flow around the world. These new realities are making it possible to manage and manipulate massive amounts of data, which is disrupting business, politics, and public policy. Henry Kissinger, whom people in China know well and followed closely, famously said that "being a policymaker is like being at the end of a fire hose," which for those of you who are not familiar with the term is a high pressure and high volume hose that is used to fight fires. Policy-makers and the public are faced with a flood of issues, ideas, and actors, which have served to intensify competition, conflict, and to certain extent cooperation. This never-ending flood of competing ideas and information makes it difficult to process all the different ideas, options, and alternatives. How do we determine which product or policy is the best one? It is no surprise that in this environment, traditional approaches, in terms of ideas and information, are overlooked for the outrages and the outlanders. These forces have created a crowded and competitive global marketplace of ideas and policy advice. This poses very new and very challenging strategic and operational challenges for think tanks.

In the last 4 years, the trends outlined above have been compounded by two new forces that have intensified and accelerated the winds of change, and are likely to transform think tanks, policy advice, and public policy in ways that we previously could not imagine. One is the effort to discredit and undermine experts, policy advice, and think tanks. The second is the Covid-19 pandemic. These two additional trends have accelerated and compounded the transformation that is taking place and will force all think tanks to respond.

Furthermore, the dawn of the fourth industrial revolution is upon us, and will require think tanks to manage change, access, policy issues, and trends, and make recommendations more quickly than ever before. The pandemic has intensified those operation and think tanks of all types and size have never felt so much pressure to rethink how they operate to fit the changing environment. The Covid-19 pandemic and increased velocity of information and policy flows will continue to accelerate factors like digitalization, globalization, automatization, and analytics. What this means is that think tanks must become smarter, better, faster, more digital, more adaptive, and more agile if they have any hope of surviving.

It is precisely during these turbulent times when experts and their advice are being undermined. More importantly, the significant policy and technology disruptions calling into question the value and efficacy of policy advice has led to my conclusion. It is critical that we pause and reflect on the future of think tanks and policy advice.

# 5   The Vital Need for a New Breed of Think Tanks

Think tanks are crucial to conducting research, engaging scholars, and building partnerships. The rationale means dialogues, partnerships, and cooperation, embraced by think tanks, become essential in the face of many complex global challenges.

This is why think tanks in China, in the US, and around the world matter and matter more than ever before, and that is why we must work to make sure that think tanks are fit for an uncertain future.

Think tanks must face the reality that there will be no new normal, only a series of extraordinary events that will create a world where disruptions and the abnormal will be the norm. Only those think tanks that are smarter, better, faster, tech-savvy, and agile will be able to weather the storm. The mission of the think tanks and civil societies program at the Lauder Institute of the University of Pennsylvania is to help think tanks prepare to survive the storm so they can continue their service in the post-COVID era.

The impact of technology; big data and artificial intelligence; competition from advocacy groups and public relations firms; increased polarization of politics; major changes in how think tanks are funded; and the impact of the COVID-19 pandemic on think tank operations are all major issues that affect think tanks around the world. Think tanks must be smarter, better, faster and more agile, innovative, and tech-savvy if they are to survive. I would like to now turn to a few issues that Chinese think tanks, in particular, face in addition to these more universal, global issues.

## 6 Think Tanks the New Great Wall in China and Why Modernization and Reform is a National Imperative

There are now over 11, 175 think tanks in our database and we have also collected in a very systematic way and identified 1415 think tanks in China. This reflects a dramatic increase in the number of think tanks in China and constitutes the most significant number of think tanks among the think tank leaders or leading countries in Asia: India, Korea, Australia, and Vietnam. Even more impressive is that over 600 of these think tanks have been established since 2000. However, there are a number of unique issues facing Chinese think tanks and hinder their integration into the global environment.

First, there are many blanks and gaps in the information that we have on Chinese think tanks, specifically on staffing, size, budget, and even basic information about their research programs. This is a huge information gap. The missing information highlights the lack of transparency surrounding the nature and operation of think tanks in China. Thirdly, the number of think tanks or the largest number of think tanks is still in Beijing which outnumbers the rest of think tanks proportionally in every other city in China. There are, as I said, 500 think tanks in Beijing, which makes about one-third of the total think tanks in China. This makes sense because Beijing is the political center, but more cities need to create think tanks to help with their regional or provincial issues.

There are a number of areas for improvement. First, the vast majority of think tanks in China do not have functional websites. In many respects, they are blackholes that have little or no information on them. For those that do, they are not updated on any regular basis. Scholars and research programs are not listed and no contacts for key staff and scholars. The majority of think tanks do not have bi-lingual (Chinese and English) and just a hand full have multilingual websites which limits the access and the ability to have impact on regional or global policy issues and debates. So, if the aspiration is to create great think tanks in China and to have influence around the world, English and multilingual websites are essential.

The last two I think are fundamental and require attention to the reform and modernization of think tanks in China. There is a complete lack of access to data by scholars at think tanks which undermines the credibility of what is produced. Many scholars and think tanks in China regularly complain that ministries and other government agencies have little or no access to the critical data that they need for their research.

Finally, there is a severe lack of adherence to the universally practiced social science research methods and standards. There is no access to data or the research methods which limits the ability to replicate studies that are produced and raise questions about the quality of the research. All of these basic, universal, and internationally accepted standards are not practiced or adhered to in China and that needs to change if Chinese think tanks are to "rival the great think tanks in the West." They must modernize and become smarter, better, and faster, if they have any hope of having national, regional, and global impact.

Those standards signify that accessing to data and the ability to replicate studies that are produced. All of these basic, universal, and internationally accepted standards are not practiced or adhered to in China. That needs to change if Chinese think tanks are to be smarter, better, faster, and to have both national, regional, and global impact.

China should join other think tanks around the world by adopting a set of basic standards for public policy research like ones that are now being considered by think tanks in every region of the world.

For centuries scholars, scientists, and think tanks around the world have embraced the scientific method and what have become known as social science research methods. These standards include a set of core elements that guide the quality and integrity of research around the world. The basic standards include the following: 1. the research should be based on empirical evidence and have a rationale for conducting it. More specifically, evidence should be provided to justify the key findings, results, and conclusions; 2. the empirical research should be transparent, that is, reporting and the data sources should make explicit the logic of inquiry, the funding supporting it, and activities that led to initial interest in the issue, topic, problem, or research question, through the definition, collection, and analysis of data or empirical evidence to the articulated and support the outcomes of the study. Disclosing and reporting of the research methods takes these principles into account and enables other scholars, practitioners, and the public to understand the research, prepares that work for public scrutiny, and enables others to use the research for further research and for practical applications in policy. These standards are therefore intended to promote empirical research findings that are warranted and transparent. The reporting standards are divided into eight general areas: problem formulation; design and logic of the study; sources of evidence and data; measurement and classification; analysis and interpretation; generalization; ethics in reporting; and title, abstract, and headings.

# 7 Advice for Think Tanks and Policy-Makers

Covid-19 will influence all think tanks on several key points in a broader context. As I alluded to earlier, the disruptive and transformative dimensions of this crisis will have and will continue to alter all aspects of our lives and livelihood. We will not return to a new normal or any normal after this crisis. It is so transformative. The crisis has become the great accelerator, transformer, and terminator. What I mean by that is changes are accelerated and institutions are transformed. Many institutions will cease to exist as a result of this pandemic. 25 to 30% of certain organizations, private enterprises, and think tanks will close and not reopen.

Additionally, governments will have to take on huge and decimated budgets while also facing rising social, political, and economical challenges. Those institutions that have taken steps and this is important and a key message for think tanks in China. Those institutions that have taken steps to modernize their operations and implement digital and other strategies are more likely to survive the crisis. Key sectors such as higher education, medicine, travel and leisure, and information-based organizations will be most adversely affected.

This crisis and the economic impact it has are different from previous economic downturns because in the past the negative economic impact of a downturn such as the oil crisis plus the 2008 economic crisis hit both the rich and the middle class at about the same level. The COVID-19 crisis has widened the gap and created a huge gulf between rich and poor. That trend is likely to have long-term and destabilizing effects in countries around the world. Like all great wars, this crisis will create a global power shift, and China at the moment seems to be the only country, ironically, that is emerging from this crisis in a commanding economic position. That seems certain to have a highly transforming global and geopolitical impact.

Finally and most importantly, this is a massive wake-up call for all organizations to accelerate modernization and reform. Failure to respond and understand the forces that have been released means the very survival of many organizations is at stake. Every organization must embed into its goals to be smarter, better, faster, more agile, and more digital. If we come together as a community of think tanks and innovate and cooperate, we will beat this invisible beast and be better for it.

# References

McGann JG (2004) Scholars, dollars and policy advice. Think Tanks and Civil Societies Program, pp 6–15

McGann JG (2007) Think tanks and policy advice in the US. Routledge, London. https://doi.org/10.4324/9780203963203

McGann JG (2012) Chinese think tanks, policy advice and global governance. Indiana University Research Center for China Politics and Business. http://www.dragon-report.com/Dragon_Report/home/home_files/mcgann-rccpb-21-think-tanks-march-2012.pdf

McGann JG (2014) China's first think tank summit was hosted in Shanghai by the Think Tanks and Civil Societies Program and the Shanghai Academy for Social Sciences. https://www.thedp.com/article/2014/07/chinese-think-tank-conference

McGann JG (2015a) Going global: what Chinese think tanks need to do to have global reach and impact. Think Tanks and Civil Societies Program, University of Pennsylvania

McGann JG (2015b) Expert advises China to build innovative think tanks. https://www.linkedin.com/pulse/expert-advises-china-build-innovative-think-tanks-james-mcgann/?articleId=7795707204265141347

McGann JG (2016a) The fifth estate: think tanks, public policy, and governance. Brookings Institution Press, September

McGann JG (2016b) 2016 China global think tank innovation forum. https://repository.upenn.edu/ttcsp_china_reports/4/

McGann JG (2016c) Think tanks in action: foreign policy case studies. In: The fifth estate: think tanks, public policy, and governance. Brookings Institution Press, Washington, DC, pp 114–148. http://www.jstor.org/stable/10.7864/j.ctt1gpccjc.8. Accessed 16 Oct 2020

McGann JG (2017a) 2017 China global think tank innovation forum. https://repository.upenn.edu/ttcsp_china_reports/3/

McGann JG (2017b) 2016 global go-to think tanks report. University of Pennsylvania

McGann JG (2018a) 2018 China global think tank innovation forum. https://repository.upenn.edu/ttcsp_china_reports/2/

McGann JG (2018b) Thinking aloud. Beijing Review. https://www.bjinforma.com/Current_Issue/2018/202102/t20210204_800235116.html

McGann JG (2019a) 2018 global go-to think tanks report. University of Pennsylvania

McGann JG (2019b) 2019 China global think tank innovation forum. China.org.cn. https://repository.upenn.edu/cgi/viewcontent.cgi?article=1000&context=ttcsp_china_reports

McGann JG (2019c) Promoting development of China's think tanks through global vision. http://www.china.org.cn/china/2019-05/31/content_74841640.htm

McGann JG (2019d) Think tanks: the new policy advisors in Asia. Brookings Institution Press, Washington, DC

McGann JG (2020a) Let 1000 think tanks bloom in China. Speech presented at Think Tank Leader Knowledge Exchange Program in Beijing, China

McGann JG (2020b) 2019 global go to think tank index report. TTCSP global go to think tank index reports. https://repository.upenn.edu/cgi/viewcontent.cgi?article=1018&context=think_tanks

McGann JG (2020c) Global think tank town hall report. University of Pennsylvania, April-July

McGann JG (2020d) Chinese think tank landscape workshop. University of Pennsylvania

McGann J, Whelan L (2020) Global think tanks: policy networks and governance. Routledge, London. https://doi.org/10.4324/9780429298318

McGann JG (2021) The future of think tanks and policy advice around the world. Palgrave Macmillan

**James G. McGann** is Director, Think Tanks and Civil Societies Program, Wharton School and School of Arts and Sciences; Senior Fellow, Fels Institute of Government, University of Pennsylvania. He has served as a Consultant and Advisor to the World Bank, the United Nations, and the Asian Development Bank to name just a few. He earned his M.A. and Ph.D. from the University of Pennsylvania. He has authored over 17 books on think tanks and is the Creator and Editor of the annual Global Go To Think Tank Index. He has traveled on assignments and programs to 114 countries.

**Open Access** This chapter is licensed under the terms of the Creative Commons Attribution-NonCommercial-NoDerivatives 4.0 International License (http://creativecommons.org/licenses/by-nc-nd/4.0/), which permits any noncommercial use, sharing, distribution and reproduction in any medium or format, as long as you give appropriate credit to the original author(s) and the source, provide a link to the Creative Commons license and indicate if you modified the licensed material. You do not have permission under this license to share adapted material derived from this chapter or parts of it.

The images or other third party material in this chapter are included in the chapter's Creative Commons license, unless indicated otherwise in a credit line to the material. If material is not included in the chapter's Creative Commons license and your intended use is not permitted by statutory regulation or exceeds the permitted use, you will need to obtain permission directly from the copyright holder.

# Global Talent Mobility: Trends, Challenges and Proposed Global Governance Solutions

Lu Miao

**Abstract**  A compelling case can be made that *talent migration makes a very significant contribution to global economic development*, but the *global governance of talent migration has been sorely neglected* compared to other economic sectors such as international trade and finance. This essay makes the case for *the value of creating a new global infrastructure for talent migration*. The focus of this new agency would be on the *optimal management of talent migration* to realize its great potential for the mutual benefit of all mankind. Global migration, especially of highly skilled talent, has pushed forward scientific and technological discoveries. However, many existing *challenges impede global talent migration*. Meanwhile, the world economy has reached a critical point in which many *major economies with aging populations and declining birth rates might lose the engines that drive economic development*. Competition for talent has become increasingly fierce and the accumulation, or loss, of talent can have a significant impact on the balance of power in international relations. In the short term, the physical mobility of international talent has been limited by COVID-19. In the long term the frequency of *online intellectual mobility provides an alternative way to replace physical international mobility*.

**Keywords**  Talent migration in global economic development · Global governance of talent migration · New global infrastructure for talent migration · Optimal management of talent migration · Challenges to global talent migration · Engines that drive economic development · Online intellectual mobility

## 1 The Need for International Infrastructure to Optimize Talent Migration

There is a compelling case to be made that talent migration makes a very significant contribution to global economic development. But the global governance of talent migration is very neglected compared to other sectors of the economy such as the management of international trade and finance. This essay makes the case for the

L. Miao (✉)
Center for China and Globalization (CCG), Beijing, China

© The Author(s) 2021
H. Wang and A. Michie (eds.), *Consensus or Conflict?*, China and Globalization,
https://doi.org/10.1007/978-981-16-5391-9_18

value of creating a new global infrastructure for talent migration, the focus of which would be on the development of the great potential of optimal management of talent migration for the mutual benefit of all mankind.

Since the end of World War II, global flows of goods, capital, and human resources have become an increasingly free, driving development and boosting mobility of talent around the world. According to the United Nations International Migration Stock 2019, the total number of migrants worldwide was expected to reach 272 million in 2019. That makes up around 3.5% of the world's population, which is an increase from 173 million in 2000 and 222 million in 2010. Global migration, especially of highly skilled talent, has pushed forward scientific and technological discoveries. It has also raised new issues for global governance, which must be addressed to promote the overall welfare of the global community.

The study of global talent migration and its governance can be traced back to the "push-pull" theory,[1] which views talent migration as driven by the dual effects of a "push" out of origin countries and a "pull" towards destination countries. Later, the theory of transnational migration emphasized the rapid development of transportation links and communications technology, which allows for highly mobile migrant groups to travel more frequently between their homelands and new destinations, forming a kind of "brain circulation." These highly mobile migrants engage in a variety of economic, cultural and political activities, including processes of learning, communication and exchange.[2] Transnational migration theory highlights "de-borderization" and migration networks in the context of globalization and is particularly prevalent among groups of highly skilled migrants.

Many countries have adopted specific policies and measures to adapt to the emerging trends of global migration in the 21st century. The goals of these practices include nurturing human capital, especially highly skilled workers, and attracting international talent with professional experience or certain qualifications through policies that emphasize skilled labour and investment. These countries usually offer a pathway to permanent residency and eventually full citizenship. Countries like Australia, Canada and New Zealand also continuously refine immigration policies to integrate new immigrants into their labour markets. These include regulations that support international students to accumulate work experience, which facilitates their transition from short-term to permanent residence. In China, government, business and educational institutions have been active in launching new policies to attract international talent. Many Chinese nationals that have studied or worked abroad have returned to China for career opportunities, resulting in recent waves of "return migration" and "brain circulation"[3]

While there has been significant progress in both theoretical work and practical application regarding global talent migration and its governance, many existing challenges still impede global talent migration, limiting the potential contribution that these human resources could make toward economic and social development. This

---

[1] www.futurelearn.com/info/courses/migration-theories/0/steps/35073.
[2] Dutt-Ballerstadt (2010), Tsuda (2012).
[3] Lu and Zong (2017), Lu (2009).

points to the need for an international infrastructure to facilitate discussion and address a range of crucial questions, including how to better leverage the role of globally mobile talent; how to ensure and regulate reasonable talent mobility; how to balance the interests of origin and destination countries and so find ways to resolve current and future problems.

## 2  Global Talent Mobility

While transnational movements of talent have existed as long as nation-states, the scale, modalities and characteristics of these migration flows have varied greatly during different historical periods. Over the past 20 years, enhanced links among countries through globalization has enabled the rapid expansion of transnational talent flows in both scope and scale. According to the 2018 Global Talent Mobility and Wealth Management Report by Forbes, the four most common forms of international talent migration were overseas study and employment, skilled migration, periodic migration and return of talent. In recent years, with the development of the global economy, transnational talent mobility has demonstrated the following distinct characteristics.

### 2.1  Unprecedented Scale and Speed

The world economy has reached a critical point in which many major economies with aging populations and declining birth rates might lose the engines that drive economic development. Foreseeing such challenges, many countries have introduced measures to attract international talent to fill in the demand for human resources. At the same time, the extensive outreach of transnational corporations that have integrated human capital on a global scale propels more frequent movements of talents across borders.

Meanwhile, advances in transportation infrastructure have also provided the conditions for increasingly convenient international travel. By the end of 2018, there were 15,684 scheduled passenger flights between China and other major countries each week, and the number of international routes opened in a single year exceeded the total opened in 30 years before the launch of reform and opening-up.

According to the latest United Nations report, the total number of transnational migrants reached 258 million in 2017, of which 71% went to high-income countries and 74% were workers aged between 20 and 64.

## 2.2  High Demand and Intense Competition for High-Tech Talent

As big data and artificial intelligence enter a phase of wider application and pioneer the development of Industry 4.0, the demand for high-tech talent is increasing in the global labour market and leading to a shortage of capable individuals in related fields.

According to the Global AI Talent Report released by LinkedIn,[4] the number of AI positions published on LinkedIn skyrocketed from 50,000 in 2014 to 440,000 in 2016, which is a nearly eight-fold increase. Meanwhile, in 2016 China's Ministry of Industry and Information Technology disclosed to the media that China faced an AI talent shortage of over 5 million.

Aiming to win in the global competition for talent, many countries have implemented talent development strategies, such as the "Strengthening American Competitiveness for the 21st Century" program in the United States, the "2.4 million Science and Technology Talent Development Comprehensive Promotion Plan" in Japan, the "Innovation and Skills Plan" in Canada, the "young professional system" in Germany[5] and the "Brain Korea 21 Program for Leading Universities & Students" in the Republic of Korea. This reflects an intensification of the competition to attract international talent in different countries.

China has also made great strides in making its talent pool more international, whether in terms of cultivating new talent, attracting talent from abroad or how talent is being used and incentivized, particularly high-tech talent. However, you 'cannot change the plant without changing the soil' and China must create a more international 'soil' for talent to grow and thrive. China must also ultimately cultivate more "renaissance scholars"—those that are not driven by the singular goal of being a scientist or economist but have a range of interests that inspire them to innovate and create in technology and other fields.

## 2.3  Widespread "Brain Drain"

Global North–South competition for skilled workers such as scientists, engineers, professors, administrative talent and start-up entrepreneurs is not a new thing. Better living and working conditions and strong policies to attract talent give developed countries an advantage in the battle for talent, while developing countries continue to lose many skilled workers because of their lack of competitiveness.

In countries such as Angola, Burundi and Kenya, 33–55% of people with higher levels of education have left to work in member countries of the Organization for Economic Co-operation and Development (OECD). As a Canadian economics

---

[4] https://economicgraph.linkedin.com/blog/global-ai-talent-trends-looking-back-at-ai-impact-in-2019-to-understand-the-challenges-and-opportunities-ahead.

[5] www.asis-germany.org/en/nachwuchsfoerderung.

professor once wrote in the Wall Street Journal, "Plundering the most talented people, especially from small and poor countries, may damage the political and economic development of these countries, and even ruin them in the worst scenario."

At the same time, it should be noted that "brain drain" also exists in developed countries. Approximately 400,000 high-end skilled workers from the European Union work in the United States, while the rapid development of emerging economies such as China and India has caused a brain drain even in the United States. However, this problem is mild compared with developing countries due to the massive inflow of talent that developing countries enjoy.

## 2.4  Linkages Between Global Talent Migration and International Relations

Many countries recognize talent as a strategic resource in international rivalry. Competition for talent has become increasingly fierce and the accumulation or loss of talent can have a significant impact on the balance of power in international relations. Issues related to sensitive technical expertise can even trigger friction between countries.

These changes in geopolitics increasingly affect global talent migration. For example, China-US trade friction that started in 2018 has spread to the field of talent. The United States has made changes in policies related to Chinese students, limiting visas for Chinese students majoring in sensitive fields such as robotics, aerospace and high-tech manufacturing, to one year, while the FBI has started to scrutinize Chinese-American scientists or even American scientists who are part of China's Thousand Talents Plan. We will touch more on this later.

## 3  The Effect of COVID-19 on Talent Mobility

The relentless onslaught of the COVID-19 pandemic over the past year has also had a massive impact on talent mobility. In the short term, the focus has been on limiting physical mobility of international talent to prevent the spread of the pandemic. In the long term, however, with the development of digital links, the pandemic has contributed to an increase in online intellectual mobility, which may provide an attractive alternative to physical international mobility in the future. This trend provides huge potential for enhancing communication and cooperation among international talent pools across borders.

## 3.1 The Stagnation of the Physical Mobility

With countries closing their borders and taking measures to prevent the spread of the virus, the flow of talent across borders has been affected in a number of ways. These include regulatory barriers such as visa and travel restrictions, as well as social barriers due to stigmas attached to the pandemic.

Perhaps the most direct impact on talent mobility has been the limitations placed on travel and entry into nearly every country around the world, preventing talent from moving across borders in a practical, physical way. Since countries closed their borders, issued travel restrictions and stopped issuing visas, international travel has nearly reached a standstill, ranging from a complete barring of international flights to an extremely low number of flights with limited capacity. Statistics from the Civil Aviation Administration of China show that the number of passengers travelling on international routes hit a low of only 77,000 in April 2020, compared with 6.08 million the year before. For scientists and researchers worldwide, limited physical mobility due to extended periods of lockdown has led to the restricted access or loss of access to laboratories and research facilities, irregular communication patterns under mandated isolation requirements, cancellation of academic conferences and field works and disruptions in supply chains for essential equipment, which has altogether had an adverse impact on their productivity.

In addition, regulatory policies that were designed to halt the further spread of the corona virus and to safeguard public health became a major barrier for global talent mobility. These strict visa restrictions set up by many countries along with stringent testing and quarantine procedures have made it extremely difficult for talent to move across borders. This is especially relevant for China, which in early 2021 once again restricted all entry from medium and high-risk countries, given the third wave of infections fuelled by the new variants sweeping across Europe and America.

Another element of public administration is the ongoing shift towards restrictive immigration policies in education, which will have even more far-reaching consequences for talent mobility and is underpinned by a complex political-economic nexus. China is the largest source for international students in higher education and the US has maintained its status as their top destination country, but the number of Chinese students who choose to study and stay after graduation in the United States has fallen over the last decade and declined even more dramatically during the pandemic. Before the COVID-19 crisis, there were already instances of students being wrongfully accused of espionage by Trump administration officials, who threatened to cancel or revoke their visas. This inflammatory rhetoric has created a hostile climate and affected 3,000–5,000 Chinese students currently studying in the US.

Although border control measures were initially adopted to curb the spread of the COVID-19, in some countries political leaders with an explicit anti-immigration position have used the pandemic as an opportunity to criminalize international migration and garnered public support to restrict future flows. In recent months, the international community has witnessed a significant increase in racial discrimination and hate crimes targeting Chinese and other people of Asian descent in western countries, particularly in the United States. This rise in xenophobia and isolationism is inextricably linked to the systematic demonization of China, where COVID-19 transmission was first reported, not only by the media but also in political and public rhetoric. Negative public opinion and overt discrimination make potential talent hesitant to settle in areas where such a social climate is present and ultimately prevents them from contributing towards the host country in the long term.

## 3.2 The Development of Online Intellectual Mobility

To offset the negative impacts caused by the physical stagnation of talent exchange, the frequency of online intellectual mobility has increased considerably over the past year. The ongoing transition to remote working is expected to become the new normal, while the rise of online learning, lab-sharing, virtual webinars and conferences, which enable long-distance study, research and communication, are fostering new patterns of international talent mobility. This trend makes it easier for international talent to cooperate and overcome the limitations of geographic boundaries.

The broad application of online tools that have facilitated international talent mobility, which has grown rapidly over the past year, has not only improved online intellectual mobility but also improved a huge potential to make life easier for international talent in foreign countries. For example, the city of Hangzhou in eastern China has created smart phone applications that provide civil services such as housing, health care and public transportation for both domestic and foreign residents. These developments make all aspects of life more convenient for those living and working there.

While we can expect to see a gradual return to the physical mobility of international talent following large-scale vaccination programs and effective control of the pandemic, online intellectual mobility will also play an increasingly important role in the post-pandemic era because of its convenience. Throughout this process, the advancements in digital links, along with the digitalization of civil services, could be utilized to facilitate the integration of international talent in foreign countries and increase the competitiveness of country's ability to attract international talent.

## 3.3 The Growth of Stronger Collaborative Efforts in Science and Innovation

While the pandemic has exacerbated the divisions in global politics and eroded international systems meant to respond to the crisis, the immediacy and urgency of global challenges has strengthened connections within specialized scientific networks. This began with Chinese scientists publicly sharing the genomic sequence of the new virus and was immediately followed by international cooperation and exchanges of data and genetic and viral material among research institutions. A number of online platforms backed by publishers, foundations, firms and research labs have also committed themselves to the open access of analytical tools, scholarly articles as well as epidemiological, clinical and genomic data. According to the OECD, more than 75% of the 75,000 scientific publications on COVID-19 in the past 11 months have been made open to the public. International cooperation was also essential for vaccination research and clinical trials, allowing countries with scientific resources to acquire robust data from different regions, particularly developing countries with large vulnerable populations and limited preparedness, and accelerate the development of potential vaccines.

It is worth highlighting that while the pandemic broke out in the midst of a tense geopolitical climate that was trending toward de-globalization, the scientific community continued to actively work against isolationism. For example, in the initial months of the crisis, hundreds of Chinese and American scholars signed open letters appealing to the US government to allow cooperation with China to develop a framework for a shared global response. Despite disagreements on foreign policy, trade and technology, the United States and China, as the top producers of COVID-19 research, have had the most collaborators working on co-authored papers. Despite the influence of the pandemic and geopolitical factors, the global cooperative network created by scientists has set an example for the significant value of better and more extensive collaboration among global talent, which has to some extent laid the foundation for the creation of an international organization to coordinate and promote global talent mobility.

# 4   Regulation of Global Talent Migration Today

Mechanisms of global governance are not yet fully capable of dealing with the increasingly fierce global competition for talent, which has resulted in a dearth of regulation in the field of global talent migration and in the long term may result in the under-uses of talent and adversely affect sustainable development. Specific challenges facing the regulation of global talent mobility are outlined below.

## 4.1   Lack of a Common Consensus on Global Talent Cooperation

With the ever-expanding reach of globalization, division of labour and cooperation on a global scale is increasingly prevalent. Today, more than 35% of scientific papers are produced through joint efforts by academics from different countries. Breakthroughs and innovation often come from teams made up of talented individuals from multicultural backgrounds. Venkatraman Ramakrishnan, winner of the Nobel Prize in Chemistry and President of the United Kingdom's Royal Society, once told the media that, from the perspective of scientific research, scientific progress as a whole benefits from global talent migration. The response to this trend should not be to limit the flow of labour, but to foster a research environment in which people are willing to work in many different places.

However, individual countries are often more concerned about the competitive aspect of global talent migration. Relatively little attention, or research, focuses on the value of cooperation in international talent, leading to a lack of consensus on the topic. However, competition and cooperation are two sides of the same coin in global talent migration and, from the overall perspective of human development, cooperation is extremely important and should not be overlooked.

## 4.2 The Need for Dialogue, Coordination and Cooperation Mechanisms in Global Talent Migration

Currently, at the global level, there is a lack of mechanisms for the promotion of dialog and coordination on talent migration. Differences in labour policies and the lack of mutual recognition of professional qualifications show the need for enhanced cooperation and coordination. Some mechanisms have been implemented within the European Union and the Association of Southeast Asians Nations (ASEAN), while China and the European Union have launched the EU-China Dialogue on Migration and Mobility Support Project, but these mechanisms remain limited to the regional level, lack stability, and are often limited to certain governmental agencies.

## 4.3 Lack of Data and Resources on Global Talent Migration

Despite the increase in global talent migration, precise data on the scale, gender, age and professions of migrants is incomplete, which hinders the ability of policymakers and researchers to perform accurate analysis and develop appropriate policies.

In recent years, the rise of LinkedIn has helped to fill in this data gap. With 645 million users, LinkedIn provides a wealth of talent data. However, its status as a business also means that access to this data is restricted.

# 5 This Regulatory Void Calls for a Global Institutional Solution

The previous sections highlighted the barriers to talent mobility on various levels, which include a lack of international consensus, cooperation mechanisms and available resources regarding the management of global talent flows. This section outlines a proposed solution to address this gap, namely, an international non-governmental organization to promote global talent exchange and cooperation on talent flows. The vision for this organization is an inclusive international platform that can address challenges facing global talent migration and will resolve the following needs: facilitating dialogue between existing organizations working on talent-related issues; developing common standards; fostering innovative global governance solutions and promoting best practices.

## 5.1 Concept and Goals of the Proposed International Organization

The purpose of this organization would be to promote international talent mobility; strengthen talent cooperation; provide basic protections for talent and research support for developing countries; reinforce talent cooperation in key fields with developed countries; and improve talent mobility and talent creation in member countries.

To accomplish this, the first goal would be to create a platform for dialogue on fair competition in international talent exchanges. This means promoting global and regional conversations on the following topics: global talent migration; improving understanding of the relevant opportunities and challenges; developing and refining effective policy measures; and identifying comprehensive methodologies and measures that can support international cooperation.

The second goal of the organization would focus on the welfare of people around the world and encourage the international movement of talent. Different levels of development at the regional level mean that the available pool of international talent varies between countries. Countries blessed with an abundance of talent should support and work with less developed countries to locate and cultivate the talent needed to drive economic development through talent sharing and exchange platforms. This requires support from governments, non-governmental organizations, skilled workers and other stakeholders to utilize human capital more efficiently and promote the flow of talent between countries.

The final goal is to work to protect the rights and interests of individuals and address current gaps in the governance of global talent. Existing international organizations in this area include the International Organization for Migration, which focuses more on issues related to vulnerable groups of migrants like refugees and internally displaced persons. There is also the International Labor Organization, which works towards the protection of workers' rights. However, an organization focusing on the cultivation and sharing of highly skilled talent would ultimately be responsible for coordinating between these institutions to better guide and regulate efforts by local organizations to protect the rights and interests of international talent to ensure fair, equal and reasonable treatment.

# 6 Work That Needs to Be Done

As a platform for dialogue and cooperation on international talent mobility, the specific work carried out by such an organization would cover a wide range of far reaching issues. There is currently a paradox in the field of international talent mobility: despite the pandemic, the world is more interconnected and mobile than at any other moment in history. The importance of this work on talent mobility, which will provide a foundation for the next stage of globalization and economic development, places it on par with other issues like trade negotiations, environmental issues and health crises that the world is currently facing.

The first bit of work this organization would need to carry out would be to forge a consensus. As a coordinating body for international talent, it would be the role of this organization to establish a general consensus for the international community to follow in order to expand exchanges on international talent and promote international cooperation.

Once this consensus is reached, the second step for this organization would be to set up mechanisms for dialogue, coordination and cooperation. These mechanisms would first focus on the active promotion of discussion and research on various aspects of global talent cooperation and development through a Global Talent Conference and Summit. This would set the stage for discussions that would feed into the development of actual services. For example, mutual recognition of academic qualifications; certification of professional qualifications; quotas on future immigration and management of international students.

Finally, this organization would assess and guide policies and development efforts to promote the orderly flow of talent through a range of services centred on the collection and sharing of information.

The results produced by these efforts must also be made available on a platform that would: (1) collect information on talent pools and demand, serving as an official point of access for data, information and guidance; (2) publish annual reports on developments in global talent and related industries; (3) manage a database on global human resources, country statistics and services; (4) post-event information on annual meetings, conventions, forums, trade fairs and other activities; (5) facilitate and strengthen exchange and cooperation among members, cities and even countries on topics of talent development and mobility and (6) organize training to cultivate talent, improve talent management and enhance talent services provided by governments and institutions.

One last key function of such an international organization would be to collect and integrate information. Specifically, this task relates to the analysis of various aspects of international talent that leverage big data and internal, as well as external database resources, to provide authoritative information on global talent. This information would serve governments in policy making and the development of methodology, as well as approaches and tools to improve the governance of international talent.

Talent is one of the most valuable resources in promoting international dialogue and cooperation, which is essential to the promotion sustainable development and tackling global issues such as climate change, food security and public health. The exceptional collaboration during the development of the COVID-19 vaccine has proven the great value of enabling easy exchange of ideas across borders. This trend can be even further leveraged through the creation of the international organization proposed in this essay. This agency would provide a permanent international infrastructure for cooperation in international talent and could potentially overcome the friction and tensions of geopolitics and policy issues that we currently face by enabling the free flow of ideas and talent; by enabling scientists, researchers and entrepreneurs alike to better communicate with each other; promote the development of science and technology and tackle global issues in a better way. The outcome can be a positive return, which might promote multilateral cooperation between nation states and contribute to a more sustainable future.

To conclude, whether in terms of goods, capital or talent, globalization is a trend that we are confident will continue to build momentum in the long-term. The challenges to talent mobility that currently exist are partially due to short-term global events or changes in policies and attitudes in certain countries. But evidence shows that the broader trend is toward increased exchanges and cooperation in the field of talent development. This requires an administrative body to coordinate between the various countries and regions among which talent is shared. Only by establishing standards and channels for communication can talent better be allocated and applied, which will ultimately benefit not only the host country, but individuals as well.

**Lu Miao** is Secretary-General of CCG, Young Leader for Munich Security Conference (MSC) and the Deputy Director General of the International Writing Center of Beijing Normal University. She received her Ph.D. in contemporary Chinese studies from Beijing Normal University and has been a visiting scholar at New York University's China House and the Fairbank Center at Harvard University. Dr. Miao is a co-author of many Chinese Social Science Academy blue books and Chinese Social Science Foundation's research project reports. Dr. Miao has published a number of books in Chinese, which detail China's outbound business and global talent. Her latest publications in English are: *International Migration of China: Status, Policy and Social Responses to the Globalization of Migration* (2017); *Blue Book of Global Talent*; *Annual Report on the Development of Chinese Students Studying Abroad* and *China's Domestic and International Migration Development* (2019).

**Open Access** This chapter is licensed under the terms of the Creative Commons Attribution-NonCommercial-NoDerivatives 4.0 International License (http://creativecommons.org/licenses/by-nc-nd/4.0/), which permits any noncommercial use, sharing, distribution and reproduction in any medium or format, as long as you give appropriate credit to the original author(s) and the source, provide a link to the Creative Commons license and indicate if you modified the licensed material. You do not have permission under this license to share adapted material derived from this chapter or parts of it.

The images or other third party material in this chapter are included in the chapter's Creative Commons license, unless indicated otherwise in a credit line to the material. If material is not included in the chapter's Creative Commons license and your intended use is not permitted by statutory regulation or exceeds the permitted use, you will need to obtain permission directly from the copyright holder.

# A Life-Long Inspiration from the 'Willow Pattern'

Sir Anthony Seldon

**Abstract** *Story telling lies at the heart of both Chinese and British cultures. Stories impart truths which academic rigorous texts might not achieve.* This essay uses the *Chinese 'Willow Pattern story' that is deeply embedded in British culture* as an example of *the importance of 'people to people' exchange.* This is also a study of *the value of links between Chinese and British schools.* It is impossible to quantify quite how formative exposure to another country early on in someone's life can be. But it seems that it can only be formative. *Four reasons present themselves for prioritising educational links between nations.* Where divides exist in the world, be they ideological, religious or ethnic, those on both sides, and especially the young, need all the more urgently, opportunities to meet each other. The deeper the divide between China and Britain becomes in the 2020s, the greater the need for schools to cooperate. *The shared history between China and Britain* is a second reason. Both *China and UK have much to learn from each other*, is a third reason. Finally, *China is predicted to become the world's biggest economy* within a decade. It is folly not to find ways of trading more with it, and befriending it, for all the difficulties and differences of opinion.

**Keywords** Story telling lies at the heart of both Chinese and British cultures · Stories impart truths which academic rigorous texts might not achieve · Chinese 'Willow Pattern story' that is deeply embedded in British culture · The importance of 'people to people' exchange · The value of links between Chinese and British schools · Four reasons present themselves for prioritising educational links between nations · The shared history between China and Britain · China and UK have much to learn from each other · China is predicted to become the world's biggest economy

I must have been four or five when I first saw the image. There it was staring at me from out of my reading book, but it was also on my plate at lunch. I recall very clearly—perhaps my first memory—asking my father what it meant. There was

A. Seldon (✉)
University of Buckingham, Buckingham, UK

© The Author(s) 2021                                                                                      205
H. Wang and A. Michie (eds.), *Consensus or Conflict?*, China and Globalization,
https://doi.org/10.1007/978-981-16-5391-9_19

*something* here, I could not explain it, but it seemed to be a story that needed decoding for me. How funny, I thought, a *story in time* printed is still blue ink—on a plate.[1]

My father explained it to me—you all know the story—though I am not certain I understood it even then. An angry and powerful father had rejected his daughter because she would have fallen in love (he might have skipped over that bit) with one of his servants. A marriage is to take place, but with someone more suitable, and the daughter is not happy: the blossom is to fall. The servant persists in his suit, elopes with the daughter, and they are chased over the bridge by the father, whip in hand—I *definitely* remember that bit—till they boarded a boat and land on a faraway island to live happily, but not for ever after. The angry father has them slain, and they become doves.

I was smitten. This was China, and I was avid to learn more, a strange world apart, and I loved the exotic *difference* to the safe world of the home counties.[2] Yet, except with snippets, my appetite for China was not fed: I was told, puzzlingly, that, if everyone in China was to walk past me, they would never stop. But there was nothing about the Chinese on the move, nor indeed standing still, in school—no Chinese history, no music nor culture. I had to wait for my appetite to be quenched, quite literally when a restaurant, the Sun Du, was set up in Sevenoaks, my home town. Every Friday lunchtime, I would go there with fellow gap-year assistants from the local bookshop. In one exotic meal, we regularly blew the entire week's allowance of luncheon vouchers.

This was the Cold War and China was the enemy of the west. The United States filled our television and cinema screens, and the Commonwealth and Europe, especially after Britain joined the EEC in 1973, were the limits of the horizon. China was all but invisible. It was strange, then, that my father, a free-market intellectual and writer, was an enthusiast for *mahjong*, the ivory-tiled game with colourful Chinese characters and symbols printed on them. On Sunday evenings, the 144 tiles would burst out all over the dining room table from the faux leather case that contained them. I cannot explain why the game assumed the importance it did in our family, while it did not in others; but I have no doubt that it helped shape my perceptions and thinking about the world.

# 1  Early Personal Intimations

I had been asked to leave my school for organising a demonstration against the pupil military cadet force organised within the school. Our target of protest was also the war in Vietnam. We noted wryly that, while the former continued to operate, the latter ended shortly after our school demonstration. So, a victory of sorts, we

---

[1] Since the late eighteenth century Chinese designs in still blue ink colour on plates and dinner services have been highly popular in the UK, where they are designs are described as the 'Willow Pattern'.

[2] 'Home counties' refers to the immediate districts surrounding London.

'revolutionaries' thought. The school authorities took a dim view of our youthful exuberance, and I remember being quizzed by the headmaster about whether we had been inspired to rebel by Chairman Mao's 'Little Red Book'. I had absolutely no idea what he was talking about, but I was certainly now eager to find out all about it.

Arriving in Oxford, where I studied Politics, Philosophy and Economics, there was no Chinese Politics, Philosophy nor Economics. No Chinese anything in fact. When I went on to the London School of Economics for my doctorate, I came across Chinese students wearing grey uniform suits, with inscrutable expressions, walking and talking in groups along the wide corridors. I wanted to engage with them, but I had no idea how to break through the barriers. I wanted to understand more about their culture and influences: I had started meditating daily with an eastern tradition a short while before, which opened my eyes to Confucianism. But I could find no one with whom to discuss it.

I began my career as a schoolmaster in 1983, teaching Politics and History. But of China, there was nothing on the syllabus, with the exception of sideways glances when teaching the Vietnam War. *Empire of the Sun* exploded in our cinemas in 1987, based on JG Ballard's novel of 1984, which opens with an English schoolchild in Shanghai separated from his parents at the start of the Second World War. That same year, Bertolucci's film, *The Last Emperor,* was also released. I sent all the students I taught to see them. This was China seen through the eyes of the west, not the real China, but my deep yearning to know more about the real China was only further stimulated.

Fast forward to 1997. I had become head teacher of a boarding school at Brighton College in Sussex. For the first time, I was responsible for students from China! Mostly, they joined in the sixth form, to study maths, physics, chemistry and economics. They were prodigiously bright and naturally did no harm to our league table position. But what concerned me was that they hardly integrated. They were with us, but not fully with us. They rarely played team sports and the only form of arts they became involved in was music. At breakfast, lunch and dinner, they would sit together in groups at the end of the long tables. I knew I should be doing a better job making them feel welcomed and integrated, but had no idea how to set about it.

## 2   Building School Bridges, the UK and China

In 2005, I was appointed to take over Wellington College. Having been too inward looking at Brighton, before I joined, I travelled with my wife Joanna to ten countries to understand what leading state and independent schools were doing elsewhere in the world. I did not want to see schools, however successful were their exam results, writhing to the martial music beat of tests and exams. I wanted to see real schools that were thinking for themselves. First country on my wish list was China, where I wrote to heads of schools in Shanghai and Beijing to ask to visit.

The trip felt like a homecoming and stands out as one of the most inspiring of my life. In the lobby at the Peace Hotel in Shanghai, I met Simon Mackinnon, a future Wellington parent who was a leading figure in the city's Anglo-Chinese community. '*China is the future*,' he told me, and '*you have to reach out to it to understand why.*' I needed little encouragement, but also needed better communication and language skills. At Beijing No. 1 High School, considered one of the most prestigious in the country, I had an underwhelming conversation with the principal. He spoke no English and I spoke no Mandarin. It was a painful hour during which I asked increasingly banal questions and became frustrated at my ineptitude. Lesson number one learned: I have to find a way of communicating better.

I returned to the UK determined to make Wellington College one of the country's leading schools in its outreach to China. As part of that, Wellington branch campuses should be set up in China. Ralph Mainard at Dulwich College, which paved the way in doing just this, was an invaluable guide, as were so many others. After several false starts, the yearned-for email arrived on my Blackberry during a long meeting. "*I have a school in Tianjin and I'm looking for an English partner. Could it be you?*" It most certainly was. That was in 2008, and in 2010, we opened our school in a new residential district in this fascinating coastal city on the Bohai Sea, close to Beijing.

I had visited a number of nondescript international schools around the world, some sponsored by English schools, with no tangible connection nor family resemblance to the mother ship. So, from the outset it was established that the new school buildings should physically resemble Wellington College, which had been founded by Queen Victoria in 1859 as the national memorial to the Duke of Wellington. Key features of that elegant architecture, including brick colour, windows, edifice design and towers, were replicated 7,000 miles away in China. We adopted the names of the houses, and other distinctive characteristics of Wellington, such as our belief in 'eight intelligences'.[3] The DNA of Wellington College had to be implanted, if it was to be a true collaboration. Wellington College has now inspired six international and bilingual schools in China, and by 2022 that will be eight, located in Shanghai, Hangzhou and beyond. The whole enterprise would never have happened without immensely supportive governors, including two successive chairs, Sir Anthony Goodenough, a former diplomat who immediately got it, then Sir Mike Rake, at the time president of the CBI, and governors at large, including Peter Frankopan, author of *The Silk Roads*. The parents, who included many who had worked in the Far East, were uniformly supportive. My task would have been much harder had they not been.

Overseas branches were not enough. It was important to encourage *other* schools, as well as universities and Britain's leading cultural bodies, to set up in China. So, we organised three conferences at Wellington, addressed by HRH Prince Andrew, as well as by government ministers and leading figures at the University of Nottingham, the first university to establish a campus in China. The objective was to explain how and why this should be done and to encourage others to follow suit. It was not an easy sell.

Transplanting British school DNA into China was only half the story. It was imperative that China was implanted into the UK, specifically at Wellington College in

---

[3] The eight intelligences at Wellington College are: Moral, Spiritual, Logical, Linguistic, Physical, Cultural, Social and Personal.

Berkshire. Thus, was born the idea of the Mandarin Centre within Wellington College, opened in May 2012 by the Chinese ambassador, H.E. Liu Xiaoming. Chinese to every plank of its red woodwork, the Mandarin Centre has its own bow-shaped bridge over water to access it (the 'Willow Pattern' no doubt a subliminal influence), and its own Chinese garden with *feng shui* flowing water. The classrooms were dedicated to the teaching of Mandarin, which the school threw resources at, inspired by Richard Cairns, the headmaster at my former school, Brighton College, who had announced that every student would learn Mandarin.

Language proficiency was key, and it seemed important to lead from the front. So, I announced—one of my greatest follies—that I would be learning Mandarin alongside a group of my students, that I would sit GCSE with them, and challenge them to beat me. Oh, my goodness, the hubris! By the second lesson it was evident that they had a much greater ability to understand the different sounds and to write the different shapes. As week followed agonising week, my misery grew. I experienced the deep anxiety that struggling students everywhere feel, of inadequacy, distress and personal failure. By the second term, I knew that it was not going to finish happily. I simply did not have the ability. My students were streets ahead of me, and their effervescent willingness to explain the sounds and characters to me was as touching as it was humiliating. The lesson I drew—apart from the obvious one—was that the younger people start learning Mandarin, the easier.

Only now did I meet a real live head of a Chinese school, with whom I could build a close personal relationship. I had forged the creation of a group of heads at some of the most innovative state and independent schools around the world, called the G20 schools (the political leaders' G20 had yet to be formed), and invited Beijing's High School attached to Renmin University (also known as RDFZ) to join. The principal was the formidable Madame Liu Xiaohui. Her English may have been as convincing as my Mandarin, but we spoke through translators and had an instinctive bond that ran deep. The relationship was founded over table tennis. I foolishly responded in the affirmative to a question from the translator about whether I played the game. What I had not expected was to find that Madame Liu and I were going to be playing a match in front of a large group of spectators, and I was being billed as some kind of former champion. My opponent rarely moved her feet during the entire match, which made my total defeat all the more painful. But it was a reminder how sport, like music and dance, can break through all linguistic barriers.

I was reminded of this when I directed a production of *Othello*, which I was touring with Wellington College students in the Far East. We performed in Beijing at Madame Liu's school. The reaction from an audience, full of spontaneous gasps and sighs, was visceral. This had less to do with the quality of the acting, than with the universal truths of Shakespeare, which cross all frontiers and all time. After the production, the students remained in the large lecture hall in their raked seats, asking question after question probing the meaning. As a board director of the Royal Shakespeare Company (RSC), it made me all the more eager to support our work in China, not least with education. In June 2011, when Premier Wen visited Stratford-upon-Avon with Culture Secretary Jeremy Hunt (who has a Chinese wife), he said; *"We're working with writers, translators, academics and theatre organisations in the UK and China as part of a cultural exchange to share classical Chinese stories written in English with today's audiences"*. The RSC's first major tour of China came in 2016, with Gregory Doran's superb productions of *Henry IV Part I*, *Part II* and *Henry V*. Translations of Shakespeare's plays into Mandarin, and collaborations with writers, translators and academics in both countries followed. New educational partnerships, including with Dulwich International School in Shanghai, have been forged by the RSC's education department. The British Library is another major British institution reaching out to China, showing the way for other bodies to follow.

## 3   Why Cooperation Between Schools is Important

The urgency of links between Chinese and British schools became clear as a direct result of all these encounters. We can never know quite how formative exposure to another country early on in someone's life can be. But it seems that it can only be formative. Four reasons in particular present themselves for prioritising educational links between both countries.

Where divides exist in the world, be they ideological, religious or ethnic, those on both sides, and especially the young, need all the more urgently, opportunities to meet each other. By doing so, they will experience commonalities, rather than reasons for suspicion and mistrust. Children on either side of the Catholic and Protestant divide in Northern Ireland, as from black and white families in the southern states of the United States, or from Muslim and Jewish communities in Israel and Palestine, always gain from this. Lifelong friendships and understandings are forged, and the potential for personal respect grows. The deeper the divide between China and Britain becomes in the 2020s, the greater the need for schools to cooperate.

The shared history between China and Britain is a second reason. Relationships, often far from happy, began in the early seventeenth century. Concessions in Tianjin and Shanghai, the cession of Hong Kong, the two Opium Wars and the Boxer Rebellion, defined and shaped the relationship between both countries. Britain, for better or worse, has been a significant feature in Chinese life for centuries, more so than any other western country. Critics of China in Britain rarely seem to reflect how Britain might have felt had China treated it as Britain treated the Chinese in the nineteenth century. The ubiquitous 'Willow Pattern', which began to be used widely in ceramics and art work in Britain from the 1790s, is just one of many indicators of how deep China permeated British consciousness. Both countries are inextricably intertwined, which is a reason for strong educational links to continue and deepen.

Both countries have much to learn from each other, a third reason. One does not have to be a cynic to recognise that the welcoming of western school and university branches in China is partly because the government wants to learn from them. In my experience, such readiness to learn has been far greater in China than in the west, specifically Britain. In 2015, much excitement was generated when the British government brought in mathematics teachers from Shanghai into Britain. The initiative emphasised how much can be learned from mutual exchange, but also how shallow and transactional the vision of the government on cooperation currently is. In truth, much mutual benefit would come in *every* subject, as well as in extracurricular activity and in education technology if there were to be a much greater exchange. After becoming Vice Chancellor of the University of Buckingham in 2015, we tried to launch the British-Sino Institute in London, to encourage educational and cultural links: it was a difficult time to achieve it, but the quest continues.

Finally, China is predicted to become the world's biggest economy within a decade. It is folly not to find ways of trading more with it, and befriending it, for all the difficulties and differences of opinion. In the future, the more young people in Britain learn Mandarin, and grow in understanding about Chinese culture and customs, given the importance in business relationships of empathy, the more Britain will flourish in its political and trading links with China. The flow is not just one way. Britain might be only the world's fifth biggest economy, and possibly shrinking, but it is still the number one soft power in the world, and its language, its creativity, its universities, cultural bodies and system of government have much to offer China. It has 300 years of contacts and relationships on which to build. China has as much to gain from deepening educational, and broader links with Britain, as vice versa. And China could learn how a pluralist country works in the 21st century. History shows us that, without exception, attempts to hold down a population will never succeed.

# 4   Models for Future School Cooperation

Since the heyday of UK–China relations of the David Cameron and George Osborne era (2010–2016), the drawbridge has been pulled up on British-Chinese relations. The Theresa May government (2016–2019) arrived in power with a deep suspicion of Beijing. I was one of many whom Chinese Ambassador Liu Xiaoming asked about how to thaw relations, to no avail. Influential elements of the right-wing in particular now see no good in China and want nothing to do with it. The treatment of the democracy movement in Hong Kong, the Uighurs in Northwest China, and China's global ambition are among the reasons given. But their suspicion goes far beyond these very troubling concerns.

Regarding China like Britain did Albania in the Cold War is one option, and this will be where we end up if we continue on the current trajectory. This approach implies zero contact between schools in both countries. This strategy is a counsel of despair: a new Cold War will be the result, from which no one will gain. British universities, which depend heavily on Chinese international students, will lose far more than revenue. Research collaborations, student friendships and academic relationships will all be sacrificed and may not be regained.

Very limited contact is a second option, as occurred in the 1980s and 1990s under Deng Xiaoping. Periodic exchanges of students and staff, maybe, but only at a minimal level.

The third option, and the one I favour, envisages a wide and generous school relationship, the most meaningful that China enjoys with any western country, and that Britain has with any country overseas. Exchanges between schools and teachers in both countries could be very significant stepped up in, with every British school encouraged to partner digitally with a school in China, and shared activities between them. But, and this is the significant point, there should be protection guaranteed for the safety and integrity of each British and Chinese student and teacher, agreed understandings about intellectual property, and an absence on both sides of any attempt to proselytise.

The final option is to enjoy this very full level of exchange, but without the safeguards. This would be a mistake. China needs to understand, and respect, that exchange with the liberal west means respect for the individual and for property.

## 5  *Just* a Fable?

Story telling lies at the heart of both Chinese and British cultures. Stories impart truths which the most impeccable and academically rigorous texts might not achieve. Why is it that the Chinese 'Willow Pattern' has had such an enduring hold on our imaginations today?

There are many interpretations of the story, but let us consider it from the point of view of the young—they are the servant and his lover. The love of the servant for the daughter of the powerful man, and her for him, is real and deep. The attempt by father to deny them this fails, as the young couple, from totally different backgrounds, abscond, and find much joy in each other's company, until the powerful father destroys them.

The young in both countries should not have their opportunities to know each other extinguished by those in power in either country. The desire and rights of the young cannot be suppressed forever, and the attempt to do so will ultimately fail because that desire will only rise, dove like, again, until it triumphs.

**Sir Anthony Seldon** is a leading world authority on contemporary British history and education. He is a former Vice-Chancellor of the University of Buckingham. He was formerly Master of Wellington College, one of the world's most famous independent schools. He is author, or editor, of over 40 books on contemporary history, politics and education and is the author on, and honorary historical advisor of, the office of the British Prime Minister at Number 10 Downing Street. He has written books with penetrating insights into the last six past British Prime Ministers. He is governor of several bodies, including the Royal Shakespeare Company, and is Chair of The Comment Awards.

**Open Access** This chapter is licensed under the terms of the Creative Commons Attribution-NonCommercial-NoDerivatives 4.0 International License (http://creativecommons.org/licenses/by-nc-nd/4.0/), which permits any noncommercial use, sharing, distribution and reproduction in any medium or format, as long as you give appropriate credit to the original author(s) and the source, provide a link to the Creative Commons license and indicate if you modified the licensed material. You do not have permission under this license to share adapted material derived from this chapter or parts of it.

The images or other third party material in this chapter are included in the chapter's Creative Commons license, unless indicated otherwise in a credit line to the material. If material is not included in the chapter's Creative Commons license and your intended use is not permitted by statutory regulation or exceeds the permitted use, you will need to obtain permission directly from the copyright holder.

# Global Governance Trends and Dealing with the Digital and Biosphere Revolutions

# Cross-Border Data Policy: Opportunities and Challenges

**Robert D. Atkinson and Nigel Cory**

**Abstract** *Data governance* and the *management of global digital data* flows pose immense challenges for *global governance*. International digital data agreements must be embedded in revisions of the *global "rules based" order* that emerged out of *Bretton Woods* in the aftermath of World War II to manage global economic issues. In that spirit, the countries that value a *rules-based global digital economy* need to come together to enact *new global data management rules*. It is becoming more and more critical to treat data as the key driver of today's global economy. Creating new rules will require policymakers to alter their current approaches, which have led to a stalemate in making progress on *frameworks for the global internet*. China should revise its restrictive approach so that it can play a more constructive role in debates and negotiations between like-minded countries. On *China and internet rules*, if the Chinese Government retains its restrictive approach to data, AI, and digital trade, it will increasingly find itself excluded or marginalized in global discussions on digital issues. Many other countries see the Chinese approach as far from the baseline of emerging global norms and as self-serving for China from a trade perspective.

**Keywords** Data governance · Management of global digital data · Global governance · Global "rules based" order · Bretton Woods · Rules-based global digital economy · New global data management rules · Global internet frameworks · China and internet rules

## 1 Introduction

Global data and digital economy governance are increasingly critical to every country's efforts to support innovation and productivity. Yet, it is an area where little progress has been made at the international level in building a framework for an open, rules-based global digital economy.

R. D. Atkinson (✉) · N. Cory
Information Technology and Innovation Foundation (ITIF), Washington, DC 20001, USA

© The Author(s) 2021
H. Wang and A. Michie (eds.), *Consensus or Conflict?*, China and Globalization,
https://doi.org/10.1007/978-981-16-5391-9_20

These conflicts arise over a myriad of issues, such as free speech, intellectual property, privacy, cybercrime, consumer protection, taxation, commercial regulation, and others. This means the Internet has ended up being guided by both formal and informal rules by international, national, and subnational bodies (whether governmental or non-governmental) throughout its history (Castro 2013).

How a country's domestic regulations impact how its firms and consumers can access and use the Internet and other digital technologies is emerging as a key differentiator in the global race of economic and innovation advantage—which both China and the United States want to win. However, China's restrictive approach to data governance and the digital economy needs to change if it wants to win that race.

China's approach to digital policy is one among many. The key question today is how a world, extremely diverse in income levels, cultures, and types of government, will deal with global technologies and global firms. The differences are significant. Some, including China's data and digital economy governance framework, prioritizes government control, domestic firms and domestic digital economic growth and innovation. The United States and many other nations more easily allow firms and consumers to freely access global markets, platforms, and new and innovative digital products. China should rebalance its approach to allow greater openness for commercial and trade-related digital engagement, lest it miss out on maximizing the benefits of the Internet and working with trading partners on building a new open, rules-based digital economy.

## 2   The Need for a Universal Internet Architecture

There has not been much progress on building a framework for a global digital economy as the push for a single, universal approach to the Internet is embedded within many early discussions, initiatives, and frameworks for the global digital economy. As this essay explains, a universal approach to managing the technical architecture of the Internet is needed, otherwise the Internet will not work. However, as it relates to the policy layer in how laws and regulations affect how people and firms use the Internet, data, and digital technologies, there can be policy differences in how countries manage the Internet. However, where there are substantive shared interests—whether for economic or social reasons—countries should ensure these are aligned. In the global digital economy, key areas for cooperation involve cross-border data flows related to trade, actions against cyber crime, and competition policy.

The United States and China are both leaders in the global digital economy. The reason is that they have a key natural advantage in the global digital economy—scale of their economies and populations. Because digital industries, especially information (including search engines and social networking) and e-commerce, are characterized by scale and network effects, US and Chinese firms are able to capitalize on early leads to be competitive in the global market (Foote and Atkinson 2020). Yet, despite their success, China and the United States' conflicting approaches to managing the domestic and global digital economy demonstrate the current stalemate over Internet policy. China's domestic data governance and digital economic policy is based on state control and keeping most data inside China's borders, while the United States' approach is defined by openness, light-touch regulation, and digital globalism. Yet, these differences do not mean that a new mutually beneficial and acceptable approach to the global digital economy cannot be developed—one that more specifically acknowledges that countries can take conflicting approaches to Internet policy, while working together where there are shared economic benefits.

Every country benefits from a global digital economy framework that supports data-driven innovation and digital trade. While China's digital economic model differs from that of the United States (as well as the European Union), it does not mean that these nations and regions cannot find areas—such as digital trade—that are mutually beneficial, and thus, worthy of building alignment. This essay makes the case that China should reform its current approach to build a clear, mostly open, and innovation-friendly data and digital economy governance framework. China's current model will entail growing costs in the future, as more and more countries seek to work with like-minded partners to build an open and rules-based global digital economy. China's impressive digital economic development would be at a disadvantage if it were to miss the chance to compete in the next phase of the global digital economy.

## 3   Why China Needs to Help Build a Clear, Mostly Open, and Innovation-Friendly Data Governance Framework: A State-Controlled Internet Only Goes so far

China should revise its current approach—with restrictive national security interests outweighing economic competition, innovation, and trade interests—as the cost of this approach will only grow as digital technologies become central to global innovation and trade (Shen 2016). A number of nations, including Australia, Canada, Chile, Peru and Singapore, are pursuing new international digital economy agreements to put in place new rules and regulatory cooperation to ensure their firms and digital economies are more integrated, innovative, and competitive. As domestic digital economic frameworks become more common and mature around the world, more countries will be looking to see which of their trading partners are willing to work together on mutually beneficial digital economy arrangements. Piece-by-piece, these represent an emerging opportunity for countries like China to ensure its firms and consumers can benefit from access to each other's digital economies.

There are also increasing discussions around a global digital trade framework such as former Japanese Prime Minister Shinzo Abe's initiative for "data free flow with trust," launched at the G20 (Cory et al. 2019). More countries are joining the Asia-Pacific Economic Cooperation's Cross-Border Privacy Rules, which is an adaptable approach to ensure that firms are held accountable for managing local data wherever they transfer it. In addition, there are ongoing negotiations among 70-plus countries at the World Trade Organization (WTO) on new e-commerce and digital trade rules.[1] And the Organization for Economic Co-operation and Development (OECD), has emerged as a central hub for research and debates about many global digital economy issues.

A common theme among all these initiatives is that countries can maximize the benefits of the digital economy when they cooperate. However, China is not central to these initiatives. As such, it risks being left behind.

# 4 Key Internet Conflicts

The key question is how different countries deal with the internet and global firms using it. There are several areas of conflicts over global Internet policy: internet governance, data and AI governance and ethics, content moderation, and government surveillance or censorship. To build a new global digital economic framework, countries will need to address these by building compatible approaches that are not overly restrictive of digital trade and data-driven innovation. China, the European Union (EU), and the United States provide three differing models and approaches.

## 4.1 Internet Governance—Differences Between China, the US, and the EU

Internet governance refers to the norms, rules, and technologies that govern the working of the Internet internationally. China advocates for a state-controlled Internet, including at the International Telecommunication Union and other forums it supports, such as the China-hosted World Internet Conference (Segal 2020; Eichensehr 2014). China's limits on allowing free flow of data across borders means it largely avoids making any commitments on these issues in its trade agreements. It has also opposed language on these issues at the G20 and elsewhere.

The United States advocates for a multi-stakeholder-based approach to the Internet that is based on a voluntary, industry-based, and bottom-up standards process, which pushes back against government efforts to dictate how the global internet should work. It advocates for this approach at the ITU, the Internet Corporation for Assigned Names and Numbers (ICAAN, responsible for coordinating databases related to the namespaces of the Internet), and the Internet Governance Forum (Yang 2019). The United States also pursues new trade rules to support data flows and digital trade in bilateral, regional, and multilateral forums and agreements, such as the United

---

[1] "Australia-Singapore Digital Economy Agreement," https://www.dfat.gov.au/trade/services-and-digital-trade/Pages/australia-and-singapore-digital-economy-agreement; "Digital Economy Partnership Agreement," https://www.mti.gov.sg/Improving-Trade/Digital-Economy-Agreements/The-Digital-Economy-Partnership-Agreement.

States–Mexico–Canada trade agreement. The United States' global digital economic policies are often fused with broader efforts to support human rights, like freedom of speech, on the Internet.

At the heart of the EU's international strategy is the push for other countries to also adopt the precautionary principle and to harmonize their data privacy laws to its General Data Protection Regulation (GDPR). GDPR imposes a general prohibition on transfers of EU personal data to only a small group of foreign countries (mainly former colonies) it has determined provide an "adequate" level of protection equal to data protection at home (Atkinson 2015). The EU also supports certain policies that it wants applied to global Internet, such as the impact that GDPR has had on certain ICANN functions (such as identifying domain name holders for criminal investigations and other purposes) and the "right to be forgotten" (which allows a person to have private information removed from Internet searches and other directories, which the EU wants applied not just domestically, but to the global Internet). Overall, the EU tends to support the multi-stakeholder approach to other global Internet issues, but where these conflict with its own laws, it is willing to undermine global cooperation to enact its own (conflicting) approach.

## *4.2   Data and AI Governance Conflicts*

Data governance is the most prominent global conflict within Internet policy. This involves data privacy and protection, portability and sharing, cybersecurity, and government access to data (whether for law enforcement investigations, national security, or political purposes). However, AI governance is also fast emerging as a growing flashpoint. This involves debates about AI development, ethics, and accuracy and explainability.

China's domestic data governance is based on the goal of "cyber sovereignty." China's commercial data privacy framework is evolving and rebalancing from a largely laissez faire approach to how firms use data by adding greater consumer protection (Shi 2020). China requires a range of data to only be stored locally and for the government to have wide ranging access and control over it and the broader digital economy.[2] While the desire for government access to data can make sense, China can achieve this goal by requiring copies of data to be maintained in China, while still allowing data "exports." China also has pursued an active "digital industrial policy" to support growing digital economy firms. However, this has usually meant that Chinese firms have benefited more than foreign digital firms. Some of the world's leading digital firms, including many from the United States, are banned or blocked in China (Cory 2020). While China's approach to AI ethics/governance is still at a

---

[2] Recently reinforced in the draft Personal Information Protection Law, which would expand data localization requirements beyond the "critical information infrastructure" (CII) operators covered in the Cybersecurity Law, requiring non-CII operators in general to store personal data locally if the amount of such data reaches certain thresholds set by the government (Article 40); Cory, "Why China Should Be Disqualified From Participating in WTO Negotiations on Digital Trade Rules."

very early stage, it is heading in a similar direction, given its focus on self-sufficiency (Laskai and Webster 2019).

The United States is focused on a light-touch approach to Internet regulations, such as privacy and AI. From the Clinton administration Internet governance principles crafted by Ira Magaziner, to efforts by the Trump White House supporting a light-touch approach to AI regulation, the US government has generally avoided innovation-harming regulatory regimes and sought to convince other nations of the wisdom of this approach (Thierer 2012).

The EU has embraced the "precautionary principle" where new innovations are approached from a "glass half empty" view, with the urgent need to form a commission of experts—largely academics and "civil society" representatives with little connection to actual R&D and commerce—to study the innovation and how it could be harmful (Kop 2020). The dominant narrative in Brussels is that the strict regulation of privacy, AI, and other emerging technologies is required in order to boost consumer trust, which in turn will give EU firms a leg up over their American and Chinese competitors (McQuinn and Castro). The EU's emerging AI governance framework is applying a similarly restrictive and protectionist approach in favoring local (over foreign) AI and standards.

The EU's all-consuming fears about government surveillance—following the European Court of Justice decisions in *Schrems I* and *II*—means that its evolving data governance framework makes it increasingly difficult to transfer EU personal data outside the region, which acts as a barrier to trade for foreign firms (Cory et al. 2020). The EU singles out the United States for actions that it does not even restrict among its own member states (in terms of surveillance and government access to data). However, recent data and AI-related policies show that this is expanding to include firms from China and other countries. In the context of foreign AI developed by foreign firms (especially China), Commissioner for the Internal Market, Thierry Breton, said firms that develop and use AI could be forced to "retrain algorithms locally in Europe with European data," adding that, "We could be ready to do this if we believe it is appropriate for our needs and our security." Mobike and TikTok have already attracted greater regulatory scrutiny. This will likely continue as Chinese tech firms and their products become more prominent in Europe and elsewhere around the world.

## 4.3  Content Moderation and Censorship

The conflict over online content moderation and censorship is essentially a proxy for the broader conflict over the role of government and human rights in the digital economy. How countries define what content is legal and illegal online and assign legal responsibility (or protection from liability) to Internet platforms and other intermediaries is changing around the world. This is a massive challenge: every minute, more than 500 hours of video are uploaded to YouTube, 350,000 tweets are sent, and 510,000 comments are posted on Facebook (Karanicolas 2020). Yet, how countries go about making their respective approaches as clear, predictable, and as targeted as possible is necessary. This is due to the growing role that digital (creative) content creators and Internet platforms and intermediaries play in global trade and innovation.

Many countries are trying to address a range of legitimate issues, such as hate speech, disinformation, copyright infringing material, child pornography, terrorism-related material, and other issues (Liang and Lu 2012). But beyond efforts to address specific types of content, many democratic nations share a concern about countries like China that remove or block access to content for political purposes (Rayburn and Conrad 2014; Zittrain and Edelman 2003). Conflicts arise as the global nature of the Internet means that content that is legal in one country can be illegal in another. For example, content that is considered hate speech in Germany or is considered politically sensitive in China or Vietnam would be protected as free speech in Australia, the United States and many other countries.

The clearest conflict between the United States and China is over free speech and political censorship. The United States advocates an open internet where nearly all content on the Internet is available to citizens, because of the belief in the ultimate democratizing and empowering force of information. The United States has also created a legal framework that provides legal liability protection for Internet-based intermediaries if they take reasonable steps to remove illegal content, such as via the Digital Millennium Copyright Act and Section 230 of the Communications Decency Act. However, the debate in the United States (and internationally) is often about where to draw the lines around legal and illegal content online. This dialogue is distorted as many cyberlibertarians and open Internet advocates misguidedly equate any efforts to address, block, or remove illegal content online as censorship.

While both the United States and China block content that they deem illegal, the definition of that content is much broader in China. The 'Great Firewall' of China blocks thousands of foreign websites and limits domestic content (Griffiths 2019). Even though political and social concerns may be a central motivation, some have argued that China's internet censorship has served its economic ends in blocking foreign platforms and digital goods.[3]

## 4.4 Government Surveillance and Requests for Data for Law Enforcement Investigations

Government access to data—both law enforcement and surveillance-related—is emerging as a major point of conflict.

---

[3] Testimony to the U.S. Senate Subcommittee on Trade Regarding Censorship as a Non-Tariff Barrier to Trade | ITIF.

Countries have used the specter of foreign government surveillance—both real and imagined—to justify restrictions on data and international data flows.[4] Policymakers fear that data is being accessed directly through a firm's in-country facilities or indirectly via extraterritorial requests for data or operations that target data transferred and stored overseas.

The 2013 Snowden disclosures about US surveillance were the initial catalyst for policy changes around the world, especially in China and Europe. (In 2013 Edward Snowden leaked a vast amount of secret data from the US National Security Agency). The irony is that many of the same Western and democratic countries that denounced US surveillance on the behalf of their citizens, have enacted their own surveillance regimes (Cate and Dempsey 2017). Furthermore, the debate on national security and data flows is often misleading and disingenuous, as countries use national security in a broad and vague manner to enact restrictions on a growing range of data and digital services that are largely commercial, and not directly tied to national security.

Some countries have used the fear of foreign government surveillance to enact restrictive data governance systems that help them control data for political and social ends, which at times means cutting themselves off from the global Internet. China's broad use of national security permeates its data governance, cybersecurity, and related laws.[5] The vague and sweeping nature of Chinese law, combined with the lack of legal checks and balances, gives China the capability to pursue a broad range of data, but it is unclear as to what extent it actually uses this power.

Government concerns over cross-border access to data for law enforcement investigations is another emerging point of conflict. As the threat of global cybercrime rises, there is an increasing need for a better process to manage cross-border requests for data. Yet, cross-border digital law enforcement cooperation is complicated. Requests can involve data that implicates multiple stakeholders, people, and jurisdictions. This may cover the nationalities of the individuals or organizations that own the data, the service providers storing the data, the individuals or organizations accessing the data and, if the data contains personally identifiable information (PII), the individuals described in the data. In today's digital world, it is not hard to see how criminal investigations in one country may involve an email stored in another country and a bank account in yet another.

There are significant differences in how different countries' legal systems facilitate data sharing for law enforcement purposes. Existing legal tools (such as mutual legal assistance treaties) are out-of-date and slow, yet new tools are emerging, such as the US's CLOUD Act agreements (which will make the process much more efficient, while keeping legal safeguards in place) (McQuinn and Castro 2017). Rather than seeking to improve domestic and international legal frameworks to improve cross-border law enforcement cooperation, some policymakers in Brazil, China, India and

---

[4] Surveillance is defined as: "the focused, systematic and routine attention to personal details for purposes of influence, management, protection or direction (Lyon 2007)."

[5] China's Cybersecurity Law states that key IT services only store "important data" within China, which includes "data that, if divulged, may directly affect national security, economic security, social stability, or public health and safety" (Creemers et al. 2018); Although China's government tries to caveat this by stating it does not generally include firm-related data (Tai et al. 2019).

elsewhere have supported data localization as they think it is the only way to get local and foreign firms to respond to requests for data from law enforcement and other agencies. This stems from the mistaken belief that firms can avoid oversight and requests for data by simply transferring data out of the country.

## 5   What is at Stake—A More Integrated and Prosperous Global Digital Economy or Chinese Digital Mercantilism?

Maximizing the benefits of digital technologies will take countries working together to create new norms, rules, and frameworks. On one side: China, the EU and Russia are creating their own walled-off digital economies. On the other side: Australia, Canada, Chile, Japan, Mexico, New Zealand, Peru, Singapore, the United Kingdom, the United States and others are working towards new rules and governance. In the middle: the vast majority of countries who have not yet decided which model they want to follow.

Central to China's challenge is the recognition that its domestic economic interests—characterized by the rise of Baidu, Alibaba, Tencent and other innovative firms—increasingly align with the needs to create a framework that allows greater global data flows and digital trade (Ramamurti and Hillemann 2018; Xinyi and Gereffi 2018). The alternative—a "Balkanized" fragmented global Internet that gives nations the right to act as they please—will inevitably hurt China and its firms.

## 6   Building a More Pragmatic and Integrated Global Digital Economy

Nations are struggling to address cross-border Internet policy issues. One reason is that efforts are not guided by a coherent policy framework. Four principles should guide these efforts.

### 6.1   Principle 1: Adopt a Pragmatic Framework for Cross-Border Internet Policy

Countries need to recognize that when it comes to policies about how the Internet is used, there can be differences among nations. Figure 1 offers a four-cell typology of issues where there can and cannot be consensus and policy issues that involve public benefits and public harms. An example of a policy that can be based on consensus, and involves harms, is restricting child pornography. Every nation agrees with this

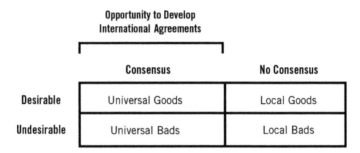

**Fig. 1** Typology of Internet policy goals affecting individuals outside the country

goal. The clearest example of a universal good, and thus the need for universal rules, pertains to frameworks on core Internet architecture and protocols, as the Internet needs commonly shared global standards. A multi-stakeholder approach to maintaining this goal is desirable, as debates and disagreements over the technical architecture and protocols of the Internet can only be resolved with stakeholder consensus. Because there is a presumed global consensus on trade—as evidenced by membership in the World Trade Organization—there should, at least in theory, be able to be a consensus on digital trade issues.

In contrast, issues of data privacy involve a local good, and will be difficult to generate global consensus. Likewise, Internet content moderation is usually a local bad (blocking harmful or objectionable content), but there is unlikely to be consensus among countries (besides on specific content, like child pornography) on what content should be blocked. However, policymakers can still agree that whatever framework a country adopts does not act as a barrier to trade.

A central challenge is that many countries associate data governance with political and social control. Therefore, these countries will oppose global efforts to harmonize rules on data privacy (such as the EU's GDPR). Given the current values-based approach to global Internet policy, these countries are likely to be intractable in coming up with principles and mechanisms that allow robust encryption, privacy, and content moderation and related issues. Every nation needs to recognize that not every country it deals with on the global digital economy will share its values. This is a distinction that policymakers already acknowledge offline with traditional trade.

Ultimately, policymakers need to recognize the critical policy distinction—between policies with global consensus and those without. In many cases, this consensus will (at best) be widespread but not unanimous. Given this reality, it is better that a consensus-based approach be ambitious, but pragmatic, in seeking shared principles and agreements among a like-minded group of countries that represent a substantial part of the global economy and value a mostly open, rules-based global digital economy (see Fig. 1) (Castro and Atkinson 2014).

## 6.2 Principle 2: Data Governance—Focus on Accountability and Legal Nexus, not the Geography of Data Storage

Perhaps the most challenging global internet policy issue relates to cross-border data flows. Rather than tell firms where they can store or process data, policymakers should hold firms that have legal nexus within their borders accountable for managing data they collect, regardless of where they store or process it. This expectation could be made clear in law by declaring that companies doing business in a country are legally responsible for any failures to manage data from that country, regardless of whether those failures are the fault of the firm in that country or abroad, or an affiliate or business partner in that country or abroad. In other words, a country's data-protection rules would travel with the data. The accountability principle is based on the fact that modern technology, especially the Internet and cloud data storage, means that each country's domestic regulatory regime for data (such as for privacy) needs to be globally interoperable given that each country faces the same challenge in applying its laws to firms that may transfer data between jurisdictions. Interoperable privacy frameworks are the international extension of this accountability-based approach such that data is still able to flow between different privacy regimes, and countries data protection rules flow with it.

Interoperability is already at the heart of many countries' data privacy frameworks and at global discussions on data privacy, such as at the OECD and the Asia-Pacific Economic Cooperation's Cross-Border Privacy Rules system.[6] As per ITIF's typology, interoperability is fighting to be the global consensus, as it is a mutually acceptable and beneficial principle to countries, regardless of their political system, their approach to data privacy, or level of development (as opposed to the disadvantages of harmonization and localization). Such an interoperable system would focus on "global protections through local accountability."

While the EU's data protection rules have gained some global traction over the past year (in its efforts to push for a global, harmonized approach to data privacy), there is no reason to suspect that in the future another country or region might not put forth competing rules. For example, imagine if China created its own set of data protection rules and declared that any country wanting to do business in China must have identical data protection laws. Such a scenario would potentially force countries to choose one privacy regime or another. Such a clear divergence would simply deepen the splinternet. This is why it is unrealistic and impractical to demand universal rules on privacy. A better option would be to create an interoperable, accountability-based system that works for all countries and the various ways they enact data privacy and protection.

---

[6] "OECD Privacy Guidelines," https://www.oecd.org/sti/ieconomy/privacy-guidelines.htm; "Current Developments in Privacy Frameworks: Towards Global Interoperability," OECD website, November 1, 2011, http://www.oecd.org/digital/ieconomy/currentdevelopmentsinprivacyframewor kstowardsglobalinteroperability.htm.

## 6.3   Principle 3: Apply Domestic Regulation to Address Challenges of Unwanted Digital Services and Products

Many nations and regions, especially Europe, are pushing for a regime of global AI regulation, rightly understanding that not all AI systems will comport with EU values or laws.[7] And while global efforts to develop and implement AI governance principles (such as that AI systems should minimize undesirable AI bias) are useful and warranted, going further and codifying these into some kind of international legal agreements would be not only difficult to do, but also likely harmful to innovation. It would be difficult to do because just like privacy, it is unlikely that all nations will agree to a single standard. It would be potentially harmful because it is likely that the most restrictive rules would be put in place, limiting the ability of digital and AI developers to innovate.

Just as nations now have the right to regulate the safety of material products (such as cars, food, pharmaceutical drugs) and limit imports that do not meet these standards, they have the same right to do the same with digital products, including ones with AI in them. There is no global standard on genetically modified organisms (GMOs), for example, which is a good thing because it means that countries that take a science-based approach to GMO-based crops, are able to produce and sell to other like-minded nations. While there is no single, harmonized approach to regulating these and other trade-related issues, countries have shown that they can agree upon shared principles and processes in how they regulate these issues so that they share commonalities and that a country's system is generally interoperable with those in other countries. For example, the World Trade Organization's core principles of non-discrimination, most-favored-nation, and transparency and the OECD's privacy principles.[8] These shared principles help ensure countries can address legitimate public policy objectives, but in a way that ensure that domestic regulation is not used as a de facto trade barrier. For digital issues, this would mean that countries could pursue different domestic policy regulatory regimes that are interoperable and supporting digital trade as they form part of an integrated global digital economy.

## 6.4   Principle 4: Recognizing, Reconciling, and Addressing Conflicts over Valued-Based Digital Content

It is critical to recognize that countries can have conflicting rules and regulations regarding values-related digital content (in terms of how each country determines what is and is not illegal online). Countries that are realistic about the task of building

---

[7] https://www.sciencemag.org/news/2020/02/europe-plans-strictly-regulate-high-risk-ai-techno logy.

[8] "OECD Privacy Guidelines," https://www.oecd.org/sti/ieconomy/privacy-guidelines.htm; "Principles of the trading system," World Trade Organization website, https://www.wto.org/english/the wto_e/whatis_e/tif_e/fact2_e.htm.

a broad rules-based global digital economy need to accept (even if they do not necessarily like) the fact that some countries censor information on the Internet for political and social purposes. Indonesia blocks websites and apps for displaying "harmful" material, such as pornography, terrorism-related material, or that related to the lesbian, gay, bisexual, and transgender community (Davies and Silviana). The EU does not have the same commitment to freedom of speech as the United States does. For example, online access to *Mein Kampf* is blocked in Germany, but not in the United States. Any global solution imposed on either country would violate key principles and values. Policymakers and advocates also need to recognize that the practice of authoritarian nations to limit access to certain websites and web pages does not constitute the breaking of the internet. The architecture is still the same and enables cross-border communication, just not all of it.

This principle is also based on the central recognition that not all website blocking constitutes a threat to the open internet. When talking about a data-driven global digital economy, it is important to recognize that not all data flows should be treated the same, as some data flows are rightly illegal. For example, over 30 countries (including many democratic, rule-of-law countries) use website blocking to prevent access to websites engaged in large-scale copyright infringement, illegal gambling services, financial fraud, and child pornography (Cory 2018).

A pragmatic global digital economy strategy will require changes from everyone. The United States needs to move away from an idealist view of digital international relations to a realpolitik one, which is focused more on protecting key economic interests rather than acting as a global ambassador of complete and unfettered Internet openness. Countries do and will continue to take differing approaches to moderating and blocking content online. Countries should develop clear, predictable, and non-discriminatory legal and administrative frameworks for all firms—both foreign and domestic—to use so that they know what online content is and is not illegal.

# 7 Conclusion

Just as there was a set of institutions, agreements, and principles that emerged out of Bretton Woods in the aftermath of World War II to manage global economic issues, the countries that value the role of an open, competitive, and rules-based global digital economy need to come together to enact new global rules and norms to manage a key driver of today's global economy: data. But doing so will require policymakers to make careful changes to their current approaches, which in many instances, have led to the current stalemate in terms of making progress on new rules, norms, and frameworks for the global Internet.

China should revise its restrictive approach to data and digital policies so that it can play a constructive role in debates and negotiations between like-minded countries. If China retains its restrictive approach to data, AI, and digital trade, it will increasingly find itself excluded or marginalized in global discussions on digital issues as other countries will see its approach as far from the baseline of emerging global norms and as self-serving (and not mutually beneficial) from a trade perspective.

# References

Atkinson R (2015) Don't just fix safe harbor, fix the data protection regulation. Euractiv. https://www.euractiv.com/section/digital/opinion/don-t-just-fix-safe-harbour-fix-the-data-protection-regulation/. Accessed 18 Dec 2015

de Bossey C (2005) Report of the working group on internet governance (ITU). https://www.wgig.org/docs/WGIGREPORT.pdf

Castro D, Atkinson R (2014) Beyond internet universalism: a framework for addressing cross-border internet policy (ITIF). http://www2.itif.org/2014-crossborder-internet-policy.pdf. Accessed Sep 2014

Castro D (2013) A declaration of the interdependence of cyberspace. ComputerWorld. https://www.computerworld.com/article/2494710/a-declaration-of-the-interdependence-of-cyberspace.html. Accessed 8 Feb 2013

Cate F, Dempsey J (2017) Bulk collection: systematic government access to private-sector data. Oxford University Press, Oxord. https://www.oxfordscholarship.com/view/10.1093/oso/9780190685515.001.0001/oso-9780190685515

Cory N (2018) The normalization of website blocking around the world in the fight against piracy online. Innovation Files, blog post. https://itif.org/publications/2018/06/12/normalization-web site-blocking-around-world-fight-against-piracy-online. Accessed 12 June 2018

Cory N (2020) Testimony to the U.S. Senate Subcommittee on trade regarding censorship as a non-tariff barrier to trade (ITIF, testimony). https://itif.org/publications/2020/06/30/testimony-us-senate-subcommittee-trade-regarding-censorship-non-tariff. Accessed 30 June 2020

Cory N, Atkinson RD, Castro D (2019) Principles and policies for "Data Free Flow With Trust" (ITIF). https://itif.org/publications/2019/05/27/principles-and-policies-data-free-flow-trust. Accessed 27 May 2019

Cory N, Dick E, Castro D (2020) The role and value of standard contractual clauses in EU-U.S. Digital Trade (ITIF). https://itif.org/publications/2020/12/17/role-and-value-standard-con tractual-clauses-eu-us-digital-trade. Accessed 17 December 2020

Creemers R, Triolo P, Webster G (2018) Translation: cybersecurity law of the People's Republic of China. DigiChina blog post. https://www.newamerica.org/cybersecurity-initiative/digichina/blog/translation-cybersecurity-law-peoples-republic-china/. Accessed 29 June 2018

Davies E, Silviana C (2018) New Indonesia web system blocks more than 70,000 'negative' sites. Reuters. https://www.reuters.com/article/us-indonesia-communications/new-indonesia-web-sys tem-blocks-more-than-70000-negative-sites-idUSKCN1G30KA. Accessed 19 Feb 2018

Eichensehr K (2014–2015) The cyber-law of nations. Georgetown Law J 103:317–380

Foote C, Atkinson R (2020) Chinese competitiveness in the international digital economy (ITIF, November 23, 2020)

Griffiths J (2019) The Great firewall of China: how to build and control an alternative version of the internet. Zed Books Ltd.

Karanicolas M (2020) Moderate globally, impact locally: a series on content moderation in the Global South. Yale Law School. https://law.yale.edu/isp/initiatives/wikimedia-initiative-interm ediaries-and-information/wiii-blog/moderate-globally-impact-locally-series-content-modera tion-global-south. Accessed 5 Aug 2020

Kop M (2020) Quantum technology and the law. European Commission website. https://futurium.ec.europa.eu/en/european-ai-alliance/document/quantum-technology-and-law. Accessed 16 Nov 2020

Laskai L, Webster G (2019) Translation: Chinese expert group offers 'Governance Principles' for 'Responsible AI'. DigiChina blog post. https://www.newamerica.org/cybersecurity-initiative/digichina/blog/translation-chinese-expert-group-offers-governance-principles-responsible-ai/. Accessed 17 June 2019

Liang B, Lu H (2012) Fighting the obscene, pornographic, and unhealthy: an analysis of the nature, extent, and regulation of China's online pornography within a global context. Crime Law Social Change 58(2):111–130

Lyon D (2007) Surveillance studies: an overview. Polity Press, Cambridge

McQuinn A, Castro D (2017) How law enforcement should access data across borders (ITIF). https://itif.org/publications/2017/07/24/how-law-enforcement-should-access-data-across-borders. Accessed 24 July 2017

McQuinn A, Castro D (2018) The scholarly evidence is quite clear that strong regulations deter innovation and don't spur more adoption. ITIF. https://itif.org/publications/2018/07/11/why-stronger-privacy-regulations-do-not-spur-increased-internet-use. Accessed 11 July 2018

Ramamurti R, Hillemann J (2018) What is "Chinese" about Chinese multinationals? J Int Bus Stud 49:34–48. https://doi.org/10.1057/s41267-017-0128-2

Rayburn M, Conrad C (2014) China's internet structure: problems and control measures. Int J Manag 21(4):471–480

Segal A (2020) China's alternative cyber governance regime (Council on Foreign Relations). https://www.uscc.gov/sites/default/files/testimonies/March%2013%20Hearing_Panel%203_Adam%20Segal%20CFR.pdf.Accessed 13 Mar 2020

Shen H (2016) China and global internet governance: toward an alternative analytical framework. Chin J Commun 9(3):304–324. https://itif.org/publications/2020/11/23/chinese-competitiveness-international-digital-economy

Shi M (2020) China's draft privacy law both builds on and complicates its data governance. DigiChina blog post. https://www.newamerica.org/cybersecurity-initiative/digichina/blog/chinas-draft-privacy-law-both-builds-on-and-complicates-its-data-governance/. Accessed 14 Dec 2020

Tai K, Laskai L, Creemers R, Shi M, Neville K, Triolo P (2019) Translation: China's new draft 'Data Security Management Measures'. DigiChina blog post. https://www.newamerica.org/cybersecurity-initiative/digichina/blog/translation-chinas-new-draft-data-security-management-measures/. Accessed 31 May 2019

Thierer A (2012)15 Years on, President Clinton's 5 principles for internet policy remain the perfect paradigm. Forbes. https://www.forbes.com/sites/adamthierer/2012/02/12/15-years-on-president-clintons-5-principles-for-internet-policy-remain-the-perfect-paradigm/?sh=30b1c6fb7170. Accessed 12 Feb 2012

Xinyi W, Gereffi G (2018) Amazon and Alibaba: internet governance, business models, and internationalization strategies. Int Bus Inf Digit Age 13:327–356

Yang Y (2019) Mixed messages at China's tech summit. Financial Times. https://www.ft.com/content/b7d48d5e-ff65-11e9-be59-e49b2a136b8d. Accessed 6 Nov 2019

Zittrain J, Edelman B (2003) Internet filtering in China. IEEE Internet Comput 7(2):70–77

**Robert D. Atkinson** is the Founder and President of the Information Technology and Innovation Foundation (ITIF), a global top think tank for science and technology policy. He is an internationally recognized scholar and author whom The New Republic has named one of the "three most important thinkers about innovation." He holds a Ph.D. in city and regional planning from the University of North Carolina, Chapel Hill, where he was awarded the prestigious Joseph E. Pogue Fellowship. He earned his master's degree in urban and regional planning from the University of Oregon, which named him a distinguished alumnus in 2014.

**Nigel Cory** is an associate director covering trade policy at (ITIF). Cory holds a master's degree in public policy from Georgetown University and a bachelor's degree in international business and commerce from Griffith University in Brisbane, Australia.

**Open Access** This chapter is licensed under the terms of the Creative Commons Attribution-NonCommercial-NoDerivatives 4.0 International License (http://creativecommons.org/licenses/by-nc-nd/4.0/), which permits any noncommercial use, sharing, distribution and reproduction in any medium or format, as long as you give appropriate credit to the original author(s) and the source, provide a link to the Creative Commons license and indicate if you modified the licensed material. You do not have permission under this license to share adapted material derived from this chapter or parts of it.

The images or other third party material in this chapter are included in the chapter's Creative Commons license, unless indicated otherwise in a credit line to the material. If material is not included in the chapter's Creative Commons license and your intended use is not permitted by statutory regulation or exceeds the permitted use, you will need to obtain permission directly from the copyright holder.

# Technology, Sovereignty and Realpolitik

Hermann Hauser

**Abstract** This analysis exposes how the *current revolution in the digital and biospheres* creates *threats to national sovereignty* in new ways. The view of *sovereignty built on military strength* is outdated. Sovereignty of a nation is defined as the "*supreme authority in a territory*", but it is better understood by examining the freedom from one-sided dependencies and military or economic coercion. In the past, sovereignty was mainly associated with military dependency and the resulting coercion by foreign states. This has changed with the *rise of technology and its importance to the economy*. *Dependence on critical technologies* can lead to *economic coercion by states* and large companies which are as effective as the military one. In the future, every nation or group of nations must ask itself three questions: Do we have *control over critical technologies*? If not, do we have *access to critical technologies* from a number of independent countries? If still not, do we have guaranteed, unfettered, long-term (more than 5 years) access to monopoly or oligopoly suppliers of a single country (Typically this will be the US or China)? If the answer to all three questions is no, then that nation is open to *economic coercion that is no less severe than the military coercion* of yesteryear.

**Keywords** Revolution in the digital and biospheres · Threats to national sovereignty · Sovereignty built on military strength · "Supreme authority in a territory" · Rise of technology and its importance to the economy · Dependence on critical technologies · Economic coercion by states · Control over critical technologies · Access to critical technologies

## 1 Introduction and Definition

Sovereignty is defined as the "*supreme authority in a territory*". But it is best understood by examining the freedom from one-sided dependencies and military or economic coercion. In the past, sovereignty was mainly associated with military dependency and the resulting coercion by foreign states. This has changed with the

H. Hauser (✉)
Amadeus Capital Partners, Cambridge, UK

© The Author(s) 2021

H. Wang and A. Michie (eds.), *Consensus or Conflict?*, China and Globalization, https://doi.org/10.1007/978-981-16-5391-9_21

233

rise of technology and its importance to the economy. Dependence on critical technologies can lead to economic coercion by states and large companies which are as effective as the military one.

It became clear during the COVID-19 crisis how dependent the world was on Chinese manufacturing of masks and PPE, while the Trump administration made the world aware that China was dependent on the USA for chip design software and the global dollar-based payment infrastructure.

## 2 The 3 Key Questions on Technology Sovereignty

In the future, every nation or group of nations must ask itself three questions:

1.  Do we have control over critical technologies?
2.  If not, do we have access to these technologies from a number of independent countries?
3.  If still not, do we have guaranteed, unfettered, long term (more than 5 years) access to monopoly or oligopoly suppliers of a single country (Typically this will be the US or China)?

If the answer to all three questions is no, we lay ourselves open to economic coercion that is no less severe than the military coercion of yesteryear.

## 3 An Ideal World

To better understand the situation we are in, let us examine an ideal utopian world. This is where most major nations, or federation of nations (like the EU), enjoy the following characteristics:

1.  Every region has most, or all of the critical, technologies and access to most, or all of the relevant, supply chains. Each area can manufacture products based on these technologies and has the software, logistics and payment systems to make it work for their economy, their government and for export.
2.  There are open worldwide standards and IP arrangements for each of the technologies to ensure healthy competition between the regions resulting in vibrant global trade between all regions. This creates many dependencies, but they are all symmetric ensuring they do not lead to coercion whereas withholding technology or products from one region would produce a reciprocal action in the opposite direction.
3.  There is no dependency on a single region for anything.

The reality is very far from this ideal state as most advanced critical technologies are concentrated in a small number of nations, namely, the US, EU, China, Japan and Korea.

# 4   Analysis Tools

An excellent report on technology sovereignty (Edler et al. 2020) by the Fraunhofer Gesellschaft, a world leading research institute, helps us with analysis.

Firstly, we need to determine whether a technology is critical. That means determining if a technology is indispensable, now or in the future, and how access to that technology could be threatened by external shocks. These shocks can be natural like the COVID-19 crisis or man-made by states exercising extra-territorial coercion.

Secondly, we need to examine the functional context in which a technology is critical. Is it economic competitiveness, meeting social needs such as healthcare, energy supply, communications infrastructure, transport and logistics, or sovereign tasks like the security of citizens.

Thirdly, we need to define the spatial-political system boundaries, in which technology sovereignty can be achieved.

Fraunhofer lists the following tools and methods to decide whether a region is technologically sovereign:

- The number of patents and percentages of world patents that a region holds in a particular technology sector;
- The number of publications and contributions to world standards of a region, which indicates the degree of autonomy, it has in shaping the future of a specific technology;
- Technology and resource-specific production statistics that enable the identification of the regional availability of relevant resources and production capacities;
- Technology specific export shares which provide information about the international competitiveness of the production of a state or a federation of states.

The following helps us understand the dependencies and access to competencies and resources from other regions.

- International standards, patent pools and open-source repositories which provide information about internationally available technologies that can be used;
- Trade balances grouped and analysed by technology provide information about the dependence of a state or a federation of states on technology-specific imports (resources and components), and their distribution;
- Complexity indices make it possible to estimate the dependence of relevant geographical areas on specific technologies and how these technologies are integrated into local or regional innovation and value chains;
- Analyses of World Trade Organisation (WTO) compliance enable a concrete assessment of the reliability of potential partner nations in specific issues;
- Analyses of the World Bank's World Governance Index, various corruption indices and indices on the form of governance make it possible to assess the basic reliability of potential partner nations.

## 5   Examples of Critical Technologies

The following examples were chosen to illustrate these issues: 5G, 5 nanometer semiconductor fabs, virus technology and payment systems.

### *5.1   5G*

This is a global standard which originated in Europe as Groupe Speciale Mobile (GSM). Setting global standards is one of Europe's strengths as it had to accommodate the requirements of many different European nations in the European Union. The EU is the only major region in the world that has a significant government structure above the nation state. The EU marshalled this edifice having realised that much is to be gained by giving up a small amount of national sovereignty for the benefit of all EU citizens. Although this has also caused some problems, as Brexit has shown, it is the best working example we have that can guide us towards nations sharing some technology sovereignty for the benefit of mankind as a whole.

To understand any critical technology like 5G we have to look at standards, fundamental patents, research capabilities, innovation, manufacturing capacity, software, logistics and payment infrastructure.

At present, Chinese companies, especially Huawei and ZTE, account for 33% of total 5G patents worldwide, South Korea comprises 27%, European companies 17%, and US/North American companies 14% (Edler et al., 2020). This produces a reasonable Herfindahl Hirschman Index (HHI) value, the accepted measure of supplier concentration, taking into account the number of players and their market share. The lead supplier with the most advanced technology and the largest market share is Huawei.

The US feels threatened by Huawei's dominance and has started a campaign against the company using American dominance in design software for semiconductor chips. As practically all the chips in the world are designed using US software and President Trump could coerce non-US companies as well as TSMC (Taiwanese Semiconductor Manufacturing Company), the main foundry supplier to Huawei, to stop supplying them with state-of-the-art chips. The US also used security concerns to coerce other countries like the UK to stop buying Huawei equipment. This example is an excellent example of how economic coercion is just as effective as military might, but much less controversial.

Imagine the following hypothetical scenario:

> Vice-Admiral Eugene H. Black III, commander of the US 6th fleet, makes a request of the British Prime Minister and pointed to the positions that his fleet had taken up in the English Channel. In this case, most people in Britain would object to this interpretation of the special relationship.

Now let us examine a real situation in 2020:

Mike Pompeo, the US Secretary of State requested that the UK Prime Minister stop using Huawei 5G products. Pompeo implied that if the UK did not comply with the ban on Huawei, the US would stop sharing intelligence with the UK. Both parties also understood that the USA controls the payment infrastructure of the City of London. In addition, US software is needed for the design of all UK electronic chips. However, there was no public outcry at this demand from Pompeo. This was despite the fact that the thorough security analysis by GCHQ, the UK's world renowned security organisation had concluded that it was safe to use Huawei products in non-critical parts of 5G infrastructure. Pompeo's coercion was equally blatant, but technological might is less visible to the public than a US aircraft carrier at the mouth of the Thames.

In the past, Britain's dependence on other nations was overlooked because it was believed that supply chains were secure. Also, the USA was considered a friendly, dependable ally. Both these assumptions have been brought into question by recent events.

## 5.2   5 nanometer (nm) Semiconductor Fabrication

The most advanced electronic devices today, including smartphones, 5G processors, and server chips for data centres all require 5 nm fabrication. Intel, which used to be the leading semiconductor processor company in the world, has recently fallen behind and there are now only two suppliers capable of delivering 5 nm chips: Taiwanese Semiconductor Corporation (TSMC) and Samsung in Korea.

This is clearly an unacceptable concentration of suppliers. The US has asked TSMC to build a state-of-the-art factory in Phoenix Arizona,[1] so they have local access to the latest technology. Samsung is also building fabrication plants in the US. The EUR 672bn Recovery and Resilience Facility of the EU includes EUR 145bn for semiconductor and processor technologies.[2] China has made it a national priority to develop an independent semiconductor technology and is willing to spend even larger amounts.[3] However, unless each region develops its own design software, the dependence on the US will remain.

By using the US monopoly on chip design software as a weapon, Trump has caused the rest of the world to scramble for alternatives. As is so often the case with short term populist thinking, the result will be the opposite of what was intended. Both the EU and China will develop their own software to ensure independence from the US and the ability of the US to export their software and use it for economic coercion will disappear.

---

[1] https://www.bloomberg.com/news/articles/2020-11-19/tsmc-wins-approval-from-phoenix-for-12-billion-chip-plant.

[2] https://ec.europa.eu/info/business-economy-euro/recovery-coronavirus/recovery-and-resilience-facility_en.

[3] https://www.brookings.edu/techstream/lagging-but-motivated-the-state-of-chinas-semiconductor-industry/.

## 5.3   Anti-virus Technology

The COVID-19 pandemic has shown the world how dependent many nations are on Chinese manufacturing. If COVID-19 had been more deadly, and all transport had to be shut down to stop infections from spreading, most nations would have had to go without masks and PPE. This is a clear dependency that is unacceptable and local manufacturing needs to be set up to prevent this from happening in the future. In this case, the technology involved is not advanced and it should be a straight forward goal to achieve.

When it comes to vaccines themselves, the world has shown amazing ingenuity and resolve to come up with new vaccines in record time. While the first vaccines have come from technology leaders like Germany, the UK, the US, China and Russia, there are now 200 vaccines in development in many different countries. It is unlikely that this will result in dependence, but there is a great deal of controversy of manufacturing capacity, speed of delivery and how to help developing nations cope if they cannot afford to purchase vaccines.

## 5.4   International Payment Systems

The U.S. walked away from the Iran agreement. Europe has not and would like to do some trade with Iran, but they are being bullied by the U.S. Treasury," said Gary Smith, founder of Sovereign Focus, a consultancy based in London. "So, having an alternative payment system that Europe can use without falling foul of the U.S. Treasury is something that probably has some appeal.[4]

Last year, the US State Department put the Hong Kong Chief Executive, Carrie Lam and other senior executives on a list that bars them from accessing the US financial system. Even China's largest state-run banks operating in Hong Kong have had to comply to ensure access with crucial dollar funding. Major lenders with operations in the US, including the Bank of China, China Construction Bank and China Merchants Bank have become cautious on opening new accounts for the officials on the list, including Lam, Bloomberg News reported in August.[5]

These dramatic extraterritorial powers of the US have forced the rest of the world to look for an alternative to the US dollar dominated financial system. Central Bank Digital Currencies (CBDC) are seen as a way to become independent from US control of the financial sector. China has the most advanced CBDC, which has already been rolled out in four Chinese cities and will play an important role in the Belt and Road initiative (BRI). At the same time, Europe is also working on an electronic version of the Euro—the e-Euro.

---

[4] https://www.nasdaq.com/articles/cbdcs-could-challenge-us-dollars-dominance%3A-deutsche-bank-2020-09-30.

[5] https://www.bloombergquint.com/global-economics/chinese-banks-move-to-comply-with-u-s-sanctions-on-hong-kong.

The former head of the Bank of England, Mark Carnie, proposed Synthetic Hegemonic Currencies (SHC)[6] at the 2019 Jackson Hole Economic Policy Symposium attended by the heads of the world's major central banks. This proposal by Carnie was as a response to private stable coin initiatives like the Facebook Libra. One of the objectives was to "*dampen the domineering influence of the US dollar on global trade*". The SHC would consist of a basket of the main trading currencies in the world proportional to the trading volume in a particular currency rather than having the majority of international transactions denominated in dollars despite the US only accounting for 15% of world trade.

Unfortunately, the US is not alone in using economic coercion to promote its agenda. Australia has also been pushed by China:

> China has slapped punitive tariffs on Australian barley, restricted beef imports and begun an anti-dumping inquiry into wine exports. Chinese importers have warned their Australian partners that wine, lobster, timber, sugar, coal and copper would face trade disruption from last Friday, according to verbal briefings delivered by Chinese authorities. (Financial Times 2020)

These powers of economic coercion are no longer wielded by governments alone but are increasingly exercised by technology monopolies, which states have allowed to surreptitiously grow into the behemoths they are today. The list of these quasi-monopolies, with powers that often exceed those of the state, has grown frighteningly large and covers many aspects of our daily lives. These include Google, Facebook, Twitter, Netflix and Amazon in the US and the Chinese companies Alibaba, Tencent and Baidu.

There is no alternative to breaking up what are, in reality, monopolies. In the US, control must be returned to the people through their elected government by creating a number of competitive players and curbing the excessive power they accumulate by buying up every successful company vaguely related to their sector.

Thomas Philippon's book *The Great Reversal—How America Gave Up on Free Markets* (Philippon 2019) documents the decline of anti-trust activities in the US due to the power of lobbying in the US politics. This has allowed some of these companies to become de facto monopolies.

The recent activity in China against ANT, owner of Alipay and affiliate of Alibaba Group, is a good example of state intervention as ANT became so large that it was a potential threat to the stability of the entire financial system in China.

---

[6] https://www.bankofengland.co.uk/-/media/boe/files/speech/2019/the-growing-challenges-for-monetary-policy-speech-by-mark-carney.pdf.

## 6 Territories with Technology Sovereignty

I would now like to address the issue of how big a territory has to be to enjoy technological sovereignty.

Let us start with a household. A typical family has sovereignty over their home. They can decide when and what to drink and eat, when to turn on the lights or the vacuum cleaner and what to watch on TV and when to use the Internet and what websites to visit. Or do they?

For most people in the world, drinking requires a water supply and food comes from the supermarket, as 50% of the world's population now lives in cities. Electricity is delivered by the power company through power lines and the Internet needs telephone lines or mobile infrastructure connections. From this perspective, a household's sovereignty is actually very limited and all but the most determined hermits have decided to share their sovereignty over water, food, electricity and the Internet with other people in their village or city. As they have to pay for all these goods, they are also dependent on a national payment infrastructure.

Can cities be sovereign? Many cities have their own water supply, but depend on national supermarket chains and their logistics for the food supply. Electricity is often generated locally, but in order to ensure the supply is not disrupted, they are often linked to a national power grid. The need of people to communicate and travel outside individual cities, there are also national telecoms and transport infrastructures that are based on approved standards.

So, can nations be sovereign? This is where technology makes a big difference. Most developed nations have managed to create their own water production systems and power networks, and many even produce a significant portion of their food supply.

But the latest critical technologies like 5G, 5 nm semiconductors, global payment infrastructures etc. are not available to most nations. The key question then becomes which territories have the ability to be technologically sovereign in ALL critical technologies. The obvious answer is that there are only three such regions in the world: the US, the EU and China. This poses a dilemma for nations outside these three blocks as they are dependent on one of the three for at least some of these technologies, which are critical for the functioning of their economy and government. This creates dependence that can lead to economic coercion, which is precisely what happened in the UK with 5G.

The only stable long-term solution is to try and get closer to the utopian vision of technology sovereignty by sharing advanced technologies amongst regions on a reciprocal basis. This strategy is the exact opposite of the "America First" concept. We should help China and others to gain access to 5 nm semiconductor technology in exchange for building factories, say in Europe for the European market and share jointly developed future IP with partners. The principle of reciprocity is the key enabler of this strategy. This worked well for the Japanese car industry in Europe. It is only through mutual dependence that we can achieve a stable long-term state in technology sovereignty. This is particularly important for new technologies, which will be critical to the proper functioning of our economies and governments in the next decade or two.

These new technologies include: AI and machine learning, quantum computing, synthetic technology, and blockchain technologies. It is important that we again set global standards in these fields and promote an open research community to share in the latest breakthroughs and then make sure that new one-sided dependencies are not created by either excluding nations from certain technologies or allowing overbearing tech companies to appear and monopolise a particular sector.

Globalisation and the division of labour across the world is clearly beneficial to all but as COVID-19 has shown supply chains can be disrupted. Building resilience into the system is a key requirement for the adoption of these powerful new technologies.

# 7 Conclusion

Technology sovereignty has become a dominant issue for the coming decade. The absence of such sovereignty can lead to one-sided technological dependencies which in turn can lead to economic coercion. In order to avoid a new era of economic colonialisation based not on military occupation, but on technological dependencies, we establish global technical standards and a fair exchange of new technologies through licensing and sharing of manufacturing knowhow that is reciprocal. This will avoid one-sided dependencies and the stresses caused by trade wars.

# References

Edler J et al (2020) Technology sovereignty. Fraunhofer Gesellschaft
Financial Times (2020) https://www.ft.com/content/b764e4c9-cc38-43b6-848c-dba0cbc6475a. Accessed 11 Nov 2020
Philippon T (2019) The great reversal—how America gave up on free markets. Harvard University Press

**Hermann Hauser** has contributed to the translation of science into business for over thirty years. He has successfully developed and financed over 100 high-tech companies. These include Acorn Computers in 1978 and ARM Holdings in 1990. He went on to co-found Amadeus Capital Partners in 1997. As the author of a 2010 influential report, he called for the UK government's investment in a network of technology and innovation centres. This led to the creation of 'Catapult' Centres. He is a Fellow of the Institute of Physics and of the Royal Academy of Engineering and an Honorary Fellow of King's College, Cambridge. He is also Vice-Chair of the European Innovation Council.

**Open Access** This chapter is licensed under the terms of the Creative Commons Attribution-NonCommercial-NoDerivatives 4.0 International License (http://creativecommons.org/licenses/by-nc-nd/4.0/), which permits any noncommercial use, sharing, distribution and reproduction in any medium or format, as long as you give appropriate credit to the original author(s) and the source, provide a link to the Creative Commons license and indicate if you modified the licensed material. You do not have permission under this license to share adapted material derived from this chapter or parts of it.

The images or other third party material in this chapter are included in the chapter's Creative Commons license, unless indicated otherwise in a credit line to the material. If material is not included in the chapter's Creative Commons license and your intended use is not permitted by statutory regulation or exceeds the permitted use, you will need to obtain permission directly from the copyright holder.

# Trends in the Global ICT Industry—Globalization, Competition and the Internet of Things

Peter Nolan

**Abstract** This essay provides an analysis of *the Internet of Things.* The facts provided differ greatly from the opinions that dominate media both inside and outside of China. The Internet of Things needs to be considered in terms of not just a single part of the architecture, but rather, in terms of the comprehensive structure of global data transmission, storage and analysis. Huawei has a significant role within one segment of that structure. However, within the whole structure, *Huawei has a small role in the Internet of Things.* So far, the entire structure of the Internet of Things is dominated by firms from high-income countries, especially the US. Three super-large firms—*Amazon, Microsoft and Alphabet-Google—have leveraged their dominant position* to establish an early lead in cloud computing software and services. These three behemoths account for 38% of the total R&D spending and 34% of the net sales revenue for the 321 firms in the G2500 ICT software and services sector. Collectively, they account for almost 60% of global revenue from software services for the public cloud. *Huawei is China's only high technology company with a significant global market* share outside China.

**Keywords** The Internet of Things · Huawei has a small role in the Internet of Things · Amazon, Microsoft and Alphabet-Google—have leveraged their dominant position · Huawei is China's only high technology company with a significant global market

## 1 Background

Since the 1980s, a revolution has taken place in information and communication technology (ICT). The revolution has penetrated every sector of the economy and society. It has transformed the way in which governments function. It has transformed financial services. It has also transformed every part of non-financial services, including

The data in this paper are from P. Nolan, *China and the West: Crossroads of Innovation,* Routledge, 2022 (forthcoming).

P. Nolan (✉)
China Centre, Jesus College, Cambridge University, Cambridge, UK

© The Author(s) 2021                                             243
H. Wang and A. Michie (eds.), *Consensus or Conflict?*, China and Globalization,
https://doi.org/10.1007/978-981-16-5391-9_22

telecommunications, retail, travel and tourism, entertainment, mass media, professional services, health care and education. It has transformed every part of the world's manufacturing system, including aerospace, automobiles, beverages and biomedical products. The revolution has transformed the internal operations of global companies, enabling them to overcome managerial diseconomies of scale. It has even transformed the nature of the R&D process, the nature of their products, as well as the relationship of the systems integrator firms with their supply chain and with their customers. The pace of the ICT revolution is accelerating with the advent of cloud computing, Artificial Intelligence, Machine Learning and the Internet of Things.

The modern ICT revolution began in the 1970s. Intel was founded in 1968, and in 1971 it produced the world's first commercial microprocessor chip. In 1973, Hewlett Packard produced the first desktop micro-computer with a keyboard and mouse. In 1977, Apple launched the first mass-market ready-assembled personal computer. The sales of PCs reached 71 million in 1996, soaring to 366 million in 2011.

The ICT revolution accelerated with the emergence of the World Wide Web and the modern Internet in the mid-1990s, but its penetration has greatly increased in recent years: the number of Internet users increased from 390 million (16% of the world population) in 2000 to 4.6 billion (59% of the world population) in 2020.

The share of telecommunications information carried over the Internet increased from 1% in 1993 to 51% in 2000, climbing to 97% in 2007.

Easily usable search engines began to emerge at the end of the 1990s: Yahoo was established in 1995 and Google in 1998. The combination of the PC, the World Wide Web and the web browser for access to the internet transformed a significant fraction of modern life, both business and personal.

The first mass-market mobile phone was produced by Nokia in 1992. The first mass-market smartphone was launched by Apple (the iPhone) in 2007.

E-commerce took off in the new millennium: Amazon's revenues increased from USD 2.4 billion in 2004 to USD 34 billion in 2010, before accelerating to USD 281 billion in 2019.

Social media hardly existed before 2000. Facebook was founded in 2004 and YouTube in 2005. The number of 'active users' of social media increased from 970 million in 2010 to 3.8 billion in 2020. In July 2019, Facebook and YouTube both had over 2 billion 'active users'.

Servers have been a vital part of information technology networks throughout the modern information technology era. Advances in software and semi-conductors have combined with new generations of servers to produce a new era of information technology.

Clusters of private servers for local clients within firms and institutions have been increasingly superseded by public 'cloud' computing, based on giant data centres distributed across the world, connected by 'dark fibre' submarine and terrestrial communication networks.

Cloud computing services for data storage and analytics are paid for on a 'per service' (IaaS, PaaS and SaaS).[1] Revenues from cloud computing have increased

---

[1] 'Infrastructure as a Service', 'Platform as a Service' and 'Software as a Service'.

from less than USD 6 billion in 2008 to over USD 200 billion in 2019. Development of the 'cloud' has been greatly accelerated by the development of the 'Internet of Things' (IoT), with a huge expansion of embedded semi-conductors in almost every piece of complex machinery, from in-car infotainment systems to refrigerators. The global market for semi-conductors increased from USD 340 billion in 2015 to USD 440 billion in 2019, and is predicted to reach USD 650 billion in 2025. Advances in machine learning and artificial intelligence are likely to stimulate even further development of cloud computing.

The ICT sector has been at the leading edge of innovation in the recent era and it will be even more important in the years ahead. It is the sector in which by far the greatest amount is spent on R&D, amounting to over two-fifths of total R&D spending by the world's top 2,500 companies.[2] Firms with their headquarters in the USA account for 55% of total R&D spending on ICT hardware and software by G2500 companies. The dominance of American firms is especially noticeable in software and services: they account for 72% of total R&D spending in this sector by G2500 firms.

The ICT industry has been characterized by a high number of mergers and acquisitions, which has contributed to a high level of industrial concentration in the industry, which is heavily research-intensive. In 2018/2019, R&D spending in the ICT hardware and equipment sector amounted to 8.4% of net sales revenue and in the computer software and services sector, it amounted to 10.8% of sales revenue.

The ICT sector has evolved at tremendous speed. The innovations made by scientists and engineers in the firms within this broad sector have transformed the modern world, driven by high levels of R&D spending and ferocious oligopolistic competition from the top to the bottom of the ICT value chain. Since the introduction of the semi-conductor and the PC, a wide array of new sectors have emerged within the ICT industry, but within each sector, an oligopoly has rapidly developed.

# 2   Computer Software and Services

There are 321 firms on the G2500 list that are in the computer software and services sector, of which the top 20 firms account for 67% of R&D spending and 70% of sales revenue.

Microsoft has maintained its dominant position in PC operating systems, which it attained early on, for many years.

In the Enterprise Resource Planning (ERP) sector, the top five firms account for around one-half of the global market. With the exception of China, Google established its dominant position among the various search engines, while Facebook established a dominant position in social media, which they have maintained since then. Google

---

[2] The G2500 companies are the world's top 2500 companies ranked by R&D spending. They account for around 90% of global corporate spending on R&D (EU, 2019, *The 2019 EU Industrial R&D Investment Scoreboard*, Brussels: EU).

and Facebook account for over one-half of global digital advertising revenue. Google (Android) has around three-quarters of the global market for smartphone operating systems.

Cloud computing has grown rapidly over the past five years and is the foundation of the Internet of Things. Three super-large firms—Amazon, Microsoft and Alphabet-Google—have leveraged their dominant position in other parts of the digital world to establish an early lead in cloud computing software and services. These three behemoths account for 38% of the total R&D spending and 34% of the net sales revenue for the 321 firms in the G2500 ICT software and services sector. Collectively, they account for almost 60% of global revenue from software services for the public cloud.

The customers for the giant cloud companies' services are drawn from a wide array of sectors, including financial services, automobiles, energy systems, pharmaceuticals, health care, media and entertainment, retail, hospitality, manufacturing and government. They provide on-demand data storage, data analysis and machine learning for a wide array of sectors as well as on-demand cloud services for consumers, which means that they can avoid investing in their own 'private cloud', which may operate at less than full capacity. Their customers benefit from state-of-the-art network infrastructure purchased by the giants' cloud computing companies.

The vast size of their network means that they can acquire equipment, which includes servers, routers and switches, more cheaply than small-scale private cloud systems. They play a vital role within the 'Internet of Things' that connects embedded semi-conductors across a wide array of machines. They also invest heavily in data security, including the security advantage of their closed-loop global dark fibre networks. They require a network of routers and switches to link the centres together, and need huge amounts of electricity to keep the server farms cool. It is estimated that 50% of the electricity used by data centres is devoted to keeping them cool.

## 2.1 Amazon

Amazon's AWS (Amazon Web Services) division increased its revenues from USD 1.5 billion in 2010 to USD 36 billion in 2019. By 2019, it accounted for around one-third of global revenues from cloud services. The rapid growth of Amazon's web services division was greatly helped by Amazon's leading position in e-commerce outside China and the consequent rapid growth of its revenues. Information technology is centrally important for Amazon's vast e-commerce business, including third-party sales. Amazon's revenues increased from USD 34 billion in 2010 to USD 280 billion in 2019. Its R&D investment increased alongside its increased sales revenue, rising from USD 1.7 billion in 2010 to USD 35.9 billion in 2019, by which point Amazon was by far the largest global company in the world in terms of the size of its R&D budget. Amazon has invested a significant proportion of its revenue in building data centres across the world: it has eight in the Americas, six in

Europe/Middle East and eight in Asia-Pacific. Each centre consists of thousands of servers and Amazon's global system contains a total of 1.4 million servers.

## 2.2 Microsoft

Microsoft's cloud business is built on the foundation of Microsoft's long-held dominance of PC software, in which it still has around three-quarters of the global market. Microsoft's total revenues increased from USD 94 billion in 2015 to USD 126 billion in 2019. Microsoft consistently invests around 13% of its revenues in R&D, which has supported its powerful competitive position in cloud services, the revenues of which are the fastest-growing part of Microsoft's revenue stream. Microsoft's total revenues from the 'Intelligent Cloud' reached USD 40 billion, within which cloud services made up USD 33 billion. Microsoft Azure, Microsoft's cloud service subsidiary, benefits from Microsoft's global network of data centres, including 14 in the Americas, eight in Europe and 15 in Asia-Pacific. Microsoft owns and operates its own Wide Area Network (WAN) of 'dark fibre' which connects its data centres with each other. During 2017–2020, Microsoft increased its WAN network seven-fold. It claims that its Software-Defined Network (SDN) is the 'fastest network of any in the public cloud'.

## 2.3 Alphabet (Google)

Google's Chrome search engine is the foundation of Alphabet's business. Outside China, Google's search engine 'dominates the market in all countries on any device, whether desktop, mobile or tablet', with a market share of over 90%. As Alphabet's revenue has grown rapidly, it has maintained a high rate of investment in R&D. Between 2014 and 2019, Alphabet's revenues increased from USD 66 billion to USD 161 billion, over 80% of which comes from Google Search, and investment in R&D grew from USD 10 billion to USD 26 billion. Google Cloud software services division is linked closely to Google's global network of data centres: it has eight centres in the Americas, six in Europe and seven in Asia-Pacific. Google's public cloud software business has evolved out of its existing ICT-based businesses, including its Google Chrome search engine, Android operating system for smartphones, which it acquired in 2005, YouTube, which it acquired in 2006, Gmail and Google Maps. Google's global infrastructure serves six billion hours of YouTube video per month and provides data storage for one billion Gmail users.

## 2.4  Other Cloud Competitors

Although these three behemoths have dominated the early phase of cloud computing, they face fierce rivalry from competitors who already have a strong position in the ICT industry. For example, IBM has a powerful platform from which to attack the market in cloud computing. IBM maintains a long-held monopoly over mainframe computers, which are still a significant source of revenue and profits. It also has a leading position in the server market. However, despite its continued strength in key components in the computer hardware market, IBM has made a long-term transition away from hardware. By 2019, two-thirds of its revenues came from software and services. IBM systems service 90% of the world's credit card transactions, and over four-fifths of the world's telecom companies are its customers. Since 2012, IBM has invested over USD 30 billion in capital expenditures and USD 45 billion in R&D, much of it cloud-related. In 2019, it completed its acquisition of Red Hat to the tune of USD 34 billion in order to advance its competitive position in cloud computing.

## 3  Technology Hardware

There are 477 firms in the G2500 data set from the technology hardware sector. Of these, the top 20 firms account for 51% of R&D spending and 66% of sales revenue.

Two firms (Samsung and Apple) account for three-fifths of the global market for smartphones (by revenue).

Servers are the workhorses of the whole ICT system, including the private and public cloud. Half a dozen firms, led by HPE and Dell, dominate the global server market.

In advanced TVs, Samsung alone accounts for over one-half of the global market (by sales revenue).

In telecom equipment, Huawei alone accounts for around one-third of the global market and the top five firms account for two-thirds. The value chain of these industries is also highly consolidated. One firm (Cisco) accounts for around one-half of the global market for telecoms routers and switches.

The semi-conductor sector also is highly concentrated. Five firms account for about one-half of the whole market, but levels of industrial concentration are even higher in most sub-sectors of the chip industry. Intel accounts for around three-quarters of the global market for PC microprocessors. Two firms (Qualcomm and Apple) account for three-fifths of smartphone processors. One firm (Samsung) accounts for almost one-half of the global market for DRAM chips and a third of the market for NAND chips. Five firms account for around three-fifths of the global market for Wi-Fi chips. Five firms account for one-half of auto semi-conductors. Moreover, four firms account for two-thirds of the global market for semi-conductor equipment, which is a vital part of the innovation process in the semi-conductor industry.

The technology hardware sector embraces a wide range of sub-sectors in terms of their R&D intensity. PCs, printers and servers typically involve relatively low R&D intensity. Leading technology hardware companies from the first generation of the ICT revolution, such as IBM and HP, have divested their PC and low-end server divisions in order to focus on other parts of the ICT industry, which have higher margins and profitability.[3]

Smartphones and tablets involve the medium intensity of R&D spending. However, they require high innovation skills in terms of product design and customer understanding. They also require the capability of integrating sophisticated systems. Manufacturing these products requires complex value chains across the world as well as a wide array of sub-systems and components, including software, semi-conductors, screens, batteries and camera lenses. This drive also requires considerable investments in marketing and branding.

Telecom equipment typically requires a high degree of R&D intensity. Telecom equipment is typically customer-specific and innovation needs to closely integrate design, manufacturing and customer knowledge.[4] The brand image and reputation of telecom equipment companies are strongly affected by the level and quality of customer support they provide after the sale has been completed.

Within the ITC hardware industry, semi-conductors are known for the intense research carried out to drive innovation. Of the top 30 ICT hardware firms, half are specialist semi-conductor manufacturers. However, besides making complex electronic and telecom equipment, Samsung, Apple and Huawei also are significant semi-conductor producers.[5] In 2018, Samsung's revenues from semi-conductors were over USD 60 billion, making it the world's second-largest chip-maker. A significant share of its huge R&D budget of EUR 15 billion (2018) is devoted to driving technological capabilities in DRAM and NAND chips. In 2018, Samsung's semi-conductor division accounted for over three-quarters of its total profits. If we include the semi-conductor equipment sector, then 22 out of the top 30 ICT hardware companies in terms of R&D spending are in the semi-conductor sector, either as pure-play chip makers or companies with large semi-conductor sub-divisions. Semi-conductors are a crucial part of the whole ICT industry and the sector has been at the centre of the transformation of the modern world since the 1980s, but it will become even more important as the transition to the Internet of Things, Machine Learning and Artificial Intelligence continues. At the core of this 'connected world' will be 'hundreds of billions' of sensors and smart devices, which will result in a huge increase in the amount of data that will be generated, transmitted, stored, processed and analysed.

---

[3] Hewlett Packard was one of the earliest pioneers of the ICT revolution. In 2015, it divided into two: HP, which focused on low R&D intensity PCs and printers, and HPE, which focused on high-end servers and other cloud-related technologies.

[4] A key part of Huawei's competitive success can be attributed to the mindset revolution produced by Huawei's Chairman Ren Zhengfei. Around the year 2000, he engaged a team of consultants from IBM at high cost to transform the thinking of Huawei's R&D department away from a narrowly 'engineering' approach and focus on the individual customer's particular needs. In Ren's view, Huawei needed to 'cut its Chinese feet to fit American shoes'.

[5] Huawei's subsidiary, Hisileon is a semi-conductor maker.

# 4   Conclusion

The role of Huawei in the Internet of Things has been one of the most fiercely argued issues in international relations in recent years.

In 2012, I described the rise of Huawei in my book *Is China Buying The World?* (Polity Press). The following excerpts from the book might provide some insight into Huawei, and in turn the degree of Chinese influence in ICT around the world.

> In almost every discussion about China's 'catch-up' at the level of the firm, the case of Huawei arises. It has advanced from a minnow in the highly concentrated global telecom equipment industry to a giant firm with revenues in 2010 of $27.1 billion and an operating profit of over $4.3 billion. In the late 1990s Huawei comprehensively re-engineered the company, engaging IBM at great expense to lead the transformation from a technology-based to a customer-based approach. The reprocess was so painful that its CEO likened it to 'cutting our feet to fit American shoes'. Huawei's foreign sales grew from $100 million in 1999 to almost $18 billion in 2010. Although its sales in developing economies are far greater than those in high-income countries, Huawei has made significant inroads into markets in the latter, especially in Europe. In 2005 it was certified as a qualified supplier to both BT and Vodafone, which required it to submit to the deepest scrutiny of its products and processes and all aspects of its performance, including not just technical issues but also its compliance with internationally accepted practices in terms of corporate social responsibility. Among large Chinese firms Huawei is unique in having met the most severe standards of global competition among customers in the high-income countries: it stands alone in being 'inside us'. It is unusual among large Chinese firms in terms of the continuity of its top management, its focus on core business, the high share of revenue allocated to R&D, the large share of its employees engaged in R&D, the large share of foreign workers among its employees, the open and transparent system of organization and remuneration of its workforce, the intellectual and physical attractiveness of the work environment, and the internationalization of its culture, including the use of English throughout the upper reaches of the company.

The recent attempts to thwart the international rise of Huawei, particularly in 5G development outside of China, is nothing new. This is evidence from what I wrote in 2012 in *Is China Buying The World?*.

> A succession of possible international acquisitions by Huawei were all abandoned. In 2005 it was rumoured that it was in negotiations to acquire Marconi, the venerable but loss-making UK telecoms equipment maker. This prompted intense discussion in the UK mass media and rumours that the deal would be referred to the US government's Committee on Foreign Investment in the United States (CFIUS). Huawei made no formal offer to acquire Marconi, and eventually it was sold to Ericsson for $2.1 billion. In 2010 Huawei made a bid to acquire the tiny niche telecoms software company 3Leaf for $2 million, a minuscule transaction in global terms. The deal was blocked by CFIUS on national security grounds. An alternative to full-scale takeover is the acquisition by Chinese companies of substantial minority shares in leading Western companies. In 2007–8 it was proposed that Huawei would acquire 3Com, the US telecoms equipment company, jointly with the US private equity firm Bain Capital. Despite the fact that Huawei would own only a small minority share, and despite the fact that 3Com is a relatively small company, the proposal led to an intense US media furore focusing on Huawei's 'threat to US national security', and the case was referred to CFIUS. Before a formal ruling was reached, the acquisition offer was withdrawn by Bain and Huawei. In 2010 HP acquired 3Com for $2.2 billion.

Huawei is China's only high technology company with a significant global market share outside China. The company has been relentless in expansion in telecom equipment and is widely accepted to be the tech leader in 5G telecom equipment. Its global market share in 5G transmissions equipment may be as high as 35%, more than the combined share of its closest competitors, Nokia and Ericsson.

However, the role of Huawei needs to be analysed in relation to the overall structure of the fast-developing Internet of Things.

Each segment of this vast architecture has become highly consolidated, with a few companies, almost all from high-income countries, which dominate each part of the architecture. The Internet of Things is made up of a massive overarching ICT architecture that requires a huge network of base stations as well as a global network of 'dark fibre', a widely distributed global network of data centres full of servers, a cloud computing software system (notably IaaS, PaaS), a global array of billions of smartphones, semi-conductors and software within the smartphones, and hundreds of billions of semi-conductors embedded with 'connected devices'.

Huawei has a relatively minor position in operating the global structure of massive data centres and dark fibre and secure global networks that connect them. Huawei is also relatively negligible in other areas, including its global market share in the server hardware that comprises cores of data centres, its role in the cloud computing software services as well as its market share of the various markets for semi-conductors, which are embedded in countless millions of 'connected devices'. Huawei also does not have much influence in global search engine and browser systems that produces a vast amount of data.

Huawei has developed a significant, but far from dominant market share in smartphone handsets, but the core operating systems inside almost all smartphones, including Huawei's devices, are dominated by Google-Android. The wide array of semi-conductors and software systems inside the world's billions of smartphones are also dominated by a small group of high technology companies with their headquarters in the high-income countries, led by the US.

Global security in the Internet of Things needs to be considered in terms of not just a single part of the architecture, but rather, in terms of the comprehensive structure of global data transmission, storage and analysis. Huawei has a significant role within one segment of that structure. However, within the whole structure, it has a small role. So far, the entire structure is dominated by firms from high-income countries, especially the US.

**Peter Nolan** is the Founding Director of Cambridge University's Centre of Development Studies and the Director of Jesus College's China Centre. He is the Director of the Chinese Executive Leadership Programme (CELP), which each year brings chief executives from China's largest firms to the University of Cambridge to attend training programmes taught by academics and the leaders of international firms. The Financial Times commented: "Nolan knows more about Chinese companies and their international competition than anyone else on earth, including in China". Peter Nolan has researched, written and taught on a wide range of issues in economic development, globalisation and the transition of former planned economies.

**Open Access** This chapter is licensed under the terms of the Creative Commons Attribution-NonCommercial-NoDerivatives 4.0 International License (http://creativecommons.org/licenses/by-nc-nd/4.0/), which permits any noncommercial use, sharing, distribution and reproduction in any medium or format, as long as you give appropriate credit to the original author(s) and the source, provide a link to the Creative Commons license and indicate if you modified the licensed material. You do not have permission under this license to share adapted material derived from this chapter or parts of it.

The images or other third party material in this chapter are included in the chapter's Creative Commons license, unless indicated otherwise in a credit line to the material. If material is not included in the chapter's Creative Commons license and your intended use is not permitted by statutory regulation or exceeds the permitted use, you will need to obtain permission directly from the copyright holder.

# China's International Science and Technology Trends and the US–China Relationship

Denis F. Simon

*Only if core technologies are in our own hands can we truly hold the initiative in competition and development.*
PRC President Xi Jinping's Speech to the Chinese Academy of Sciences/Chinese Academy of Engineering, Beijing, June 2014.

**Abstract** *The twenty-first century represents a new, dynamic period in world history in terms of the conduct of international science and technology (S&T) affairs.* It is a *"new era of science diplomacy".* The ability of science diplomacy to thrive has been aided by the onset of globalization. *Globalization has enabled the almost unhindered movement of people, products and services, and knowledge across borders.* Clearly, *China has been a major beneficiary of globalization,* utilizing access to the world's leading corporations, best universities, most dynamic research institutes, and government and non-governmental international organizations and scholarly bodies as a way to support and advance its own modernization efforts. For most of the last 40 years, China has had increasingly unencumbered access to these critical repositories of know-how and information, though Chinese leaders also have felt steadily more and more anxious about *the degree to which the openness of the world economy would continue to work in China's favor.* This essay analyzes *China's evolving strategy, policies, and practices regarding its international S&T relations*, with special emphasis on the US–China relationship. The essay also highlights China's strategic posture and footprint in terms of its goal of becoming a player of growing influence in the shaping of international S&T affairs.

**Keywords** The twenty-first century represents a new dynamic period in world history in terms of the conduct of international science and technology (S&T) affairs · "New era of science diplomacy" · Globalization has enabled the almost unhindered movement of people, products and services and knowledge across borders · China has been a major beneficiary of globalization · The degree to which the openness of the world economy would continue to work in China's favor · China's evolving strategy, policies, and practices regarding its international S&T relations

D. F. Simon (✉)
Duke's Fuqua School of Business, Duke University, Durham, USA

© The Author(s) 2021                                         253
H. Wang and A. Michie (eds.), *Consensus or Conflict?*, China and Globalization,
https://doi.org/10.1007/978-981-16-5391-9_23

# 1 Introduction

The above statement by Chinese President Xi Jinping could not have been more prophetic as just four short years later, China found itself embroiled in both a deleterious "trade war" and destructive "technology war" with the United States and several of America's allies.[1]

The twenty-first century represents a new, dynamic period in world history in terms of the conduct of international science and technology (S&T) affairs. One might even designate it a "new era of science diplomacy."[2] The ability of science diplomacy to thrive has been aided by the onset of globalization. Globalization has enabled the almost unhindered movement of people, products and services, and knowledge across borders. Clearly, China has been a major beneficiary of globalization, utilizing access to the world's leading corporations, best universities, most dynamic research institutes, and government and non-governmental international organizations and scholarly bodies as a way to support and advance its own modernization efforts.[3] For most of the last 40 years, China has had increasingly unencumbered access to these critical repositories of know-how and information, though Chinese leaders also have felt steadily more and more anxious about the degree to which the openness of the world economy would continue to work in China's favor.[4]

This essay analyzes China's evolving strategy, policies, and practices regarding its international S&T relations, with special emphasis on the US–China relationship. The essay highlights China's strategic posture and footprint in terms of its goal of becoming a player of growing influence in the shaping of the contemporary international S&T system. Finally, the essay concludes with a discussion of the changing landscape of the international S&T system, with a focus on the ways in which the US–China relationship might alter the evolving structure and operation of the system in the coming years.

# 2 China's Evolving Global S&T Footprint

With the founding of the People's Republic of China (PRC) in 1949, the Ccommunist Party of China (CPC) formulated and implemented a bilateral S&T cooperation agreement with the former Soviet Union—a relatively short-lived arrangement that was followed by the policy of self-reliance (*zili gengsheng*) in response to Moscow's termination of technology assistance in 1960. The relationship between Moscow and Beijing had been highly asymmetrical as China was very dependent on the former USSR for massive inflows of industrial equipment and managerial know-how to jump-start the Chinese economy after the end of the civil war with

---

[1] Buckley (2014).

[2] Ruffini (2017).

[3] Samuelson (2018).

[4] Zukus (2017).

the Kuomintang in 1949. Beginning in the late 1970s, China's leadership shifted its focus to rapid economic and S&T development under the so-called "four modernizations" program. In terms of China's international S&T relations, guidelines were adopted to lay the foundation for expanded global engagement and a more proactive international participation, including significant growth in the level of international S&T cooperation. By the end of the twentieth century, China had achieved full-scale implementation of an international S&T cooperation system focused on acquiring foreign technology and fostering cooperative arrangements with leading international scientific institutions.

With the reform and opening up policy inspired by Deng Xiaoping, and general abandonment of the policy of self-reliance, China joined numerous international and regional S&T organizations, and promoted foreign plant, equipment, and technology imports. During the first two decades of the twenty-first century, the government has pushed for more mutually beneficial international S&T cooperation, developing more well-articulated programs designed to achieve greater symmetry of results and more well-defined mutual benefit. Currently, China is playing an increasingly active role in international organizations—encompassing major global science and engineering programs, while at the same time strengthening technical assistance to developing countries.[5] Since 2012, China has sought to plan and promote innovation with what it now characterizes as a global vision, embodied in various key national policies.[6] China's so-called "vaccine diplomacy", as a response to the COVID-19 global pandemic, is a good example of how Chinese leaders hope to use science and technology as an instrument of foreign policy.[7]

At present, China is in the process of transforming itself from primarily a technology importer to a technology importer and exporter, as it pursues a strategy of promoting indigenous innovation as well as global engagement.[8] It is no longer simply a technology learner but also is a knowledge provider, especially within new promising efforts such as the Belt and Road Initiative (BRI). Overall, central to its efforts to move from imitator and copy-cat to an innovation-driven nation are a series of policies and initiatives associated with becoming a more central player in international S&T affairs.[9] By mid-2020, China had established S&T cooperation partnerships with 161 countries and regions and executed 114 inter-governmental agreements on S&T cooperation. In addition, the PRC has joined over 200 inter-governmental international S&T cooperation and research organizations. It has appointed over 150 S&T diplomats for its 70+ overseas offices in 47 countries. And, as of the beginning of 2018, over 400 Chinese scientists were holding office

---

[5] Cheng (2008).

[6] For example, the "Opinions of the CPC Central Committee and State Council on Deepening S&T Reform and Speeding Up the Building of a National Innovation System," the 13th Five Year Science and Technology Plan, the Innovation-Driven Development Strategy, and the Belt and Road Initiative on building international S&T cooperation networks.

[7] Wang (2020).

[8] Central Committee and State Council, "Outline of the National Strategy of Innovation-Driven Development," Beijing: May 20, 2016.

[9] Xie et al. (2014).

in international S&T-related NGOs, including approximately 30 as chairman and 50 as vice-chairman. Among the world's 48 major cross-border big science programs and projects, four have been initiated by China and 17 have China's official participation; China also serves as an observer in three programs. This all demonstrates that China's presence in the structure and organization of global S&T governance is becoming more meaningful and steadily expanding.

# 3   The Administrative Structure of China's International S&T Policies

The S&T governance structure for China's international S&T engagement is comprised of a number of key state agencies and organizations. Three organizations have emerged as the most important in organizing and managing China's international S&T relations: the Ministry of Science and Technology (MOST), the Chinese Academy of Sciences (CAS), and the China Association for Science and Technology (CAST).[10]

## 3.1   Ministry of Science and Technology (MOST)

The Ministry of Science and Technology is the predominant entity that plans and implements China's overseas S&T activities, providing the overarching framework for international S&T cooperation and exchanges at different levels and by increasingly diverse actors. Since its mission is to foster economic growth and technological advancements, MOST coordinates basic research, frontier technology research, and the development of key and advanced technologies.

In March 2018, the State Administration for Foreign Experts (SAFEA) was placed under the oversight of MOST. SAFEA, heretofore, has been responsible over several decades for bringing to China a broad range of experienced scientific and technical experts from abroad to assist their Chinese counterparts with various developmental problems and issues. It also has sent large numbers of PRC delegations abroad, especially to the US, Western Europe, and Japan for training in management and an assortment of technical fields.

---

[10] Others include the Foreign Affairs Leading Group of the CPC, and the Inter-Ministerial Coordination Mechanism, which includes the Ministry of Agriculture (MOA), Ministry of Education (MOE), the international cooperation departments of local governments, the China Association for International Science and Technology Cooperation, and enterprises. MOST also commands some 20 affiliated agencies, including the Institute of Scientific and Technical Information of China, the High-Tech Research and Development Center, the Intellectual Property Rights Center, the Supervision Service Center for Science and Technology Funds, and the National Science and Technology Venture Capital Development Center.

As part of the same change, the China National Natural Science Foundation (NNSFC) also was moved under the direct oversight of MOST. The NNSFC oversees support for much of the research in basic science that occurs within China. Its creation was modeled after the US National Science Foundation; the onset of serious peer review in the submission and awarding of grants helped improve the reliability and credibility of the funding system. The NNSFC has developed extensive links with the top scientists around the world and has included members of the international S&T community in the periodic reviews of its operational performance.

## 3.2 Chinese Academy of Sciences (CAS)

The Chinese Academy of Sciences, directed by President Hou Jianguo, is structured as a comprehensive, integrated R&D network. It is the nation's high-end think tank, a merit-based learned society as well as a system of higher education and has long functioned as the linchpin of China's national and global S&T ambitions.

Since its inception, the CAS has made significant progress in fostering international S&T cooperation relationships.[11] It has succeeded in developing extensive and diverse partnerships with research institutes and scientists across the globe, and is well-positioned to play a central role in shaping China's S&T diplomacy from a substantive point of view.[12] To take some key examples, CAS has accomplished the following:

- set up 20 collaborative groups with the German Max Planck Society for the Advancement of Science in areas including astronomy, life sciences, and materials science;
- implemented several talent programs (such as the CAS Fellowship for Senior and Young International Scientists), attracting over 1,000 foreign scientists and engineers to conduct R&D activities at its institutes;
- initiated a BRI action plan in 2016 calling for international S&T cooperation, training, and cultivating more than 1,800 S&T management and high-tech personnel for relevant countries;
- plans to become the spearhead and central hub for an Asia-Pacific, Eurasia, and Asia-Africa collaborative innovation network system.[13]

Among its major overseas initiatives are (a) the South America Center of Astronomy, (b) the Sino-Africa Joint Research Center, (c) the China-Sri Lanka Joint Center for Education and Research, and (d) the CAS Innovation Cooperation Center in Bangkok.

---

[11] Bai (2017a).
[12] Poo and Wang (2014).
[13] Bai (2017b).

### *3.3   China Association for Science and Technology (CAST)*

Founded in 1958, the China Association for Science and Technology (CAST) is under the direct jurisdiction of the Secretariat of the CCP's Central Committee. Its role includes promoting S&T exchanges and indigenous innovation, protecting and advancing the interests of science workers, organizing S&T professionals to participate in formulating national S&T policies, and facilitating non-governmental international S&T exchanges and cooperation through developing liaisons with foreign S&T associations and scientists.

## 4   China's International S&T Strategy and Policies

Since Deng Xiaoping's reform and opening up, the Chinese government has been consistent in encouraging Chinese organizations to engage abroad to better leverage international S&T resources as well as formulating a series of policies to guide its S&T engagement with other countries.[14] Today, these policies reflect the growing emphasis on strengthening indigenous innovation, especially in view of the negative impact of the so-called US–China trade/tech war on PRC access to advanced technologies. From China's position, indigenous innovation is necessarily coupled with an outward-looking strategy that calls for S&T partnerships and international collaborations. International S&T relations are thus best understood as constructed to serve China's goal of becoming a global innovation leader, especially in key technologies such as clean energy, artificial intelligence, and life sciences.[15] Not only are scientific and technological advances sought to promote long-term economic development, but they also are viewed as an important component of national wealth and influence, especially as the centrality of technology as a tool of state power in international relations has increased.

Generally speaking, China's state-led efforts to achieve indigenous innovation have not been well received by Western rivals.[16] The 15-Year Medium-to-Long-term Plan for Science and Technology (MLP) launched in 2006, for example, was roundly denounced in a US Chamber of Commerce-sponsored report bearing the title, *China's Drive for Indigenous Innovation: A Web of Industrial Policies* (McGregor 2010).[17] The report accused China of "hunkering behind the 'techno-nationalism' moat", switching "from defense to offense" in light of its economic ascendance as well as its fear of foreign domination.[18] The MLP, according to the report, "is considered by many international technology companies to be a blueprint for technology theft on

---

[14] Bound et al. (2013).

[15] Cao and Suttmeier (2017).

[16] Atkinson et al. (2017).

[17] Ministry of Science and Technology, National Medium- and Long-Term Science and Technology Development Plan (2006–2020)," Beijing, 2006 (in Chinese).

[18] McGregor (2010).

a scale the world has never seen before." The report obviously contains a great deal of hyperbole; nonetheless, the MLP's policies did provoke a strong reaction from China's major trade and technology partners that has not dissipated over time.

For China, the emphasis on indigenous innovation, however, is not analogous to self-reliance as was the case in the 1960s. Rather, it always has been seen as a pathway to strengthen China's leverage in the international technology market.

Budgetary allocations for international S&T cooperation have grown apace with domestic S&T spending, especially at the local level.[19] As suggested above, China's emphasis on indigenous innovation should not obscure the fact that the government has spared no efforts to deepen and enlarge bilateral and multilateral S&T partnerships. The 13th Five-Year S&T Plan,[20] in contrast to its predecessors, designated specific tasks and goals that serve Beijing's strategy of science diplomacy, transforming itself from passive recipient to active donor. The 14th Five-Year Plan (2021–2025) continues to place similar, if not greater, emphasis on the continued expansion of international S&T engagement.

China's international S&T cooperation strategy is carefully differentiated according to a categorization of partners into developed, developing, and neighboring countries. The current effort calls for increased openness of China's national S&T programs, including offering governmental support to overseas experts who are expected to take the lead—or at least participate in—national S&T program strategic research. It also calls for deepening international cooperation on an equal basis with international partners (a claim which has been met with some skepticism). To achieve its goals, China has initiated and organized significant international S&T programs and projects; has become more actively involved in helping to set global S&T agendas; has accelerated the sharing of global large-scale scientific research information; and begun active participation in global S&T governance, including the formulation of international S&T cooperation rules. Chinese scientists have increased their participation in scientific exchange programs, as well as seeking official positions in major international scientific and technological organizations. China's most recent—and clearly most dramatic—diplomatic move in the science field is the BRI S&T cooperation network, which calls for promoting technology transfer and assisting countries in training young scientists—a clear indication, as noted, that China plans to play a central role in the international S&T landscape as a technology exporter as well as importer.[21]

Despite comments from foreign critics that the PRC appears to be becoming more "techno-nationalistic", China clearly continues to look outward—out of both conviction and necessity—as it plans its S&T future. Its recent steps toward greater technology self-reliance must be understood in the context of the changing global political situation rather than a purposeful, fundamental Chinese turn inward.

---

[19] OECD, "China Headed to Overtake EU, US in Science & Technology Spending, OECD Says," Paris, December 11, 2014.

[20] See in particular the 13th Five-Year Plan Special Program on International S&T Cooperation (Beijing, MOST, 2016)

[21] Zou (2018).

# 5   China's Bilateral S&T Relations with the United States

Over the last four decades, S&T cooperation has been one of the foundational elements in the Sino–US relationship. While some modest renewal of S&T exchanges occurred in the aftermath of "ping-pong" diplomacy and the now infamous Nixon visit to China in the early 1970s, the 1979–89 period featured the formal inception of China–US S&T cooperation. The 1979 agreement on science and technology has functioned as the overall framework under which the two governments have promoted S&T cooperation in various forms and through a large number of channels.

Bilateral S&T cooperation experienced rapid growth during the early years as it was new and exciting; the two parties invested significantly to support joint programs. Nevertheless, it is important to bear in mind that the two sides also had quite different objectives. The US intended to counter the former USSR by developing rapport and trust with China, and the US technical community was interested in the distinctive natural and social phenomena in China. The Chinese side, however, assumed that engagement with the international science and technology system, especially with the US, would be a useful vehicle for promoting economic construction and catching up with the world's leading powers (Suttmeier 2014).

From 1990 to 1999, bilateral S&T relations witnessed some apparent decline, followed by resumption of activity. Due to the events in Tiananmen Square on June 4, 1989, many programs were curtailed, including China–US space cooperation. Gradual resumption of bilateral S&T cooperation began in 1994. With China's accession to the World Trade Organization in 2001, the possibilities for a new growth spurt began to appear.[22]

From 2000 to 2015, China–US relations were characterized by comprehensive and rapid development. President Hu Jintao remarked in 2012 that S&T cooperation had become an important driving force for Sino–US relations, and a critical component of people-to-people exchange. This cooperation fell into six main areas: energy and physics, health and life science, ecology and environmental science, agriculture and food science, science education, and meteorology. It is worth noting that, beginning in 2006, the agenda for bilateral S&T cooperation took on a heightened awareness of the urgent need to explore interdisciplinary research themes, frontier science, and international hot issues such as global warming, new and clean energy, carbon capture, and aggregation. In other words, the rising salience of these global issues altered the context for both sides to think about how S&T cooperation might proceed. A series of new initiatives were taken that were based on high-level political commitments. The Strategic Economic Dialogue (SED) that came into place in 2006 and later the Strategic and Economic Dialogue (S&ED) produced an enormous expansion of activities and functions. The latter launched the Ten-Year Framework on Energy and Environment Cooperation in 2008, designating clean water, clean air, clean vehicles, and energy efficiency as key areas with high priority for cooperation. By 2011, China had risen to become the top collaborating partner of the US,

---

[22] Richard Suttmeier and Denis Simon, "Conflict and Cooperation in the Development of US-China Relations in Science and Technology," in Mayer et al. (2014).

outpacing the UK, Japan, and Germany—nations that have been long-time partners of the US in science.[23] By the end of the decade, in jointly authored scientific papers, Chinese scientists claimed the first authorship much more frequently than their US counterparts.[24]

One of the key elements of these new dialogues was the initiation of the China–US Innovation Dialogue, which actually began in 2008 as part of a discussion about how the Chinese side could improve the performance of its own innovation system. The Innovation Dialogue had great potential when it started because it might have served as a useful vehicle for exchanging meaningful information about the evolving requirements for successful innovation in the twenty-first century. An Experts Group represented by top-level Chinese and American scholars from both countries served as a vehicle for ensuring the right issues were placed on the agenda and that the discussions were focused on the key topics of relevance to both sides. Unfortunately, the Innovation Dialogue ended up being neither a real dialogue nor about innovation. On the US side, growing disenchantment with China in the US Congress led to constraints being placed on the White House Office of Science and Technology (OSTP) about the expansion of S&T cooperation; funding was tightly controlled. Moreover, the innovation agenda was hijacked by the US Trade Representative Office (USTR) and made to focus on extracting concessions from the Chinese side on pressing trade matters. The bulk of discussions ended up concentrating on dismantling Chinese policies regarding the promotion of indigenous innovation. On the Chinese side, the prize still remained in sight, though their side also was often distracted from the core innovation-related issues that they expected to drive the Innovation Dialogue.

Starting at the tail end of the Obama Administration, more and more questions were raised about China's willingness to play by WTO rules and to adhere to related commitments about IPR protection, etc. Under the former Trump administration, however, the anti-China rhetoric built up great momentum; a number of major steps were taken to alter the essential dynamics of the overall China–US S&T relationship. Certain things have become clear as the two countries have attempted to find a way around their ongoing trade war—which essentially has been centered on technology issues. Because of tensions over trade, technology transfer, the South China Sea, and human rights (e.g., Hong Kong and Xinjiang), the prevailing political environment will barely support the status quo, let alone an expanded S&T relationship. In fact, the newest iteration of the bilateral S&T agreement did not experience a smooth renewal process during the last set of negotiations; the final decision to renew the agreement was done under the shadow of darkness and given a very low profile from both governments. The decision by the Trump Administration in March 2018 to invoke special legislation under the US Section 301 laws concerning trade and investment with China brought on the beginning of "a trade war" with China over programs such as Made in China 2025 as well as technology theft and other related

---

[23] Suttmeier (2014).

[24] Wagner et al. (2015).

IPR issues positioned at the center of American concerns.[25] It also became the focal point of critical comments by Christopher Wray, the Director of the Federal Bureau of Investigation, in early 2018 when he warned American higher education institutions about the vulnerability of their institutions to "non-traditional" collectors of critical scientific and technical information coming from China. The onset of the COVID-19 virus in Wuhan in early 2020 and its transition into a major global pandemic further exacerbated the tensions between the Trump administration and the Chinese leadership under President Xi Jinping. Finger-pointing, accusations about blame and lack of transparency, and even racism have traveled across the Pacific in both directions, thus further damaging the possibilities for rekindling the kind of relationship that existed in the past. To say that there continues to be a fundamental lack of trust between both sides would be a serious understatement.

## 6 Key Outstanding Issues and Challenges

In spite of the overall progress China has made in institutionalizing its international S&T cooperation structure and expanding its cross-border S&T relationships, numerous challenges remain. IPR protection has been, and will continue to be, a serious concern for foreign S&T partners—in both public and private sectors. As China is increasingly viewed as a steadily growing serious competitor, relations have become more difficult across a broad spectrum of issue areas.[26] For example, given China's plans for massive investments in the development of artificial intelligence, will Western countries be willing to collaborate with China and perhaps put their technology at risk? China's increasingly prominent position across the global innovation landscape has made it increasingly difficult for China still to play the role of the learner in its cooperation with developed countries. Clearly, China is in the process of re-defining its role—one where it desires more of a co-equal partnership in terms of cooperation and contribution. This will require China to afford far greater IP protection for foreign partnerships. President Xi Jinping's heightened attention on IPR issues reflects this reality as well as the fact that with Chinese innovation on the rise, China now has more skin in the game insofar it has its own IPR to protect.[27]

China's role in international S&T cooperation is evolving from learner to partner and rule maker. We expect to see increasing proactive participation by China in global S&T governance, as Chinese scientists hold a growing number of positions at major international S&T organizations, and more Chinese-initiated "big science" projects and advanced research facilities that attract scientists from all over the world.

---

[25] USTR, "Special 301 Report on Intellectual Property Rights." Office of the United States Trade Representative, Washington, DC, 2017.

[26] Friedberg (2020).

[27] For a somewhat different conclusion, see Baark (2014), who argues that China does not yet possess the excellence that positions its scientific research institutions as world-leading, even if research in key organizations may be able to support leading and original research achievements.

Under the specific reforms that were part of the recently completed 13th Five-Year STI Plan and Strategy of Innovation-Driven Development, China has put forth a strategic vision for future international S&T cooperation that includes very ambitious goals and innovative mechanisms.[28] If reforms are successfully implemented, they should increase the openness of China's S&T programs, resulting in the growing demand for international cooperation. Through comprehensive reforms, some of the internal issues that have thus far hindered S&T cooperation, such as restrictions on travel abroad and the use of funds, might be resolved.

Nonetheless, the Chinese government needs a clearer definition of its key role—one that improves the quality of its services to China's major innovation actors. It already is reinforcing its international S&T cooperation strategy through such efforts as promoting innovation dialogues, expanding cultural and educational exchanges, upgrading the scale of communications, and involving an expanded number of stakeholders such as universities, research institutes, and private enterprises. The government also is setting up special funds and programs, with different purposes and characteristics, to promote international S&T cooperation. More resources are being channeled and leveraged from central and local governments, as well as the growing private sector. In the long run, China needs to develop a more coherent strategic plan and policy umbrella that will better guide its international cooperation activities and design more innovative mechanisms to better meet the country's changing needs. The 14th Five-Year Plan promises to launch additional reforms that will foster more mutually beneficial international S&T cooperation; these reforms will provide more incentives to potential and existing foreign partners that ideally will overcome present anxieties and uncertainties that too often have constrained the growth of new activities.

The bottom line looking ahead is a simple one—there is no major international S&T-related issue whose meaningful solution will not require close cooperation and collaboration with China.[29] Climate change, clean energy, global pandemics, water, and other such issues are central to China's future and mission-critical for the world if the human race is to avoid major disasters like the COVID-19 pandemic in the coming years. China's decision in 2017 to step up on global climate change despite the US decision (under former President Trump) to withdraw from the Paris Accord signed during the Obama Administration marks an important turning point in China's role in the international S&T system. The decision by the Biden Administration to renew the US participation in the Paris Accord certainly will provide China with added incentives to stay the course in terms of its stated commitments. That said, China's willingness to take on a leadership role on this issue portends an expanded Chinese presence across multiple similar issue areas. Chinese behavior is starting to re-shape the global S&T and innovation landscape. How countries such as the US,

---

[28] Ministry of Science and Technology, "The 13th Five-year National Plan for Science, Technology and Innovation of the People's Republic of China," Beijing: August, 2016.
[29] Manmadov (2020).

the UK and Japan as well as the EU will deal with this new Chinese posture remains one of the key challenges facing the international S&T system.[30]

Overall, however, there remain two outstanding issues for Beijing. The first revolves around the immediate impact of the COVID-19 pandemic on the Chinese economic trajectory. In May 2020, it was announced that the national budget for science would be cut by 9.1%; this stands in contrast to the 13% increase that occurred in 2019.[31] The gap is to be filled by local governments, so that the net result still will be a 3% increase in public R&D expenditures. MOST Minister Wang Zhigang specifically noted that international cooperation would still be a major high priority. In the 14th Five-Year Plan, R&D spending will increase around 7% or more annually, accompanied by a hefty increase in spending on basic research.

The second issue deals with the impact of the COVID-19 experience on the prevailing structure and operation of the global supply chain and the evolving Chinese role in the global value chain. Lots of rumors have emerged about how the US and other multinational firms will begin a significant retreat back home as their degree of dependence on China and Chinese suppliers have come to be viewed as a high-risk factor. While initial indications from many multinationals are that there is a great deal of hyperbole surrounding many of the initial media reports, the fact remains that there are likely to be some pronounced shifts over the coming 2–3 years that could alter China's plans to become a high value-added manufacturer and new source of design and innovation in the near future. Xi Jinping's pronouncements in summer-2020 about China's need to pursue a so-called "dual circulation" strategy that gives greater attention to the Chinese domestic economy highlights the fact that China is already preparing for potential discontinuities, including the increased difficulties that it will have gaining access to advanced foreign know-how.[32] This is particularly true with respect to semiconductors and integrated circuits as well as the equipment and software needed to design and manufacture advanced chips.

Looking ahead, given that the country aims to deepen engagement in global S&T innovation governance, we likely will see more Chinese efforts in agenda-setting for global innovation systems and more emphasis on rule-setting for key international S&T projects focusing on key global challenges including food security, energy security, environmental protection, climate change, public health, etc. It remains unclear, however, whether the international S&T community will welcome an enhanced Chinese presence without a series of concomitant gestures from Beijing with respect to prevailing norms and values in areas such as Internet freedom, cyber security, IPR protection, and research ethics. The verdict is not out yet on just how bumpy the road ahead will be for China's international S&T relations if present concerns are not addressed head-on by Beijing.

---

[30] Wagner (2020).

[31] Chen (2020).

[32] Lelyveld (2020).

# 7    Where Are US–China S&T Relations Headed?

Given the huge stakes involved and before any further costly missteps occur, there is much to be gained from the Biden Administration along with the US Congress stepping back to take a new, fresh look at the role and value of the S&T relationship with China. The framework that supported the bilateral S&T relationship requires a re-think and re-adjustment. Both sides need to reach a new accommodation based on the new evolving realities. The shift from asymmetry to greater parity in many key S&T fields indicates that the hierarchical relationship of the past must give way to a more balanced relationship where the concept of mutual benefit has more tangible meaning. In essence, a new road map is needed to define the rules of the road for the next 40 years, one that considers the growing synergies as well as the growing differences and changing priorities between the two countries.

Why take this important step back instead of just following on with the approach adopted by the former Trump Administration? As noted, the basic dynamics of the Sino–US bilateral S&T relationship have shifted, particularly because of a narrowing of the technological gap between the US and China. In addition, S&T cooperation along with scholarly exchanges no longer sit on the safe margins of the relationship between Beijing and Washington; they are now center stage as the competition between the two countries heats up. Everyone recognizes that we live in a world of high-speed technological change and rapidly accelerating innovation. For the first time in four decades, China's progress in science and technology provides an opportunity for there to be real reciprocity and mutual benefit going in both directions—from the US to China (as in the past) and now from China to the US. In addition, as noted earlier in this essay, many critical global problems, including climate change, clean energy, and global pandemics, are tied to S&T whose meaningful solutions will depend on the close US–China collaboration. The need for cross-border collaboration and cooperation is not just something nice to pursue; it has become a growing necessity. A renewal of the bilateral S&T relationship in an environment of greater transparency and better defined "rules of the road" could help to re-build confidence and restore trust in the political sphere. In turn, constructive engagement regarding S&T cooperation could prove to be one of the key missing ingredients that will take the two countries away from the current problem-plagued situation into the future in a smoother, less tension-filled manner.

# References

Atkinson RD, Cory N, Ezell SJ (2017) Stopping China's mercantilism: a doctrine of constructive, alliance-backed confrontation, information technology and innovation foundation (ITIF)

Bai C (2017a) International S&T Cooperation Network will be established by 2030. National Natural Science Foundation of China

Bai C (2017b) ORI network of International S&T Cooperation to be established by 2030, Beijing, Xinhua

Baark E (2014). Is China Becoming a Science and Technology Superpower, and So What? Discussion paper presented at conference entitled' "The Evolving Role of Science and Technology in China's International Relations," 3–4 April 2014, Arizona State University, Tempe, AZ.

Bound K, Saunders T, Wilsdon J, Adams J (2013) China's absorptive state: research, innovation, and the prospects for China-UK collaboration. NESTA, London

Buckley C (2014) Xi urges greater innovation in core technologies. NY Times

Cao C, Suttmeier RP (2017) Challenges of S&T system reform in China. Science 335:1019–1021

Chen S (2020) Two sessions: China cuts science budget by 9 per cent but national R&D still tipped to grow. South China Morning Post

Cheng R (2008) China's international science and technology cooperation strategy and policy evolution in 30 years (in Chinese). China S&t Forum 7(26):7–11

Friedberg A (2020) An answer to aggression: how to push back against Beijing. Foreign Affairs 150–164

Lelyveld M (2020) China unveils new strategy for economic growth—analysis. Eurasia Rev

Manmadov S (2020) China is tapping into its intellectual potential. GCTN, Beijing

Mayer M et al (2014) The global politics of science and technology. Springer International Publishing, Berlin

McGregor J (2010) China's drive for indigenous innovation: a web of industrial policies. US Chamber of Commerce Global Regulatory Cooperation Project, Washington DC

Poo M-M, Wang L (2014) On CAS Pioneer initiative—an interview with CAS President Chunli Bai. Natl Sci Rev 1:618–622

Ruffini P-B (2017) Science and diplomacy: a new dimension in international relations. Springer International Publishing, Paris

Samuelson RJ (2018) China's breathtaking transformation into a scientific superpower. Washington Post

Suttmeier RP (2014) Co-inventing the future? Science diplomacy and the evolution of Sino–US relations in science and technology. Discussion paper presented at conference entitled "TheEvolving Role of Science and Technology in China's International Relations", 3–4 April 2014, Arizona State University, Tempe, AZ

Wagner CS, Bornmann L, Leydesdorff L (2015) Recent developments in China–US cooperation in science. Minerva 53(3):199–214

Wagner C (2020) The Trump administration is curtailing visas for Chinese scientists. That may backfire. Washington Post

Wang Z (2020) Provide strong support for the global fight against the pandemic with pragmatic and efficient scientific and technological cooperation. Qiuzhi (Truth)

Xie Yu, Zhang C, Lai Q (2014) China's rise as a major contributor to science and technology. Proc Natl Acad Sci 111(26):9437–9442

Zou L (2018) The political economy of China's Belt and Road initiative. World Scientific Publishing, Singapore

Zukus J (2017) Globalization with Chinese characteristics: a new international standard. The Diplomat

**Denis F. Simon** is Senior Adviser to the President for China Affairs at Duke University and Professor of China Business and Technology at Duke's Fuqua School of Business. He has more than four decades of experience researching business, competition, innovation and technology strategy in China and was awarded the Chinese Government's prestigious 'Friendship Award' medal in 2006. He previously served as Executive Vice Chancellor at Duke Kunshan University in China, General Manager of Andersen Consulting in Beijing and the Founding President of Monitor Group China. He has published several books: *Corporate Strategies Towards the Pacific Rim, Techno-Security in an Age of Globalization (1996)* and *China's Emerging Technological Edge: Assessing the Role of High-End Talent (2009)*. Dr. Simon received his Ph.D. and MA degrees from UC Berkeley. He speaks and reads Mandarin Chinese.

**Open Access** This chapter is licensed under the terms of the Creative Commons Attribution-NonCommercial-NoDerivatives 4.0 International License (http://creativecommons.org/licenses/by-nc-nd/4.0/), which permits any noncommercial use, sharing, distribution and reproduction in any medium or format, as long as you give appropriate credit to the original author(s) and the source, provide a link to the Creative Commons license and indicate if you modified the licensed material. You do not have permission under this license to share adapted material derived from this chapter or parts of it.

The images or other third party material in this chapter are included in the chapter's Creative Commons license, unless indicated otherwise in a credit line to the material. If material is not included in the chapter's Creative Commons license and your intended use is not permitted by statutory regulation or exceeds the permitted use, you will need to obtain permission directly from the copyright holder.

# Global Governance Perspectives from Africa, Asia, North America and Europe

# Can Europe Help Prevent a Bi-polar World?

Jean-Christophe Bas and Richard Higgott

> *The contribution which an organized and living Europe can bring to civilization is indispensable to the maintenance of peaceful relations.*
> Declaration on the creation of a European Coal and Steel Community.
> Robert Schuman, May 9, 1950.

**Abstract**  This essay is built on three assumptions. Assumption one is that the *American led "rules-based world order"* is waning. Assumption two is that the world is witnessing an accompanying trend towards a *growing geo-political bifurcation* in two distinct global political ecologies; one under *US suzerainty* and the other under *Chinese suzerainty*. This essay proposes that *Chinese suzerainty is not inevitable*. Other major players must be engaged in this process and the European Union must be among them. Assumption three is that it is essential to *block the drift towards a bi-polar world*. That means that *European Union foreign policy* efforts must take a much more proactive and strategic role in revising the *American led "rules-based" world order*. To-date, Europe is struggling to develop a coherent position towards these challenges. This paper suggests the idea that the EU Commission should be (i) a "geopolitical commission" operating in an increasingly geo-political world and (ii) a continued the commitment of the EU to the values of multilateralism and *cooperative, collective action problem-solving*. While not necessarily contradictory, these are messages that do not normally sit easily together.

This chapter is the product of a major re-writing and updating of a Working Paper by Richard Higgott and Luk Van Langenhove, "The EU and the Unravelling of the World Order in Times of the COVID-19 Pandemic", https://cris.unu.edu/sites/cris.unu.edu/files/WP20.1%20-%20Higgott%20and%20Van%20Langenhove.pdf. Copyright is held by the authors and permission is hereby granted to Higgott and Bas to use material from the Working Paper.

J.-C. Bas (✉)
The Global Compass, Paris, France

R. Higgott
University of Warwick, Coventry, UK

© The Author(s) 2021
H. Wang and A. Michie (eds.), *Consensus or Conflict?*, China and Globalization,
https://doi.org/10.1007/978-981-16-5391-9_24

**Keywords** American led "rules-based world order" · Growing geo-political bifurcation · US suzerainty · Chinese suzerainty · Chinese suzerainty is not inevitable · Drift towards a bi-polar world · European Union foreign policy · American led "rules-based" world order · Cooperative, collective action problem-solving

# 1 Introduction

This short paper is built on three assumptions. Assumption one is that the American led world order is waning.[1] Assumption two is that we are witnessing an accompanying trend towards a growing geo-political bifurcation in two distinct global political ecologies; one under US suzerainty and the other under Chinese suzerainty. The paper does not assume this second trend is inevitable, but we do assume it is likely without positive intervention to ward it off. To mix metaphors, the ball is, of course, very much in the court of the two major players; but the ball is not for them alone to run with. Other actors must be engaged in this process and the EU must be among them. So, the third assumption of the paper is that if we are to have any hope of containing the drift towards a bi-polar world, then the European Union[2] must, to use a final sports metaphor, "step up to the plate".

This paper investigates two core issues.

(i)  At a strategic level, it investigates the thinking of the major actors—the US and China—towards this trend. Depressingly, we argue that the bi-polar dynamic is increasingly driving the strategies of both powers and is unlikely to change in the near future. President Biden, we assume, may soften the rhetoric of bifurcation but not the practices—such as decoupling—that are in motion and will continue.

(ii) At an applied policy level, the paper identifies the core issue areas in which processes of bifurcation are taking place; especially in the domains of security, economics, commerce and technology (especially AI, digitalization and cyber) embedded in a wider growing ideological-civilisational contest.[3]

At a regional level, we look at how the European Union is addressing the process of bifurcation. Its role will be examined as a series of both reactive and proactive responses to the challenges of pending bi-polarity. The first part of the paper sets out briefly these assumptions. The second half of the paper looks at them through European lenses. It sets both the challenges for Europe and the tasks that face Europe in mitigating them.

---

[1] Always a problematic, the idea of "order" is used here descriptively not normatively. For a discussions See Acharya (2017).

[2] Europe and the EU are used interchangeably in this proposal.

[3] This tendency is discussed in some detail in the 2019 Rhodes Forum Report. See Dialogue of Civilisation Research Institute, *States, Civilisations and World Order*, https://doc-research.org/2019/09/civilisations-states-and-world-order.

## 2  Bifurcation and Its Implications

A drift towards bi-polarity is a multidimensional process. It is built on the growing competition between the USA and China in a range of distinct policy areas: broadly speaking security (military hard power), economy (trade, finance and infrastructure), technology (AI and cyber) and ideology (education, science and culture). In combination, these areas are building towards a generic level contest between the world's two dominant powers that in some of the more alarmist analyses is leading us inexorably towards a new Cold War. If not a new Cold War, then at least a new *geopolitical order* is in the process of evolution with major implications for USA-China competition and implications and challenges for Europe.

To-date, Europe is struggling to develop a coherent position towards these challenges. It welcomes the arrival of Joe Biden, but it is wary of a full-blown recommitment to the trans-Atlantic relationship in the wake of four years of Donald Trump in which the US came to be seen as an untrustworthy ally. But Europe is also cognizant of what is perceived by many as the bullying and ruthless nature of China's growing global influence captured recently for example in the rise of its "wolf diplomacy" during 2020. Thus, the EU—which was at the epicentre of the first bipolar world during the Cold War—is yet to formulate a recognisable cohesive strategy to address the current trend. Pew recently found European views of both the USA and China to be more negative than positive. In brief, European (especially German) distrust of China as a country and Xi Jinping as a leader is at an all-time high.[4] This growing lack of trust in China reflects the same lack of trust in the USA that developed in the EU during the Trump Administration.

The structure of a future world order is a work in progress. Currently, the EU seems to think it can cover the spectrum from being a genuine good liberal internationalist multilateral citizen at one end to being a realist geo-political strategic actor at the other.[5] The issue for the EU in 2021 and beyond is how to manage the relationship with these two superpowers as they force a bifurcation of world order. The early signs are that this emerging order will be very different from the constituent form that dominated during the Cold War. If China, or perhaps more precisely, Xi Jinping's diplomacy, has over-reached in recent years with attendant negative consequences and trust issues for China, then Biden's desire to secure a new alliance of liberal democracies via a Summit for Democracy to "renew the spirit and shared purpose of the nations of the Free World" is equally fraught with the danger of over-reach following four years of Donald Trump's wrecking-ball diplomacy.[6]

A good idea in principle, the proposed summit nevertheless risks looking like an attempt to put the genie back in the bottle by simply rehashing a G7+ view of world order. Like it or not, allusions to the "free world" no longer carry the moral authority they might once have done when Joe Biden first entered the US Senate forty-seven years ago. Adding several other countries to his summit—for example,

---

[4] Silver et al. (2020).

[5] For an early articulation of this argument see Higgott and Van Langenhove (2020).

[6] See Stiglitz (2020) and Biden (2020).

Australia, South Korea and India–would make it look no less elitist or exclusionary. Other inclusions or exclusions will only make the enterprise seem more problematic. America's unipolar moment has passed.

In an op ed published in *The Guardian* 22 December 2020 entitled *"Biden wants to convene an international 'Summit for Democracy'. He shouldn't"*, David Adler and Stephen Werteim argued:

> …the summit will not succeed. It is at once too blunt and too thin an instrument. Although the summit might serve as a useful forum for coordinating policy on such areas as financial oversight and election security, it is liable to drive US foreign policy even further down a failed course that divides the world into hostile camps, prioritizing confrontation over cooperation … If Biden is to make good on his commitment to 'meet the challenges of the 21st century', his administration should avoid recreating the problems of the 20th. Only by diminishing antagonism toward the nations outside the 'democratic world' can the US rescue its democracy and deliver deeper freedom for its people.

Unlike the bi-polarity of the US-USSR Cold War, any new bifurcation will not be built around hard and fast politico-ideological blocs. China does not represent the existential threat of mutually assured destruction that drove strategy and diplomacy in the earlier bi-polar era. Rather its challenges arise more in the domains of technology and economy. Moreover, smaller global actors in the current era—state and non-state alike—are not simply waiting for the US to return to provide their security. They can be expected to flow between either the US or the Chinese spheres, traversing specific issue areas in a manner that was not the case in the twentieth century Cold War. A potential further unintended consequence is that talk of democracy alliances could exacerbate the bifurcation process by driving Moscow and Beijing closer together.

Much stock—indeed far too much stock we believe—is being placed on the potential of the new administration in the United States to address this trend. But how the Biden Administration will change both the rhetoric and practice of international order can only be assumed at this stage. For sure, the rhetoric will change, as will some US practices—especially with regard to a range of multilateral activities such as the Paris Agreement, and the WHO to name but two—but we can only speculate at this stage regarding the degree to which policy will halt, let alone roll back, the wider *structural geo-political* and *geo-economic* trends currently in motion. Biden, one can only assume, will rapidly come to the conclusion that he needs to deal with the world as it is, not as it was prior to Donald Trump. But this will require a shift in thinking for the incoming administration away from a Trumpian transactional approach towards a system in which delusions (for that is what they are in the 2020s) of American exceptionalism should no longer drive US foreign policy.

A disagreement on values, culture and modes of governance should not prevent cooperation on fundamental issues to guarantee peace and stability, the fight against terrorism, sustainability of the planet and health safety. Nor should it be impossible to find a path to agreement on a reformed multilateral framework to achieve the indispensable goals of development and prosperity. Bifurcation does not only not correspond to the aspirations and well-being of humanity but also makes cooperation difficult if not impossible. Alternative approaches other than bifurcation must be explored. Alternatives on offer are captured well in an article in *The Atlantic* in

July 2020. Then, President of the Carnegie Endowment, William Burns (President Biden's new head of the CIA) proposed that:

> The United States must choose from three broad strategic approaches: retrenchment, restoration, and reinvention… We can't afford to just put more-modest lipstick on an essentially restorationist strategy, or, alternatively, apply a bolder rhetorical gloss to retrenchment. We must reinvent the purpose and practice of American power, finding a balance between our ambition and our limitations…

# 3 The European Dimension

Joe Biden has expressed a desire to reassert American trans-atlantic leadership in dealing with China economically and Russia militarily. Yet an optimistic view of a diplomatic reset is problematic. After four years of Donald Trump, both Europe's leaders and its general public have indicated that they will only cautiously and selectively support American rapprochement. As a recent German Marshall Fund survey found, there is little support from the French or German public for their governments to get involved in a number of current international issues central to US policy.[7] Indeed, despite its expressed preference for global multilateral cooperation, Europe's leaders have indicated an intent to hedge geopolitically when faced with a growing bifurcation of American and Chinese positions in key policy domains such as ecology and climate, trade, investment, finance, infrastructure, digital, military, education, culture and science.

Rhetorically, for example, Emmanuel Macron has advocated: "European solutions for European problems", and Josep Borrell, the EU High Representative for Foreign Affairs and Security Policy, has more pointedly called for EU, "strategic autonomy".[8] The rhetoric of strategic autonomy is increasingly reflected in EU policy behaviour. On the one hand, the EU signed an investment agreement with China that has disappointed the incoming Biden Administration, seeking to establish a common position against what it regards as malicious Chinese behaviour. However, the agreement has been welcomed by some prominent American analysts.[9] On the other hand, British and French aircraft carriers have conducted freedom of navigation operations in the East and South China Seas, much to China's ire and America's delight. But one-off examples of individual policy behaviour do not represent a consistent approach to diplomacy. It would be naïve to believe that a European strategy could be built on a process of issue-by-issue hedging between China and the US.

Multilateralism may be instinctively preferable for Europeans, but there are no simple panaceas in a world of prospective growing spheres of influence. First, establishing operational strategic autonomy requires the EU selectively developing a

---

[7] Transatlantic Trends, 2020, https://www.gmfus.org/sites/default/files/TT20_Final.pdf, pp. 12–13. See also Stokes 2020.

[8] Brzozowski (2020), Borrell (2020).

[9] See Sachs (2020).

member state consensus on the best ends, ways and means to consolidate an independent yet complementary position between the two behemoths. Secondarily, but still significantly, EU policy will need to develop a coherence with a post-Brexit UK if it is to be successful. This will require a greater flexibility of strategic thinking and diplomacy than either side of the Channel demonstrated in the final stages of the Brexit negotiations. Both will require skill and a nuanced use of material resources—adaptable to a variety of contexts. But the prospects of managing the US will be enhanced only the unlikely event of the EU and the UK proving capable of aligning their respective approaches to their transatlantic ally.

To address the limitations in its coherence and capacities and to avoid sending out mixed messages to the wider international community, Europe must address two major issues in its diplomacy:

(i)   The development and viability of the core elements beyond simply the rhetoric of European *strategic autonomy* as a means to combat global bifurcation. The priorities, forms and limitations of that EU strategy must be articulated.
(ii)  The tools that the EU has at its disposal, and those that it will need to build, if it is to succeed as a diplomatic actor enhancing its economic and military security in the increasingly bifurcated world, will also need to be articulated and honed.

## 4   How is the EU to Avoid "Mixed Messaging"?

The EU is surely correct to adopt a more strategically independent approach towards a troubled and competitive world order. But a full-bore commitment to a *geopolitical* strategic disposition is at odds with the path the EU has taken over the last several decades, especially in its commitment to collective problem solving in multilateral institutional settings. For all the challenges it faces, multilateral collaboration is still the best approach for the EU to articulate and propagate. Not withstanding setbacks along the way, it has served the EU well as it has developed over the last sixty years. Moreover, all things considered, multilateralism remains the best option for a more peaceful, stable and prosperous world order.[10] Objections to the rationalist, liberal multilateral endeavour of course exist, but realists describe attempts to secure common, collective action solutions to global challenges as no more than globalist-cosmopolitan meanderings.[11]

In an era when populist leaders try to normalise the nationalist postures of the realist, it falls to the EU to provide the intellectual and practical leadership necessary to halt this trend. It will best do so by reasserting the core liberal values that underpin the European project. We present seven propositions as to how this might be done.

---

[10] Although this argument can only be asserted here we have fully elaborated it in the 2020 Rhodes Forum report: *Can Multilateral Cooperation be Saved?* https://doc-research.org/wp-content/uploads/2020/12/Rhodes-report_Download-file2.pdf.

[11] See for example Mearsheimer (2018).

We propose these seven in a way that resists both the populist-nationalist discourse and, in turn, mitigates the geopolitical discourse of traditional realism with which the Commission was dabbling throughout 2020:

*4.1 The US is looking a less reliable actor and long-term partner. Thus the EU— while embracing the US security relationship—should do more to defend itself.* There are damaging long-term splits in the EU's relationship with the US that need to be repaired. The future of NATO, the strategy towards Iran, trade and protectionism, the importance of international institutions (especially the UN and WTO) and global environmental policy are all in need of priority attention. A strategy of European Defence can coexist with NATO, especially with the EU buying more than 80% of its military hardware from the US. Russia should also be engaged, but in a European way. On an issue such as Russian readmittance to the G7, we need to adhere to President Macron's view of re-engagement with "necessary prerequisites", rather than former President Trump's condition-free approach.

*4.2  Europe must lead the reform and (re)-strengthening of multilateralism in the absence of either US or Chinese leadership.* This is especially poignant as we celebrate the 75th anniversary of the creation of the UN. As both High Representative Borrell and President Von der Leyen have noted, multilateralism comes naturally to the EU. As she says "Cooperating and working with others is what our Union is all about". But multilateralism must change. It needs to adapt to the growing hybridity in international relations, become less bureaucratic and be more open to non-state actors. A new multipolar system will require new rules, or at least reform of the old rules. Sensitively espoused and properly contextualised, "rules-based order" preferences emanating from long-standing liberal democratic norms still have considerable purchase power and Europe remains a laboratory of multilateralism and multi-level governance. It must act as a defender of these principles and support the reform of institutional practice where necessary.

The venues of diplomacy and dialogue need reinvigoration or, as with the WTO, they will continue to atrophy. The challenge is to get the balance right between a tired-looking international institutional technocracy and the need for a multilateral diplomacy to provide public goods in a nuanced and moderated fashion. This should be a diplomacy that exhibits an appropriate compromise, reflecting the demands of *all* major players in the modern order and taking advantage of modern communicative technologies. The EU must support multilateralism with all the vigour it can muster. It must put real support, not just rhetoric, behind the Franco-German led *Alliance for Multilateralism*. But while the EU must stand firm in the pursuit of modern-day multilateralism, it must also tread softly and deftly.

*4.3 The EU should strengthen its inter-regional multilateral relations, especially in its own neighbourhood.* In a world drifting away from global multilateralism, inter-regional relations will become increasingly important. This is especially true regarding Eurasia, East Asia, the Middle East and North African (MENA) and Sub-Saharan Africa regions. EU-Asia relations will grow as trans-Atlantic relations become more strained. The EU understands the global "China issue". But in contrast to US policy towards China, the EU should work towards accommodation, not confrontation. This does not mean accepting everything that China does that may be questionable. Cautiously nurturing the relationship is not the same as either passive acceptance or aggressive rejection.

The EU should treat the concept and practice of Eurasia seriously. It is gaining momentum as both an economic and a geopolitical fact of life. The relationship between Russia and China might be fitful, but it would be imprudent to assume that it will not consolidate in the security or the economic domain in the near term, especially since the relationship is now developing more on the basis of strategic pragmatism rather than, as in the past, ideology.

The EU should recognise that events across the Mediterranean will have an adverse impact in the longer run if sustainable governance and growth and development strategies cannot be put in place to contain the pressures of economic and political migration. Less talk of Europe as a "cultural superpower" and more talk of pragmatic partnership and business potential that takes the relationship beyond a residual colonial legacy will change the atmospherics of the relationship. The two continents are going to be more integrated across a range of economic and political issue areas in the years to come. Now is the time to think comprehensively about a systemic strategy that balances both optimism and pessimism about the future of the continent. The development of a "continent to continent" relationship, with North and Sub-Saharan Africa treated as a single entity, should be an important development.

*4.4 The EU needs to take the lead in combating climate change*: The European Green Deal is premised on the assumption identified in the 2019-24 *New Strategic Agenda for the EU* that climate change is "an existential threat". The EU cannot solve this challenge on its own. It is a foreign policy issue. The new Commission has the impressive ambition to combine growth with sustainable development. In theory, the proposed EUR 100 billion deal will cut emissions while also creating jobs and improving quality of life. But to do so it will require massive investment in infrastructure, research, innovation and green technologies, as well as a commitment to stimulate a circular economy. Moreover, it will also need policies to decouple economic growth from resource depletion and environmental degradation. This implies levying carbon taxes on imports, becoming carbon neutral by 2050 and developing the various technologies needed to get there as the EU becomes the partner of countries also wishing to address the climate change challenge. This task is not simply an internal affair, but also one that will change the EU's external policy. Its ambition here will, for example, affect EU trade policy and its policy of scientific and technological cooperation.

*4.5 Dealing with digitalisation and digital disruption must be another EU priority*. These issues are foreign policy and international relations questions as much as internal questions that the EU must resolve. The need and desire of states to preserve their "information sovereignty" is a major policy issue, as issues of sovereignty and jurisdiction compete with freedom and openness. The EU will need to respond to both the *hierarchical* behaviour of the digital "superpowers" (the US and China) and the aspiring great powers (notably Russia and India) and the *hybridity* of the principal non-state digital players that have driven digitalisation in the twenty-first century: notably Google, Apple, Facebook, Amazon and Microsoft (GAFAM) companies in the US and Tencent, Huawei, Baidu, Alibaba and Weibo in China.

The major states are now harnessing privately developed technological platforms of power to enhance their rhetoric and practice of nationalism in the battle to safeguard (and control) national digital economies. Current tensions over design, governance and jurisdiction reflect broader global fissures. In the current era, the US and China are creating two sharply defined technological and online systems—or separate *digital ecologies*. The American system is still primarily private sector-driven, while China's is state-driven. But both systems envelop the development of AI, big data, 5G and instruments of cyber warfare. The European President appears to understand the implications of this for the EU, especially the digitalisation of finance. Importantly here, it is time for the EU to get over its inferiority complex vis-à-vis the US dollar, especially as the US now uses it as an economic weapon. As Russia and China look to trade in roubles and renminbi, the EU should ensure that European financial instruments are used strategically to enhance Europe's leadership and influence in the world of digital practice and governance.

*4.6 The EU must not follow the US in seeking a major decoupling of manufacturing and industrial sectors.* Decoupling in the name of national security is a US response to China as a strategic competitor. China is also showing signs of a decoupling strategy. But supply chain integration is much greater than vocal "decouplers" appreciate and support for this trend is still alarming. Integrated supply chains are still one of our best hopes for avoiding a new Cold War. Europe lacks the clout to contest US, Chinese or Russian politico-strategic power. The EU should be a major player *but* has to-date "muddled through", so it must now make the best of the economic and trade assets to remain the champion of global commerce.

As a top three global trader, regardless of how painful it might be, the EU must deal with US protectionist recklessness and a preference for transactional/bilateral negotiation if an open trading regime is to survive. It will not be alone. Others will support the EU position, especially states along the East Asian seaboard from China down through Japan, South Korea and into the major Southeast Asian trading states. Support will also be found in outward facing Africa, Latin America and Oceania. The EU should show resolve towards excessive Chinese intrusion into its affairs, especially in AI and digital information technologies. But it should equally avoid decoupling from China simply to conform to American wishes and pressure.

*4.7 The EU needs to acknowledge that for many people in Europe, migration is the major policy challenge.* Therefore, coherent, humane and fair policies are needed. But to do this Brussels must now deal with the principal opponents to a sensible migration policy—populists and nationalists. Not only have they grown more politically powerful, they *are becoming internationalist in their outlook*. While still strongly Eurosceptical, the new populist-nationalists are learning to harness a pan-European identity to further their goal of a racially pure, white Christian continent. Nationalists have done this by adopting a broader "civilisational" outlook on international relations which ironically focuses on European, not nationalist, culture.

Conflict is moving in a nationalist cross-cultural civilisational direction, although nationalist views of European values focus less on issues of freedom, democracy, equality, the rule of law and respect for human rights than racial and ethnic identity politics and a privileged status for Judaism and Christianity.

Adjusting old narratives to new environments will not be enough to restore the liberal order. New mindsets will need to take into account the impact of modern communicative technologies on international relations as we strive to maintain an open (and increasingly digitally networked) new order. Digital communication changes the nature of state bargaining and cooperative strategies. The governance dilemma is no longer simply democracy *versus* autocracy; it is also *open* governance versus *closed* governance. This applies in particular to the role of those self-empowered international civil society networks outside the scope of governments and for whom many traditional liberal values remain salient. There will (must) still be a place for democracy (of many variants), freedom of thought, rule of law and human rights. Europe must be their advocate. But these values will have to exist within a context of greater respect for national values and civilisational identity. In an open order we should expect power to be distributed more horizontally—both publicly and privately and with flatter, reciprocal structures—than in the past. So-called soft power will become increasingly, not less, important and increasingly digital in its application.

# 5 Conclusion

The world is drifting, *faut de mieux*, towards a US-China bi-polar world. The European Union must decide what strategy might best allow it to resist this drift. What should its strategic message be? This paper has suggested that to outside observers two competing views might appear to emanate from its senior leadership: (i) The idea that the new Commission will be a "geopolitical commission" operating in an increasingly geopolitical world and (ii) a continuing commitment by the EU to the values of multilateralism and cooperative, collective action problem solving. While not necessarily contradictory, these are messages that do not normally sit easily together.

Sometime soon, choices will need to be made. The EU should not become a purely *Realpolitik*-driven player—implicit in the first view—if it really believes in and intends to stick to its internationalist values, expressed in the second view. It must behave better than the great powers if it is to lead by example. A geopolitical road needs to be resisted for a geo-sustainable strategic agenda that offers innovative ways to deal with climate change, digital disruption and migration and that strengthens multilateralism as a way to securing greater inter-regional and intercultural cooperation and an open, non-protectionist global trade regime in the face of the protectionist and decoupling urges of its major trans-Atlantic ally. Only by privileging its internationalist message can Europe hope to play a significant role in the mitigation of the trend towards bi-polarity.

# References

Acharya A (2017) *The end of American world order*. Cambridge, Polity

Biden J (2020) Why America must lead again: rescuing US foreign policy after Trump. Foreign Affairs. https://www.foreignaffairs.com/articles/united-states/2020-01-23/why-america-must-lead-again

Borrell J (2020) The pandemic should increase our appetite to be more autonomous. European Union External Action. https://eeas.europa.eu/headquarters/headquarters-homepage/82060/pandemic-should-increase-our-appetite-be-more-autonomous_en

Brzozowski A (2020) In Munich, Macron presents EU reform as answer to 'weakening West'. Euroactiv. https://www.euractiv.com/section/future-eu/news/in-munich-macron-presents-eu-reform-as-answer-to-weakening-west/

Higgott R, Van Langenhove L (2020) The EU and the unravelling of world order in the time of COVID-19. http://cris.unu.edu/eu-covid19-unravelling-world-order

Mearsheimer J (2018) The great delusion: liberal dreams and international realities. Yale University Press, New Haven

Sachs J (2020) Europe and China's year end breakthrough. Project Syndicate. https://www.project-syndicate.org/commentary/eu-china-investment-agreement-by-jeffrey-d-sachs-2020-12?utm_source=Project+Syndicate+Newsletter&utm_campaign=10de40350f-sunday_newsletter_01_03_2021&utm_medium=email&utm_term=0_73bad5b7d8-10de40350f-107044401&mc_cid=10de40350f&mc_eid=d775e5422c

Silver L, Devlin K, Wang C (2020) Unfavourable views of China reach all time highs in many countries. Pew Research Center: Global Attitudes and Trends. https://www.pewresearch.org/global/2020/10/06/unfavorable-views-of-china-reach-historic-highs-in-many-countries/

Stiglitz JE (2020) Reclaiming America's Greatness. Project Syndicate. https://www.project-syndicate.org/commentary/reclaiming-american-greatness-by-joseph-e-stiglitz-2020-09?barrier=accesspaylog

Stokes B (2020) Joe Biden must think about the transatlantic alliance if he wins. The Hill. https://thehill.com/opinion/international/505312-joe-biden-must-think-about-the-transatlantic-alliance-if-he-wins

**Jean-Christophe Bas** is the CEO of The Global Compass. He was previously CEO of the Dialogue of Civilizations Institute in Berlin; Director of Democratic Citizenship and Participation at the Council of Europe; deputy head of the United Nations Alliance of Civilizations in New York; Head Development Policy Dialogue at the World Bank. He is the author of *Europe à la carte* (2009). He is regularly invited to give speeches on issues related to multiculturalism and identity; democracy and participation; cultural diversity; leadership and global affairs.

**Richard Higgott** is Distinguished Professor of Diplomacy in the Brussels School of Governance at the Vrije Universiteit Brussels, Emeritus Professor of International Political Economy at the University of Warwick and Visiting Professor in Political Science at the University of Siena. His latest book, *States, Civilisations and the Reset of World Order*, published in September 2021.

**Open Access** This chapter is licensed under the terms of the Creative Commons Attribution-NonCommercial-NoDerivatives 4.0 International License (http://creativecommons.org/licenses/by-nc-nd/4.0/), which permits any noncommercial use, sharing, distribution and reproduction in any medium or format, as long as you give appropriate credit to the original author(s) and the source, provide a link to the Creative Commons license and indicate if you modified the licensed material. You do not have permission under this license to share adapted material derived from this chapter or parts of it.

The images or other third party material in this chapter are included in the chapter's Creative Commons license, unless indicated otherwise in a credit line to the material. If material is not included in the chapter's Creative Commons license and your intended use is not permitted by statutory regulation or exceeds the permitted use, you will need to obtain permission directly from the copyright holder.

# Did the United States Miss Its Chance to Benefit from Ongoing Asia–Pacific Trade Agreements?

Wendy Cutler

**Abstract** This essay contends that it is in the US interest to become fully engaged in the Asian economic landscape. Twenty years ago, Asia accounted for less than a third of global output. Twenty years from now, Asia will account for more than half the world's total economy. Today, *Asia is home to a burgeoning middle class* and and a growing and dynamic market to many of the countries and companies that will shape the global economy for years to come. As most countries in the region have moved to put in place extensive trade agreements, including the Regional Comprehensive Economic Partnership *(RCEP),* the Comprehensive and Progressive Agreement for Trans-Pacific Partnership *(CPTPP)*, and numerous bilateral and sectoral agreements, the US has substantially withdrawn from participating. Since the *US exit from the Trans-Pacific Partnership (TPP)* in 2017, there has been *a steady march of new trade agreements across the Asia–Pacific region* that do not include the United States. If this trend continues, there is a serious danger that the US will miss its window of opportunity to shape trade rules and norms within the largest and most rapidly growing region in the world.

**Keywords** US strategic foreign trade policies · Asia is home to a burgeoning middle class · RCEP · CPTPP · US exit from the TPP · New free trade agreements (FTA's)across the Asia–Pacific region

W. Cutler (✉)
Asia Society Policy Institute (ASPI), Washington, D.C., USA

© The Author(s) 2021
H. Wang and A. Michie (eds.), *Consensus or Conflict?*, China and Globalization,
https://doi.org/10.1007/978-981-16-5391-9_25

283

Twenty years ago, Asia accounted for less than a third of global output. Twenty years from now, it will account for more than half the world's total economy. Asia is today home to a burgeoning middle class and a growing and dynamic market to many of the countries and companies that will shape the global economy for years to come. As most countries in the region have moved to put in place extensive trade agreements—including the RCEP,[1] the CPTPP,[2] and numerous bilateral and sectoral agreements—the US has substantially withdrawn from participating. Since the US exit from the TPP in 2017, there has been a steady march of new trade agreements across the Asia–Pacific region that do not include the United States. If this trend continues, there is a serious danger that the US will miss its window of opportunity to shape trade rules and norms within the largest and most rapidly growing region in the world.

# 1 The RCEP Confirms Rules-Based Trade

As the United States largely retreated from economic engagement in Asia over the past four years, fifteen countries in the Asia–Pacific region, including China, Japan, Australia and ASEAN members, signed a major new trade agreement, the Regional Comprehensive Economic Partnership (RCEP), which covers thirty percent of global GDP. Beijing has been a promoter of RCEP since day one. Then, as the US backed away from the regional stage and pursued a trade policy based on unilateralism and bilateral negotiations, Chinese leaders used that vacuum to portray Beijing as the reliable partner of choice for economic growth, trade, and investment. But to describe RCEP as a China-led trade initiative misses broader trends in Asia, where countries are focused on diversifying trading partners, solidifying supply chains, and achieving economic and job growth through trade agreements.

The RCEP negotiations were grueling. They went on for eight long years with many ups and downs. Most notably, RCEP members were confronted with a major setback when India withdrew from the negotiations. While India's exit was not a welcome move, in many respects it made the deal easier to conclude because New Delhi was blocking progress on many important issues, including market access, intellectual property protection, and investment.

Overall, the RCEP is less ambitious than the Comprehensive and Progressive Agreement for Trans-Pacific Partnership (CPTPP) with respect to market access (including tariffs) and trade and investment "rules." That said, the effects of RCEP are impressive and likely to be far-reaching despite not being as rigorous as the

---

[1] RCEP is the Regional Comprehensive Economic Partnership and is a free trade agreement that was signed on 15th November 2020. The nations that signed were Australia, Brunei, Cambodia, China, Indonesia, Japan, Laos, Malaysia, Myanmar, New Zealand, the Philippines, Singapore, South Korea, Thailand and Vietnam. The 15 member countries embraced about 30% of global GDP at the time of signing.

[2] TPP is the acronym for Trans-Pacific Partnership. The history and outcome of TPP is described in the main body of this essay.

CPTPP. It incentivizes supply chains across the region while also putting many political sensitivities to the side.

Being arguably the largest free trade agreement in history connecting 30% of the world's people and output, and mainly an ASEAN-centered agreement also means that the RCEP is likely to improve and expand over time as other regional agreements have. That said, it falls short on e-commerce, and is silent on labor, the environment and state-owned enterprises—all key chapters in the CPTPP. However, regardless of their differences, both the RCEP and the CPTPP are powerful responses to growing protectionism and put Asian countries on the map as key trade rulemakers. By signing the RCEP agreement, the member countries made a forceful statement in favor of trade liberalization, open markets, and the importance of rules to govern flows of goods and services.

Furthermore, trade agreements, especially those concluded between multiple parties, are not just about tangible market access benefits and the wording of rules provisions. RCEP promotes the further integration of the member economies through common rules and lower tariff rates. It solidifies bonds between trade negotiators and ministers, from Beijing to Jakarta to Wellington, which will carry over to other fora and initiatives. And we can also expect geopolitical impacts as the fifteen countries chose to work together under the RCEP framework regardless of their differences and their disputes with other parties in the region.

Finally, RCEP is another reminder that our Asian trading partners have developed a confidence about working together without the United States. This is a far cry from the early days of the Trump Administration when the remaining TPP members were doubtful of their ability to go forward without Washington.

## 2   The Future of the CPTPP

Many expected the Trans-Pacific Partnership (TPP) to die a quiet death after the United States exited the agreement in the first week of the Trump administration. That didn't happen. Instead, the regional trade deal lives on internationally as the CPTPP, as well as in numerous provisions of the United States-Mexico-Canada Agreement (USMCA) and the US-Japan phase one trade agreement.

The US exit put the brakes on US participation in a 12-country agreement whose members represented nearly 40 percent of global economic output. It included 30 chapters and state-of-the-art rules on such topics as customs administration, services, technical standards, intellectual property protection, e-commerce, investment, labor, and the environment. It also provided members with unprecedented access to each other's markets by eliminating or lowering tariffs and non-tariff barriers across all sectors, including agriculture. The TPP was envisioned as an open platform that would welcome other participants that could meet its high standards.

For the remaining 11 TPP signatories, the exit of the United States at first threw the agreement into disarray. The loss of the world's biggest market diminished the TPP's appeal, collapsing the share of global Gross Domestic Product (GDP) covered by the deal from 40 to 13 percent. However, these remaining countries were also divided. Australia announced that it wanted to move forward without the United States but raised the possibility of including other partners such as Indonesia and China. Chile said that it would pursue bilateral trade deals with Beijing instead.

Japan was especially disappointed and stated that, "The TPP would be meaningless without the United States," adding that the US departure, "destroys the basic balance of gains" from the deal. With time, however, Japan reversed course after a bilateral meeting in February 2017, which resulted in a joint statement that gave Japan tacit approval from Washington to go ahead with the TPP without the United States.

In March of that year, Chile hosted the remaining TPP members, as well as South Korea and China, and by May, the 11 original TPP members were determined to move forward among themselves. While Japanese, Australian, and Vietnamese leadership pushed the negotiation toward a conclusion, others, particularly Canada, began to drag their feet. Ultimately, the 11 countries regrouped and were able to work through their remaining differences, including Canada's concerns that the revised deal did not go far enough in addressing progressive issues, particularly labor rights. Following months of negotiation, the most crucial discussions took place on the margins of the November 2017 APEC (Asia-Pacific Economic Cooperation) Economic Leaders' Meeting in Da Nang, Vietnam and were close to reaching an agreement on what would eventually be called the Comprehensive and Progressive Agreement for Trans-Pacific Partnership, or CPTPP.

The CPTPP members surprised skeptics and concluded their revised agreement in March 2018. The amended agreement put aside some of Washington's core concerns and suspended 22 provisions from the original TPP, a small fraction of the lengthy and detailed text, which included provisions that were most important to the United States and those that had drawn concerns from other countries. Procedural adjustments were also made including the schedule for the agreement's entry into force and accession as well. They also exchanged side letters to address specific concerns. Yet the overwhelming majority of the TPP provisions, including the elimination or reduction of tariffs and increased market access, remained untouched, making the CPTPP one of the broadest and most state-of-the-art trade agreements ever signed.

Ratification followed swiftly in Mexico, Japan, Singapore, New Zealand, Canada and Australia, and the CPTPP officially entered into force between those members in December 2018. Vietnam joined a few weeks later. Three of the CPTPP members— Brunei, Chile and Malaysia—have yet to ratify the deal and bring it into force. This is largely due to domestic politics, but the US absence most likely made ratification less urgent. A number of countries have expressed varying degrees of interest in acceding to CPTPP, with the UK taking the first formal step earlier this year.

# 3   Possible Chinese Participation in the CPTPP

China has also raised its interest in the CPTPP privately and publicly in recent years. But, recent statements from the most senior leaders have garnered international attention. The motivation and timing of these remarks are curious and could be interpreted seriously or with skepticism. Regardless, they cannot and should not be ignored, particularly by the United States.

At the November 2020 meeting of APEC, President Xi Jinping stated: "We must stay as determined as ever to support the multilateral trading system with the World Trade Organization at its core, promote free and open trade and investment, and make economic globalization more open, inclusive, balanced and beneficial to all. Continued efforts are needed to press ahead with regional economic integration for the early realization of a Free Trade Area of the Asia-Pacific (FTAAP). China welcomes the signing of the Regional Comprehensive Economic Partnership (RCEP) and will favorably consider joining the Comprehensive and Progressive Agreement for Trans-Pacific Partnership (CPTPP)."

From Beijing's perspective, CPTPP accession would allow China to further integrate its economy with others in the region while also reducing its reliance on the US market and its vulnerability to US tariffs and other forms of retaliation. Replacing the United States in this signature Asian trade deal would also represent a major public relations coup.

CPTPP countries are unsure of what to make of Beijing's interest. China is a major trading partner of virtually every country in the Asia–Pacific region with two-way trade with China surpassing two-way trade with the United States for most CPTPP members. That said, China would have a long way to go to demonstrate its CPTPP "readiness," particularly with respect to digital trade, labor, and SOEs.

In the early days of original TPP negotiations, which included the US, the word in Beijing was that it was a US strategy to contain China by enlisting its neighbors in a trade deal without the largest Asian economy. This view changed, however, as negotiations proceeded, an evolution captured in a statement by a Foreign Ministry spokesperson who conveyed China's "open-minded attitude toward TPP."

I will always remember my first trip to Beijing in early 2016, soon after ending my almost three-decade career in the Office of the United States Trade Representative. The TPP talks had just concluded and other countries were lining up to express interest in joining. The lengthy text had been translated into Chinese, and in my meetings with officials from the Chinese government, academia and business community, I was peppered with questions on specific provisions and what they might mean for China, should it consider joining.

But once the US left the deal, the TPP looked dead. Remarkably, with Japan's leadership, the other members decided to go forward without US participation rather than squander all the political will and work they had invested, bringing the CPTPP into effect among seven of the 11 members over two years ago.

Since then, China has quietly approached certain CPTPP members to learn more about the agreement and informally explore their views on possible Chinese accession. While these overtures have not yet led to anything concrete, they demonstrate a continuing interest, which appears to have risen to a new level with Xi's statement.

A number of considerations seem to be motivating China. First, with the US on the sidelines and with the signing of the RCEP, it would provide another avenue for China to integrate its economy with others in the Asia–Pacific region.

Secondly, it could help reduce China's reliance on the US market and its vulnerabilities to further tariffs and other sanctions emanating from Washington. At the same time, acceding to CPTPP could provide external pressure, similar to the role that World Trade Organization accession played two decades ago, for Beijing to proceed with certain needed domestic reforms, particularly in the services sector.

Finally, it could be a great public relations coup for Beijing to try to convince the world that it is serious about trade liberalization and structural reform while the US remains hesitant in entering into new trade agreements.

Of the eight CPTPP members that have ratified the agreement, Singapore has been most vocal in support of Chinese accession. In an interview with the Nikkei Asian Review a year ago, Prime Minister Lee Hsien Loong said, "Singapore's view is that we welcome China to join."

Japan has been more cautious. A Japanese trade official told Caixin, the Chinese media group, last year, "CPTPP members welcome everybody who is willing to take on the high standard of market access commitments and the high standard rules," but he added that "it is up to China, not CPTPP members, to decide whether China is willing to take on those CPTPP rules."

In a January 2019 meeting, CPTPP members established a detailed accession process that spelled out benchmarks for joining the pact. In particular, they asked candidates to show that they could "comply with all of the existing rules contained in CPTPP." Furthermore, they called for comprehensive market access commitments.

Fulfilling both requirements would be an enormous challenge for China, especially as its economy becomes more state driven. Bringing Chinese practices in line with CPTPP commitments on such matters as state-owned enterprises, labor, e-commerce and IPR would be a heavy lift for China, as would Beijing achieving the high rates of tariff liberalization met by other countries.

This should not mean that working toward accession is a futile exercise, albeit one with a long time horizon. If China were to actually implement the market-opening actions over time to match the positive attitude expressed by Xi, this would be a welcome step. Time will tell whether there is any substance behind Xi's words on CPTPP.

# 4 Agreements with the European Union

The EU's renewed pursuit of trade deals in the region is notable as well. The EU concluded the Economic Partnership Agreement with Japan in July 2018, establishing the world's largest bilateral trade agreement. The EU also concluded agreements with Singapore in 2018 and put in place its agreement with Vietnam in 2020. Long-running negotiations with ASEAN and certain individual ASEAN members are in various stages, along with more recent negotiations with Australia and New Zealand.

From an economic and geopolitical point of view, the recently announced China-EU Investment Agreement (CAI) is most challenging. How might it affect the Biden Administration's work towards building a coordinated trans-Atlantic strategy to counter China's growing assertiveness?

While it won't derail trans-Atlantic cooperation, the CAI which is now not moving forward at the time of writing this essay, it may present some challenges. One of the biggest challenges is that the EU, should it reverse its current position, will need to be in a selling and promotional role as it seeks approval for the CAI from the European Parliament. In doing so, the EU will likely refer to China as an important and trusted partner, running counter to the narrative that the Biden administration will be proposing as it looks to work with Europe and other allies and partners in coordinating a China strategy. Furthermore, the EU may be reluctant to robustly use the measures in its new toolbox against China as European companies expand their investments in China in fear of retribution and counter-retaliation.

As a result, it is important that the US and EU open a dialogue on establishing a joint China strategy early on. In doing so, the Biden team will benefit from listening closely to evolving European views on China, including on the CAI, and work to shape a coordinated strategy that takes these views into account.

# 5 The Way Forward

President Biden has emphasized the importance he attaches to working with allies and partners and through international institutions to achieve policy objectives, rather than to rely on the "go it alone" approach that characterized the Trump presidency. As the Biden team re-engages globally it will find a different Asia than that of four years ago. This is most evident on trade, where RCEP now joins CPTPP as two major regional trade agreements concluded since 2015, and where the large and growing Chinese market has become increasingly important to the countries in the region. US re-engagement in Asia will require recognition and appreciation of, and respect for, these changes before the United States puts new ideas and initiatives on the table. It is essential that the US finds new and effective ways to become fully engaged in the Asian economic landscape.

**Wendy Cutler** is Vice President at the Asia Society Policy Institute (ASPI) and the managing director of the Washington, D.C. office. She joined ASPI following a distinguished career of nearly three decades as a diplomat and negotiator in the Office of the US Trade Representative (USTR). During her USTR career, she worked on a range of bilateral, regional, and multilateral trade negotiations and initiatives, including the Trans-Pacific Partnership, US-China negotiations, and the WTO Financial Services negotiations. She has published a series of ASPI papers on the Asian trade landscape and serves as a regular media commentator on trade and investment developments in Asia and the world.

**Open Access** This chapter is licensed under the terms of the Creative Commons Attribution-NonCommercial-NoDerivatives 4.0 International License (http://creativecommons.org/licenses/by-nc-nd/4.0/), which permits any noncommercial use, sharing, distribution and reproduction in any medium or format, as long as you give appropriate credit to the original author(s) and the source, provide a link to the Creative Commons license and indicate if you modified the licensed material. You do not have permission under this license to share adapted material derived from this chapter or parts of it.

The images or other third party material in this chapter are included in the chapter's Creative Commons license, unless indicated otherwise in a credit line to the material. If material is not included in the chapter's Creative Commons license and your intended use is not permitted by statutory regulation or exceeds the permitted use, you will need to obtain permission directly from the copyright holder.

# The Pandemic, Governance and the Year of the 'Great Transition'

**Martin Jacques**

**Abstract** The book called *When China Rules The World* was published in 2009. In this essay, the author updates his original statements based on his thoughts in the 12 years since publication. Great stress is placed on his belief *that China and its governance system are little understood by the world* outside of China. In particular, the author stresses how scholars deeply mislead the world with studies that attempt to *compare the communism of the Soviet Union with the communism of China.* There is a special focus on the *Communist Party of China and how it has continually adapted* to changes in the world. The latest change triggered by COVID-19 has increased awareness of how China is leading the world in economic development and innovation. This acceleration is described as the '*great transition*', which was in turn also caused by a '*test of governance' forced by COVID-19.* In that test, China scored well, while the EU and US failed. The evidence is in how the Chinese economy was able to achieve an annual growth rate of 6% by early 2021, while EU nations and the US were still struggling to control the pandemic.

**Keywords** *When China Rules the World* · China and its governance system are little understood by the world · Compare the communism of the Soviet Union with the communism of China · Communist Party of China and how it has continually adapted · 'Great transition' · A 'test of governance' forced by COVID-19

In June 2009, the book called *When China Rules the World* was published, I wrote the book to capture profound global changes. This was the synopsis to describe the book's argument:

> For over two hundred years we have lived in a western-made world, one where the very notion of being modern was synonymous with being western. The book argues that the twenty-first century will be different: with the rise of increasingly powerful non-Western countries, the west will no longer be dominant and there will be many ways of being modern. In this new era of 'contested modernity' the central player will be China.
>
> Martin Jacques argues that far from becoming a western-style society, China will remain highly distinctive. It is already having a far-reaching and much-discussed economic impact,

M. Jacques (✉)
Department of Politics and International Studies, Cambridge University, Cambridge, UK

© The Author(s) 2021

H. Wang and A. Michie (eds.), *Consensus or Conflict?*, China and Globalization, https://doi.org/10.1007/978-981-16-5391-9_26

but its political and cultural influence, which has hitherto been greatly neglected, will be at least as significant. Continental in size and mentality, and accounting for one-fifth of humanity, China is not even a conventional nation-state but a 'civilization-state' whose imperatives, priorities and values are quite different. As it rapidly reassumes its traditional place at the centre of East Asia, the old tributary system will resurface in a modern form, contemporary ideas of racial hierarchy will be re-drawn and China's ages-old sense of superiority will reassert itself. China's rise signals the end of the global dominance of the west and the emergence of a world which it will come to shape in a host of different ways and which will become increasingly disconcerting and unfamiliar to those who live in the west.

For the purposes of this essay, I aim to share some of my thinking more than a decade after *When China Rules The World* was first published. I will do this through three talks I have delivered in the intervening years.

# 1 The Challenge the CPC Presents the World as a Very Different Form of Governance in the Era of Globalisation

There is a profound ignorance in the West about Chinese governance. The dominant attitude is still essentially dismissive. There are two main reasons for this. The first is that Chinese governance is based on entirely different values and principles to those that inform Western governance. The idea of Western democracy has been the main calling card of the West since 1945 and, for countries like the US and the UK, much longer. In Western eyes, the legitimacy of any political system is measured by the extent to which it approximates universal suffrage, a multi-party system, the separation of powers and the rule of law. Such is the commitment to these notions that it is not an exaggeration to suggest that Western democracy is viewed in terms that are akin to the 'end of history'. They are regarded as indispensable for good governance and cannot be improved upon in their essentials. The second reason is the legacy of the cold war, which continues to exercise a profound influence on Western thinking—and elsewhere too, though usually to a rather lesser extent. Communism and Communist Parties are still deeply associated in the Western mind with the history, experience and fate of the Communist Party of the Soviet[1] Union (CPSU).

The rise of China has served to shift Western views about China to some degree,[2] most obviously respect for the country's economic progress and the huge reduction in poverty; in terms of attitudes towards Chinese governance, though, there has been, if anything, a marked deterioration. This is evident in a number of ways: the priority given in the West to the Chinese record on human rights, the speed with which China is condemned and demonised for its present policy in Xinjiang and the gathering hostility towards China in the United States, with its political system occupying a

---

[1] Communist Party of China (CPC).

[2] *This talk was delivered by Professor Martin Jacques at the Third Symposium on International* Ccpology at Fudan University on November 24, 2018.

crucial place in the increasing antagonism. The conclusion I would draw from this is that any fundamental shift in Western attitudes towards Chinese governance in a more sympathetic or benign direction is very unlikely over the next decade and probably much longer.

And yet there are much deeper forces at work that will require—and will eventually serve to compel—precisely such a shift in Western attitudes. These can be summarised as follows.

First, the extraordinary economic rise of China cannot be separated from China's governance. On the contrary, China's governance has been absolutely fundamental to this achievement. It could not have been attained without it. This irresistible fact will continue to gnaw away at perceptions of China: in the long term, facts speak far louder than ideological prejudices and assumptions.

Second, the West is in deep relative decline which has been greatly accelerated by the Western financial crisis from which it has barely emerged. The Chinese economic crisis that was widely forecast in the West never happened—instead, it happened in the West. And, as we have seen, this then predictably led to a profound political crisis in Europe and the United States. The people have lost faith in the governing elites and their institutions, and the consequences of this still remain deeply unclear. The political systems in the West now face by far their greatest challenge since 1945.

Third, we should look at these two developments in a broader context. The rise of the West to a position of global hegemony lent Western political leaders and institutions great status and prestige amongst their peoples. The authority, power and influence they enjoyed on the global stage served to greatly enhance their position at home. The precipitous decline of the West, in contrast, is having—and will have—exactly the opposite effect, serving to undermine, weaken and diminish the status of their leaders at home. My own country, the UK, is a classic example of this phenomenon. British political leaders enjoy the hugely diminished status and power and influence both internationally and nationally. This can only serve to weaken the respect, trust and faith that people have in their political systems and institutions. Exactly the opposite is the case in China. The rise of China has greatly enhanced the respect the Chinese people have for their leaders and institutions. The fact that China now has the second largest economy in the world, that it enjoys a quite new kind of global influence and that the country feels increasingly aligned with the great achievements of earlier periods of Chinese history lends its leaders and institutions, above all the Chinese Communist Party, a new kind of authority, charisma and respect which is only likely to strengthen further as China's rise continues in the future.

These three factors together are bound to progressively weaken the standing of Western governance and enhance that of Chinese governance, both at home and abroad. In other words, we must see attitudes towards Western and Chinese governance in the context of a much longer timescale and in an essentially dynamic way. Western attitudes may seem to be relatively static, even frozen, but from the vantage point of, say, 2040, it will surely look very different.

Which brings me to an analysis of the Chinese Communist Party (CPC). Comparisons with the Soviet Communist Party (CPSU) serve to obfuscate rather than enlighten. They are profoundly different just as, if you like, Russia and China are profoundly different. One of the most important differences, probably *the* most important, is that the CPSU never enjoyed widespread popular support—it was concentrated in the very small industrial proletariat and extremely limited amongst the peasantry who constituted the great majority. The CPC was exactly the opposite: its support was overwhelmingly amongst the peasantry and very limited in the very small proletariat. The CPC, as a result, had very broad support and very deep roots, which gave it great confidence. In contrast, the CPSU from the outset depended on coercion and authoritarian rule to get its way.

A classic illustration of the CPC's strength was Deng's reforms in 1978. China, at that point, was not in a good place and yet Deng felt able, willing and had the courage to introduce what represented a fundamental shift in CPC philosophy. Such profound shifts can only be undertaken by parties that are deeply rooted and enjoy great historical self-confidence. This, of course, brings us directly to what might be described as the birth of the modern era of the Chinese Communist Party.

The significance of Deng's reforms has, in historical terms, been greatly underestimated. They involved two major changes in communist thinking. Hitherto, socialism had been seen as synonymous with the state and planning. Deng now redefined socialism to include the market. His second innovation was to abandon the idea of socialism in one country, or socialist autarchy, and embrace the concept of a single world with China seeking to integrate itself and become interdependent with the rest of the world. The novelty and courage enshrined in this shift were to have huge consequences, economic, political and intellectual. It required so much to be rethought, not just economically but also politically. A different kind of state had to be constructed, with a different role based on a different mindset and skills. Deng's radical thinking unleashed a quite new intellectual energy which over time was to utterly transform the thinking and energy of the people. It was to create a new mentality, in effect a new people. It is impossible to explain China's rise without understanding the intellectual dynamism and innovation that lay at the heart of the reforms.

One of the great problems of the communist tradition had been the tendency for it to ossify, to become backward-looking and to become akin to a tablet of stone, the belief that victory was inevitable, that success was historically guaranteed. This was the very antithesis of Deng's thinking: nothing was guaranteed, China had to make and invent its own future. The result was not only the transformation of China but increasingly the transformation of the world as well. While the West betrays growing signs of a hardening of the arteries, a retreat into the past and a failure to embrace the future other than as a retread of the past and present, China is exactly the opposite. This is a huge achievement of the Chinese Communist Party.

It is inconceivable that Western countries could adopt a Chinese-style political system—it runs counter to their history, traditions and beliefs—just as, for the same reasons, China cannot and should not be expected to move towards a Western-style political system. Western countries can and should learn from the Chinese way of doing things, as China has over time learnt much from the West. Over the last two centuries, the major direction of travel has been from the West to China. Increasingly that will be reversed, as China rises and becomes the home of modernity, and the

West declines. And the Chinese political system, including the pivotal importance of the Chinese Communist Party, will be no exception to this.

What are the key attributes of the Chinese Communist Party in this respect?

First, the most challenging single aspect of Chinese governance is the demographic size and geographical spread of the country. Finding ways to bind such a huge country together and ensure inclusivity, an area where the US and the UK, far smaller though they may be, have been found deeply wanting, is one of the great strengths of Chinese governance, and of which it enjoys a unique understanding. The fact that China, moreover, is, in effect, a sub-global system in its own right, accounting for one-fifth of the world's population, means that the CPC has a special insight into the demands of governance in the era of globalisation, as the Belt and Road project illustrates.

Second, the Chinese Communist Party's ability and capacity to transform a developing country is second to none: it is the exemplar for all others. In an era in which the imperative of transforming the developing countries, home to 85% of the world's population, is arguably the greatest task of our era lends a unique significance and special responsibility to the role of the CPC.

Third, it is clear that the Westphalian system faces a growing and multifarious crisis. The nation-state form was a Western invention, specifically a European invention, which spread as a result of Western influence to assume an almost global universality, though in many respects it was, and has proved to be, a poor fit for many countries outside the West. The fact that China is primarily a civilization-state and only secondarily a nation-state gives it a special insight into and sensitivity about this question. As China's global influence grows apace, these attributes will become increasingly important in seeking to find ways of resolving a myriad of problems around the world. Again, this lends the CPC a special role and capacity.

Fourth, it is becoming increasingly clear that China is at the fore in the practice and the concept of modernity: its bold and ambitious attitude towards and relationship with technological innovation and the industries of the future; its recognition of the pivotal importance of climate change to the future of humanity and its embrace of globalisation, multilateralism and the developmental challenge are three examples. This stands in stark contrast to the trend in the United States, epitomised by Trump, which rejects globalisation, climate change and even reason and sees America's future in terms of a return to some golden age in the past.

Fifth, the CPC has pioneered a new kind of competence in statecraft which has raised the global bar in terms of governance. All countries will need to learn from China in this respect. A combination of accountability, experience, competence, education and meritocracy has underpinned the remarkable achievements of the Chinese government with, of course, the CPC being the key to this.

Finally, a word of caution. The rapid deterioration in relations between the US and China is very unlikely to be a temporary phenomenon. We have almost certainly entered a new era characterised by growing enmity between the two countries, thereby bringing an end to the long period of relative cooperation which dates back to 1972. We can already feel the draughty winds of a new cold war-like assault on China emanating from Washington. An integral part of this will be an attempt to demonise and smear the Chinese Communist Party. So far, the rise of China has taken place in relatively benign conditions; for the foreseeable future, something more like the opposite is likely to be the case. This will present the CPC with a great challenge, one very different from both the Deng era and the Xi period between 2012 and 2016. China will be faced with the imperative of seeking friends and building bridges with as many countries as possible as the US seeks to isolate it.

## 2   No Time for Wishful Thinking

There is no point in building castles in the air.[3] We must live in the here and now. I am sure the great majority of us wish we were not where we are. We would prefer that the era, beginning in the late 1970s, of globalisation and multilateralism, and that was characterised by relative stability and cooperation in the relationship between the US and China, was still in place. It is not. And it will not return for a very long time. The reason for the breakdown in that old order is profound, as is invariably the case with great historical shifts. We need to understand the causes.

The period between the late 1970s and 2016 was marked by three underlying features: a new phase of globalisation, the hegemony of neo-liberalism in the West and a stable *modus vivendi* between China and the United States. Two things served to undermine this era, one was an event, the other a much longer-term process. The event was the Western financial crisis in 2007–8, the worst since the 1930s. It fatally wounded neo-liberalism in the West and led to many years of supine economic growth, a stagnation in living standards in most Western countries and a backlash against globalisation. The result was the undermining of the authority and credibility of Western governing elites and the governing institutions, together with the rise of anti-establishment populism. In the United States, it created the conditions for the rise of Trump and a profound shift in US policy both domestically and internationally.

The longer-term process I referred to concerns the changing balance of power between China and the United States. In the late 1970s, the Chinese economy was tiny compared with the US. And it never imagined that the Chinese economy would one day come to rival the size of the US economy. Furthermore, the US believed that unless China became a Western-style country, with a Western-style political system, its modernisation would prove unsustainable. After the financial crisis, the US slowly began to realise that on both counts it was profoundly mistaken: China was no longer a relatively insignificant junior partner, but now a peer competitor, and China's political system was far more robust than it had assumed. This dawning realisation persuaded the US establishment that China's rise had to be resisted, at a minimum slowed. While Trump was the initiator of this turn against China, it is important to recognise that it has widespread bipartisan support.

The Trump administration sought to reverse the norms of the previous era from the late 1970s until 2016: to weaken globalisation, undermine global trade by embracing

---

[3] This is the transcript of a talk that Professor Martin Jacques gave at a Forum organised by China Daily at the G20 in Osaka on June 25, 2019.

protectionism, displace multilateralism in favour of US power, sideline the WTO and wound China through the imposition of tariffs and the introduction of sanctions against its tech industries, most notably Huawei. It is a sobering reminder that history never travels indefinitely in one direction. In 1914, it was generally believed that the trend towards globalisation that had dominated the period after 1870 was irreversible: they were wrong. The world was soon to be ravaged by two world wars, protectionism, the division of the world into autarchic economic blocs, and the worst-ever economic crisis. The world can go backwards as well as forwards. Trump's economic policy marked a reversion to the nationalistic and isolationist thinking that informed US policy in the nineteenth century and in the twentieth century prior to the Second World War. It was America's response to its declining position in the world and the fear that its dominant position would be usurped by China.

How does the rest of the world respond? In the longer run, the trend towards globalisation will be resumed. An increasingly globalised world means the growing interdependence of nations in a multitude of ways, from economic and cultural to environmental and the overarching challenge of climate change. These arguments and imperatives have not gone away even if they have now been displaced to some degree by the tide of nationalistic populism. At the heart of America's shift is the question of China. How does China respond?

The shift in America's position towards China is not for the short term. It is the beginning of a new era that seems likely to last for twenty years or more; bear in mind, in this context, that the previous era from 1970 to 2016 lasted for rather more than four decades. China will have to learn to live in a world that is increasingly divided and in which the US seeks to isolate it. We will all be casualties of this new regime, including, of course, China and the US. In my view, though, the US will be a much bigger loser than China. The US will cut itself off from China, the world's biggest, most dynamic and competitive market, and its competitiveness will suffer greatly as a consequence. China is the rising power, the US the declining power. The US's retreat into autarchy and isolationism will only serve to hasten its decline. At some point, still a long way in the future, it will come to recognise this fact that it needs China and that a new relationship with China must be based on equality between the two countries.

China is patient. This is one of its great strengths. In contradistinction to the US, it thinks long term. It understands now is not forever. China will be a very different and new kind of great power. Its rise has been remarkably peaceful in a way that the equivalent rise of the US, or indeed the UK, France, Germany and Japan, was not. They all fought many wars of expansion: China has not. It has a different way of thinking born of a very different history. China will find a way to resist America's attempts to weaken and isolate it: we can be sure of that. China's rise will continue. But at the same time, it will, and should, keep its lines of communication with the US open, to avoid giving the US any reason or excuse to further poison their relationship. China's caution is already manifest. It has responded to America's protectionist moves against it, and its attempts to hobble Huawei, but very cautiously, seeking not to exacerbate the relationship and give the US cause to further up the ante. This is most important and aligns with China's practice of valuing long-term over short-term gain. China, meanwhile, must intensify its efforts to build bridges and strengthen its relations with as many countries as possible. In this way, it will seek to resist the US's attempts to isolate it while at the same time demonstrating to the world its multilateral objectives and values.

# 3   2021 and Beyond

From the vantage point of history, certain years are invested with enormous importance, marking, as they do, some kind of turning point, perhaps the end of an era or the beginning of a new one. I expect 2020 to be one of those special historic years. The pandemic has clearly been a highly exceptional event, the worst pandemic since the Spanish flu in 1918, almost exactly a century ago. The manner in which the pandemic has encompassed the whole world, the scale of the disruption and the debilitating economic consequences and the way in which it has tested governments to the limit are unparalleled in peacetime. Indeed, the challenges of war perhaps bear a closer resemblance to those of the pandemic than what we normally experience in peacetime. It is inevitable that such a monumental event will have a huge effect on the world, far greater than the last major such event, the Western financial crisis in 2008.

Every economy, bar China's, will start 2021[4] smaller than it was a year earlier: France and the UK will be around 10% smaller, likewise India, the Eurozone will contract by 8% and the US by 4%. Most countries will face much higher unemployment. The Western countries will be confronted with huge increases in their debt. Inequality has grown dramatically. Young people, the biggest sufferers, have lost close to a year's education. These consequences have been far from uniform across countries. The most striking divergence is that between East Asia on the one hand and the West on the other. Much of East Asia, most notably China, has been far more successful at eliminating COVID-19 than the West. Economic disruption across most of East Asia, as a result, has been much less severe and shorter in duration than in the West. At the end of 2020, the vast majority of the West found itself still mired in the pandemic, while China, in contrast, has already been growing rapidly for several months.

Unlike the 2008 financial crisis, which was primarily economic in nature, the pandemic has, first and foremost, been a test of governance. The West has failed miserably. Indeed, without a vaccine, it is very doubtful whether the West would ever be able to eliminate the virus in the manner that China has. The reasons are fundamental: governments have lacked strategic clarity, they are shorn of the necessary levers of power, they are ill-informed, they do not enjoy sufficient support amongst the people, they have constantly yo-yoed between fighting the pandemic and reviving the economy and there are endless debates about individual rights versus the role of

[4] This is the transcript of a video interview Professor Martin Jacques gave for People's Daily on January 18, 2021.

government, while social cohesion and solidarity amongst the people have been too weak to foster and sustain the necessary social discipline. In other words, in the face of a new and profound crisis, Western societies have displayed a fundamental lack of resilience, the United States being the stand-out example.

The disparity between China's performance and that of the West has been nothing short of a chasm. This is a hugely important moment in the story of China's rise and the West's decline. Hitherto this has overwhelmingly been seen and calibrated in economic terms. No longer. The pandemic, in stark contrast, has fundamentally been a test of governance. History will come to see 2020 as the year of the Great Transition, the moment when large numbers of people around the world came to see China, rather than the US, as the global leader and exemplar. If in 2021, the year of the vaccine, China is able to shoulder much of the burden of providing a vaccine at a relatively low cost for many in the developing world, then this will serve to further consolidate how China is seen by the world. We can be sure that America will absent itself from any such role or responsibility.

One of the things that has poisoned the atmosphere around the fight against the pandemic has been Trump's barrage of racially charged attacks on China. I doubt that Biden will engage in such abuse and there is likely to be a calmer and more predictable response from the White House. But that does not mean we will see a return to the status quo ante. If the deterioration in the relationship between China and the US was at the behest of the latter, with China very much on the defensive, from 2021, in contrast, we would see a very different picture. China has drawn the lesson that it cannot rely on the US and that it must become more self-reliant. Dual circulation rather than opening up is the new mantra. Accompanying this new emphasis on the Chinese economy will be a stronger and closer relationship with East Asia, as illustrated by the recent RCEP trade agreement. As a result of the pandemic, the US economy and the West in general will find themselves much smaller relative to the size of the Chinese economy; they will also become increasingly aware that they are growing less important to the Chinese economy and they will matter that bit less. The price the West will pay, over time, for its short-sighted turn against China will be a significant diminution in its relative size, presence and influence on the global stage. This will be one of the hallmarks of the Great Transition.

But this will not be the only, or even the main, consequence of 2020 for the West. Cast your mind back to the rather less significant 2008 financial crisis. The Western economies contracted and took a long time to recover; real living standards have, in many cases, barely returned, if at all, to their 2007 levels; the huge loss of trust in governments, the governing elites and the political systems; the rise of nationalism and populism; the election of Trump; the turn against China; the polarisation of US politics to the point of virtual paralysis and, to the shock of the West, the emergence of a serious threat to the survival of American democracy. The consequences of the 2008 financial crisis were clearly very profound. But 2008 was a far less damaging event than the pandemic. So imagine what kind of damage might over time be wrought on the West in the wake of the pandemic?

With seriously weakened economies, the abject failure of governance, reduced living standards, mass unemployment, heightened inequality, the loss of hope and a young generation that has lost out badly, Western societies will be highly troubled, unstable, riven with conflict, inward-looking, volatile and unpredictable to an extent not previously witnessed since 1945. We see the first signs of this in 2021, but the long-term effects of the pandemic will dominate the West during the 2020s with consequences that we cannot foresee. For sure, the West will emerge much weaker as a result.

**Martin Jacques** is the author of the global best-seller *When China Rules the World: the End of the Western World and the Birth of a New Global Order*. It was first published in 2009 and has since been translated into fifteen languages and sold over 350,000 copies. Martin is a Visiting Professor at Tsinghua University, Beijing; Fudan University, Shanghai; and the Lee Kuan Yew School of Public Policy, Singapore. Until recently, he was a Senior Fellow at the Department of Politics and International Studies, Cambridge University. He was also formerly the editor of the renowned London-based monthly Marxism Today and was co-founder of the think-tank Demos.

**Open Access** This chapter is licensed under the terms of the Creative Commons Attribution-NonCommercial-NoDerivatives 4.0 International License (http://creativecommons.org/licenses/by-nc-nd/4.0/), which permits any noncommercial use, sharing, distribution and reproduction in any medium or format, as long as you give appropriate credit to the original author(s) and the source, provide a link to the Creative Commons license and indicate if you modified the licensed material. You do not have permission under this license to share adapted material derived from this chapter or parts of it.

The images or other third party material in this chapter are included in the chapter's Creative Commons license, unless indicated otherwise in a credit line to the material. If material is not included in the chapter's Creative Commons license and your intended use is not permitted by statutory regulation or exceeds the permitted use, you will need to obtain permission directly from the copyright holder.

# Globalization's Future Is Asian

**Parag Khanna**

**Abstract** *At the heart of Southeast Asia is Singapore*, a global center for finance and technology. This essay delivers an analysis of the future of the world from an *Asian perspective*. The analysis stresses core trends: first, *imagination and creativity* will be crucial as the world changes faster and faster. *Technologies from AI to gene therapy* are evolving at revolutionary speeds and are colliding in novel and unexpected ways. Second, *complexity must be embraced*. The chain reactions across economics, geopolitics, climate, and demographics make a mockery of linear projections. Asia represents more than half the world population and nearly fifty percent of global GDP in PPP terms. Coming out of the COVID-19 pandemic, only Asia will grow beyond pre-COVID levels in the immediate aftermath. This means the world will become ever more shaped by Asia. But what will the Asian world look like? Can Asians embrace a cartographic pragmatism similar to what they have achieved in the economic and social spheres? What can be done to resolve *Asia's numerous legacy conflicts*? What strategies might lead both to conflict resolution as well as to building a new and more stable Asian equilibrium?

**Keywords** At the heart of Southeast Asia is Singapore · Asian perspective · Imagination and creativity · Technologies from AI to gene therapy · Complexity must be embraced · Asia's numerous legacy conflicts

## 1 Scenarios for Asia's Future

When conjuring up visions for the Asia of 2050, two lessons from countless scenario exercises are essential to bear in mind. First, we must be imaginative. History is accelerating. Technologies from AI to gene therapy are evolving far more rapidly than we previously thought and are colliding in novel and unexpected ways. Second, we must embrace complexity. The chain reactions across economics, geopolitics, climate, and demographics make a mockery of linear projections.

P. Khanna (✉)
FutureMap, Singapore, Singapore

© The Author(s) 2021
H. Wang and A. Michie (eds.), *Consensus or Conflict?*, China and Globalization,
https://doi.org/10.1007/978-981-16-5391-9_27

Two decades ago, when the US invaded Afghanistan and Iraq, pundits were quick to declare an eternal extension of American "hyperpower." Yet here we are, nearly twenty years, into the spectacular delegitimation of the Anglo-American system. Meanwhile, Europe, which even Western analysts dismissed as a geopolitical museum, has embarked on a fiscal compact to match its monetary union, trades more with Asia than it does with the US, and leads the world in climate-resilient investments. Any holistic approach to measuring power and influence does more than look at military assets.

We already live in an Asian world. Asia represents more than half of the world's population and nearly fifty percent of global GDP in PPP terms. Coming out of the COVID-19 pandemic, only Asia will succeed in returning to pre-COVID-19 levels in the pandemic's immediate aftermath. Thus it remains fairly certain that the world will become ever more shaped by Asia. But what will the Asian world look like?

## 2 The Asian System

The rise of the modern Asian mega-system can be traced back around thirty years to the collapse of the Soviet Union. Since that time, numerous milestones have propelled an acceleration of pan-Asian interdependence. The commodities "supercycle" of the 1990s meant that West Asian energy exporters such as the Arabian Gulf countries began exporting far more oil and gas eastward across the Indian Ocean than westward to Europe and America. The 1998 Asian financial crisis forced emerging Asian countries to undertake major reforms in monetary policy and regulation and to open more to trade with each other. By the mid-2000s, intra-Asian trade had exceeded trade with countries outside the region. This provided a very important cushion to the demand shock of the global financial crisis.

Since 2008, not only has Asia led the world in economic growth, manufacturing, and infrastructure investment, but it has also been negotiating major trade liberalization agreements such as the Regional Comprehensive Economic Partnership (RCEP), which has created the largest open trade zone in the world. According to a McKinsey report, 60 percent of trade across all Asia is already internal to the continent. Here again, integration proves to be an important source of resilience against major global shocks such as the COVID-19 pandemic.

Along the way, deeper aspects of integration have also accelerated. The Belt and Road Initiative encompasses nearly all countries in Asia and has contributed massively to infrastructure finance across the region. The Asian Infrastructure Investment Bank (AIIB) also shows how Asians are capable of developing and driving their own institutions. But what about the geopolitical dynamics of the Asian system?

# 3   A Technocratic Peace?

In recent years, commentators have been far too quick to project that China's Belt and Road Initiative heralded the inevitable return of the Ming dynasty's tributary system of hierarchy across Asia. But rather than resurrect a Chinese version of the British East India Company (another common analogy for the BRI), a strong backlash has already eroded China's ability to coerce. Major powers such as the US, Japan, Australia, and Europe have erected significant barriers to Chinese investment while demanding reciprocal market access, formed a "quad" coalition of navies to maintain a free and open Indo-Pacific region, and are working with weaker states to offer alternative lifelines of credit to dilute China's "debt trap" diplomacy.

Both cases embody geopolitical complexity: the reaction to one power's actions proves to be more decisive than that power's original action. What it took the British nearly 300 years to learn, China is experiencing in the span of three years. China has told us what it wants its place to be in 2049. History will have a different opinion.

Envisioning Asia's future by way of linear projection is therefore dangerous, and so too is using static analogies and antiquated (if not outright irrelevant) theories. Western history teaches that unipolar orders are more stable, but Asia's four thousand years of history have been almost exclusively *multipolar*, with diverse and dispersed civilizations focusing more on commercial ties and cultural exchange than conflict. The most recent power to violate that norm was twentieth-century Japan, an experience of which China is well aware.

Extreme scenarios grab headlines: US Hegemony 2.0, China Takes Over the World, New Cold War, or World War III—take your pick. But if global history is any guide, we would be better served by drawing on precedents from Asia's broad past while infusing disruptive elements coming at us from the future.

As the world gravitates more toward regional constructs than frictionless globalization, the most salient template harkens back to the pre-colonial world, namely the fifteenth- and sixteenth-century Afro-Eurasian system that spanned the Indian Ocean. Today once again, the Indian Ocean region is the center of gravity in global trade, linking highly complementary regions from East Africa to ASEAN in an ever more fluid milieu. This is complemented by the revival of another pre-colonial artifact, the "Silk Roads" stretching from Arabia to the Far East. The resurrection of this trans-regional connectivity (across all of Eurasia) has far more to do with the collapse of the Soviet Union three decades ago than the rise of China, hence we can expect these new Silk Roads to flourish in all directions irrespective of China's influence over the Asian system.

The most fundamental test then of whether Asia's principal powers can maintain stability is whether they can resolve outstanding territorial disputes. Asia has managed three post-Cold War decades of great power stability, keeping major escalations from crossing the point of no return. From the South China Sea and Taiwan to North Korea and the Senkaku Islands, many flashpoints that have elevated fears that World War III would break out in Asia have not yet come to pass. But past success does not guarantee future stability: Asia's evolution into a mature system is far from guaranteed. On the contrary, Asians have not developed sufficiently robust dispute resolution mechanisms to keep conflicts from boiling over.

The biggest risk of conflict in the twenty-first century thus stems from not settling the conflicts of the twentieth century. Can Asians embrace a cartographic pragmatism similar to what they have achieved in the economic and social spheres? The answer will play a key role in determining whether today's Asian arms race can give way to the type of stable multipolar equilibrium that has characterized Asia's most prosperous eras.

What can be done to resolve Asia's numerous legacy conflicts? What strategies might lead both to conflict resolution as well as to building a new and more stable Asian equilibrium?

Asians have the capacity for collective foresight with the aim to eliminate the need for such tactics in the first place. What has been missing is a process suited to taking advantage of these propitious conditions. Asia requires its own version of the prevalent Western paradigm known as "Democratic Peace Theory," which states that democratic societies do not wage war against each other. Democratic peace theory is both inspirational and aspirational, but either way, it is of limited applicability to Asia given its dissimilar regimes (including non-democracies such as China) and cultures. An approach more suited to Asia might be what I call "Technocratic Peace Theory." Less than a predictive hypothesis, it suggests that expert arbitration is the approach to permanent dispute resolution best suited to the region's heterogeneous landscape. Given that Western scholars and diplomats lack the empathy to grasp both their own and Asian perspectives simultaneously, much less the creativity to reconcile them, it is up to Asians to do this themselves.

An important virtue of a technocratic approach is that it is not biased toward legal conventions or frameworks that not all parties view as legitimate. In the border dispute between India and China, as well as over the South China Sea, boundary demarcations have their origins in late nineteenth- and early twentieth-century colonial-era conventions. These conflicts, then, are effectively pre-legal with respect to contemporary international law. Until sovereignty is settled, how is the law of nations to apply? Western diplomats often speak of the need for a rules-based international order, but in many conflict formations, the rules have yet to be agreed on in the first place.

There is no ideal way to resolve international conflicts, especially given their diverse historical origins, power asymmetries, and diplomatic posturing. But in conflict resolution, the perfect should never be the enemy of the good. And good approaches involve sharing sovereignty, sequencing solutions, and setting boundaries in order to achieve greater collective security. Without prescribing a specific end-state, these tools can deliver a roadmap to peace for Asia. Leaders know that the same back-of-a-napkin approach that caused so many of today's territorial tensions can also just as easily be used to resolve them. This decade is a good time to do just that.

# 4  Factoring in Complexity

Now let us infuse some unprecedented variables into our construct of the Asian future. First, demographics. The world is headed not toward rampant overpopulation as many feared two decades ago, but rather a plateau of perhaps no more than nine billion people—followed by a rather precipitous collapse. China, Japan, South Korea, Singapore, and other Asian nations are aging rapidly and have fallen below replacement fertility levels. Their need to import foreign manpower is evident in Japan now home to nearly three million foreigners, including legions of young Vietnamese and Indians. It turns out that the country least known for welcoming outsiders has become an immigrant magnet. China too has a very cautious approach toward immigrants, yet beneath the radar is also heavily importing Southeast Asians to fill its growing labor shortages. We are witnessing a new era of Asian mass migrations from young to old societies, reinforcing the melting pot nature of the region.

Another driver of this demographic swirl is climate change. One of the most compelling virtues of the recent *2219: Futures Imagined* exhibit at the Singapore ArtScience Museum was that it made a radical scenario—Singapore as a high-rise Venice, with canals, hanging gardens, and vertical farming—appear entirely plausible. But 2219 could well be 2119, or even sooner. From remote work to travel bubbles, the coronavirus pandemic has taught us to speed up our acceptance of the "next normal." Singapore's own "30 by 30" plan to generate thirty percent of our fish and vegetable consumption through local aquaponic farming by 2030 has been brought forward to 2023.

The estimated ten million Indonesians working in Malaysia (in sectors such as agriculture and construction) already represent the largest cross-border community in the region. What will happen as rising sea levels engulf Indonesia's coastlines, drought scorches its agriculture, and heat effects broil its population? No place on earth is immune to climate effects, but IPCC models are more favorable toward upper peninsular Malaysia, Myanmar, Japan, and even Mongolia than equatorial latitudes. We should not be surprised to find tens of millions of Bangladeshis in northern Myanmar and perhaps hundreds of millions of Chinese in Siberia several decades from now. I once called this emerging blended zone "Sino-Siberia," and one only has to look at a map of the fourteenth-century Yuan dynasty to realize how plausible a scenario it is.

Today's technological breakthroughs befit a world of people more on the move than our more recent sedentary period. We are moving from reliance on heavy and polluting hydrocarbon energy toward more localized renewable and alternative resources such as wind and solar. We are recycling, desalinating, and drawing freshwater from the air and building aquaponic facilities wherever food is needed. We can 3D print homes and buildings and tow them on hydrogen powered trailers should some places be threatened by natural disaster. Thousands of satellites circulate in orbit and portable 5G base stations can be erected anywhere. A large share of the workforce is telecommuters, and immunity certifications (even chips under our skin) will be the new passports as countries compete for talent to fuel their societies. We all have e-wallets and crypto-currencies that work seamlessly across borders.


# 5 Asia's AI Advantage

The rapid acceleration in artificial intelligence (AI), research, and commercialization also points to growing dynamism across the breadth of Asia. From Japan to Singapore, AI start-ups and research clusters are emerging rapidly, a harbinger of the technological leapfrog that is to come. Asia has been home to tech pioneers for decades. Leading tech companies in Japan and South Korea, for example, have some of the highest numbers of AI patent filings, according to the World Intellectual Property Organization. The success of these and other East Asian conglomerates is also a testament to the quality of their talent and ability to commercialize research. Asians are placing emphasis on scaling applications in industrial and home robotics, self-driving cars, and smart city projects such as one large automotive manufacturer's planned development in the foothills of Mount Fuji.

China now leads the world in annual R&D spending with nearly USD 275 billion (just above 2% of GDP), but other Asian nations are also above the 2% mark, including Japan (roughly USD 176 billion), South Korea (USD 70 billion), and Singapore (USD 13 billion). By comparison, US federal R&D spending is roughly USD 131 billion. While these figures capture a wide range of sectors from biotech to materials to computer science, all are driven by AI. Japan's large-scale push into the Internet of Things (IoT) sensor deployment across Asia should be understood as part of its AI strategy given the data it will generate. As the first country with widespread 5G deployment, South Korea has an edge in gathering data that will deepen its AI prowess in areas such as smart manufacturing, immersive gaming, and autonomous vehicles.

Though its R&D spending is much lower than other countries in the region, Singapore stands out for its ambitious vision for AI and success in execution. Singapore's recently announced AI strategy includes all the key ingredients to become a leading AI hub for Asia: application to urban problems, investment capital for start-ups, training for citizens, and regulatory framework for data protection. Singapore's holistic approach to innovation has helped it rank as the third most innovative country in the world. (Korea is second; the US is ninth.)

While Singapore remains a small market, it has positioned itself as the most dynamic emerging region of Southeast Asia (ASEAN), home to 600 million people with a lower median age and per capita income than China. This zone of nearly 10 countries between China and Singapore is also a highly collaborative one. Leading companies in Japan, China, South Korea, and Singapore are all lead investors in one of Singapore's most promising start-ups, with services ranging from ridesharing to e-payments. One e-commerce and gaming unicorn, SEA Group, also launched in Singapore with funding from a Chinese multinational conglomerate and in 2017 became the region's first tech company to conduct an initial public offering on the New York Stock Exchange.

As foreign investment in manufacturing shifts from China to Southeast Asia, companies are putting AI to work to bring automation to the industrial landscape of Indonesia, Malaysia, Thailand, and Vietnam. These countries are home to major investments from Chinese tech giants, which have opened up AI labs in the region. This trend shows no sign of slowing as venture capital funds invested over USD 3.4 billion in ASEAN in the first half of 2019 and China's investment in the region increased fourfold.

While India lags behind East Asian states in R&D spending and patent filing, it ranks second only to China in the number of computer science graduates it produces each year. By further training software engineers to become data scientists and machine learning specialists, India almost doubled its AI workforce from 40,000 in 2018 to 72,000 in 2019. This labor pool is deeply involved in national initiatives such as a universal identification project—which has already registered more than 1 billion citizens—and a new facial recognition database for law enforcement agencies. Many global companies have set up AI research centers in Bengaluru while one multinational AI company has raised more than USD 325 million to boost enterprise efficiency with AI.

Pakistan is another young and fast-growing Asian market with an increasing emphasis on nurturing deep tech. In 2019, Pakistan was ranked as the region's fastest-growing country for digital freelancers. The government also recently appointed a Massachusetts Institute of Technology trained executive to head its Digital Pakistan initiative.

# 6   Conclusion

There may still be all manner of tensions across Asia and globally. Armed interventions and land grabs to claim and cultivate fertile habitats may be the new territorial geopolitics. Access to climate oases may be restricted while others scavenge in a more neo-medieval landscape. On top of this, bio-therapies and other preventative medical treatments could exacerbate inequality, both economic and genetic.

The more unpredictable the future appears, the more individuals seek refuge in islands of stability such as Singapore, well-governed enclaves that offer the virtues of security and connectivity humans innately desire. Already Singapore has enough housing stock to support a population of seven million or more, and demographic transition makes higher immigration an eventual necessity. At the same time, becoming a leader in sectors ranging from advanced manufacturing to vaccines requires fresh minds and knowledgeable technicians, as well as manpower to export innovations to a global society that constantly craves upgrades.

There is a saying that "only the paranoid survive." This means being prepared for a wide range of scenarios since the future is almost never either/or; it is far more often both/and. That means it is neither all utopia nor all dystopia, not all hyper-globalization nor all hyper-localization. Our global system evolves the way humanity does, not through grand design or random accident but adaptation to changing realities. The faster we react to an accelerating world, the better our chances of shaping the future to our benefit.

**Parag Khanna** is a leading global strategy advisor, world traveler, and best-selling author. He is founder & managing partner of FutureMap, a data and scenario based strategic advisory firm. He holds a Ph.D. from the London School of Economics. He is author of a trilogy of books on the future of world order: *The Second World: Empires and Influence in the New Global Order* (2008), *How to Run the World: Charting a Course to the Next Renaissance* (2011), and *Connectography: Mapping the Future of Global Civilization* (2016). Parag's newest book is *MOVE: The Forces Uprooting Us* (2021), which was preceded by *The Future is Asian: Commerce, Conflict & Culture in the 21st Century* (2019).

**Open Access** This chapter is licensed under the terms of the Creative Commons Attribution-NonCommercial-NoDerivatives 4.0 International License (http://creativecommons.org/licenses/by-nc-nd/4.0/), which permits any noncommercial use, sharing, distribution and reproduction in any medium or format, as long as you give appropriate credit to the original author(s) and the source, provide a link to the Creative Commons license and indicate if you modified the licensed material. You do not have permission under this license to share adapted material derived from this chapter or parts of it.

The images or other third party material in this chapter are included in the chapter's Creative Commons license, unless indicated otherwise in a credit line to the material. If material is not included in the chapter's Creative Commons license and your intended use is not permitted by statutory regulation or exceeds the permitted use, you will need to obtain permission directly from the copyright holder.

# Globalization Is Dead! Long Live Globalization!

**Kishore Mahbubani**

**Abstract** *Globalization has done more to improve the human condition over the past few decades than any other force in human history.* Yet, many are predicting its imminent demise, especially in the West. This essay analyzes this paradox. *The West has made three strategic mistakes in its management of globalization*, the majority of which have been made by the US. These have been compounded by *the failure of the second most powerful Western economic force, the European Union*, to help and guide the US. *The first mistake was made by the elites, the top 1% in the US.* They reaped huge rewards from globalization, but they failed to help the bottom 50% in the US. *The second mistake was to weaken governmental institutions.* This mistake was made during the famous Reagan-Thatcher revolution. *The third mistake was for the top 1% to create a functional plutocracy in America.* The essential difference between a democracy and a plutocracy is that, in a democracy, you have a government of the people, by the people, and for the people, while in a plutocracy, you have a government of the 1%, by the 1%, and for the 1%. *Most Americans react with disbelief to the claim that their society has functionally become a plutocracy.*

**Keywords** Globalization has done more to improve the human condition over the past few decades than any other force in human history · The West has made three strategic mistakes in its management of globalization · The failure of the second most powerful Western economic force · the European Union · The second mistake was to weaken governmental institutions · The third mistake was for the top 1% to create a functional plutocracy in America · Most Americans react with disbelief to the claim that their society has functionally become a plutocracy

We have all heard the refrain: "The King is dead; Long live the King!" The newest version of this is "Globalization is dead; Long live globalization!" This new refrain captures well the central paradox about our times. Globalization has done more to improve the human condition over the past few decades than any other force in human history. Yet, instead of celebrating globalization, many in the world are predicting its

K. Mahbubani (✉)
Asia Research Institute of National University of Singapore, Singapore, Singapore

© The Author(s) 2021  309
H. Wang and A. Michie (eds.), *Consensus or Conflict?*, China and Globalization,
https://doi.org/10.1007/978-981-16-5391-9_28

imminent demise, especially in the West, even though it was the West that launched our foray into globalization.

How do we explain this paradox? Why has the West turned against its most benevolent contribution to humanity? The simple explanation is that the West has made three strategic mistakes in its management of globalization. More accurately, the mistakes have been by the largest Western power, the United States. Nonetheless, these American mistakes have been compounded by the failure of the second most powerful Western economic force, the European Union, to help and guide the US when the US was making these three strategic mistakes. The passivity of the Europeans contributed significantly to the problem.

# 1   Three Mistakes the US Made

So what were the three strategic mistakes made by the US? The first mistake was made by the elites, the top 1% in the US. They reaped huge rewards from globalization, but they failed to help the lower half of Americans who suffered from the inevitable disruptions (or, more accurately, "creative destruction") caused by globalization. The second mistake was to weaken the government and governmental institutions when they should have been strengthened instead. This mistake was made during the famous Reagan-Thatcher revolution when Ronald Reagan famously said, "Government is not the solution to our problem, government is the problem." The consequences of this belief were disastrous. Three decades of defunding, delegitimization, and demoralization of key public service agencies followed it. The third mistake was for the top 1% to create a functional plutocracy in America. What is the essential difference between a democracy and a plutocracy? In a democracy, you have a government of the people, by the people, and for the people. In a plutocracy, you have a government of the 1%, by the 1%, and for the 1%. Most Americans react with disbelief to the claim that their society has functionally become a plutocracy. Yet eminent figures like Paul Volcker, Joseph Stiglitz, and Martin Wolf have confirmed this development.

Another paradox surrounds these three strategic mistakes made by the US. The country with the largest strategic thinking industry in the world (embedded in the universities, think tanks, consultancies, non-governmental organizations) is the US. Yet, even though these are the three major strategic mistakes, there is no public acknowledgment in the American body politic that these mistakes have been made. Nor has there been much discussion of it in the very influential op-ed pages of leading newspapers like the New York Times and Washington Post, the Wall Street Journal, and The Economist. Future historians will have to investigate and explain this curious phenomenon of massive self-ignorance in the American body politic.

Since many Americans would vehemently deny that these strategic mistakes have been made, it is necessary to explain in greater detail how each of these mistakes was made This is what this essay will try to accomplish, while also suggesting some solutions to the problems and mistakes that are identified. This essay will also end with the optimistic conclusion that all three strategic mistakes can be rectified and the US can emerge again as the number one champion of globalization, as it once was. After that, Tom Friedman, Jagdish Bhagwati, and Martin Wolf can come out with new editions of *The World is Flat*, *In Defense of Globalization* and *Why Globalization Works* in 2021.

## 1.1 Strategic Mistake One

The first strategic mistake was the failure of the elites in the US to protect the working classes from the inevitable disruptions caused by globalization. Why did this happen? Was it a result of the greed and callousness of the elites in America? Or were there larger historical trends that also contributed to this final strategic mistake?

As usual, the answers to these questions are complicated. Yet, it is also clear that larger historical trends contributed to this mistake. Future historians will see more clearly than we do that the working classes in America suffered because of an unfortunate coincidence of two major moments of history. The first moment was "The End of History" moment captured in the famous essay by Francis Fukuyama. The second moment was "The Return of History" moment, also in the early 1990s, when China and India decided to wake up. The unfortunate result of the coincidence of these two moments is that the West chose to go sleep at precisely the moment when China and India (and the rest of Asia) decided to wake up.

How and why this happened has been documented in my book, *Has the West Lost It?* Here's a brief summary. Francis Fukuyama didn't intend to put the West to sleep. However, when he suggested that Western civilization had reached the end of the road of political and economic evolution, he certainly created the impression among many Western minds, including some leading minds, that Western societies no longer needed to make any serious structural or strategic adjustments to a new world. Only non-western societies had to adjust and adapt. This message inevitably created arrogance, hubris, and complacency in Western societies. As a result, almost no one in the West noticed that the moment the West chose to go to sleep was the moment when it should have woken up instead.

Wake up to what? The West should have seen in the early 1990s that after having essentially gone to sleep for almost two hundred years, China and India decided to wake up. Why was their awakening significant? From the year 1 to 1820, the two largest economies in the world were China and India (see Fig. 1). Hence, when China and India decided to once again wake up, it was inevitable that they would shake the world. As China emerged as a manufacturing superpower, producing better quality goods at lower prices, it was inevitable that some industries in the US would shut down and American workers would lose their jobs. None of this should have been surprising. It is called "creative destruction" in Western economic theory.

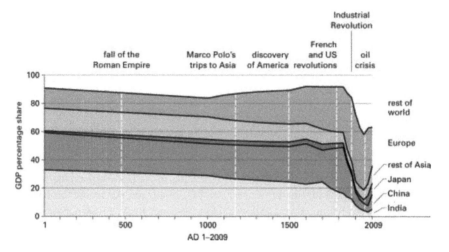

**Fig. 1** Share of total world GDP[1]

Let me acknowledge here that there is some debate among economists whether the emergence of the new industries in China caused job losses in the US. Some economists reject this claim. Yet there are at least two strong and credible economists who have documented how American workers lost jobs as a result of new competition from China. They are Daron Acemoglu of the Massachusetts Institute of Technology and Robert Scott of the Economic Policy Institute. Scott et al. (2018) states that 3.4 million jobs were lost in the US post 2001, while Acemoglu et al. (2016) estimate a 2–2.4 million job loss from 1999–2011 due to Chinese import competition.[2,3]

Significantly, while all this was happening, the Clinton Administration made no effort to launch programs to help workers who lost jobs. After the Clinton Administration left office in January 2001, there was once again an unfortunate coincidence of two historical events. The big event that the Bush Administration paid attention to was the attack on the US by Osama bin Laden on September 11, 2001 (remembered as 9/11). Quite naturally, this caused a lot of anger in the American body politic. Consequently, the Bush Administration became involved in two major wars in Afghanistan starting October 7, 2001, and in Iraq starting March 20, 2003. In their anger over the 9/11 attacks, the American people and policymakers didn't notice that something more significant and earth-changing happened in 2001: China's entry into the World Trade Organization (WTO) on December 11, 2001.

As more Chinese exports to the US and the rest of the world obtained duty-free access, it was inevitable that Chinese exports would surge following their entry into the WTO. Indeed, Fig. 2 shows clearly how China's trade with the rest of the world, including the US and Europe, increased significantly after 2001. Clearly, if US

[1] Mahbubani (2018).

[2] Scott and Mokhiber (2018).

[3] Acemoglu et al. (2000).

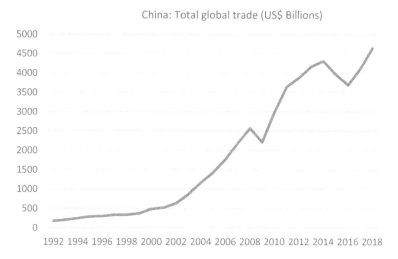

**Fig. 2** China: increase in global trade, 1992–2018[4]

policymakers had been more vigilant, they would have paid attention to the increasing plight of American workers. Sadly, they didn't. So this was strategic mistake number one: ignoring the needs and interests of the working classes as they experienced "creative destruction" caused by the return of China, India, and the rest of Asia.

## 1.2 Strategic Mistake Two

Strategic mistake one was clearly compounded by strategic mistake two: the weakening of government institutions, especially in the US. The Reagan-Thatcher revolution of the 1980s left behind two intellectual legacies. The first was the belief that markets knew best. Hence, if an economic problem emerged, the markets would find a solution to it. The second was the belief, as indicated earlier, that "Government is not the solution to our problem, government is the problem." Hence, the idea that governments should play a role in helping workers hurt by economic competition was considered taboo. The markets would create and provide new jobs to workers.

Curiously, even though in theory the Reagan Administration was not in favor of government interventions against market forces, the Reagan Administration intervened at least twice when it believed that free-market forces would hurt American companies. When American automobile companies complained that they could not compete against Japanese automobile manufacturers, the American government arm-twisted the Japanese government into accepting "Voluntary Export Restraints" (VERs) on Japanese car exports to the US. The VERs were implemented in 1981. In

---

[4] World Bank, *World Integrated Trade Solution*, https://wits.worldbank.org/Default.aspx?lang=en.

K. Mahbubani

addition to VERs, the Reagan Administration also took a second step to protect American companies from Japanese competition: it arm-twisted the Japanese government into accepting a significant upward revaluation of the yen from 240 to the dollar in 1985 to 120 to the dollar in 1988. Clearly, this made Japanese exports uncompetitive. As an aside, let me mention that one unintended positive outcome of the forced revaluation of the yen was that the Japanese companies began to manufacture more in the US and in third countries, including ASEAN countries.

The Reagan Administration, therefore, left behind a contradictory legacy in the US. In theory, it opposed government interventions in markets. In practice, as demonstrated in its actions against Japanese industries, the Reagan Administration actually supported government interventions. Unfortunately, the government intervention it favored was "negative" intervention: using strong-arm tactics to stop Japanese competition. It did not carry out any "positive" intervention, like retraining workers who lost jobs in the face of economic competition.

In this regard, the American attitude of letting market forces take care of creating new jobs is different from both European and Asian approaches. Indeed, the governments of the European Union and several East Asian governments (including Japan, South Korea, Taiwan, and Singapore) invest in worker-training programs. This American antipathy to have government intervention in worker - training programs also extends to opposition to trade unions to protect worker interests. Singapore discovered this when it laid out the red carpet for American multi-national companies (MNCs) to invest in Singapore. in the 1960s and 1970s. These American MNCs insisted that they would only invest in Singapore if the Singapore government prevented Singaporean workers from joining trade unions because, in their eyes, trade unions interfered with market forces. It took some persuasion but, in the end, the American MNCs accepted the Singapore government's argument that the Singapore trade unions could help to create better relations between workers and management in the factories.

This American disdain for setting up schemes and institutions to help workers was also part of a larger philosophical outlook which was captured in a famous statement made by Milton Friedman: "the business of business is business." In short, the only thing that mattered was the bottom line of the companies. If workers had to be fired to improve the profitability of the companies, so be it. Profits were more important than people.

It would be unfair to blame only Milton Friedman for this ethos. One of America's most august institutions is the Harvard Business School (HBS). For several generations, HBS also spread the philosophy that the primary responsibility of firms was to generate greater profits. Hence, only one stakeholder mattered: the shareholders. All the other stakeholders, including the workers and the community, were deemed to be less important. By contrast, the World Economic forum advises firms to pay attention to multiple stakeholders, including "employees, customers, suppliers, local communities, and society at large."[5]

---

[5] World Economic Forum (2019).

## 1.3 Strategic Mistake Three

This antipathy of the American business elites to paying attention to larger societal concerns may also be a contributing factor to the third strategic mistake made by the US: the creation of a functional plutocracy that has effectively undermined the American democratic system. In short, the US has gone from having a government of the people, by the people, and for the people toward having a government of the 1%, by the 1%, and for the 1%. What is truly lacking is that even though there is overwhelming evidence that the US has become a plutocracy, there is a powerful resistance to calling the US a plutocracy, even though eminent voices like the late Paul Volcker, Joseph Stiglitz, and Martin Wolf have done so. Since there is a lot of political and intellectual resistance to "calling a spade a spade" on this issue, I devoted a whole chapter in my book, *Has China Won?* to explain in careful detail how the US has evolved toward becoming a plutocracy.

Significantly, some of the most wealthy Americans have begun to acknowledge this. Ray Dalio runs the largest, most successful hedge fund in the world, which has succeeded through rigorous empirical research. Dalio has now applied this research to understanding poverty and inequality in America. On his LinkedIn page, Dalio spells out the dramatic decline in the living standards of the majority of Americans and points out that "most people in the bottom 60% are poor" and cites "a recent Federal Reserve study [that showed that] 40% of all Americans would struggle to raise \$400 in the event of an emergency."[6] Worse, Dalio notes that "they are increasingly getting stuck being poor... the odds of someone in the bottom quintile moving up to the middle quintile or higher in a 10-year period... declined from about 23% in 1990 to only 14% as of 2011." The data on social deterioration in America is undeniable. It undercuts the claims that America is a society where hard work brings rewards. For most people, the rewards have dried up. The platitude "virtue is its own reward" turns out to be grimly and limitingly true.

## 2   America's Road to Plutocracy

Why has America performed so badly? The simple explanation is that it demonstrates that a fundamental change has taken place in America's political arrangements, without the American people noticing it. Every two to four years, Americans go to the polls to elect their congressmen, senators, governors, and state legislative assembly representatives. And yet, under the surface guise of a functioning democracy, with all the rituals of voting, America has become a society run by a moneyed aristocracy that uses its money to make major political and social decisions. As a

---

[6] Dalio (2019). See also Board of Governors of the Federal Reserve System, Report on the Economic Well-Being of U.S. Household in 2017, May 2018, https://www.federalreserve.gov/publications/files/2017-report-economic-well-being-us-households-201805.pdf, quoted in Dalio.

result, this class has been able to enact the greatest transfer of wealth that has ever taken place in American society.

The great American philosopher, John Rawls, warned of this danger. He said, "The liberties protected by the principle of participation lose much of their value whenever those who have greater private means are permitted to use their advantages to control the course of public debate." Almost fifty years ago, he warned that if those with "greater private means" are allowed to control the course of public debate, American democracy would be subverted.

This is exactly what happened when the US Supreme Court overturned, in a landmark ruling in *Citizens United v. Federal Election Commission (FEC)* (2010) and in other decisions, many of the legislative restraints on the use of money to influence the political process. The impact of this and other Supreme Court decisions was monumental. Effectively, they helped to transform the American political system. Martin Wolf says that "the Supreme Court's perverse 2010 'Citizens United' decision held that companies are persons and money is speech. That has proved a big step on the journey of the US toward becoming a plutocracy."

Two Princeton University professors have documented how ordinary American citizens have lost their political power and influence. Martin Gilens and Benjamin Page studied the relative influence that the views of average Americans and mass-based interest groups have on policy outcomes versus the views of the economic elite in 1,779 cases. They found that:

".....economic elites and organized groups representing business interests have substantial independent impacts on U.S. government policy, while average citizens and mass-based interest groups have little or no independent influence. [. . .] When the preferences of economic elites and the stands of organized interest groups are controlled for, the preferences of the average American appear to have only a minuscule, near-zero, statistically non-significant impact upon public policy. [. . .] Furthermore, the preferences of economic elites (as measured by our proxy, the preferences of "affluent" citizens) have a far more independent impact upon policy change than the preferences of average citizens do. [. . .] In the United States, our findings indicate, the majority does not rule—at least not in the causal sense of actually determining policy outcomes."[7]

They reach the following alarming conclusion:

"Americans do enjoy many features central to democratic governance, such as regular elections, freedom of speech and association, and a widespread (if still contested) franchise. But we believe that if policymaking is dominated by powerful business organizations and a small number of affluent Americans, then America's claims to being a democratic society are seriously threatened."

In the past, the broad middle classes of America had a strong say in determining the fundamental directions of American society. Today, they no longer do. The decisions of the US Congress are not determined by the voters; they are determined by the funders. As a result, America is becoming functionally less and less of a democracy, where all citizens have an equal voice. Instead, it looks more and more like a plutocracy, where a few rich people are disproportionately powerful.

---

[7] Gilens and Page (2014).

A 2018 study by scholars Alexander Hertel-Fernandez, Theda Skocpol and Jason Sclar of the School of International and Public Affairs, Columbia University, further argued that:

"......since the mid-2000s, newly formed conservative and progressive Donor consortia—above all the Koch seminars [founded by brothers Charles and David Koch] and the DA [Democracy Alliance]—have magnified the impact of wealthy donors by raising and channeling ever more money not just into elections but also into full arrays of cooperating political organizations. . . . The Koch seminars… allowed donations to be channeled into building a virtual third political party organized around AFP [Americans for Prosperity], an overarching political network able not only to electorally support the Republican Party but also to push and pull its candidates and office holders in preferred ultra-free-market policy directions… To the degree that wealthy donor consortia have succeeded in building organizational infrastructures, they have shifted the resources available for developing policy proposals, pressing demands on lawmakers, and mobilizing ordinary Americans into politics… When plutocratic collectives impose new agendas on political organizations seeking to attract financial resources, the funders reshape routines, goals, and centers of power in U.S. politics well beyond the budgetary impact of particular grants."[8]

The authors thus conclude:

"Our analysis of the Koch and DA consortia highlights that a great deal of big-money influence flows through mechanisms other than individual or business donations to the electoral and lobbying operations…To understand how the wealthy are reshaping U.S. politics, we need to look not just at their election and lobbying expenditures but also at their concerted investments in many kinds of political organizations operating across a variety of fields and functions. Only in this way can we account for the stark inequalities in government responsiveness documented by researchers such as Martin Gilens, Larry Bartels and Benjamin Page."

In theory, the American people would revolt if their votes were taken away from them. Yet, their votes have effectively been hijacked by the rich—but most Americans haven't noticed it yet. Anand Giridharadas, a former *New York Times* columnist, has documented in great detail in *Winners Take All* how the dream of the American middle class has effectively evaporated. As he says:

"A successful society is a progress machine. It takes in the raw material of innovations and produces broad human advancement. America's machine is broken. When the fruits of change have fallen on the United States in recent decades, the very fortunate have basketed almost all of them. For instance, the average pretax income of the top tenth of Americans has doubled since 1980, that of the top 1 percent has more than tripled, and that of the top 0.001 percent has risen more than seven fold—even as the average pretax income of the bottom half of Americans has stayed almost precisely the same. These familiar figures amount to three and a half decades' worth of wondrous, head-spinning change with zero impact on the average pay of 117 million Americans."[9]

American scholars on political systems are fond of quoting Lord Acton's famous quip: "Power corrupts. Absolute power corrupts absolutely." After quoting him, they probably whisper under their breaths, "Thank God, we are a democracy with

---

[8] Hertel-Fernandez et al. (2018).
[9] Giridharadas (2018).

separation of powers. This couldn't happen to us." All those scholars should consider this variation on Lord Acton instead: "Money corrupts. Absolute money corrupts absolutely."

The corrupting effect of money on political processes should be more prominently highlighted in American political discourse. In most societies, when individuals or corporations use money to influence public policy decisions, it is called out as corruption. Even people in third world countries that suffer from widespread corruption know it is illegal, though they often do not have the means to oppose it. But in America, it is not considered corruption to use money to influence public policy decisions because the Supreme Court has legalized it.

In legalizing the use of massive amounts of money to influence public policy decisions, the Supreme Court had clearly ignored the advice of John Rawls, who warned that if, "those who have greater private means are permitted to use their advantages to control the course of public debate," this would be the corrupting result:

> "Eventually, these inequalities will enable those better situated to exercise a larger influence over the development of legislation. In due time they are likely to acquire a preponderant weight in settling social questions, at least in regard to those matters upon which they normally agree, which is to say in regard to those things that support their favored circumstances."[10]

This is precisely what has happened over the past few decades: the affluent have gained, "preponderant weight... in regard of those things that support their favored circumstances." There has been a relative transfer of wealth and political power from the vast majority of America's population to a privileged superminority. Hence, there is no doubt that America has become a plutocracy.

## 3   Simple Solutions and Hard Decisions

So to quote Lenin, "What is to be done?" in response to these three strategic mistakes. The good news is that they can be fixed. Here are three simple steps that can be taken. The first step is for the West, especially the US, to acknowledge that the wounds it has suffered from globalization are self-inflicted, as documented in the three mistakes made. The second step, a natural consequence of the first, is to take remedial measures against the self-inflicted wounds. The third step would be for the West and the East, especially the US and China, to reach a new comprehensive understanding of how to cooperate in managing the common challenges faced in globalization.

Sadly, even though these steps are "simple" in theory, in practice they will be difficult to implement. The first step may be the hardest to take. Most societies, including the US, would prefer to believe that other societies are responsible for their problems. Hence, when Donald Trump launched his trade war against China, few American voices spoke up to say the undeniable truth: America's trade deficits were

---

[10] Rawls (1999).

a result of a domestic, not external, factors. The imbalance between consumption and savings was the main reason for the trade deficit. Indeed, even if the trade deficit of the US with China went down, its trade deficit with the rest of the world would not go down. This is exactly what happened between 2017 and 2019, the years of the Trump trade war. In 2019, the US deficit with China dropped from USD 375 billion in 2017 to USD 345 billion in 2019, but its overall trade deficit with the world went up from USD 792 billion in 2017 to USD 854 billion.

Therefore, unless the US acknowledges that its problems with globalization are the result of self-inflicted wounds, it will be difficult for it to take the necessary remedial steps, especially the rebuilding of strong and effective institutions to manage the inevitable challenges of globalization and the reversal of the moves (including the Supreme Court decision legitimizing the unlimited amount of corporate funding for political donations) that have led to the development of plutocracy in the US. In short, the first step and second step are connected. Just as we cannot cure a medical ailment until we acknowledge that we have an ailment, the US cannot reverse the problems it has developed with globalization until it acknowledges that its problems are the result of self-inflicted wounds.

While it is working on a difficult first two steps, the US can begin taking action on the third: reaching a new understanding with China on how to manage the challenges of globalization together. Here too, in theory, the interests of the US and China in this area may appear irreconcilable. However, as I have documented in great length in the final chapter of *Has China Won?*, there are no fundamental conflicts of interest between the long-term interests of the US and China.

Indeed, there are five "non-contradictions" between the US and China and here's the first non-contradiction. If the primary goal of the US government is to improve the well-being of the American people (as it should be) and if the primary goal of the Chinese government is to improve the well-being of the Chinese people (as it should be), there is no fundamental contradiction between these two goals. Indeed, both governments are more likely to succeed in achieving their respective goals, if they cooperate, rather than engage in a zero-sum game of geopolitical competition. The main obstacle to such win–win cooperation is a belief among many influential voices in Washington DC that the primary goal of the US should be to preserve "primacy" in the global system. However, between "primacy" and "people", clearly the interests of the American people are more important. Sheer common sense makes this clear.

The election of Joe Biden as President provides a tremendous opportunity to reset the US–China relationship. In theory, Biden's hands are tied since a rock-solid anti-China consensus has gripped the Washington elite. However, if Biden is politically shrewd, he can navigate this difficult domestic environment in the US by appearing publicly critical of China while privately enhancing cooperation in the areas of mutual benefit between the US and China. He could use the excuse of COVID-19 to remove some trade sanctions against China. This would encourage China to buy more from America, especially in agricultural products. If the farmers in the mid-West swing toward supporting Biden, he would have undercut a significant base from the Republicans before the 2022 and 2024 elections. Hence, paradoxically, economic cooperation with China could help Biden win votes domestically.

In short, even though it appears inconceivable in today's political context that the US and China can cooperate for mutual benefit, the reality is that they can and should do so, especially after the election of Joe Biden. Both sides, especially both governments, should not lose sight of the fact that their primary responsibility is to improve the well-being of their people. They can achieve this by working with each other, not against each other.

# References

Acemoglu D, Autor D, Dorn D, Hanson GH, Price B (2016) Import competition and the great US employment sag of the 2000s. J Labor Econ 34(S1):S141–S198

Dalio R (2019) Why and how capitalism needs to be reformed (part 1). LinkedIn. https://www.lin kedin.com/pulse/why-how-capitalism-needs-reformed-ray-dalio/

Gilens M, Page BI (2014) Testing theories of American politics: elites, interest groups, and average citizens. Perspect Polit 12(3):564–581. https://scholar.princeton.edu/sites/default/files/mgilens/files/gilens_and_page_2014_-testing_theories_of_american_politics.doc.pdf

Giridharadas A (2018) Prologue. In: Winners take all: the elite charade of changing the world. Alfred A. Knopf, New York

Hertel-Fernandez A, Skocpol T, Sclar J (2018) When political mega- donors join forces: how the Koch network and the democracy alliance influence organized U.S. politics on the right and left. Stud Am Polit Develop. 32(2)

Mahbubani K (2018) Has the west lost it? A provocation. Penguin UK, London, p 5

Rawls J (1999) A theory of justice, rev. Belknap Press, Cambridge, MA, p 225

Scott RE, Mokhiber Z (2018) The China toll deepens. Economic Policy Institute, Washington, DC. https://epi.org/156645

World Economic Forum (2019) Davos manifesto 2020: the universal purpose of a company in the fourth industrial revolution. https://www.weforum.org/agenda/2019/12/davos-manifesto-2020-the-universal-purpose-of-a-company-in-the-fourth-industrial-revolution/

**Kishore Mahbubani** is a former President of the UN Security Council (January 2001 to May 2002) and is a Distinguished Fellow at the Asia Research Institute, National University of Singapore. He has had two acclaimed careers with thirty-three years in diplomacy and fifteen years in academia. He was the Founding Dean of the Lee Kuan Yew School of Public Policy in Singapore. He lived in New York for over ten years as Singapore's ambassador to the UN. In 2019, he was elected to the American Academy of Arts and Sciences. He has authored several books the most recent being: *Has China Won? The Chinese Challenge to American Primacy* (2020).

**Open Access** This chapter is licensed under the terms of the Creative Commons Attribution-NonCommercial-NoDerivatives 4.0 International License (http://creativecommons.org/licenses/by-nc-nd/4.0/), which permits any noncommercial use, sharing, distribution and reproduction in any medium or format, as long as you give appropriate credit to the original author(s) and the source, provide a link to the Creative Commons license and indicate if you modified the licensed material. You do not have permission under this license to share adapted material derived from this chapter or parts of it.

The images or other third party material in this chapter are included in the chapter's Creative Commons license, unless indicated otherwise in a credit line to the material. If material is not included in the chapter's Creative Commons license and your intended use is not permitted by statutory regulation or exceeds the permitted use, you will need to obtain permission directly from the copyright holder.

# Could This Be the African Century?

**Carlos Lopes**

**Abstract** *Demography will shape Africa's future.* Africa's *current population is 1.3 billion.* Some forecast that, it will double by 2050. This essay contends that *narratives about Africa tend to be negative.* If Africa is home to 2.6 billion people, or a quarter of the world's population, *Africa will play a decisive role in shaping the future of the world.* A number of socio-economic indicators support an *African Century narrative,* which would result in a shift from policies driven by perception to those driven by reality. *The youth bulge in Africa,* if managed properly is, for instance, not just a fuel for African economies, but also for the rest of the world, especially Europe. *Chinese investors in Africa* adjust to the local context extremely quickly, and are not perceived as expatriates having living standards way above the rest. They instill an entrepreneurial "can do" attitude against adversity. *Chinese perception of risk is also very different* from traditional western investors. These characteristics make China a good partner for the industrialization policies being pursued by African countries.

**Keywords** Demography will shape Africa's future · Africa's current population is 1.3 billion · Narratives about Africa tend to be negative · Africa will play a decisive role in shaping the future of the world · African Century narrative · The youth bulge in Africa · Chinese investors in Africa · Chinese perception of risk is also very different

Narratives about Africa tend to be negative. Embedded in historical simplifications and dismissiveness the current changes being observed on the mainstream views about the continent have a lot to do with a stronger agency and significant achievements. While the 'Africa Rising' storyline tends to on about new business opportunities, more voices admit the possibility of an African century.

The adoption of the UN's Millennium Declaration—and its companion Millennium Development Goals—inaugurated a new era. Prescriptive structural adjustment policies were replaced by goals, meaning different ways of attaining objectives or, in economic jargon, policy space. Around the year 2000, Africa started to demonstrate a

C. Lopes (✉)
Mandela School of Public Governance, University of Cape Town, Cape Town, South Africa

© The Author(s) 2021
H. Wang and A. Michie (eds.), *Consensus or Conflict?*, China and Globalization,
https://doi.org/10.1007/978-981-16-5391-9_29

different pattern of economic behavior. For the last decade, African countries systematically dominated the list of the top-10 fastest-growing economies in the world. In 2019, the IMF forecasts indicated that *six of the ten fastest-growing economies in the world would be in Africa* [1](Ethiopia, Ghana, Ivory Coast, Rwanda, Senegal, and South Sudan). Economic growth resulted in Africa doubling its Gross Domestic Product (GDP) within a period of 12 years. Even though growth has slowed down due to a challenging global context, the continent's performance is second only to Southeast Asia.

A number of socio-economic indicators have also fueled the African Century narrative. By 2010, the middle class had risen to *34% of Africa's population,*[2] up from 27% in 2000. Such growth—of 3.1%—in the middle class between 1980 and 2010 is higher than the 2.6% growth rate of the total population. The middle class, although arguably still vulnerable, is viewed as fuel for the economies of the continent. In 2017, household spending reached USD *1.6 trillion*[3] after passing the USD 1 trillion mark in 2010. This is on par with large economies such as China. By 2025, household spending is projected to reach USD 2.5 trillion according to estimates by McKinsey Global Institute and the Brookings Institute.[4]

However, growth experience alone is indeed not sufficient to claim the twenty-first century. Africa grew quickly, but transformed slowly, putting in jeopardy many of the gains so far registered. The *forecasted 4% GDP growth for 2019*[5] remains far short of the 7% minimum percentage required to double the average income in a decade. This is partly due to the fact that too many African economies still depend on the production and export of primary commodities.

# 1 Growth with Transformation

The good news is that attractive solutions are known. Translating growth into meaningful developments for African countries will require an aggressive industrialization agenda. Africa is not a desert when it comes to manufacturing and industrialization. Attempts to industrialize in the 1960s and 1970s by adopting an import-substitution model of industrialization had mixed results. While this led to some remarkable progress, it quickly showed the limits of state-led production rather than state-led facilitation. Manufacturing value addition as a percentage of the GDP has been declining since the introduction of liberal policies promoted by structural adjustment programs. However, since the overall economy has grown considerably, the

---

[1] https://www.bloomberg.com/news/articles/2019-04-10/ghana-is-the-star-in-imf-s-2019-economic-growth-forecast-chart.

[2] https://www.afdb.org/fileadmin/uploads/afdb/Documents/Publications/TheMiddleofthePyramid_TheMiddleofthePyramid.pdf.

[3] https://qz.com/africa/1486764/how-big-is-africas-middle-class/.

[4] https://www.brookings.edu/research/africas-consumer-market-potential/.

[5] https://www.afdb.org/en/knowledge/publications/african-economic-outlook/.

value addition percentage hides the fact that the real production of manufactured goods has gone up significantly too. Yet the concentration of such industrial bases in a few countries and sectors demonstrates that an overall structural transformation is still missing in action.

The quest for industrialization is not over in Africa. Domestic manufacturing in Africa doubled between 2000 and 2010 according to the African Development Bank and continues to increase thanks to investments in the retail clothing manufacturing sector by the likes of H&M, Primark, and Levi's; car manufacturing by the likes of Volkswagen, Mercedes, Renault, Peugeot, among others; Seemahale Telecoms in the mobile phone segment; and by the aviation and automobile parts sector in countries like Morocco and Tunisia. Local investors have also boosted the manufacturing sector on the continent notably in electronics (mobile phone, computers) by manufacturers such as Algeria's Condor Electronics and the Mara Group in Rwanda; the pharmaceuticals sector—a *sector valued at USD 65 billion*[6] by 2020 , therefore, matching India's pharmaceutical sector—with companies such as Algeria's Saidal, Biofarm, and Merinal Laboratories, among others, which produce 47% of locally purchased medical products, South Africa's Aspen and Adcock Ingram, Tunisia's laboratories which managed to increase local production from 14% in 1990 to 45% in 2010. And the list goes on to include companies elsewhere on the continent in countries including Angola, Cameroon, Egypt, Ethiopia, Ghana, Kenya, Lesotho, Mauritius, Morocco, Nigeria, Tanzania, and Uganda.

Agro-processing, delocalization of low value-added manufacturing in Southeast Asia due to labor costs rise there, as well as commodity-based industrialization hold the key for a more radical transformation.

For African countries endowed with natural resources, focusing energies on exploiting and transforming the wealth of the country can be far more promising than trying to diversify away from commodities. Despite criticism of this model of industrialization, largely due to the argument that it is unlikely to promote linkages, experiences from other resource-rich countries such as Argentina, Malaysia, Thailand, Australia, Norway, and Scotland show that such model can deliver economic growth. Examples from within Africa itself demonstrate that such a model can be promising in terms of developing elements of an ecosystem that promotes innovation, value addition as well as quality employment.

Agriculture represents also an important vehicle for resource-based industrialization. Agriculture accounts for almost 65% of Africa's employment and 75% of its domestic trade. In addition, the agri-food sector has already made some strides on the continent and has significant potential with estimates putting its value at USD *1 trillion by 2030.*[7] The sector can generate significant productivity gains in rural areas with vibrant hubs of agri-business and linkages across value chains.

---

[6] https://www.mckinsey.com/industries/pharmaceuticals-and-medical-products/our-insights/afr ica-a-continent-of-opportunity-for-pharma-and-patients.

[7] https://agra.org/agribusinesses-and-african-smallholders-seize-1-trillion-food-market-as-meals-replace-minerals-to-restart-african-economic-growth-new-report/.

To fully reach this potential, it will be important to improve land productivity. Africa's land productivity is stuck at 1.5 tons per hectare, while in countries like India, land productivity has grown from 0.95 tons/ha to 2.53 tons/ha over the past 50 years. This is despite the fact that agricultural land in Africa is three to six times higher than in countries like China and India, both of which have successfully managed to secure food for their "bottom billion" despite having much lower available agricultural land per capita, while Africa continues to be the world's most food-insecure region.

Small-scale farmers will be important players in this transformation. But they need support and innovation. Most African farmers have not benefited from initiatives and programs aimed at improving farming techniques, farm equipment, seeds, fertilizers, post-harvest technology, and agricultural financing. But some interventions, although still too timid and sparse, stand out as possible routes to enable the integration of small-scale farmers in the quest for higher productivity in African countries. For example, the interventions of the government of Ghana to introduce mechanized farming systems and make block farming a reality for small-scale farmers have successfully turned the country into an established food basket. Egypt's rice yield today stands at nine metric tons per hectare, making it the best rice output in the world. Water harvesting in Tanzania has been successfully scaled up in the lowlands, where seasonal rainfall can amount to as much as 600–900 mm, improving the Majaluba rain-fed rice farms. With the help of low-cost individual pump schemes, Nigerian farmers have turned to small-scale irrigation by using shallow groundwater recharged by rivers and lifting it with *shadouf* and *calabash* in the dry season to grow vegetables for city dwellers.

Transforming African economies through resource-based industrialization will not be easy. It will require innovation, skills, robust knowledge base of the industry structure and global value chains. It would also require African countries to be particularly attuned to the global trading landscape, including barriers and preferential policies. However, boosting intra-Africa trade remains imperative for creating the markets that are needed for successful industrialization.

The entry into force of the African Continental Free Trade Area (AfCFTA) in May 2019 is potentially an important game changer. From this year, Africa has the largest free trade area in the world by size—with its 1.2 billion person consumer market. The combined consumer and business spending is expected to hit USD *6.7 trillion within the next 10 years*.[8] The Economic Commission for Africa expects AfCFTA intra-African trade (currently standing at 20%) to expand by 52% by cutting tariffs on 90% of goods traded across the continent to zero.

Admittedly, the transition will not be without consequences—at least for some time. Experiences in countries that have undergone such transformations show that there is a strong historical pattern of worsening income distribution between rural and urban economies during the initial stages of structural transformation. As the urban population in Africa is projected to double in size to eventually reach 2.3 billion people over the next 40 years, it is likely that such a pattern would be further accentuated. However, we also know from historical data that absolute poverty does

---

[8] https://www.weforum.org/agenda/2018/03/capturing-africa-s-high-returns.

not necessarily worsen during such episodes, therefore, reducing the risk that the strides made in fighting extreme poverty in Africa over the last two decades are unlikely to be reversed.

## 2   Changing Perceptions

Transformation requires capital, which will need to be generated in international markets, through foreign direct investment. Yet, Africa remains marginal as a destination for foreign investors. Such reluctance is often justified by exaggerated risk perceptions, often dominated by security and governance concerns.

The turn of the century witnessed some progress in Africa in the area of political governance, peace, and security. Despite pockets of violence, there is consensus that the nature of politics in Africa is changing. The appetite of the continent's population for political participation has increased as demonstrated by the increase in political contestation on the continent from the events we have seen this year in Sudan and Algeria to the events of the Arab Spring, Burkina Faso, and many other countries on the continent. Youth, particularly those residing in urban areas operate in political spaces in *similar ways to their counterparts*[9] elsewhere in the world. In addition, conflicts have receded across the continent largely driven by improvements in political governance across the continent. Although recent years saw increases in violent incidents, incidents of violent death as a result of conflict remains significantly lower than what the continent witnessed in the early 1990s. Furthermore, the increase is largely attributed to global dynamics and especially the *rise and expansion of the Islamic State in the Sahel and West Africa.*[10]

Yet, despite the decline in the number of conflicts in Africa, the continent continues to be viewed as conflict-ridden. Unlike Asia, conflicts in Africa are not seen as isolated. The conflicts in Mindanao do not shape the image of the Philippines. The Sabah insurgency does not shape the image of emerging Malaysia. There were about 29 piracy attacks in 2009 off the coast of Somalia as compared to 150 attacks in the strait of Malacca, between Malaysia and Singapore, in 2005. The Naxalite insurgency and the issue of Kashmir do not shape investors' image of a rising India. And South Korea remains unaffected by its proximity to its belligerent sister state to the north. Indeed, despite the widespread nature of conflict in Asia, the region is branded as dynamic rather than unstable.

Perception shapes engagement (public and private) in different ways. Structural transformation requires a different type of engagement that taps into the potential of the continent rather than seeing it as a high-risk region or at best a charity basket case. Development aid, albeit still important in specific cases, cannot single-handedly

---

[9] https://afrobarometer.org/sites/default/files/publications/Working%20paper/AfropaperNo136. pdf.

[10] https://reliefweb.int/sites/reliefweb.int/files/resources/Conflict%20Trends%20in%20Africa% 2C%201946%E2%80%932017%2C%20Conflict%20Trends%20Report.pdf.

transform African economies at a time when the demography of the continent requires bold action. Africa's youth can be an asset, but that requires a different form of engagement. In West Africa for instance, the sub-regional grouping ECOWAS estimates that more than *2 million youth who enter the market every year do not have access to jobs.*[11] The African Development Bank estimates that *10 to 12 million youth enter the workforce*[12] each year, but that only 3.1 million are absorbed. Support to agriculture, which would play a key role in transforming African economies and integrate a large portion of the labor force, did not benefit from strategic investments. Numbers do not mean impact. For example, in 2002, Africa received almost double the amount of ODA for agriculture (USD 713.6 million) that was given to the countries of East and Southern Asia (USD 479.8 million). However, this did not translate into per-dollar greater returns largely because it was treated in isolation of the infrastructure and technological innovations that would stretch impact.

Tapping into the potential offered by Africa's growing population and consumer market means engaging through investments in key enabling sectors. Despite the perceived challenges, China, besides being Africa's main trading partner, has become Africa's main infrastructure financier and builder. Concerns about the indebtedness of African countries to China have been raised, but it is important to remember that, despite the recent surge in debt, the debt to GDP ratio in Africa has not dramatically increased and remains the lowest in the world after that of the rich Gulf States region, if reserves are taken into consideration, is sometimes negative.

The COVID-19 pandemic was yet another crucial moment in defining Africa's relationship with the world. Global economic governance was seriously disrupted and the African position suffered consequently. Debates about the socio-economic impact of the pandemic outpaced the preoccupations with the sanitary dimensions, given the fact that the continent registered lower levels of infections and lethality. The lessons learned from growing protectionism, disruption of supply chains, the drastic drop in demand, and paralysis in the informal sector all pointed to the need to accelerate Africa's industrialization and regional integration. Trade emerged as a key element for the continent to get its act together and better negotiate. Without a common position in major debates, Africa appears weakened in light of exogenous shocks as amply verified during the pandemic.

## 3  Benefiting Africa and Beyond

Reaching Africa's full potential requires the political courage to ask all international partners to look beyond. For example, African countries fought hard to obtain preferential rules of origin for the least developed countries at the nineteenth Ministerial Conference of the WTO in 2013. Yet, they have not called for the implementation of

---

[11] https://www.youtube.com/watch?v=D3ZmaGLNuaU&app=desktop.

[12] https://www.afdb.org/fileadmin/uploads/afdb/Images/high_5s/Job_youth_Africa_Job_youth_Africa.pdf.

those preferential criteria in their bilateral negotiations with the EU under Economic Partnership Agreements (EPAs) or requested the same under the African Growth and Opportunity Act (AGOA) with the United States.

It is time for engagement with international partners to shift from policies and frameworks driven by perception to those driven by reality and a common vision for the future. The youth boom in Africa, if managed properly, will not only drive African economies, those in the rest of the world, especially Europe. A recent study by the Bertelsmann Foundation, for instance, shows that intra-EU migration will no longer be able to satisfy the needs of *Germany's economy, requiring it to rely on 146,000 workers per year from non-EU countries.*[13] Yet, the migration of African youth is currently viewed largely as a threat rather than an opportunity, with the EU caving in to pressure from its right-wing politicians. The reality, however, shows that Africans are far from making up the majority of non-EU migrants entering Europe. The rate of Chinese migration to Europe is double that of Africans and the proportion of African nationals in Europe is similar to numbers in the 1970s. Those wishing to migrate also tend to be more *educated*.[14] Concerns about refugees are also unjustified as Africa continues to bear the brunt of wars with 80% of refugees remaining in Africa.

A future-focused engagement also requires international partners to move beyond classical development aid models. Limiting Europe's engagement with Africa to mechanisms of aid disbursements that have been in place since the 1970s does not bode well for the future. Where the EU sought to be innovative, it developed initiatives without consulting African countries, isolated from the plethora of initiatives and mechanisms in place in Africa as well as Europe. These fragmented approaches to dealing with Africa do not only risk inefficient use of the resources to the detriment of both Europe and Africa, but further jeopardizes the close relationship between the two continents by further undermining Africa's own efforts and agency in its development agenda.

# 4   The Role of China in the Promotion of African Agency

China's relationship with Africa is changing. From what was once a narrative built on the sale of primary commodities to fuel China's booming economic growth, it is increasingly being defined by an emerging, confident Africa with its own socio-economic and political priorities. Many African countries are now demanding tangible and credible benefits beyond rent seeking based on natural resource exports. In short, China's relationship with Africa has transformed into one defined by dynamism and African agency, lessening the hold the former previously had.

---

[13] https://www.dw.com/en/study-germany-needs-260000-immigrants-a-year-to-meet-labor-dem and/a-47470731.

[14] https://www.afrobarometer.org/blogs/african-migration-whos-thinking-going-where.

China's Africa Policy is best analyzed from its unique political and economic perspectives. Although China reaps considerable economic gains from Africa, it would be simplistic to regard those benefits as the sole driver of China's policy.

Media outlets and Western scholars often suggest that China's relationship with Africa is built on its dependency on natural and energy resources, as well as markets, and investment opportunities for its booming industries and job-seeking workers. Indeed, China has often been criticized for taking advantage of Africa's vulnerability. This perception, however, fails to take into account that China is no different from any global player: it defends its interests; it does it in its own terms; and cannot avoid tensions between those interests and values. It also shows a condescending attitude toward Africans, assuming that they need someone to help them coordinate relationships according to a moral compass defined by well-meaning outsiders.

China can no longer be expected to subordinate its commercial and strategic interests to others. Most African countries that have benefited from China's increasing trade, investment, and debt relief, are not endowed with mineral wealth, offering fewer investment opportunities for Chinese enterprises. They are interesting for China for other reasons.

Even though Africa remains a relatively marginal player when it comes to China's overall trade with the rest of the world, its trading relationship with China has important implications for both. Africa serves as a low-value consumer market for Chinese goods, particularly for loss-making state-owned enterprises, which have set up shops across the continent. Increased labor costs in China have created new opportunities for the delocalization of low-margin Pearl River manufacturing sectors to other parts of the world. Chinese entrepreneurs have knowledge of supply chains, contacts with major world retailers, possess the capital and investment appetite to deal with difficult environments, and can now replicate their processes in hubs in Africa at will.

Chinese investors are good politicians that adjust to the local context extremely quickly and are not perceived as expatriates demanding living standards far above local levels. They tend to be hard workers and instill the market with an entrepreneurial "can do" attitude. Perhaps their biggest difference is their perception of risk, which is very different from traditional western investors. These characteristics make China a good partner for the industrialization policies being pursued by African countries.

Ultimately, it is the responsibility of African leaders to devise a strategy for their relations with China; not for China to be responsible for a mutually beneficial relationship. It is important to retain a more nuanced view of the relationship, which is more of a two-way road. The interest and motivation of Africans to expand their presence in China is also real, but less reported.

**Carlos Lopes** is a Professor at Nelson Mandela School of Public Governance, University of Cape Town; Visiting Professor at Sciences Po, Paris, and Associate Fellow at Chatham House, London. He was a 2017 Fellow at Oxford Martin School, University of Oxford. Previously he Chaired the Lisbon University Institute Board and occupied prominent positions such as UN Assistant

Secretary-General and Political Director for Secretary-General Kofi Annan and Executive Secretary of the UN Economic Commission for Africa. He is currently the African Union High Representative for Partnerships with Europe and a member of the African Union Reform Team. Widely published, he has received many awards and honorary doctorates and has integrated 20 times the lists of most influential Africans of the main pan-Africa media.

**Open Access** This chapter is licensed under the terms of the Creative Commons Attribution-NonCommercial-NoDerivatives 4.0 International License (http://creativecommons.org/licenses/by-nc-nd/4.0/), which permits any noncommercial use, sharing, distribution and reproduction in any medium or format, as long as you give appropriate credit to the original author(s) and the source, provide a link to the Creative Commons license and indicate if you modified the licensed material. You do not have permission under this license to share adapted material derived from this chapter or parts of it.

The images or other third party material in this chapter are included in the chapter's Creative Commons license, unless indicated otherwise in a credit line to the material. If material is not included in the chapter's Creative Commons license and your intended use is not permitted by statutory regulation or exceeds the permitted use, you will need to obtain permission directly from the copyright holder.

# Lessons from History for the Next Steps in Global Governance and Trends

# It's Just Hierarchy Between States—On the Need for Reciprocity

Daniel A. Bell and Pei Wang

**Abstract** As the *longest continuously active civilization in the world*, China *has a rich legacy in the written world* with *libraries and writings that go back three millennia*. These libraries offer scholars vast archives to analyze the past. For example, in *classical China*, political thinkers developed rich and diverse theories on international politics that took the *hierarchy between states* for granted. We believe that these ancient theories can be mined for contemporary insights, such as the ideal of reciprocity between hierarchical political communities that formed the *tributary system in imperial China*. Under this system, China guaranteed security and provided economic benefits to tributary states, but regardless of its advantages in the past, this system would be problematic in the modern world. The most obvious reason is that the tributary system, by definition gives, the vassal states a secondary status and is incompatible with the ideal of the equality of sovereign states. However, while there may be a case for paying lip service to equal sovereignty, in reality, states are neither sovereign nor equal. The most viable path toward global peace involves a *bipolar world with the United States and China* leading two regional state hierarchies that benefit the weaker states.

**Keywords** Longest continuously active civilization in the world · A rich legacy in the written world · Libraries and writings that go back three millennia · Classical China · Hierarchy between states · Tributary system in imperial China

---

D. A. Bell (✉)
Shandong University, Jinan, China

P. Wang
Fudan University, Shanghai, China

© The Author(s) 2021
H. Wang and A. Michie (eds.), *Consensus or Conflict?*, China and Globalization,
https://doi.org/10.1007/978-981-16-5391-9_30

# 1 Weak and Strong Reciprocity

There are two kinds of reciprocity.[1] One kind—let's call it "weak reciprocity"—is the idea that hierarchical relations between states should be mutually advantageous. Each state thinks from the perspective of its own position (more precisely, the rulers think of the interests of their own people), and they strike deals or make alliances that are beneficial to (the people of) both states. But weak reciprocity is fragile. Once the situation changes and the deal is no longer advantageous to one of the states, one or both can simply opt-out of the deal. For example, as the Trump administration decided to renegotiate or scrap free-trade accords.

Another kind of reciprocity—let's call it "strong reciprocity"—is the idea that both states come to think of their alliances from the perspective of both states, no longer simply from the perspective of their own state. The rulers no longer think simply in terms of benefiting their own people, and they are willing to stick with deals or alliances even if (temporarily) the deals may more beneficial to the people of other states.

We are supposed to live in an age of equal sovereign states. The Peace of Westphalia treaty in 1648 set in stone the ideal of equality between sovereign states who are supposed to respect each other's sovereignty and refrain from interfering in each other's domestic affairs.

This idea originated in Europe and slowly spread to the rest of the world. In 1945, the United Nations elevated the one person one vote principle to the level of states, with each state given equal representation regardless of size and wealth. Much theorizing in (Western) international relations is based on this ideal of formal and juridical equality between sovereign states.

In reality, however, states are neither equal nor sovereign. It takes only a moment's reflection to realize that the global order consists of a hierarchy between different states, with some states having more de facto power than others. Nobody really cares about the fact Nicaragua didn't sign for to the Paris climate change accord, but President Trump's decision to withdraw from this accord may be a global disaster because of the US disproportionate power to set the global agenda.

Even the United Nations expresses the fact of global hierarchy: The most important decisions are often taken at the level of Security Council, which distinguishes between permanent members, nonpermanent members of the Security Council, and ordinary member states. That's why rising powers such as India and Brazil fight hard (thus far unsuccessfully) for recognition as permanent members of the Security Council.

If theorists of international relations aim to develop theories that explain the behavior of states and (more ambitiously) predict outcomes in the international system, then theorizing should be more attentive to the reality of hierarchy between states.

---

[1] Abridged and adapted from *JUST HIERARCHY: Why Social Hierarchies Matter in China and the Rest of the World* by Daniel A. Bell and Wang Pei. Copyright ©2020 by Princeton University Press. Reprinted by permission.

In both classical India and classical China, political thinkers developed rich and diverse theories of international politics that took the hierarchy between states for granted.[2] We can mine these ancient theories for contemporary insights.

## 2 Hierarchical Ideals of Global Order in Ancient China

Ancient Chinese thinkers took for granted the idea of hierarchy in social life. Xunzi (ca. 310–219 BCE) most explicitly extolled the virtues of hierarchy. He is widely regarded as one of the three founding fathers of Confucianism (along with Confucius and Mencius).

Xunzi is particularly critical of economic diplomacy between states on the grounds that it can, at most, generate a weak sense of reciprocity that breaks down once the states' interests are no longer aligned:

> If you serve them with wealth and treasure, then wealth and treasure will run out and your relations with them will still not be normalized. If agreements are sealed and alliances confirmed by oath, then though the agreements be fixed yet they will not last a day. If you relinquish borderland to bribe them, then after it is relinquished, they will be avaricious for yet more. The more you pander to them, the more they will advance on you until you have used up your resources and the state has given over and then there is nothing left.[3]

If a rich country aims to gain friends just by throwing money at them, those friends will be fickle indeed. That said, Xunzi does not deny that "weak reciprocity" grounded in mutually beneficial self-interest between hierarchical powers can be relatively stable and long-lasting.

In an anarchic world of self-interested states, what Xunzi calls the "hegemonic state" (霸), can attain interstate leadership by being strategically reliable:

> Although virtue may not be up to the mark, nor were norms fully realized, yet when the principle of all under heaven is somewhat gathered together, punishments and rewards are already trusted by all under heaven, all below the ministers know what they can expect. Once administrative commands are made plain, even if one sees one's chances for gain defeated, yet there is no cheating the people; contracts are already sealed, even if one sees one's chance for gain defeated, yet there is no cheating one's partners. If it is so, then the troops will be strong ….and enemy states will tremble in fear. Once it is clear the state stands united, your allies will trust you This is to attain hegemony by establishing strategic reliability.[4]

But strategic reliability must also have a basis in hard power for the hegemon to gain the trust of its allies. A very poor or weak country cannot be trusted to keep its

[2] This essay is an abridged version of Chap. 3 from, "Just Hierarchy: Why Social Hierarchies Matter in China and the Rest of the World" written by Daniel Bell and Wang Pei and published by Princeton Press in 2020. In this essay, the focus is on the theories of Chinese political thinkers. An analysis of classical Indian political thinkers is available in Chap. 3 of the above book.

[3] Xunzi, 10, "Enriching the State" (quoted in Yan, Ancient Chinese Thought, Modern Chinese Power, 81).

[4] Xunzi, 11, "Humane Authority and Hegemony" (quoted in Yan, Ancient Chinese Thought, Modern Chinese Power, 88–89).

promises. So with a combination of wealth, military might, and strategic reliability, a self-interested but honest hegemon can establish mutually beneficial interest-based relations with weaker states. If China's "Belt and Road Initiative" provides material benefits both to China and to weaker countries in Central Asia, and China sticks to its contracts even in economically difficult times and shows that it's a trustworthy partner, the initiative can be successful in the short to medium term. Let's call this "weak reciprocity plus"—grounded in nothing more than the self-interest of states.

The most stable (and desirable) kind of international leadership, however, is what Xunzi calls "humane authority" (王), referring to a state that wins the hearts of the people at home and abroad.

At home, Xunzi stresses the need for the proper use of "rituals," combined with effective policies that secure peace and prosperity, as the key to leadership success. He states, "One who cultivates ritual becomes the humane authority; one who effectively exercises government becomes strong."[5] Setting a good example at home is necessary, but not sufficient. Humane authority can gain the hearts of those abroad by institutionalizing interstate rituals:

> If you want to deal with the norms between small and large, strong and weak states to uphold them prudently, then rituals and customs must be especially diplomatic, the jade disks should be especially bright, and the diplomatic gifts particularly rich, the spokespersons should be gentlemen who write elegantly and speak wisely. If they keep the people's interests at heart, who will be angry with them? If they are so, then the furious will not attack. One who seeks his reputation is not so. One who seeks profit is not so. One who acts out of anger is not so. The state will be at peace, as if built on a rock and it will last long like the stars.[6]

Moreover, the content of the rituals depends on the hierarchy of states: "The norms of humane authority are to observe the circumstances so as to produce the tools to work thereon, to weigh the distance and determine the tribute due." The ideal of reciprocity between hierarchical political communities informed the tributary system in imperial China, with the Middle Kingdom at the center and "peripheral" states on the outside. In this system, the tributary ruler or his representative had to go to China to pay homage in ritual acknowledgment of his vassal status. In return, China guaranteed security and provided economic benefits.[7]

In Ming China, the surrounding political communities were divided into five zones corresponding to the "Five Services" system of Western Zhou, and the frequency of ritual interaction (roughly) correlated with the degree of closeness to the center (capital) of China, which was also served to map cultural achievement.

---

[5] Xunzi, "On the Regulations of a Humane Authority" (9.5). Here we mark an area of disagreement with Yan Xuetong, who criticizes Xunzi's notion of humane authority on the grounds that he neglects to mention that it also needs a foundation in hard power. Xunzi does have an extensive discussion of domestic policies that the humane authority should try to implement, including the need for a complex bureaucracy (see especially books 9 and 13) designed to benefit the people and strengthen the state.

[6] Xunzi, "Enriching the State.".

[7] Fairbank and Teng (1941).

What's interesting for our purposes is that the system allowed for both weak and strong reciprocity. The security guarantees to the surrounding states allowed for peaceful relations that benefited both China and its vassal states.

Students of Korean and Vietnamese history will know that there were repeated incursions/invasions by China, but the big picture was relatively peaceful (again, in comparison to similar periods in European history). According to David Kang, there was only one war involving Korea, Japan and China in the five centuries the tributary system was employed during the Ming and Qing Dynasties.[8]

What's even more interesting is that borders were respected even without the notion of respect for the sovereignty of equal states: The borders between Korea, Japan, Vietnam and China were relatively fixed and did not change significantly during those five centuries.

The comparison with European imperialism is even more striking in terms of the dynamic of economic relations. Whereas European imperialism was motivated partly, if not mainly, by the quest for profit, the tribute-trade system was a net loss for China and generally benefited the tribute state.[9]

The imbalance between tribute received and gifts bestowed helped maintain the hierarchical East Asian political order centered on China because it made Chinese vassals understandably eager to have their inferior status recognized, thus entitling them to send tribute.[10]

Salvatore Babones comments that "the emperor could even punish vassals by refusing to receive tribute from them—a 'punishment' that makes sense only in terms of the disproportionate benefits accruing to the tribute-giver."[11] Clearly, these hierarchical relations satisfy the conditions for weak reciprocity, since they were mutually beneficial, and in some ways even more beneficial to the weaker surrounding states.

The central power offers material benefits and security guarantees to weaker surrounding states, and the weaker states pay symbolic tribute to the leadership of the central power, with the frequency of ritualistic interaction depending on geographical distance from the central power. Such an arrangement can be mutually beneficial, and rituals can help generate a sense of community between the strong and the weak states: What we have termed strong reciprocity.

So, should China try to re-establish the tributary system with surrounding countries today? Yan Xuetong answers firmly in the negative: "any effort to restore the tribute system will weaken China's capability for international political mobilization."[12] But why not try?

---

[8] Kang (2010).

[9] Ibid., 63, 114. See also Ge, What Is China? 138.

[10] Wang Gungwu, "Ming Foreign Relations: Southeast Asia," in D. Twitchett and F.W. Mote (eds.), The Cambridge History of China, Vol. 8: The Ming Dynasty, part 2: 1368–1644 (Cambridge: Cambridge University Press, 301–332), (quote on p. 320).

[11] Babones, American *Tianxia*, 23.

[12] Yan, Ancient Chinese Tought, Modern Chinese Power, 104.

## 3   One World, Two Hierarchical Systems?

Whatever its advantages in the past, the tributary system is problematic for the modern world, even as an ideal. The most obvious reason is that the tributary system, which symbolically enshrines the secondary status and moral inferiority of the vassal states, is incompatible with the idea of the equality of sovereign states.

In reality, as mentioned, states are neither sovereign nor equal, but there may be a case for paying lip service to the ideal of equal sovereignty even knowing it's far removed from reality (and knowing it cannot become anywhere close to reality in the foreseeable future).

The argument for hypocrisy has a long history in political theory.[13] For example, Plato (in *The Republic*) famously defended the idea of a "noble lie" to persuade those at the bottom of the political hierarchy to endorse an ideal republic run by philosopher kings and queens.

Notwithstanding a history of informal bullying by powerful countries, it has served to constrain legal takeover of territory in the post-World War II era (we prefer this formulation). China itself has become distinctly obsessed with sovereignty in the form of noninterference in the internal affairs of countries precisely because it seeks to avoid a repeat of seeing its territory carved up by foreign powers.

That said, there are limits to the idea of paying lip service to sovereignty. Most obviously, rulers lose the moral right to govern if they engage in massive abuses of the basic human rights of their own people. Earlier Confucian thinkers such as Mencius defended the view that what we'd call today "humanitarian intervention" can be justified if the aim is to liberate people who are being oppressed by tyrants,[14] and the Chinese government has recently signed up to the international accord that enshrines the "responsibility to protect" people from genocide and systematic violations of basic human rights.[15]

Second, the ideal of equality of sovereign states should not be used by powerful countries as an excuse to shirk their extra share of responsibility for dealing with global challenges. If we agree that justice requires political leaders to take into account the interests of all those affected by their policies, then political leaders in large powerful countries have a responsibility to consider how their policies affect not only just the current generation of people in the home country but also the effect on future generations, people in other countries, and the natural world.

If large countries launch major wars or make "mistakes" on such issues as climate change and artificial intelligence, it can literally be the end of the world. As one author recently put it, China "shakes the world";[16] in contrast, nobody would write a book titled "Canada Shakes the World." So it would be frankly immoral if leaders of large countries proclaim that they look out only for the interests of their own people;

---

[13] For an argument that "untruths" can be useful despite knowing they are false, see Anthony Appiah, As If: Idealization and Ideals (Cambridge, MA: Harvard University Press, 2017).

[14] See Bell, Beyond Liberal Democracy, ch. 2.

[15] Fung (2016).

[16] Kynge (2017).

even US President Trump claims that he defends the principle of "America First" rather than "America Alone."[17] In short, it's fine to pay (hypocritical) lip service to the ideal of sovereign equal states, but large states should not use that as an excuse to shirk what ought to be an extra share of global responsibilities.

There's another fatal flaw with the proposal to re-establish the tributary system in the modern world. Today, powerful countries are not necessarily the most civilized (or advanced) from a moral point of view. The tributary system was founded on the assumption that China was the center of culture and morality, and that China could and should promote its superior civilization among other nations. The closer the country (or "zone") to Beijing (the capital during the Ming and Qing Dynasties), the more civilized the territory, and conversely, the further away from Beijing, the more wild the barbarians. Nobody seriously holds this view today. However, that's not to deny the value of proximity to powerful countries. In short, the challenge is to reconstitute a de facto form of hierarchy between strong states and neighboring (weaker) states, which provides the conditions for weak and (ideally) strong reciprocity while still paying lip service to the ideal of equal sovereignty of states.

So how could China regain the trust of its neighbors? Obviously, a bellicose approach to solving regional disputes cannot be effective in the long term. At the end of the day, China must set a good model at home. As Yan Xuetong puts it, "For China to become a superpower modeled on humane authority, it must first become a model from which other states are willing to learn."[18]

As a regional leader, China would also try to provide neighboring states with mutual benefits that underpin weak reciprocity. At the very least, this would mean ensuring peace. Whatever we think of China's foreign policy, the fact that it has not launched any wars since 1979 should be a source of comfort. But China should aim for more. Ideally, it should provide the conditions for strong reciprocity by relying on Xunzi-style common rituals that generate a sense of community.

Unlike the tributary system, which implied China teaching its supposed cultural and moral inferiors, the learning curve would work both ways, with "peripheral" states learning from Chinese culture and China learning from neighboring states. The deepest ties between states in a hierarchical system are underpinned by the strongest possible form of reciprocity.

From a realpolitik point of view, the US military hegemony in East Asia is perhaps the main obstacle to the development of an East Asian *"tianxia"* hierarchy led by China.[19] But things could change.

North Korea is currently the major military threat in the East Asian region, but it is possible that the divided Korean peninsula will unify over the next few decades one form or another. At that point, the case for US troops in East Asia would be weakened and a unified Korea would fall under the "natural" influence of China

---

[17] See President Trump's speech at Davos on January 26, 2018, https://www.weforum.org/age nda/2018/01/president-donald-trumps-davos-address-in-full-8e14ebc1-79bb-4134-8203-95efca 182e94.

[18] Yan, Ancient Chinese Thought, Modern Chinese Power, 99.

[19] Xuetong (2019).

due to its proximity and superior power in East Asia.[20] China need not (and should not) send troops to Korea to replace the Americans, but it could provide security guarantees to Korea, such as protection against invasion by neighboring countries. This kind of scenario may not appeal to Koreans in favor of full sovereignty, but sometimes less powerful countries need to make the best of less-than-ideal solutions.

Canada, for example, was invaded twice by its more powerful southern neighbor (in 1775 and 1812, before Canada became an independent country) and still today many Canadians take pride in being different from Americans. But Canadians know they are a small country (in terms of population and global influence), and the government usually refrains from doing things that antagonize the bigger and more powerful southern neighbor. Canada occasionally objects to US foreign policy as in the objection by the Canadian parliament to the 2003 invasion of Iraq, but Canadians would never dream today of, say, inviting the British (or the Chinese) to build military bases in Canada as a buffer against the United States. Such arrangements also benefit the weaker party: Good ties with the Americans are good for Canadians because they don't have to spend that much on their military and the Canadian government can devote more resources to improving the welfare of the Canadian people. So, yes, Canadians are not the equals of Americans on the international stage, but what's the problem if a bit of inequality under the umbrella of an American-led regional "*tianxia*" arrangement benefits the Canadian people?[21]

Still, it could be argued that American military bases in East Asia are really meant to check China's rise. China may well become the biggest economic power in the world over the next few decades, resulting in a greater desire for status and global influence; perhaps the United States has no intention of reducing its military influence in the East Asian region. This kind of situation could lead to a disastrous war between these two major powers.

Jonathan Renshon demonstrates empirically that states attributed less status than they are due based on material capabilities are overwhelmingly more likely (than "satisfied" states) to initiate militarized disputes.[22] The policy implication should be obvious: "conflict may be avoided through status concessions before the escalation to violent conflict occurs."[23] In making this statement, Renshon is referring to Russia, but the exact same point applies in the case of China. If the United States genuinely

---

[20] For an argument that China and Korea should re-establish a Ming-like system underpinned by the principle that "Ritual lies in the deference of the small to the big and the caring of the big for the small." (春秋左氏传) But without adherence to the formal tributary system, see Orun Kihyup Kim, "Korea's Experiences with Big Neighbors," paper presented at the Berggruen Institute workshop "What Is *Tianxia*?" Peking University, Beijing, China, June 16–17, 2018.

[21] Salvatore Babones puts forward the idea of an "American *tianxia*" appropriate for the modern world, with Canada and other Anglo-Saxon allies in the zone of "internal barbarians." See Salvatore Babones, American *Tianxia*: Chinese Money, American Power, and the End of History (Bristol: Policy Press, 2017), 22. This proposal may work as a defense of an American-led *tianxia* hierarchical system in North America and Europe, but it is a complete nonstarter if China and other "wild" barbarians are meant to endorse such an order.

[22] Renshon, Fighting for Status, ch. 5.

[23] Ibid., 270.

wants to avoid war in East Asia, it should try to accommodate and make concessions to China's desire to establish a regional hierarchy with itself at the head of the table. In the 1970s, the United States courageously cut its official diplomatic ties with Taiwan in order to recognize the preeminent role of China in East Asia, but it should also be prepared to make similar concessions in the future.

In short, the most viable path towards global peace in the region involves a bipolar world with the United States and China leading two regional state hierarchies that benefit the weaker states in those hierarchical relationships. Under this model, both China and the United States would recognize each other's leadership in their respective regions and work together to solve common global problems such as climate change.

But why should other major regional powers such as the EU and Russia accept such an arrangement? The most important reason is that too many global leaders would make it more difficult to coordinate peaceful relations and work on joint global projects. It's fine if Russia and the EU are recognized as less-than-major powers with more say in their own neighborhoods, but they can't be equals with China and the United States on the world stage. There must be a hierarchy of regional hierarchical systems.

# 4   India: Challenge or Opportunity?

Perhaps the biggest challenge will be India. India's growth rate recently overtook China, and it may well achieve rough parity with China in terms of population and global clout over the next few decades.[24] So how can the two countries work together?

The situation may not look promising now as the two countries were on the brink of another border war in 2017 and China's closest partner in South Asia is Pakistan. Also Pakistan and India have always had deep tensions in their relationship. Again, we need to invoke insights that two countries with contiguous borders often regard each other as natural enemies. China went to war in 1962, and they have yet to resolve their territorial conflicts (in contrast, China has peacefully resolved territorial conflicts with eleven other neighboring countries).

But on the bright side, the two countries were both members of the nonaligned movement during the Cold War, and today China is India's biggest trading partner, thus underpinning mutually beneficial relations of weak reciprocity. Furthermore, ties between India and China have been improving since early 2018—China's President, Xi Jinping, suggested that "shared Asian values" should trump the geopolitical differences between the two countries—and India has emerged as the biggest beneficiary of the Chinese-led Asian Infrastructure Investment Bank.[25]

---

[24] See Rachman (2017).

[25] Amy Kazmin and Ben Bland, "China and India Use Summit to Push for Improved Ties," Financial Times, April 28, 2018; Kiran Stacey, Simon Mundy, and Emily Feng, "India Benefits from AIIB Loans despite China Tensions," Financial Times, May 18, 2018. More generally, China has been

History also points the way to a stronger form of reciprocity that underpins lasting peace.[26] Buddhism spread peacefully from India to China and reached a point where it became far more influential in China than in India. In the 1920s, the poet Tagore was deeply impressed with Chinese intellectual culture when he visited China.[27] The great Chinese intellectual Liang Shuming regarded Indian spiritual culture as the apex of human moral growth.[28] The learning was mutual: India benefited from China's paper, gunpowder, and silk. Perhaps China's greatest gift to India, according to Amitav Acharya, was the preservation of Buddhist texts. Chinese and Indian translators lived and worked in China and translated and preserved Buddhist texts. After Buddhism disappeared in India and original Indian texts were lost or destroyed by invaders, Chinese translations preserved Buddhist sutras that could then be re-translated into Sanskrit.[29] Buddhism would have been lost to Indians without China, just as Arabs preserved Greek texts on science and philosophy that would otherwise have been lost.

Of course, there are differences between China and India, such as the way they select political leaders, which needs to be respected. But such differences pale in comparison to what ought to be deep mutual respect between two countries, which have thousands of years of history and glorious and diverse civilizations.

The fact that India and China achieved such a high level of reciprocity in the past, begs the question of whether this could be re-established in the future? Once again, we can turn to the insights of ancient thinkers.

If the leaders of these two great Asian powers follow respectful and restrained speech and implement Xunzi's ideas for rituals that generate a sense of community, their diplomatic, cultural, and people-to-people interactions might well (re)generate a strong sense of reciprocity.

It is not impossible to imagine a future world with an Asian hierarchical system jointly led and managed by India and China, to the benefit of both countries as well as smaller neighboring and perhaps even the whole world.[30]

---

seeking better ties with its neighbors (at least partly) because the United States has been more aggressively working to counter China's rise.

[26] The point here is not that strong reciprocity should replace weak reciprocity: Strong reciprocity that is not founded on common economic interests may not be very stable (put negatively, if strong reciprocity imposes (or coexists with) severe financial constraints on one country in relation between otherwise friendly states, it may not be long lasting; we thank Zhang Feng for this point). In other words, the most stable form of reciprocity between states would be founded on both forms of reciprocity.

[27] http://english.cri.cn/12954/2016/05/05/2743s926586.htm Tagore also visited the Forbidden City for a meeting with the "last" emperor. See Reginald Fleming Johnston, Twilight in the Forbidden City (Vancouver: Soul Care Publishing, 2008), 335 [orig. pub. 1934]. We will know that India-China relations are on track for ties of strong reciprocity when leading poets and writers from India are invited to meet members of the Standing Committee of the Politburo.

[28] Shuming (2009).

[29] Email sent to Daniel on February 24, 2017.

[30] We do not mean to imply that the ideal of an Asian regional order led by the two most populous countries in Asia is the only politically realistic and morally desirable scenario for Asia's future.

# References

Fairbank JK, Teng S-Y (1941) On the Ch'ing tributary system. Harv J Asiatic Stud 6:138–139
Fung CJ (2016) China and the responsibility to protect: from opposition to advocacy. United States Institute of Peace. https://www.usip.org/publications/2016/06/china-and-responsibility-protectopposition-advocacy
Kang DC (2010) East Asia before the West: five centuries of trade and tribute. New York: Columbia University Press, p 105
Kynge J (2017) China shakes the world: a Titan's rise and troubled future—and the challenge for America, Mariner Books, New York
Rachman G (2017) Easternization: Asia's Rise and America's decline from Obama to Trump and beyond. Other Press
Shuming L (2009) 东西文化及其哲学 (Eastern and Western cultures and their philosophies). The Commercial Press, Beijing [orig. pub. 1921]
Xuetong Y (2019) Leadership and the rise of great powers. Princeton University Press, Princeton, NJ, pp 198–199

**Daniel A. Bell** is Dean of the School of Political Science and Public Administration at Shandong University and professor at Tsinghua University (Schwarzman College and Department of Philosophy). He was educated at McGill and Oxford universities, and has held research fellowships at Princeton University. He is the author of numerous books including *The China Model: Political Meritocracy and the Limits of Democracy* (2015). He writes widely on Chinese politics and philosophy for the media including the New York Times, Financial Times, Global Times and the Guardian. His articles and books have been translated into Chinese and twenty-two other languages.

**Pei Wang** is assistant professor at the China Institute at Fudan University in Shanghai.

**Open Access**  This chapter is licensed under the terms of the Creative Commons Attribution-NonCommercial-NoDerivatives 4.0 International License (http://creativecommons.org/licenses/by-nc-nd/4.0/), which permits any noncommercial use, sharing, distribution and reproduction in any medium or format, as long as you give appropriate credit to the original author(s) and the source, provide a link to the Creative Commons license and indicate if you modified the licensed material. You do not have permission under this license to share adapted material derived from this chapter or parts of it.

The images or other third party material in this chapter are included in the chapter's Creative Commons license, unless indicated otherwise in a credit line to the material. If material is not included in the chapter's Creative Commons license and your intended use is not permitted by statutory regulation or exceeds the permitted use, you will need to obtain permission directly from the copyright holder.

---

One can imagine other scenarios, e.g., a security pact between China and Russia or joint patrols of Pacific sea lanes by the United States and China, which also benefit surrounding smaller countries.

# A Return to Multilateralism—China's Reform and Opening Up in a Historical Setting

Ronnie C. Chan

**Abstract** The patterns of history provide important insights into current global political and economic trends. The ebb and flow of history illustrate that pivotal points create profound change. In the twentieth century, the obvious turning points were the two world wars. The emergence of China as an economic powerhouse, thanks to her 'reform and opening-up' policy, should be considered as the other significant event in the last century that is having a lasting impact in this century. Coupled with the United States' retreat to isolationism, the world is likely to return to a more multilateral world order.

**Keywords** Patterns of history · Ebb and flow of history · Pivotal points create profound change · The 'Reform and Opening up' of China · U.S. isolationism · China does not seek hegemony

## 1 Let's Learn from History

Before we look to the future[1], we should always review history. As Winston Churchill once said, "those who fail to learn from history are condemned to repeat it."[2] In this spirit, let's look at the two significant events that shaped the twentieth century. The first that comes to mind would be the two world wars, which had two profound effects: the invention of weapons capable of wiping out the entire human race, and a new world order ushered in after 1945 and was dominated by the United States. The other significant event of the twentieth century would be China's emergence as an economic powerhouse, thanks to her 'reform and opening-up' policy. It would

---

R. C. Chan (✉)
Asia Society Hong Kong Center, Hong Kong, China

[1] This article was written by the editing team of CCG based on the speech delivered by Ronnie C. Chan at the 2018 CCG Annual Conference in Beijing on May 20, 2018.

[2] The original quote came from George Santayana (1863–1952) the Spanish-born philosopher and critic: The Life of Reason (1905) vol. 1, ch. 12 which reads: "Those who cannot remember the past are condemned to repeat it!" In a 1948 speech to the House of Commons, Winston Churchill changed the quote slightly when he said (paraphrased), "those who fail to learn from history are condemned to repeat it."

© The Author(s) 2021

H. Wang and A. Michie (eds.), *Consensus or Conflict?*, China and Globalization,
https://doi.org/10.1007/978-981-16-5391-9_31

be worthwhile to look further into the past to see how China's current trajectory of 'reform and opening-up' fits in the ebb and flow of history.

Let us examine the past few centuries and choose two major events from each century that shaped the course of history. Starting with the fourteenth century, we saw the Black Death and the Renaissance. Then came the Conquest of Istanbul by the Ottoman Empire in the fifteenth century, thereby controlling the most critical location to control the trade routes between Europe and Asia. The outcome of that assault ultimately sparked Western Europe to send Christopher Columbus and other explorers to search for alternate sea routes to Asia, and this eventually led to the other major event of that century—the discovery of the Americas in 1492. Moving to the next century, the Reformation would be regarded as one of the two major events of the sixteenth century. This upheaval also served as a catalyst for the rise of the British Empire and her victory over the Spanish Armada in 1588. In the middle of the seventeenth century, the signing of the Treaty of Westphalia in 1648 marked the beginning of the notion of the 'nation state', and this was followed by the shameful chapter of colonialism. By the 18th century, colonialism gave way to the birth of the United States and the dawn of the Industrial Revolution. The nineteen century saw the dominance of imperialism and the United States surpassing the United Kingdom as the largest economy in the world by the 1890s. In the twentieth century, as mentioned above, there were the two world wars and the rise of China. The latter is especially important because, coupled with the United States' retreat to isolationism, the rise of China might signal a possible return to a more multilateral world order.

## 2   From Multilateral to Unilateral and Back Again

If we look at history from another perspective, we can say that some 1,400 years prior to 1945 was a period of chaotic multilateralism, while from 1945 onward, the world transitioned to a bilateral system dominated by the United States and the Soviet Union (U.S.S.R.). This period only lasted around 45 years until 1991 with the dissolution of the U.S.S.R., phasing into an essentially unilateral world dominated solely by the United States and lasting through to the present day. The increasing brevity of these periods seems to indicate that the ebb and flow in history are oscillating faster and lasting shorter. Can the current period of unilateralism sustain? Clearly, the answer is not, because of two reasons: the re-emergence of China and the retreat of the United States to isolationism.

The main reason for the United States' penchant toward isolationism is simple—fundamentally, it has always been an isolationist. The root of that characteristic is a principle upon which the young country was founded. Many events in American history pointed to this fact, for example, the Monroe Doctrine and Manifest Destiny of the nineteenth century, the Roosevelt Corollary of not joining the League of Nations, and the trade barriers of the 1920s. It was really only after World War II when the United States finally, and reluctantly, took center stage in global affairs. But even then, she was often delinquent in her United Nations dues, and has withdrawn from multilateral organizations.

History has shown that China is no stranger to isolationism. After World War II, with the United States being forced to step onto the global center stage and given the real and perceived threats of the then U.S.S.R., much of the world embarked on a long process of globalization. Only the Communist bloc was left out, while tremendous wealth was created by and for the so-called free world. Hong Kong benefited immensely, while mainland China chose isolationism.

China should have known better, but ideology got in the way. When this ancient country began to close herself off from the rest of the world in the early fifteenth century, during the Ming Dynasty, she began to wane. Attempts to open up failed, like the reforms in the early twentieth century. Subsequent civil wars and the Japanese invasion in 1931 spelled her doom. Chairman Mao's efforts to engage the United States in the late 1940s were rebuffed and the Korean War in the early 1950s sealed the country's fate to isolationism.

Leaders in Beijing knew that they were missing out, and it was not until U.S. President Richard Nixon, with the help of his then National Security Advisor Dr. Henry Kissinger, that China was given an opportunity in the early 1970s to re-engage with the Western world. To be sure, the United States had her own need for rapprochement—to contain the then U.S.S.R. Whatever the case, Beijing gladly took up the offer. This laid the foundation for the country to open her doors in 1978, which led to her prosperity of the past 40 years.

Meanwhile, the world was caught by surprise in the early 1990s when the U.S.S.R. collapsed. It gave a boost to globalization, as technologies formerly used for military purposes could now be commercialized. Modernization went to newer heights never seen before. Just consider how the smartphone alone has changed the world. The United States was free to mold the world in her own image and became her self-anointed benevolent hegemon. This enabled the United States to lead her allies and friends to form the institutions and mechanisms that shaped the current world order.

Today, the retreat of the United States to isolationism does not spell the end of the world but merely a phase in the course of history. It is in this context that we should objectively revisit history to better understand current affairs. After all, China has absolutely no intention of becoming a new global hegemon nor even be part of a "G2" with the United States. The best scenario for China would be to foster cooperation under the G20 framework, but this is not just up to China. While the United States retreats to isolationism, the world is likely to return to multilateralism.

## 3   What does China's Rise Mean to the World?

In hindsight, there were a few cultural and historic factors that played a role in China's rise, without which the miracle we see today could not have happened. This is why her emulation elsewhere in the world is doubtful. They may not have sufficient amounts of the right mix of factors. First, Confucian ethics was critical—hard work, family cohesion, and an emphasis on education. The resulting high savings rates and the willingness for delayed gratification were also absolutely necessary. The unimaginable suffering, both physical and psychological, endured during the decade-long Cultural Revolution instilled in the average citizen a powerful desire for stability, if not prosperity.

Having said that, in my opinion, the most significant impact of China's rise is it paved the way to a new world order of co-existence and co-prosperity between the East and the West. The last time this happened was around 2,000 years ago when the Roman Empire dominated Europe, while the prosperous Han Dynasty of China flourished in Asia. Of course, science and technology back then were not as advanced as they are today, hence no extensive contact between the two peoples, but it was an era in history where two major powers had co-existed and co-prospered. Thereafter, Europe had its share of rise and decline: the fall of the Roman Empire in fifth century, Renaissance in the fourteenth century, Industrial Revolution in the nineteenth century, to name just a few. In contrast, China was basically on the wane for centuries, most notably in the past 200 years.

In the current era of burgeoning co-prosperity of the West and the East, it is useful to examine the shift of economic power from the West to the East. After World War II, the first to rise was Japan, followed by the Four Asian Tigers. However, it was not until China's rise, mainly due to her 'reform and opening-up' in the past 40 years, that the world's economic center of gravity shifted from the Atlantic to the Pacific. This is why today's Belt and Road Initiative seems so intuitive—the Silk Roads, by land and sea, actually existed 2,000 years ago, so a restoration of these trade routes is not too much of a stretch of the imagination. It is simply a revival of trade and cultural interactions that existed two millennia ago. In this sense, even if China's President Xi Jinping had not proposed the Belt and Road Initiative, the same concept would have been brought forward by other nations sooner or later.

# 4 Three Major Sources of Conflict

This seismic shift in power will naturally result in some friction and possibly even conflict. I believe there are three major sources of conflict that currently plague U.S.–China relations: economics and trade, science and technology, and currency. I reckon that the current trade disputes between the United States and China are only a tertiary conflict, while the primary and secondary concerns are technological superiority leading to military supremacy, and currency domination. Recently, technology has become a far more serious issue and has replaced trade as the main battle ground.

The first source of conflict, economic and trade competition, is not a dominant concern. Disagreements in economics and trade are commonplace. It is the easiest problem to resolve between the two nations, and there is much room for negotiation.

The second major conflict is currency domination. Since the United States over-took the United Kingdom somewhere around 1890, the U.S. dollar gradually, partic-ularly after World War II, become the world's default currency. This has enabled the

United States to take out loans time and again, but the question is—can this pattern of borrowing last forever? I do believe that the U.S. dollar will remain the global currency for quite some time, but we cannot deny the increasing importance of the Chinese Yuan, especially since China has now become the world's second largest economy.

To a large extent, America's economy relies on the U.S. dollar being by far the world's most significant reserve currency. Her ability to print an inordinate amount of the greenback enables the United States to live beyond her means. It is not a stretch to say that much of the global financial system is built on the confidence on the U.S. dollar. It does not take too much imagination to see how this confidence could be shaken. When this happens, everyone will suffer, but none so much as the United States. However, we must recognize one important fact—ultimately the only country that can bring down the U.S. dollar is the United States herself.

The primary conflict, and perhaps the most contentious, is competition in science and technology. Technological advances are made with each passing day: from GPS to quantum computing and a lot more, competition has brought about innovation and invention in many areas, including the Internet, which is one of the biggest areas of competition. At the heels of technology advances is the invention and proliferation of weapons. In the past few years, the United States has targeted Huawei, China's largest hardware company. One theory I have is that the United States' monopoly in spying is being threatened.

## 5   China and US Can Learn How to Live With Each Other

China and the United States seem to be at each other's throats with a tête-à-tête that can often become intense and at times even bellicose. However, I am not too pessimistic about the future of U.S.–China relations. Let me illustrate why.

First, China simply does not want to get into a major conflict with any country, least of all the United States. I also do not believe that the United States would be able to beat China to submission, which may well be the unspoken intention of Washington, D.C. If so, the best alternative for the United States is to work with China. As the number two, China is not a challenger, except in the minds of the number one, the United States, nor does the former have the ability to be a global leader. In fact, China is very happy to play second fiddle to the United States. Sadly, the United States cannot accept that. America has never been good at compromising or at diplomacy, since she can always resort to her military and economic might.

In the coming few years, China will focus, as before, on her own domestic development. After all, she can no longer rely on the international community for her further growth. China will not close her doors, because she knows that she needs the world, just as the world needs her. However, even if there is an opportunity, Beijing will not take the initiative to play too big a role in the global arena, except to protect her own core interests. The United States is afraid that China will rise to become another hegemon like the United States was, and still is—a bully. This is rather ironic, considering how much of the rest of the world views the United States as a bully. I do not believe China would take this path, but it also seems impossible to convince my Western friends to think likewise.

Second, there are many global issues where the world needs the United States and China to work together to resolve, including climate change, environment, immigration, economic, international trade, financial security, etc.

Finally, at this point in China's development, a major conflict between China and the United States is untenable for both countries. 40 years ago, China metaphorically stood at 1.6 m, while the United States towered over her at 2.2 m. Back then, if these two friends got mad at each other, all the taller one had to do was give the shorter one a slap. 30 years ago, China grew to around 1.75 m, yet a single punch would still knock her down. A decade ago, China stood at 1.9 m, so it would take a few blows to put her in her place. Today, the United States is still 2.2 m, but China has hit the 2-m mark, which should make the United States think twice before picking a fight. If the United States is smart, she will not pick a fight with China as any physical conflict would deeply hurt both sides and could be fatal for everyone. This does not mean I view China's system as perfect. Of course, like the West, stupid things can happen. But the point made here is that if there really is a fight, both sides will lose. The United States and China are restrained by the balance of power between the two nations.

## 6    Change is Coming, but Everything Will Be Alright

The world has arrived at another pivotal moment. What happens today will change the course of the world in the coming few decades. It is akin to the onset of the Cold War after World War II, China's opening up to the world, and the fall of the Berlin Wall. For China, these three globally significant events draw parallels with three defining moments: the Korean War, U.S. President Nixon's visit, and the June 4, 1989, incident that took place the same year as the fall of the Berlin Wall. Each of these events were catalysts that changed the world.

As we contemplate at this pivotal point in history, we are experiencing popular attitudes deeply embedded in Chinese and American thinking. Many Chinese believe that the United States is on the decline. I disagree. Similarly, a good number of my American friends think that China will implode, especially with the pressures applied from the outside. I also seriously doubt this. I believe that both nations will be fine. This is why I am at ease in both places, as I am also in many other parts of the world. However, China must keep a very cool head. Chinese leaders have been very calm in the past 40 years, from the Foreign Ministry to the Ministry of Commerce. I believe that they will continue to be, and therefore the future will not as bad as many people think, especially the millions of people in the United States. If we learn from history and do what we should do, we can avoid obvious pitfalls and work toward a bright future for a co-prospering multilateral world.

**Ronnie C. Chan** is the Chair of Hang Lung Group Limited and its subsidiary Hang Lung Properties Limited. He received his MBA from the University of Southern California and honorary doctorate degrees from The Hong Kong University of Science and Technology, The Chinese University of Hong Kongand Tel Aviv University. He actively involved with non-profits, philanthropic endeavors, and educational organizations, as Chair Emeritus of the Asia Society and Chairman of its Hong Kong Center, and Co-Founder and Chair of the Centre for Asian Philanthropy and Society to name just a few. He is a Fellow of the American Academy of Arts and Sciences.

**Open Access** This chapter is licensed under the terms of the Creative Commons Attribution-NonCommercial-NoDerivatives 4.0 International License (http://creativecommons.org/licenses/by-nc-nd/4.0/), which permits any noncommercial use, sharing, distribution and reproduction in any medium or format, as long as you give appropriate credit to the original author(s) and the source, provide a link to the Creative Commons license and indicate if you modified the licensed material. You do not have permission under this license to share adapted material derived from this chapter or parts of it.

The images or other third party material in this chapter are included in the chapter's Creative Commons license, unless indicated otherwise in a credit line to the material. If material is not included in the chapter's Creative Commons license and your intended use is not permitted by statutory regulation or exceeds the permitted use, you will need to obtain permission directly from the copyright holder.

# Achieving Economic Dynamism in China

Edmund Phelps

**Abstract** *Innovation is driven by having a high degree of market competition,* governmental support of education, efficiency-enhancing regulations, and a legal structure that supports property rights. *Innovation also depends on society having people with both the desire and opportunity to exercise their creativity and their inventiveness* by coming up with original ideas and the entrepreneurial spirit to build businesses based on those ideas. China has long had high growth rates based on catching up to the world standard technologies. If China is to make the next big leap from a middle-income country into a high-income country, then *China will need to both promote indigenous innovation and continue improving its institutions.* But, at least as importantly, it will have to foster creativity, originality, exploration, and entrepreneurship. *China has taken big steps to encourage entrepreneurship in big cities, in rural areas and small cities,* and that is great. Yet, it's one thing to realize today's standards of productivity, and it's another thing to be generating new stuff all the time. *China is going to need people who demonstrate their creativity by conceiving and introducing original things.* Only this kind of indigenous innovation can lead to permanent growth.

**Keywords** Indigenous innovation · Dynamism · Mass entrepreneurship · Mass flourishing · Economic institutions · Creativity · Economic reform · Middle-income trap · Technological catch-up · Originality · Exploration · Stagnation · Job satisfaction · Productivity

Innovation depends not just on having a high degree of market competition, governmental support of education, efficiency-enhancing regulations, and a legal structure that supports property rights. It also depends on society having people, with both the desire and opportunity, to exercise their creativity and their inventiveness by coming up with original ideas, and the entrepreneurial spirit to build businesses based on those ideas.

If China is to make the big leap from a middle-income country, that has long had high growth rates based on catching up to the world standard technologies into a

E. Phelps (✉)
Columbia University, New York, USA

© The Author(s) 2021
H. Wang and A. Michie (eds.), *Consensus or Conflict?*, China and Globalization,
https://doi.org/10.1007/978-981-16-5391-9_32

high-income country with indigenous innovation, it certainly will have to continue improving its institutions. But, at least as importantly, it will have to foster creativity, originality, exploration and entrepreneurship.

The 2020 book, "*Dynamism: The Values that Drive Innovation, Job Satisfaction, and Economic Growth,*"[1] shows that indigenous innovation is rare and difficult to achieve. From the 1820s to 1960s, such innovation fundamentally changed the world economy and vastly improved living standards, first in Britain, then later in the United States, Germany and France. But, since 1945, innovation was largely driven by the United States—with little indigenous innovation even in continental Europe. And, starting in the 1970s, the economy-wide rate of innovation in the United States has slowed sharply. Today's Western nations will not be able to resume rapid growth and innovation unless they regain the spirit of originality and exploration.

In the vast majority of countries, imported innovation contributes more to productivity than indigenous innovation. That is as true of Sweden or France as it is of China, and it should be no surprise. After the launch of reform and opening-up policies starting in the late 1970s, China's innovation was predominantly imported.

But, China's sheer size might drive the need for it to stop relying on transferred technology and put more emphasis on self-directed, self-generated indigenous innovation, which, in turn, must be driven by a culture that fosters economic dynamism. As China runs out of foreign innovations it can import at an acceptable cost, its focus is now on indigenous innovation. The shift in focus in recent years from "Made in China" to "Created in China" is essential to continuing growth and transformation.

This paper does not propose to discuss all, or even most, of the issues outstanding between the world's two largest economies. It will focus, rather, on one decisive issue that bears on these tensions, namely innovation and its expression in economic development. Standard Western economic theory does not provide an adequate framework for evaluating China's challenges and opportunities, or the interaction of China with the rest of the world. Part of the source of misunderstanding between the United States and China stems from deficiencies in economic theory. A better theory—a theory of economic dynamism that leads to a better understanding of technological and economic innovation—can contribute to improved policy deliberation on US-Chinese economic relations.

It is critical to recognize that innovation is not a one-way street. China's indigenous innovation can be a spur to other world economies, which are still in the midst of a long period of declining innovation. No one can foresee the magnitude of the contribution to the world's economy by China's innovators, but I am sure they will make a significant contribution to the global economy.

---

[1] 'Dynamism—The Values That Drive Innovation, Job Satisfaction, and Economic Growth' written by Edmund S. Phelps, Raicho Bojilov, Hian Teck Hoon, and Gylfi Zoega was published by Harvard University Press in 2020.

# 1 Reforms Point in the Right Direction, but More Are Needed

In his speech at the Boao Forum in 2018, President Xi Jinping spoke of China's entering a new era of openness. Under his leadership, initiatives have been taken to boost innovation through entrepreneurship, and his discussion of "quality growth" focuses on achieving indigenous innovation.

Also, Premier Li Keqiang has spearheaded a movement to encourage the massive formation of new companies, thus providing vehicles for business people possessing innovative ideas. The process for forming a new company has been shortened, leading to an increase in the number of enterprises. Importantly, Li's policy of *shuang chuang,* innovation and mass entrepreneurship, has filtered down to local governments all around the country. Many local government officials certainly see themselves as promoters of entrepreneurship.

Vice-Premier Liu He has got behind a policy to refrain from rescuing moribund enterprises, of which there are more than a few in the State sector. This should free up individuals to start new companies, and existing companies to enter new industries. Competition solves a lot of problems—a point that is increasingly lost on the West. The key insight is that when existing enterprises are protected from new market entrants bearing new ideas, the result will be less innovation and also less "adaptation" to a changing world, to use Friedrich Hayek's term.

China's total factor productivity growth rate, which had slowed for a while, picked up after the implementation of the new policies promoting entrepreneurship, encouraging new entrants, enforcing antitrust rules, and allowing state-owned enterprises to fail.

In recent years, China's government has encouraged the creation of a new stock exchange for high-technology start-ups—the Shanghai Stock Exchange Science and Technology Innovation Board, or STAR. But, the continuing development of a financial sector oriented toward business investment by private enterprises will be necessary.

Also of note is the huge increase in the participation of foreign experts in the Chinese economy, leading to a cross-pollinization of ideas.

Monopolization is a factor in the decline of new business start-ups in the United States and in the reduction in innovation. Monopolies need to be broken up or otherwise limited in their market power. It has been said that China is going in the right direction on this.

All this is fine, but there should be a bit more emphasis on the mass innovation part of the equation. China has many, many people with new ideas, which could be used by hard-driving guys who play the entrepreneurial role. Practicing entrepreneurship is great—it's an absolutely necessary thing to do—but it will be important that people can demonstrate their originality by conceiving and producing new things.

## 2   Mass Education that Encourages Creativity is Key

China has built a vast number of schools, where Chinese children learn more about the world they will face. It has built a university system with many institutions ranking among the world's top 50 engineering schools, and it now graduates six times as many engineers and computer scientists as the United States.

Richard Nelson and I argued in 1966 that the diffusion of technical advances is hastened by investment in human capital through education. Since educational levels vary widely among countries, an improvement in education levels, that is, a deepening of human capital, allows the more developing countries to quickly import innovations created elsewhere—to catch up.

Of course, a lot of people have done a lot of things without having a great deal of formal education. But, if you want innovation all over the place, you also need to have education all over the place. And, for China to take the next step toward indigenous innovation, it needs to be education that encourages and inspires creativity.

Dynamism has to start in the school system, as early as primary school. Many children pick up musical instruments around the fifth or sixth grade, even earlier. It is perhaps not a coincidence that many Nobel Prize winners have played musical instruments. One suggestion for Chinese schools is that they give considerable attention to reading fiction and poetry and to the arts in general. It is important to encourage school children to exercise their creativity by challenging them to create original things. If that's done on a mass scale in China, there will be fruits of innovation.

Children need to have the opportunity to tinker—to build and repair things. To take a thing apart to see how it works. This applies to ideas as well as physical things. Composers might tinker a little bit before they are satisfied with the theme that they go on to develop. When the light bulb turns on and you have the idea, that's just the beginning. You then have to do a little bit of mucking around, a little testing, to see whether the idea will work. I think tinkering is integral to conceiving and implementing something on a practical level. Children need opportunities to practice this kind of tinkering.

Opportunities to be creative cannot be limited to an elite few, they need to be widespread throughout society. In the places and times when innovation was rapid and things were good, all sorts of people from all walks of life were huge contributors. For China to sustain rapid innovation, it is going to be important that the country enlists a wide swath of the population, not just a few million super-bright guys and gals in high-tech companies. The main theme of the 2013 book *Mass Flourishing*[2] is that widespread flourishing depends on grassroots innovation from the bottom up.

Development of the Western areas of China has the potential of serving as a powerful source of new waves of development and probably innovation. But that will not happen without continued emphasis on raising the educational and health levels of people in those areas. This could lead to a great increase in the average human capital in the country.

---

[2] "Mass Flourishing: How Grassroots Innovation Created Jobs, Challenge, and Change" written by Edmund S. Phelps and published by Princeton University Press in 2013.

China has been progressive toward women, but I think there is still a lot of space for women to do more and to become more active in businesses in China. They have an intuition that men do not have and they have a different perspective on the nation and the world. Women can add their intelligence and pragmatism to the pool of innovators. Adding them to the economy adds new ideas and new productivity gains.

# 3  More International Opening-Up is Needed

China also needs to continue to reinforce its policies of opening-up its markets to foreign competition. The Chinese authorities have recognized the importance of allowing more competition in the economy. By co-founding the Regional Comprehensive Economic Partnership, a trade association of 16 Asian countries, it has committed China to drastic reductions in tariffs for manufactured goods from Japan, South Korea and other countries that will compete with Chinese manufacturers.

Furthermore, China often uses a so-called "catfishing" strategy in which it strongly welcomes foreign competitors into the Chinese domestic market to force domestic firms to reach world-class standards. Tesla and Apple are examples of that.

Even so, economic and diplomatic disputes will continue to simmer. The recent trade dispute is about high tariffs and other hurdles that US companies feel they are faced with as they contemplate attempting to enter Chinese markets. China can reply that the European Union also has some pretty high tariffs, but it may be that the non-tariff obstacles are not as daunting in Europe as they are in China.

The real underlying problem is that some sectors of a national economy are hurt more than they are helped by free trade. So, all countries engage in protectionism. And China's protectionism hurts the interests of the United States, just as US protectionism hurts Chinese interests. In the United States, it is low-skilled labor that is hurt most. US administrations, regardless of party affiliation, cannot ignore stagnant wages and the resulting social pathologies, which are so well documented by Anne Case, Angus Deaton, and Robert Putnam.[3]

Of course, Scott Rozelle and his colleagues at Stanford have demonstrated similar social problems in rural areas of China.[4] So, it's important both for international relations and for China's own development that excellent education and entrepreneurial opportunities be spread widely throughout the country. This could help jump-start a beneficial cycle in which China's increasing indigenous innovation and more widespread prosperity could promote world technological innovation plus create new customers for American and other producers.

---

[3] These two books illustrate this point: "Deaths of Despair and the Future of Capitalism" written by Professor Anne Case and Professor Sir Angus Deaton and published by Princeton University Press in 2021. Also, "The Upswing" written by Professor Robert Putnam and published by Simon and Schuster in 2020.

[4] "Invisible China—How the Urban–Rural Divide Threatens China's Rise" written by Professor Scott Rozelle and Natalie Hell and published by University of Chicago Press in 2020.

It is worth saying, however, that after China achieved what Walt Rostow[5] dubbed "take-off into sustained growth" its economy soon became large relative to the countries with which it traded as measured by gross national product. As a consequence, China's gains from trade with America have generally lessened, so trade issues may become less pressing for both very large economies.

But, the world cannot ignore the opportunities created by China's move toward an economy driven by indigenous innovation. Imported innovation from America has had a net positive impact on China during the past four decades. The fact is that there is much less innovation coming out of the United States than there once was—and hardly any coming out of Europe. So China could become a major source of innovation for the global economy.

For its part, China's government is evidently supportive of Chinese businesses developing a capacity to produce indigenous innovations. It no doubt recognizes that such innovations are all the more valuable when innovation remains weak in the West, where growth in total factor productivity has continued its long slowdown.

But, thoughtful people still have questions and worries. In China, as well as the United States, a great deal of innovation is in industries making capital goods, infrastructure, or mining, but there is little innovation in industries such as clothing, housing, and healthcare. (In fact, data in the United States show that an index of prices of capital goods has been steadily falling for several decades.) It is natural to ask whether such narrowly focused innovation can go on very long. This suggests that companies aiming to innovate—in China, too—will ultimately run out of possibilities for innovation in that direction. In short, economies have to achieve broad innovation or they will have to settle for stagnation.

## 4   What Policies Can Lead to More Dynamism?

China has taken big steps to encourage entrepreneurship in the big cities, in rural areas and in small cities, and that is great. Yet, it's one thing to realize today's standards of productivity, and it's another thing to be generating new stuff all the time. So, China is going to need people who demonstrate their creativity by conceiving and introducing original things. Only this kind of indigenous innovation can lead to permanent growth.

Chinese businesspeople and entrepreneurs are increasingly showing not only the entrepreneurial drive to adapt to new opportunities but also the desire and capacity to innovate for themselves, rather than simply copying what is already out there. Indeed, more and more Chinese companies are realizing that they must innovate in order to get—and stay—ahead in the global economy. Chinese companies made breakthroughs by offering digital-age infrastructure that facilitates innovative activity, and industrial firms have recently moved into robots and artificial intelligence.

---

[5] "The Economics of Take-Off into Sustained Growth" written by Walt Rostow and published by Macmillan Palgrave in 1963.

Huawei was the first Chinese company to dominate its market segment, with a 30% global market share in the key sector of telecommunications equipment, but it surely will not be the last. But this achievement has also occasioned alarm and suspicion in the United States.

One of the big surprises of the results in *Dynamism*[6] is that during the so-called IT revolution, towering peaks either in the raw data on productivity or in our decomposed series of indigenous innovations were not detected. The United States could not restore a dynamic economy by relying on a small number of innovative firms in Silicon Valley—and the situation has worsened since those firms have become more oligopolistic and regularly employ anti-competitive practices.

When drawing up economic and social policies, we need to realize that people, in general, are capable of having original ideas, and many of these ideas might have commercial applications—not just scientists and high-tech engineers. Indeed, virtually every industry has had workers, managers, or others that hit upon new ideas at one time or another.

The implication is that indigenous innovation springs from the powers of originality and creativity among large numbers of people working in the nation's economy. In this thinking, a nation needs to possess the dynamism needed to create innovations and a willingness as a society to accept their introduction into the economy.

The sources and rewards of dynamism are tied up with the personal values that came to the fore during the period of innovation-led growth: the willingness to attempt innovation may be tied to developing conceptions of the "good life." This theory has grown out of work beginning soon after the founding of the Center on Capitalism and Society at Columbia University in 2001[7] and culminating in *Mass Flourishing* and *Dynamism*. The fundamental thesis is that people from all walks of life possess inborn powers to conceive "new things," whether or not scientists have opened up new possibilities. An innovative society allows, even encourages, people to act on newly conceived things—to create them and try them.

What kinds of governmental policies can help a country reach the difficult goal of transformative, innovation-led growth? Of course, institutional reforms in the legal and financial systems along with programs to encourage R&D and entrepreneurship are necessary, but they are not sufficient. Masses of people need to be encouraged to be innovative, creative, and dynamic. This is hard.

The exploration of new firms and new products in China in recent decades suggests that the Chinese do possess a dynamic spirit. Every time I visit China, I see energy and excitement among many people from many walks of life. But more reforms are still needed. To continue the progress and transformation, China will require leaders in government that continue to recognize the importance of both indigenous innovation as well as entrepreneurship, and, in turn, this will require policies to support people with imagination and ingenuity.

---

[6] 'Dynamism—The Values That Drive Innovation, Job Satisfaction, and Economic Growth' written by Edmund S. Phelps, Raicho Bojilov, Hian Teck Hoon, and Gylfi Zoega was published by Harvard University Press in 2020.

[7] https://capitalism.columbia.edu/about-center.

In any nation where it takes hold, innovation-driven growth is immensely powerful. It transforms the nation from agricultural to industrial, from rural to urban, and from trading to producing. China appears to be on the verge of following this transformative path but cannot be complacent. Few countries have achieved growth led by indigenous innovation. The kind of social dynamism needed for growth driven by indigenous innovation is rare and easily stifled.

History suggests that dynamic economies are largely sparked by the original ideas of ordinary people using their creativity and imagination and developed by entrepreneurial people alert to new opportunities and keen to start new businesses that develop new concepts into commercial products and methods and then sell them to potential users. This is the China that I hope will emerge.

**Edmund Phelps** was awarded the 2006 Nobel laureate in Economics. He is Director of the Center on Capitalism and Society at Columbia University. He earned his B.A. at Amherst (1955), his Ph.D. at Yale (1959). He has written on growth, unemployment theory, recessions, stagnation, inclusion, rewards of employment, indigenous innovation, dynamism and the good economy. His work can be seen as a lifelong project to put "people as we know them" into economic theory. His most recent books include *Mass Flourishing* (2013), and *Dynamism* (2020). In 2018 he was named among China's 40 most influential foreign experts by the State Administration of Foreign Experts.

**Open Access** This chapter is licensed under the terms of the Creative Commons Attribution-NonCommercial-NoDerivatives 4.0 International License (http://creativecommons.org/licenses/by-nc-nd/4.0/), which permits any noncommercial use, sharing, distribution and reproduction in any medium or format, as long as you give appropriate credit to the original author(s) and the source, provide a link to the Creative Commons license and indicate if you modified the licensed material. You do not have permission under this license to share adapted material derived from this chapter or parts of it.

The images or other third party material in this chapter are included in the chapter's Creative Commons license, unless indicated otherwise in a credit line to the material. If material is not included in the chapter's Creative Commons license and your intended use is not permitted by statutory regulation or exceeds the permitted use, you will need to obtain permission directly from the copyright holder.

# 'Soft Power' in Governance, the Burden of Debt and the Crisis of Communications

# China and the United States: Looking Forward 40 Years

Joseph S. Nye Jr.

**Abstract** This essay provides *insights into future global governance* from *the scholar who invented the concept of soft power*. China as its strategic weight grows increasingly insists on setting standards and rules. The United States resists, *global institutions like the WTO atrophy*, and appeals to sovereignty increase. *One possible future is a China-dominated world order*. China's economy could well surpass that of a declining United States by the mid-2020s. With Western economies having been weakened relative to China by the pandemic, China's government and major companies are able to reshape institutions and set standards to their liking. However, in a more universal future, *public opinion in many democracies begins to place a higher priority on climate change*. Even before COVID-19, one could foresee an international agenda in 2030 defined *by countries' focus on green issues*. If the US president introduces a *"COVID Marshall Plan"* to provide prompt access to vaccines for poor countries and to strengthen the capacity of their health care systems, much like the Marshall Plan of 1948, it could have a profound effect on shaping the geopolitics of the ensuing decade. Such leadership could *enhance US soft power* and, by 2030, could have a similarly significant geopolitical impact.

**Keywords** Insights into future global governance from the scholar who invented the concept of soft power · Global institutions like the WTO atrophy · One possible future is a China-dominated world order · Public opinion in many democracies begins to place a higher priority on climate change · By countries' focus on green issues · "COVID Marshall Plan" · Enhance US soft power

## 1 Four Phases of Recent History

Since the end of World War II, United States–China relations have gone through three phases that lasted roughly two decades each. Looking back 40 years, Jimmy Carter established diplomatic relations, but before that, hostility marked the 20 years after

J. S. Nye Jr. (✉)
Harvard's Kennedy School of Government, Cambridge, USA

© The Author(s) 2021
H. Wang and A. Michie (eds.), *Consensus or Conflict?*, China and Globalization,
https://doi.org/10.1007/978-981-16-5391-9_33

the Korean War, followed by limited cooperation against the Soviet Union during the phase that followed President Richard Nixon's famous 1972 visit.

The Cold War's end ushered in the third phase of economic engagement, with the United States helping China's global economic integration, including its entry into the World Trade Organization in 2001. Yet in the first post-Cold War decade, President Bill Clinton's administration hedged its bets by simultaneously strengthening the United States–Japan alliance and improving relations with India. After 2017, in the fourth phase, Donald Trump's National Security Strategy focused on great power rivalry, with China and Russia designated as America's main adversaries. While the election of Joseph Biden will make United States–China relations more orderly and predictable, it will not end this fourth phase any time soon.

While many Chinese analysts blame this fourth phase on Trump, Chinese leaders are also to blame. By rejecting Deng Xiaoping's prudent policy of maintaining a low international profile and by proclaiming a nationalistic "China Dream," Chinese leaders showed nationalism on the rise, and many Chinese began to proclaim American decline. These attitudes and behavior were noticed within the United States, and public opinion about China had already begun to sour before the 2016 presidential election. Trump's rhetoric and tariffs were merely gasoline poured on a smoldering fire.

The liberal international order helped China sustain rapid economic growth and reduce poverty dramatically. But China also tilted the trade field to its advantage by subsidizing state-owned enterprises, engaging in commercial espionage, and requiring foreign firms to transfer their intellectual property to domestic "partners." While most economists argued that Trump was mistaken to focus on the bilateral trade deficit, many supported his complaints about China's efforts to challenge America's technological advantage. Moreover, China's growing military strength added a security dimension to the bilateral relationship. While this fourth phase of the relationship is not a cold war, owing to the high degree of interdependence, it is much more than a typical trade dispute.

Some analysts believe this fourth phase marks the beginning of a conflict in which an established hegemon goes to war with a rising challenger. In his explanation of the Peloponnesian War, Thucydides famously argued that it was caused by Sparta's fear of a rising Athens. Some see the two countries entering a Cold War, and even argue that the two countries are destined for war. I am not this pessimistic. In my view, economic and ecological interdependence reduces the probability of a Cold War and give the two countries an incentive to cooperate and build institutions in a number of areas. At the same time, miscalculation is always possible, and some analysts even cite 1914 and the chance of "sleepwalking" into a hot war as happened with World War I. I am not this pessimistic, but humans make mistakes.

## 2   The Dangers of Miscalculation

History is replete with cases of misperception about changing power balances. For example, when Nixon's visited China in 1972, he wanted to balance what he saw as growing Soviet power, but he also interpreted as a decline what was really the return to normal of America's artificially high share of world product after World War II. He proclaimed multipolarity when what actually transpired was the end of the Soviet Union and America's unipolar moment at the end of the century. Today some Chinese analysts underestimate the resilience of the US culture and predict Chinese dominance over a declining America, but this could turn out to be a dangerous miscalculation.

It is equally dangerous for Americans to over or under estimate Chinese power, and Washington has groups with economic and political incentives to do each. Measured in dollars, China is about two-thirds the size of the American economy. Many economists expect China to pass the United States as the world's largest economy sometime in the 2030s, depending on what one assumes about the rates of Chinese and American growth. As Clinton's Secretary of Treasury Lawrence Summers posed the future foreign policy question: "Can the United States imagine a viable global economic system in 2050 in which its economy is half the size of the world's largest? Could a political leader acknowledge that reality in a way that permits negotiations over what such a world would look like?" One could add the question of whether Chinese and Americans can learn to cooperate on producing global public goods under such a future distribution of power.

Thucydides famously attributed the Peloponnesian war to two causes: the rise of new power, and the fear that it creates in an established power. Most people focus on the first half of his statement, but the second is equally important. The United States and China must avoid exaggerated fears that could create a new cold or hot war. Even if China someday passes the United States in total economic size, that is not the only measure of geopolitical power. China ranks well behind the United States in soft power indices, and US military expenditure is four times that of China. While Chinese military capabilities have been increasing in recent years, analysts who look carefully at the military balance conclude that China will not be able to exclude the United States from the Western Pacific.

On the other hand, the United States was once the world's largest trading nation and its largest bilateral lender. Today nearly 100 countries count China as their largest trading partner, compared with only 57 that have such a relationship with the United States. China plans to lend more than USD 1 trillion for infrastructure projects with its "Belt and Road Initiative" over the next decade, while the United States is cutting back aid. China will gain economic power from the sheer size of its market as well as its overseas investments and development assistance. Overall, Chinese power relative to the United States is likely to increase.

Nonetheless, the United States will retain some long-term power advantages that are likely to persist regardless of the current actions of China or the Trump Administration. One is geography. The United States is surrounded by oceans and neighbors that are likely to remain friendly. China has borders with 14 countries and has territorial disputes with India, Japan and Vietnam that set limits on its soft power. Energy is another American advantage. A decade ago, the United States seemed hopelessly dependent on imported energy. Now the shale revolution has transformed North America from an energy importer to exporter at the same time that China is becoming more dependent on energy imports from the Middle East, and transport through the Indian Ocean.

The United States also has demographic advantages. It is the only major developed country that is currently projected to hold its place (third) in the demographic ranking of countries. While the rate of American population growth has slowed in recent years, it is not shrinking in population as will happen to Russia, Europe, and Japan. China will soon lose its first-place population rank to India, and the size of its working-age population will decline in the coming decade. America also remains at the forefront in the development of key technologies (bio, nano, information) that are central to this century's economic growth, and American research universities dominate higher education. China is investing heavily in R&D, and competes well in some fields now, but those who proclaim Pax Sinica and the end of the American era fail to take the full range of power resources.

American complacency is always a danger; but, also dangerous is a lack of confidence, and exaggerated fears, that lead to over-reaction. The United States holds high cards in its poker hand, but hysteria could make the United States fail to play its cards skillfully. Discarding our high cards of alliances and international institutions is a case in point.

# 3   The Role of Institutions

Donald Trump may have despised international institutions, but his presidency reminded the world of the importance of effective and resilient ones. In the 2016 election, Trump campaigned on the argument that the post-1945 multilateral institutions had let other countries benefit at the expense of America. Of course, the populist appeal of Trump rested on far more than foreign policy. Trump successfully linked domestic resentments to foreign policy by blaming economic problems on "bad" trade deals with countries like Mexico and China, and on immigrants competing for jobs. The post-1945 liberal international order was cast as a villain.

From FDR to Trump, American presidents were never perfect institutional liberals. Nonetheless, prior to 2016, American presidents, in most instances, supported international institutions and sought their extension, whether it was the Non-Proliferation Treaty under Lyndon Johnson, arms control agreements under Nixon, the Rio de Janeiro agreement on climate change under George H.W. Bush, the World Trade Organization and the Missile Technology Control Regime under Clinton, or the Paris climate agreement under Barack Obama.

Of course, institutions can sometimes lose their value and become illegitimate. The Trump administration claimed that institutions such as the WTO had "Gulliverized" the United States: Lilliputians were using multilateral institutional threads to constrain the American giant from using the power it would have in any bilateral negotiation.

Institutions are not magic, but they do create valuable patterns of behavior. Multilateral institutions are more than formal organizations, which sometimes ossify and need to be reformed or discarded. Even more important is the whole regime of rules, norms, networks, and expectations that create social roles, which entail moral obligations, and the United States can also use such institutions to bind others to support global public goods that are on its own and others' long-term interests.

The United States needs a network of multilayered partnerships with others. Foreign partners help when they want to, and their willingness is affected not just by America's hard military and economic power, but also by its soft power of attraction, based on an open and inclusive culture, liberal democratic values and policies that are widely perceived as legitimate. Now, with less preponderance and facing a more complex world, the United States must cooperate with others, and use its soft power to attract their cooperation. America will need to exercise power with as well as power over others. The success of Joe Biden's foreign policy will depend on how quickly we can relearn these institutional lessons.

Many of the current changes in the world are directly or indirectly related to China's recent past and expected future economic growth. This makes it even more important to further strengthen and develop institutions in order to create a balance between what China presents as its "benevolent rise" that will result in shared prosperity and the perception of China in the West as a highly disruptive potential threat that must be guarded against.

## 4   An International Order Beyond the Pax Americana

During the 1990s and 2000s, neither China nor Russia could balance American power, and the United States overrode sovereignty in pursuit of liberal values. Critics describe this record as post-Cold War American hubris—Russia and China felt deceived, for example, when the NATO-led intervention in Libya resulted in regime change. On the other hand, defenders portray it as the natural evolution of international humanitarian law.

In any case, the growth of Chinese and Russian power has set stricter limits to liberal interventionism. They stress the norm of sovereignty in the UN Charter, according to which states can go to war only for self-defense or with Security Council approval.

As for economic relations, the rules will require revision. Well before the pandemic, China's hybrid state capitalism underpinned an unfair mercantilist model that distorted the functioning of the World Trade Organization. The result will be a decoupling of global supply chains, particularly where national security is at stake. China decries US restrictions on companies like Huawei from building 5G telecommunications networks in the West, consistent with sovereignty, but China has also long prevented Google, Facebook, and Twitter from operating in China for security reasons.

By contrast, ecological interdependence poses an insurmountable obstacle to sovereignty, because the threats are transnational. Regardless of setbacks for economic globalization, environmental globalization will continue, because it obeys the laws of biology and physics, not the logic of contemporary geopolitics.

In this context, it is not enough to think of exercising power over others. We must also think in terms of exercising power with others. The Paris climate agreement and the World Health Organization help us as well as others.

Since Richard Nixon and Mao Zedong met in 1972, China and the United States have cooperated despite ideological differences. The difficult question for Biden will be whether the United States and China can cooperate in producing global public goods while competing in the traditional areas of great power rivalry.

The decision President Biden now faces is not whether to restore the liberal international order. It is whether the United States can work with an inner core of allies to promote democracy and human rights while cooperating with a broader set of states, especially China, to manage the rules-based international institutions needed to face transnational threats such as climate change, pandemics, terrorism, and economic instability.

## 5   What Makes America Exceptional Now?

In July 2020, I joined 43 other scholars of international relations in paying for a newspaper advertisement arguing that the United States should preserve the current international order. The institutions that make up this order have contributed to "unprecedented levels of prosperity and the longest period in modern history without war between major powers. US leadership helped to create this system, and US leadership has long been critical for its success." Critics correctly pointed out that the American order after 1945 was neither global nor always very liberal, while defenders replied that while the order was imperfect, it produced unparalleled economic growth and allowed the spread of democracy.

Americans often see their country as exceptional and there are sound analytical reasons to believe that if the current largest economy does not take the lead in providing global public goods, such goods—from which all can benefit—will be under-produced. This is one source of American exceptionalism. Of course, if China becomes the world's largest economy, its cooperation will also be needed to create effective institutions to produce and protect global public goods.

Economic size makes the United States different, but analysts like Daniel H. Deudney of Johns Hopkins University and Jeffrey W. Meiser of the University of

Portland argue that the core reason that the United States is widely viewed as exceptional is its intensely liberal character and an ideological vision of a way of life centered on political, economic, and social freedom.

American foreign policy tends to oscillate between inward and outward orientations. President George W. Bush was an interventionist; his successor, Barack Obama, was less so. And Donald Trump was mostly non-interventionist. What should we expect from Joe Biden?

Protected by two oceans, and bordered by weaker neighbors, the United States largely focused on westward expansion in the nineteenth century and tried to avoid entanglement in the struggle for power then taking place in Europe. By the beginning of the twentieth century, however, America had replaced Britain as the world's largest economy, and its intervention in World War I tipped the balance of power. And yet by the 1930s, many Americans had come to believe that intervention in Europe had been a mistake and embraced isolationism.

After World War II, Presidents Franklin Roosevelt and Harry Truman—and others around the world—drew the lesson that the United States could not afford to turn inward again. Together, they created a system of security alliances, multilateral institutions, and relatively open economic policies that comprise Pax Americana or the "liberal international order." Whatever one calls these arrangements, for 70 years, it has been US foreign policy to defend them.

Today, they are being called into question by the rise of powers such as China and a new wave of populism within the world's democracies, which Trump tapped in 2016. A key question now is can President Biden promote democratic values without military intervention and crusades, and at the same time take a non-hegemonic lead in establishing and maintaining the institutions needed for a world of interdependence?

Public opinion polls also show public support for international organizations, multilateral action, human rights and humanitarian assistance. As I show in my recent book, *Do Morals Matter? Presidents and Foreign Policy from FDR to Trump*, no one mental map fits all circumstances. There is little reason to expect the public to have a single consistent view.

Broadly defined, intervention refers to actions that influence the domestic affairs of another sovereign state, and they can range from broadcasts, economic aid, and support for opposition parties to blockades, cyber attacks, drone strikes, and military invasion. From a moral point of view, the degree of coercion involved is important in terms of restricting local choices and rights.

Some liberals argue that the promotion of democracy is America's duty, but there is an enormous difference between the promotion of democracy through coercive and non-coercive means. The means are often as important as the ends.

Where will Biden land on the spectrum of interventions intended to promote security, democracy, and human rights? His history of good judgment and contextual intelligence are encouraging, but also bear in mind that sometimes surprises occur, and events take control.

But after international polls show that America's soft power of attraction has declined sharply over Trump's presidency, can President Biden restore that trust? In the short run, yes. A change of style and policy will improve America's standing in most countries. In contrast to Trump, Biden is a well-vetted politician with long experience in foreign policy derived from decades in the Senate and eight years as vice president. Since the election, his initial statements and appointments have had a profoundly reassuring effect on allies.

Trump chose narrow transactional definitions and, according to his former national security adviser, John Bolton, sometimes confused the national interest with his own personal, political, and financial interests, with a disdain for alliances and multilateralism, which he readily displayed at meetings of the G7 or NATO.

Biden has rejoined the Paris climate agreement and the World Health Organization, and his reassurances about NATO, will have an immediate beneficial effect on US soft power. But Biden will still face a deeper trust problem. Many allies are asking what is happening to American democracy. How can a country that produced as strange a political leader as Trump in 2016 be trusted not to produce another in 2024 or 2028? Is American democracy in decline making the country untrustworthy?

Domestically, perhaps the best demonstration of the underlying strength and resilience of American democratic culture was the 2020 election. Despite the worst pandemic in a century and dire predictions of chaotic voting conditions, a record number of voters turned out, and the thousands of local officials regarded the honest execution of their tasks as a civic duty. Contrary to the left's predictions of doom and the right's predictions of fraud, American democracy proved its strength and deep local roots.

# 6   Conclusion

The information revolution and globalization are changing world politics dramatically. On transnational issues like COVID-19 and climate change, power becomes a positive-sum game. As I argue in *Do Morals Matter?*, it is not enough to think of power over others; one must also consider power with others. Chinese and American leaders must both learn this lesson. On many transnational issues, empowering others helps a country accomplish its own goals. For example, all can benefit if others improve their energy efficiency, or improve their public health systems.

There is no single future until it happens. The fate of the United States, of China, or of the world as a whole is not yet sealed. With the election of Joe Biden, the distribution of COVID-19 vaccines, and a return to a pre-Trump semblance of normalcy in global politics, it may seem like the dust is settling a little.

However, there are many challenges that await the new international order, whether it be established by the United States or by China, or by both of them together. Chief among these are technology and the environment, which bring with them both benefits in what they can do and challenges in their management. One certainty is that global interconnectedness is here to stay and isolation is not an option. The only path forward is through cooperation and engagement.

We need not become involved in a new Cold War, much less a devastatingly hot war. As we look ahead 40 years and Chinese power grows, both countries will have to adapt. We will be involved in a "cooperative rivalry" and should not lose sight of either part of that description.

**Joseph S. Nye Jr.** is the University Distinguished Service Professor, Emeritus and former Dean of Harvard's Kennedy School of Government. He won a Rhodes Scholarship to Oxford University, and earned a Ph.D. in political science from Harvard. He has served as Assistant Secretary of Defense for International Security Affairs, Chair of the National Intelligence Council, and Deputy Under Secretary of State for Security Assistance, Science and Technology. His books include: *Soft Power: The Means to Success in World Politics* (2004); *Do Morals Matter? Presidents and Foreign Policy from FDR to Trump (2020), The Powers to Lead (2008), The Future of Power (2011)* and *Is the American Century Over? (2015).* He is a fellow of the Academy of Arts and Sciences, the British Academy, and the American Academy of Diplomacy.

**Open Access** This chapter is licensed under the terms of the Creative Commons Attribution-NonCommercial-NoDerivatives 4.0 International License (http://creativecommons.org/licenses/by-nc-nd/4.0/), which permits any noncommercial use, sharing, distribution and reproduction in any medium or format, as long as you give appropriate credit to the original author(s) and the source, provide a link to the Creative Commons license and indicate if you modified the licensed material. You do not have permission under this license to share adapted material derived from this chapter or parts of it.

The images or other third party material in this chapter are included in the chapter's Creative Commons license, unless indicated otherwise in a credit line to the material. If material is not included in the chapter's Creative Commons license and your intended use is not permitted by statutory regulation or exceeds the permitted use, you will need to obtain permission directly from the copyright holder.

# COVID-19 and Paying for the Extraordinary but Necessary Debt Accrued

**Sir Martin Sorrell**

**Abstract** *The COVID-19 pandemic shows every sign of being a watershed moment.* Months of lockdown have certainly given citizens and politicians alike plenty of time to reflect on the state of their societies. There's been *a huge upsurge of interest in the environmental and social costs that come with globalisation.* Also, deep thought is needed about what we are going to have to pay for *the extraordinary amount of debt that has been accrued to pay for COVID-19*—just as we are having to pay for the investment to tackle climate change, to counter inequalities and to equip ourselves through education and re-skilling for the disruption caused by digitisation and to continue with globalisation. *Globalisation is not going to disappear*, but it will take a more fragmented form going forward, with governments and corporations having to make tough choices about which orbit of power they want to be a part of, and where their ultimate loyalties lie. Achieving consensus and real progress on vital issues like climate change, security and economic stability will get harder, not easier. And viewed from what we used to call the West, the economic prospects look daunting. The next few years offer short-term gain—but the prognosis further ahead is going to be painful.

**Keywords** The COVID-19 pandemic shows every sign of being a watershed moment · A huge upsurge of interest in the environmental and social costs that come with globalisation · The extraordinary amount of debt that has been accrued to pay for COVID-19 · Globalisation is not going to disappear

## 1 Integration of the Pandemic and Globalisation

There is a direct link between the COVID-19 pandemic and globalisation. When the virus took off in early 2020, it was unwittingly spread around the world by tens of thousands of air travellers boarding planes to business meetings in other countries. Business travel is just one consequence of the globalisation of trade. It's

M. Sorrell (✉)
S4 Capital, London, UK

© The Author(s) 2021 375
H. Wang and A. Michie (eds.), *Consensus or Conflict?*, China and Globalization,
https://doi.org/10.1007/978-981-16-5391-9_34

no coincidence that world cities like London and New York soon found themselves at the centre of the storm.

This has been the first truly global pandemic in the modern era, but if anyone expected that it would meet a coherent worldwide response, they will have been disappointed. If anything, the pandemic has marked a setback in the progress of international co-operation and global governance on issues ranging from drug approvals to open borders.

Truth was an early casualty, with politically motivated arguments about the source of the virus quickly trumping the need for transparency and openness. And in spite of all the rhetoric about protecting the world's poorest, the unfolding story of the virus has been one of fragmentation, as countries competed with each other to secure supplies of the vaccine for their own citizens in a beggar-my-neighbour policy.

So, looking beyond the pandemic, it seems a timely moment to ask what the future is for globalisation. Is this a system, as some believe, that needs to be replaced? Or will COVID-19 come to be seen as a blip on an otherwise steady trajectory of convergence?

First, it's worth remembering that the knives were already out for globalisation long before COVID-19 arrived, with some critics arguing it had run into a dead end. They took as their evidence events such as Britain's decision to leave the European Union, the faltering of major trade agreements and the breakdown in US-China relations.

One reason for this is that we didn't always explain the benefits of globalisation when we had the chance. The reality is that Western democracies have garnered enormous benefits since Ted Levitt[1] first propounded his theory about the globalisation of markets in 1983. The windfalls of globalised trade have included rapid spread of innovation, cheaper input materials for business, access to new markets and a proliferation of low-cost manufactured goods for consumers.

But a reckoning is now overdue for the economies of Europe and North America. On the debit side, mature economies have sacrificed their manufacturing and industrial base to lower cost labour in developing countries in order to fuel an era of almost continuous economic growth. They have also willingly surrendered aspects of their sovereignty along the way. What better example than this: China controls 80 per cent of the global supply of rare earth metals, which will be central to the manufacture of the next generation of strategic products such as smartphones, electric cars and wind turbines. The US was once a leader in this field, but now its rare-earth mineral production is owned by Chinese companies and sent to China.

And notwithstanding US-China trade tensions, Apple is likewise heavily reliant on factories in Zhengzhou to manufacture its products (though it's been trying to diversify elsewhere). Ironically, the world's biggest electronics brand depends on the People's Republic to assemble iPhones and iPads at a time when dozens of Chinese tech firms are on a US trade blacklist.

---

[1] Professor Theodore Levitt in Harvard Business Review May 1983: https://hbr.org/1983/05/the-globalization-of-markets.

## 2  Business as Usual Versus Building Back Better

The pandemic shows every sign of being a watershed moment. Months of lockdown have certainly given citizens and politicians alike plenty of time to reflect on the state of their societies, and whether they want to go back to business as usual. There's been a huge upsurge in interest in the environmental and social costs that come with globalisation, whether that be destruction of rainforests, the use of child labour to stoke fast fashion, or the vast open-cast mines that scar parts of Africa. In Western economies, the destruction of the manufacturing base has left millions with curtailed working life prospects and countries with a skills vacuum, and it will be difficult to turn back the clock.

And of course, many people's horizons have contracted as a result of COVID, with international travel no longer a given, and countries looking increasingly inwards for solutions.

US-China tensions are not going to ease anytime soon, even with a change of leadership in Washington DC. After his first phone call with President Xi of China[2], US President Biden bluntly told a group of senators: "They're going to eat our lunch."[3]

US business was in favour of President Trump's crackdown on China (not least because of the appropriation of intellectual property), but it was a case of shutting the stable door after the horse has bolted. Now Xi looks set to be in power until 2035, with growing nationalism on the Chinese side and popularity of 'Made in China' among young Chinese, the difficulty for the business community is how to deal with all of this—are businesses going to have to make a choice?

Political populism around the world has been driven by inequality, and there's a widespread perception that globalisation has made the rich richer, and the poor even poorer. So, the idea of 'building back better' after the pandemic, while laudable, may prove to be a pipedream.

In countries like the UK and the US, we have a raft of serious issues to confront. There's a massive requirement for re-skilling and re-education to equip the next generation for the completely different workplace they will enter compared to their parents. And greater labour mobility will also be needed, particularly in the UK, to meet the demand from new sources of employment.

The disruption caused by globalisation in closing down industries across countries and regions is further compounded by an even more potent new disruptor: digitalisation. Sectors such as retail are feeling the brunt and face disappearing in the face of booming ecommerce, while many other service businesses are disintermediated.

Climate change is a challenge of existential proportions which, as Bill Gates recently noted, makes ending the pandemic look "very, very easy".[4] Meanwhile, companies have to tackle the agenda of 'Diversity, Inclusion and Equity', which

---

[2] www.whitehouse.gov/briefing-room/statements-releases/2021/02/10/readout-of-president-jos eph-r-biden-jr-call-with-president-xi-jinping-of-china/.

[3] www.bbc.co.uk/news/business-56036245.

[4] 15th February 2021: www.bbc.co.uk/news/science-environment-56042029.

presents an ongoing challenge to the very fabric of our society. There has been a long-term trend of the 'labour' share of income shrinking in G20 countries at the expense of 'capital', which has heightened inequality. It may be time for that to be reversed.

And in the UK, we also have the impact of Brexit to contend with. The decision to leave the EU won the popular vote, but it has increased friction in trade between the UK and EU, curtailed the freedom of movement and posed big questions about Britain's future role in the world. Brexit signifies the first serious reversal in the decade-long direction of travel of breaking down trade barriers and increasing co-operation and integration. Britain does have an opportunity to re-position itself as a free-trade 'Singapore-on-Thames'[5]—but it will need tangible steps such as lower taxes to make it happen.

## 3   The Recovery: Short-Term Gain, Long-Term Pain

All that is the background against which we are going to emerge from the pandemic.

With vaccination programmes underway and at the time of writing this essay in early 2021, the prospects look like 2021 will see a strong economic recovery taking place around the world. We can expect to see worldwide GDP growth of 5–6% this year and 4–5% next year—the last time we had growth that strong was in the 1980s. So, the short-term future looks very good, but it isn't going to last very long. What happens in 2023, when inflation may well return, and when interest rates start to rise again? Jamie Dimon, Chairman and CEO of JPMorgan Chase, says that the boom could easily run into 2023 with the benefit of Federal spending[6]—it remains to be seen whether that will be the case.

That brings us to the point at which we are going to have to pay for the extraordinary amount of debt that has been accrued to pay for COVID-19—which was of course entirely necessary—just as we are having to pay for the investment to tackle climate change, to counter inequalities and to equip ourselves through education and re-skilling for the disruption caused by digitisation and to continue with globalisation. And, of course British people may face significant costs as a price, for Brexit in the UK. At some point, we have to 'pay the piper'. And I'm not clear in my own mind how that will play out.

By 2028, China is set to become the world's largest economy, and India will become more and more important, as will Latin America. For Western Europe, meanwhile, the outlook is one of secular decline, so it is really hard to see how we are going to pay for everything, and what the grounds for optimism should be.

There will be winners coming out of the pandemic of course. It has sped up digital transformation at the consumer level, and the beneficiaries will include home games and entertainment, online grocery and essentials, online education, online financial

---

[5] The Times: www.thetimes.co.uk/article/brussels-fears-the-prospect-of-a-singapore-on-thames-after-brexit-rf3jgdss5.

[6] www.cbsnews.com/news/jamie-dimon-post-pandemic-boom-economic-growth-2023/.

services—all those industries that will do well as a result of technology. Health care will also emerge smelling of roses, because of the success in creating vaccines so quickly when many said it couldn't be done.

The tech companies themselves can expect to face increasing regulation wherever they operate—Australia's proposal to get social media companies to pay for news is one sign of that. In future, the big tech companies may have to grow organically; it is likely they will no longer be allowed to grow through acquisition as they've done in the past. So that may mean more platforms, more technology companies; Google, Facebook and Amazon will still dominate advertising, but the smaller alternatives like Twitter, Pinterest and Snap will become more interesting.

And all companies will have to pay close attention to where growth is going to be found in the post-pandemic world; brands will also have to become more focused on purpose—the pressure from investment institutions on Environmental, Social and Governance (ESG) issues will see to that.

There is also a general consensus that globalisation is not going to disappear, but it will take a more fragmented form going forward, with governments and corporations having to make tough choices about which orbit of power they want to be a part of, and where their ultimate loyalties lie.

Achieving consensus and real progress on vital issues like climate change, security and economic stability will get harder, not easier. And viewed from what we used to call the West, the economic prospects look daunting. The next few years offer short-term gain—but the prognosis further ahead is going to be painful.

**Sir Martin Sorrell** is Executive Chairman of S4 Capital plc, which is building a purely digital advertising and marketing services business for global, multinational, regional, local clients and millennial-driven influencer brands. S4 Capital plc has over 2,400 people in 30 countries, with a market capitalisation of over $1.2 billion. Sir Martin was CEO of WPP for 33 years, building it from a £1 million "shell" company in 1985 into the world's largest advertising and marketing services company. When he left in April 2018, WPP had a market capitalisation of over £16 billion, revenues of over £15 billion, profits of approximately £2 billion and over 200,000 people in 113 countries.

**Open Access** This chapter is licensed under the terms of the Creative Commons Attribution-NonCommercial-NoDerivatives 4.0 International License (http://creativecommons.org/licenses/by-nc-nd/4.0/), which permits any noncommercial use, sharing, distribution and reproduction in any medium or format, as long as you give appropriate credit to the original author(s) and the source, provide a link to the Creative Commons license and indicate if you modified the licensed material. You do not have permission under this license to share adapted material derived from this chapter or parts of it.

The images or other third party material in this chapter are included in the chapter's Creative Commons license, unless indicated otherwise in a credit line to the material. If material is not included in the chapter's Creative Commons license and your intended use is not permitted by statutory regulation or exceeds the permitted use, you will need to obtain permission directly from the copyright holder.

# Our World Is in a Communication Crisis

Alistair Michie

**Abstract** The *richness in communication networks is deepening divisions and mistrust between nations*. This trend is also *corroding the cohesion of individual societies*. If this erosion persists, it will create even more severe impediments for global society to change and introduce the measures needed to *counter challenges such as climate change*. Discord has been a dominant pattern in the history of humanity. However, past conflicts did not raise this to a *threat of catastrophe for humanity*, a threat that shows us all the urgency of tackling *the global communication crisis*. This essay contends that resolving the communication crisis is core to the challenge of climate change. The key rests with China and the US by virtue of their size and global leadership capabilities, and there can be no solution until the communication crisis between the US and China is resolved. Throughout 2020, the communication crisis deepened. One vital area is the *communication of scientific facts*. Failure to win trust through science means that reaching a consensus on remedial action will be extremely difficult. There is a *mounting breakdown of trust between politicians, the public and scientists*. China could break the deadlock. The pattern of Chinese history proves *China is capable of huge 'mindset' changes to resolve the crisis*, most recently evident in the reform and opening up policy started in 1978.

**Keywords** Richness in communication networks is deepening divisions and mistrust between nations · Corroding cohesion of individual societies · Counter challenges such as climate change · Threat of catastrophe for humanity · The global communication crisis · Communication of scientific facts

## 1 Cacophony Blocks Solutions to Shared Global Threats

The genius of a Briton, Sir Tim Berners-Lee, sparked a communications revolution in 1989. His invention means over half of humanity were active Internet users as of October 2020. Three decades on since Sir Tim invented the World Wide Web, the world gorges on a communications cornucopia.

A. Michie (✉)
International Council of the Center for China and Globalization (CCG), Beijing, China

© The Author(s) 2021

H. Wang and A. Michie (eds.), *Consensus or Conflict?*, China and Globalization,
https://doi.org/10.1007/978-981-16-5391-9_35

Immense positives have evolved from this treasure trove, where any aspect of human knowledge can be accessed at any time and anywhere, but the creation of infinite communication channels is now hurting humanity. Our world is in a communication crisis. The richness in communication networks is driving a cacophony that is deepening divisions and mistrust between nations. This trend is also corroding the cohesion of individual societies. If this erosion persists, it will create even more severe impediments for global society to change and introduce the measures needed to counter challenges such as climate change.

Discord has been a dominant pattern in the history of humanity. However, past conflicts did not raise the threat of catastrophe for humanity, a threat that shows us all the urgency of tackling the global communication crisis. This essay contends that resolving the communication crisis is core to addressing the linked challenges of climate change and viral pandemics. The key to unravelling it rests with China and the USA by virtue of their size and global leadership capabilities, and there can be no solution until the communication crisis between the USA and China is resolved.

Throughout 2020, the communication crisis deepened. In October, the respected Pew Research Centre summarised its latest research with the headline: *"Unfavourable views of China Reach Historic Highs in Many Countries."* Drivers included trade tensions between the US and China, exacerbated by President Trump's garrulous use of Twitter. COVID-19 caused continuous conflict. Constant friction on freedom of navigation in the South China Sea threatened to flare up. The US Secretary of State Pompeo left office accusing China of genocide in Xinjiang, even though State Department lawyers had advised against the use of the term. Both the UK and the USA protested new legislation in Hong Kong and when China defended its actions, communication channels began to close down, first with the UK shutting out CGTN TV and then with China blocking BBC World Service. These are all deeply serious issues.

Closing communication channels and other media, against the background of political leaders firing off a continuous barrage of conflicting invective, can never resolve the dire challenges facing humanity. The Economist on 13 February 2021 captured the conundrum by saying: *"Democracies face an unprecedented and delicate task when they deal with China, which is …. an essential partner in tackling global crises such as climate change. To refuse to engage with it is to endanger the world economy and the planet."*

If trust and understanding can be secured between the USA and China on climate change, dialogue can be turned to other issues, including the pandemic. But, making issues like Xinjiang, Hong Kong and navigation of the South China Sea conditions of that dialogue is a strategy that would *'endanger the world economy and planet'*. Instead, China and the USA need to focus on specific areas of communication changes that could fast-track progress in identifying common ground and mutual interests, and both the USA and China must strive to find mutual respect for each of their different governance systems. As Winston Churchill famously said: *"Many forms of Government have been tried, and will be tried, in this world of sin and woe."*[1]

---

[1] Winston Churchill MP, speaking in the House of Commons on 11 November 1947.

## 2    Science, Misinformation and the Communication Crisis

One vital area is the communication of scientific facts, but building common trust in science is going to be a big challenge for China and the USA. The vast majority of humanity has to trust the science that predicts the catastrophic threats from global warming or from further viral pandemics. Failure to win trust through science means that reaching a consensus on remedial action will be extremely difficult if not impossible.

In 2020, science writer Deborah McKenzie reflected the facts, trust, understanding and consensus shared by many scientists worldwide when she wrote that *"COVID-19, Ebola and worse come from destroying forests."*[2] Science provides copious evidence of the cost of reckless disrespect for nature. In her book, *The Pandemic that Never Should Have Happened, and How to Stop the Next One*, she describes how countless viruses are poised to jump from wrecked forests into humans. But the crisis in communications has resulted in mistrust of scientific facts, especially outside of China, where there are many critics that highlight the Chinese government's control of the media and the Internet. But these controls do prevent waves of scientific misinformation that flood the Internet outside of China.

Scientists continuously ring alarm bells in learned journals; from the *Lancet*: *"There is a mounting breakdown of trust. Not only between politicians and the public. But, also among politicians and publics with science and scientists;"*[3] from the Royal Society (the oldest scientific organisation in the world): *"Fakery affects science and social information and the two have become highly interactive globally, undermining trust in science"*[4].... The concern is universal, as expressed in Scientific American: *"The lack of trust in science—and the excessive trust in persuasive purveyors of misinformation—is perhaps the biggest threat to our society right now."*

Historian Niall Ferguson highlighted the immense power of the so-called *'persuasive purveyors'* in January 2021 warning that, *"Facebook, Amazon, Twitter, Google and Apple, or FATGA for short—[are] companies that have established a dominance over the public sphere not seen since the heyday of the pre-Reformation Catholic Church."*[5]

Monopoly power, as embraced by FATGA, is nothing new in the USA. In the 1900s, Presidents Roosevelt and Taft broke up many monopolies in banking, energy, railroads and agriculture, but it required very determined political leadership. President Biden faces formidable challenges in navigating through a politically polarised USA, but it is not unthinkable that the power of FATGA might be constrained. Support could come from unexpected angles. The boss of Apple, Tim Cook, clearly recognises the need for radical change when he spoke in 2021: *"At a moment of rampant*

---

[2] The Pandemic that Never Should Have Happened, and How to Stop the Next One by Deborah McKenzie published by Hachette Books in USA in 2020.

[3] The Lancet, Volume 396, issue 10,256, p. 949, 3rd October 2020.

[4] The Royal Society, 1st May 2019, https://royalsocietypublishing.org/doi/10.1098/rsos.190161.

[5] The Spectator, 16th January 2021, https://www.spectator.co.uk/article/the-tech-supremacy-silicon-valley-can-no-longer-conceal-its-power.

*disinformation and conspiracy theories juiced by algorithms, we can no longer turn a blind eye to a theory of technology that says all engagement is good engagement. It is long past time to stop pretending that this approach doesn't come with a cost—of polarisation, of lost trust and, yes, of violence. "*[6]

In the past few years, these 'rampant disinformation and conspiracy theories' have become embedded in the bilateral relationship between China and the USA, but there are reasons for hope. If President Biden tackles FATGA, then China might be the catalyst for other significant positive changes needed to conquer the crisis in global communication—especially between the USA and China—because China is capable of delivering profound and rapid change. But unlocking that potential requires effort, experience and recognition of the complexities. Professor Rana Mitter stresses that "dealing with China is a geopolitical issue perhaps more complex than any we have dealt with in the post-1945 era." He highlights how in the UK, *"most judgements are made without any very deep understanding of China itself—including by many policy-makers, both elected politicians and within the civil service."*[7] The same analysis applies to the USA.

## 3 'Reform and Opening up' of the World's Longest Continuous Civilisation

Personally, I learned almost nothing about China at school or university, an experience that was and still is typical in the UK. I was ignorant of China's history and had no idea that China had been home for millennia to almost a quarter of the global population. In 1989, Chinese friends in Malaysia awoke my curiosity, which led to a contract in 1990 with Standard Chartered Bank that enabled me to travel around China to the north, the east, the west and the south. I vividly recall the vast gap between what I saw, and the descriptions about China in books and media outside of China. For example, travelling in 1990 in China I saw Coca Cola and its products were available everywhere—even in the most remote parts of China; I visited a factory in Tianjin churning out Motorola mobile phones and another making fibre optic cable in Chengdu; travelling by air was as easy as catching a bus—and the Boeing and Airbus planes all appeared brand new. I was witnessing the impact of the first 12 years of economic 'reform and opening up' initiated in 1978 by the Chinese leader Deng Xiaoping. In the next four decades, China delivered an annual average economic growth of over 10% and, by 2009, China emerged as the world's biggest exporter of goods. During my annual visits to China, I saw first-hand how Chinese people industrialised their nation at a speed and scale that is unprecedented in human history.

---

[6] Cook (2021).

[7] 'After the Golden Age. Resetting UK-China Engagement' by Rana Mitter and Sophia Gaston—July 2020].

My experience is based on what I regard as privileged insights into China and its civilisation gathered over the past three decades, whilst working in, and studying the history of China in 28 of its 34 provinces regions and major municipalities. That means I have seen much more of China than most Chinese will see in a lifetime.

So far, this extraordinary transformation of China has failed to trigger great curiosity and deep analysis outside of China. Few outside China ask how the Chinese nation delivered over 10% annual average growth for four decades or wonder what might learn from the longest continuous civilisation in the world? If the USA and China (and other nations like the UK) are to overcome the communication crisis between themselves, then somehow they need to absorb an understanding of each other's past. China was quick to grasp this need.

Chinese Premier Wen Jiabao visiting the UK in 2011 said, *"Some leaders negotiate without understanding the history of countries they deal with. I would never want to be such a politician."* Deng Xiaoping's ideas for 'Reform and Opening up' must have been hugely influenced by his time spent in Europe. He left China in 1919 aged 15 for a work study programme aimed at learning European ideas. He returned to China via Moscow in 1927.

'Reform and Opening up' has been a huge driver for young Chinese to learn about and experience the world outside of China. By 2018, China had 662,000 of its young people studying abroad and in 2020 there were 369,548 Chinese studying in the USA alone. In sharp contrast, US government data shows there were only 11,639 American students studying in China in 2018/2019 compared with 193,422 in Europe.[8] It is ironic that such huge numbers of American students are studying in the EU, which contains less than 10% of the global population. In contrast, China is on track to be the largest economy in the world and is home to almost 19% of the global population. This is telling data that underpins the crisis in communication and understanding between the USA and China.

The UK Government does not publish how many British students are in China, but the numbers will be tiny. Charles Parton recently urged the UK Government to create and publish a strategy for UK-China relations, writing *"the number of British undergraduate students of Chinese is small, around 300. The funding and opportunities for postgraduate students is pitiful..... If the UK is to have a better understanding of China, its culture, the way its people think, then our education system needs to prepare our young for a world where China will be a big presence in all areas."*[9] These sentiments chime with my experience travelling around China, and a crucial insight in the preface to *The Search for Modern China*[10] by the eminent US-based British historian Jonathan Spence:

> *It is the contention of this book that in trying to understand China today we need to know about China in the past; but how far back we carry that search remains, in a sense, the central question. China's history is enormously long; indeed, no other society has maintained its vitality or kept so meticulous a record of its own doings over such a long span—close to four thousand years—as has China.*

[8] https://opendoorsdata.org/data/us-study-abroad/all-destinations/.

[9] 'Towards a UK Strategy for Relations With China' by Charles Parton, published by The Policy Institute, Kings College, London August 2020.

[10] 'The Search of Modern China' Jonathan Spence, published by Norton, 1990, page xix.

# 4 The 'Mindset Revolution' That Delivered 'Reform and Opening up'

When Deng Xiaoping, who led China after the death of Chairman Mao, proposed the policy of economic 'reform and opening up' in 1978, any sense of the past in China might have suggested that it was impossible. Many of his officials must have been incredulous at an idea whose core was that the Communist Party of China should embrace market socialism. This idea of 'supervised capitalism,' which called for Chinese businesses to reach out into the world to trade and learn how to industrialise China, was at variance with the practice in the preceding centuries. The reason was that Chinese rulers had made enormous efforts to cut links with the outside world, as symbolised by the thousands of kilometres of great walls of China.

Wiser officials around Deng Xiaoping might have reached deeper back in time, when China repeatedly gained from 'reform and opening' up with the world. Around 2,000 years ago, Buddhist beliefs were brought from India to China. Buddhism absorbed Chinese characteristics, but the beliefs embedded in Buddhist profoundly changed China. In history, a high point of Chinese exchange with the world was the Tang Dynasty between 618 and 907 CE. This was the golden age of the 'Silk Roads,' which facilitated a vast exchange of goods, ideas and invention between Europe and China by land and sea.

During the past couple of centuries, China turned inward and suffered from deep poverty, which dulled global interest. As universities expanded outside of China, another challenge to understanding emerged as most scholars studied Chinese civilisation through a 'liberal arts lens,' focusing on the emperors, poets, painters and political histories. In one of my journeys in China, I discovered the huge insights that emerge from understanding the science, engineering and inventions embedded in China's past. One day, whilst crossing the vast Jing-Hang Grand Canal that used to connect Beijing in the north of China with Hangzhou in the south, I learned that this waterway ran a distance equivalent to that between Miami and New York. Its history reaches back over 2,000 years, during which time ship locks were invented on the canal long before the idea spread first to Italy and then to the rest of Europe via the Silk Roads. The British scholar Dr Joseph Needham profoundly changed my understanding of China in his seven-volume *Science and Civilisation in China* published by The Cambridge University Press. The opening sentence of the volume on civil engineering hooked my attention: *"No ancient country in the world did more in engineering, both as to scale and skill, than China, yet very little has been done to making known the history of it."*[11] The writings of Needham show that China has always been a highly literate and technological civilisation and thus he explains how China was able to industrialise, after 1978, to a point over the course of 40 years that had taken the USA a century. The Chinese people were well prepared to deliver on Deng's visionary policy even though they were emerging from the traumatic impact of the Cultural Revolution. The pragmatism, ingenuity and mindset change that the

---

[11] 'Science and Civilisation in China' Volume 4 Part 2 by Dr Joseph Needham published by The Cambridge University Press.

Chinese used to industrialise provides insights into how rapidly they can respond and adapt.

That same spirit has been matched in the US in the past couple of centuries—and especially the digital revolution spawned by Silicon Valley in the past four decades. A way needs to be found to communicate between the US and China just how much greatness they share in common. Steve Jobs is a revered icon in China for what he created with Apple. But the significance of 1978 and Deng Xiaoping is lost in the USA. This means China needs to tell its story in ways people outside of China can relate to. For example, after the upheavals before 1978, China had no foreign exchange, but the leadership came up with a brilliant plan to kick start Chinese vehicle production and earn foreign currency to facilitate trade. In Beijing, there was a mothballed jeep production line built by the Russians. Ten of the unfinished jeeps were sent to Worcester in the UK, where an automotive engineer named William Riley adapted the designs to create a robust vehicle more suitable for the developing world. Riley was a highly enterprising member of the family that founded the famous British Riley automotive brand. His jeep solution used tried and tested low-cost parts that were easily available anywhere in the world—a Ford engine, ZF gearbox and Lucas electrics. The prototypes created in UK were used to restart the abandoned jeep factory in Beijing and laid the foundation of the Chinese automotive sector, which, by 2009, was making more automobiles than the EU, the USA and Japan combined. This is a story people outside of China can relate to—but it is a tale never told by the Chinese to foreigners.

I feel sure that the economic 'reform and opening up' policy of Deng Xiaoping succeeded far beyond his wildest imagination. But this immense success, and the past patterns of reform and opening up in its history, provide evidence that China is capable of another great 'mindset' shift to deliver 'reform and opening up' in communication. Such a mindset change is a crucial step to conquer the global communication crisis.

## 5  The Challenge of Conflicting Communication Styles

Another element of 'mindset' change is for Chinese people to grasp how to communicate outside China. It is very different from communicating inside China as it requires different thought processes.

I chuckle every time I hear a friend advising investors considering China; *"You can enforce contracts in China,"* he says, as relief exudes from his audience. He goes on to say that *"you will have utmost difficulty enforcing these contracts in a court of law."* Confusion and consternation break out and this insight reflects how Chinese people think very differently from US citizens. In China, business is relationship-driven—in the US, the driver is legal transactions. That is why, in China, relations are the key to enforcing contracts.

Different thinking triggers endless collisions between Chinese and foreigners. In Western society, the rights of the individual are paramount whilst Chinese people instinctively support broader community interest. In the UK, it took over twenty years to reconcile competing interests and build Terminal 5 at London Heathrow. In contrast, the much bigger Terminal 2 at Beijing Capital Airport was completed from start to opening within three years. This may also explain why control of COVID-19 has been so much more effective in China compared to the UK and the USA. Chinese people instinctively think of the community interest which optimises the effectiveness of track, trace and quarantine.

The Chinese state has always paid great attention to effective domestic communication. The invention of paper and printing in China were eagerly embraced for government communication. However, the style of communication in China has always been a directed message with little expectation of interaction. This difference in style creates a powerful conflict when used to deliver messages outside of China. In the USA and the EU communication is delivered through persuasion with a high expectation of interaction.

## 6   How China Can Optimise How It Communicates with the World

The communications 'mindset' change in China requires radical fresh thinking to take account of the fundamental differences in styles of communication outside of China. For example:

- For international messages China must stop using domestic communication styles, or models, that work well inside China but produce negative communication results outside of China;
- Websites are critical and it is vital to understand different styles. In China, web pages are very text-dense. In Europe and the USA, websites are much more image-driven;
- China has great skills in web use and development with social media having a dominant impact on the lives of Chinese people. However, their cross-border reach is very limited and that offers very great potential. Many foreigners are eager to learn about different parts of the world, but the materials about China are in a format that has very limited appeal to people outside of China;
- China very often communicates in ways that assume deep knowledge of Chinese culture. For optimal impact, in the US, for instance, messages must be multi-cultural and assume little or no knowledge of China;
- Attention to native language is vital. Often, messages become muddled and lose any impact because they are translated literally. The skills of translators from Chinese to English, and vice versa, are hugely under-rated;
- Teams in China planning and preparing international communication often consist only of Chinese team members. There is compelling evidence that teams built from a range of Chinese and foreign members are the formula that delivers the highest impact.

Evidence suggests that most of the Chinese people leading China's communications with the outside world have never had the opportunity to work in Western countries. It is little wonder that the concept of communication through persuasion is tough for them to grasp.

The result is deep frustration inside China about its lack of success in telling its story to the world despite the volume of information it produces, because most never get absorbed outside China.

There are exceptions, such as the rise of communications from the 'wolf warrior' Chinese diplomats. But, their assertive style of communications adds to the cacophony across national borders.

2021 marks the 100th anniversary of the founding of the Communist Party of China (CPC). One of the core values that differentiates the CPC from other communist parties is its ability to constantly, and successfully, adapt and adjust to global trends—for example, the introduction of 'market socialism' in 1978 and the policy of 'reform and opening up'. The CPC is known to have used innovation in communications to dramatic positive impact, but this was a long time ago in 1937. Then, the CPC used foreigners like Edgar Snow to create a great positive impact outside of China and help tell the story of the CPC to the world. Now, the CPC should adapt and innovate once again to tackle the global communication crisis. There is an urgent need for a new 'mindset' to deliver a communications 'reform and opening up'.

What is needed is a new thinking to deliver a 'mindset' change on communications inside China. This could lead to breakthroughs on all sides that seeks common ground rather than putting the emphasis on our differences. A starting point could be with the issues around climate change. China has so far failed to communicate to the world the depth and range of its commitment to 'green' issues.

For example, the consistency of messages from China about climate change since 2012 has been heard by very few outside of China. This communication gap offers a crucial step for China to bridge and start the process of building deep trust on climate change with the USA.

## 7  Utilising the Consistency of Chinese Policy

In delivering the 18th Congress Political Report on 8 November 2012, President Hu Jintao said that China must *"strive for green, circular and low-carbon development."* The text was in 'Section VIII' of the Report, the first time this kind of section was included, and it was devoted entirely to policies aimed to create a sustainable environment. It matters greatly that Section VIII, and all of the 18th Congress Political Report, was drafted under the supervision of the then-incoming President Xi Jinping. When I met President Xi in the Great Hall of the People on 5 December 2012, he explained how he chaired the committee that created the 18th Congress Political Report in November 2012. He also stressed that the Report was his 'blue-print' for governing China. In many later speeches, Xi stressed this 'blue-print' point.

The 18th Congress Political Report also stressed: *"We call for promoting equality, mutual trust, inclusiveness, mutual learning and mutually beneficial cooperation in international relations and….we should raise awareness about human beings sharing a community of common destiny."*[12] President Xi has repeated this stress on 'mutual trust and learning' and 'creating a community of common destiny' in many speeches since 2012.

At a UNESCO meeting in Paris in March 2014 President Xi said, *"History also tells us that only by interacting with and learning from others can a civilisation enjoy full vitality"* and he repeated this theme at the Boao Forum for Asia in March 2015, with the words *"we should, through efforts towards such a community for Asia, promote a community of common interest for all mankind....To build a community of common destiny, we need to ensure inclusiveness and mutual learning among civilizations."*

At Davos in January 2017, President Xi expounded China's *'goal of building a community of shared future for mankind.'* In May 2019, in Beijing at the Conference on Dialogue of Asian Civilisation, Xi used the word 'mutual' 18 times. The core messages were again totally consistent: *"We need to promote exchanges and mutual learning among countries, nations and cultures around the world, and strengthen popular support for jointly building a community with a shared future for both Asia and humanity as a whole."*

Any web search of the media in English outside of China since 2012 about President Xi Jinping is dominated by themes of autocracy and communism. But there is consistent evidence that Xi is repeatedly stressing he is willing to collaborate; and that he recognises the calamity of climate change. This mismatch of messages surely offers the leadership in the US and China the opportunity to find common ground, which they can use to deliver great imaginative initiatives to defeat the catastrophic challenges facing humanity. There is good reason to believe that this finding of common ground is possible. The first reason is the compelling evidence of the consistency of the Chinese Government about delivery of policies led by President Xi Jinping since he became President of China in 2013. Such consistency can breed confidence and trust outside of China. The second reason is the consistent commitment of President Xi Jinping since 2012 to boosting the efforts of China to invest in international communications. He strongly reinforced this commitment in a major speech he delivered on 31st May 2021 at a study session of the Central Committee of the CPC. The message was very emphatic from President Xi Jinping, that China must greatly boost its efforts in telling the 'story of China' through international communications. This speech by President Xi could be the catalyst that delivers the 'mindset' change inside China that could lead to communications 'reform and opening up.'

## 8   Lessons from History

In the early months of 2021, the enormity of the global challenge from COVID-19 was coming into focus. The question of how to vaccinate the entire global population of

---

[12] Section XI 18th Congress Political Report 8th November 2012.

over 7.8 billion people was an unprecedented task that was combined with economic damage that the world had not experienced since World War II.

Given the scale, this suggests lessons in leadership could be drawn from that War. I doubt many know that the Atlantic Charter was created in the heat of great battles in 1941. Despite the extreme pressures of all-out war, Churchill and Roosevelt created the foundations of the post-war world order. Out of the Atlantic Charter emerged the United Nations in 1945, and eventually the World Trade Organization. This same spirit of leadership travelled through later summits in Tehran, Yalta and Potsdam, which paved the way for the Bretton Woods meeting in 1944 that led to the creation of the World Bank and the International Monetary Fund.

No one can say that these new organisations were perfect, but they laid the foundation of a rules-based world order that created unprecedented global prosperity for billions of people in the seven decades between the end of World War II and when COVID-19 struck in 2020. The vital lesson from history is that, in the midst of the destruction and turmoil of war, inspired global leadership is possible.

COVID-19 and climate change are the catalyst needed for new inspired global leadership by the USA and China. Humanity needs new world organisations to match the unprecedented demands of COVID-19 and climate change. The inspiration of creating them under intense pressure can be found in the greatest heat of World War II, but any great initiative will be lost by the USA and China if they do not tackle the communication crisis that is enveloping the world. The mass of humanity will not follow the very challenging solutions required without being persuaded by compelling communication.

For the USA, this means dealing with '*rampant disinformation and conspiracy theories*' in communications as described by Apple CEO, Tim Cook.

For China, it means persuading the USA and the world to adopt a spirit of '*mutual learning*' about the deep differences between civilisations. China can do that if it embraces a new mindset about communication.

There is hope. China pioneered extraordinary fresh innovative thinking to deliver the economic 'reform and opening up' policy that utterly changed China and the world. That spirit of fresh, innovative thinking is crucial for ensuring 'reform and opening up' in communications.

It will be a huge challenge, but it is possible. China and the USA must succeed for the sake of all humanity.

# Reference

Cook T (2021) CEO of Apple, speaking in Brussels at the virtual CPDP 2021 on 28 January 2021

**Alistair Michie** is Chair of the International Council of the Center for China and Globalization (CCG). During the last three decades Alistair has visited and worked in over 28 provinces and regions of China. Alistair's work in China has focused on strategic advice to build cross-cultural understanding between the world and China. This has led to a number of advisory roles. His major advisory role is as a Director of Hampton Group, which is a global leader in strategic consulting and investment related to China. In 2013, the Chinese government awarded Alistair the 'Frienship Award' Medal.

**Open Access** This chapter is licensed under the terms of the Creative Commons Attribution-NonCommercial-NoDerivatives 4.0 International License (http://creativecommons.org/licenses/by-nc-nd/4.0/), which permits any noncommercial use, sharing, distribution and reproduction in any medium or format, as long as you give appropriate credit to the original author(s) and the source, provide a link to the Creative Commons license and indicate if you modified the licensed material. You do not have permission under this license to share adapted material derived from this chapter or parts of it.

The images or other third party material in this chapter are included in the chapter's Creative Commons license, unless indicated otherwise in a credit line to the material. If material is not included in the chapter's Creative Commons license and your intended use is not permitted by statutory regulation or exceeds the permitted use, you will need to obtain permission directly from the copyright holder.

# Index

© The Editor(s) (if applicable) and The Author(s) 2022
H. Wang and A. Michie (eds.), *Consensus or Conflict?*, China and Globalization,
https://doi.org/10.1007/978-981-16-5391-9

**Open Access** This book is licensed under the terms of the Creative Commons Attribution-NonCommercial-NoDerivatives 4.0 International License (http://creativecommons.org/licenses/by-nc-nd/4.0/), which permits any noncommercial use, sharing, distribution and reproduction in any medium or format, as long as you give appropriate credit to the original author(s) and the source, provide a link to the Creative Commons license and indicate if you modified the licensed material. You do not have permission under this license to share adapted material derived from this book or parts of it.

The images or other third party material in this book are included in the book's Creative Commons license, unless indicated otherwise in a credit line to the material. If material is not included in the book's Creative Commons license and your intended use is not permitted by statutory regulation or exceeds the permitted use, you will need to obtain permission directly from the copyright holder.

Lightning Source UK Ltd.
Milton Keynes UK
UKHW020956060122
396708UK00001B/7